WORDS AND OBJECTIONS

SYNTHESE LIBRARY

MONOGRAPHS ON EPISTEMOLOGY,

LOGIC, METHODOLOGY, PHILOSOPHY OF SCIENCE,

SOCIOLOGY OF SCIENCE AND OF KNOWLEDGE,

AND ON THE MATHEMATICAL METHODS OF

SOCIAL AND BEHAVIORAL SCIENCES

Managing Editor:

JAAKKO HINTIKKA, *Academy of Finland and Stanford University*

Editors:

ROBERT S. COHEN, *Boston University*

DONALD DAVIDSON, *Rockefeller University and Princeton University*

GABRIËL NUCHELMANS, *University of Leyden*

WESLEY C. SALMON, *University of Arizona*

VOLUME 21

WORDS
AND OBJECTIONS

Essays on the Work of W. V. Quine

Edited by

DONALD DAVIDSON

Princeton University

and

JAAKKO HINTIKKA

University of Helsinki and Stanford University

D. REIDEL PUBLISHING COMPANY

DORDRECHT-HOLLAND / BOSTON-U.S.A.

First published 1969
Revised edition 1975

Cloth edition: ISBN 90 277 0074 5
Paperback edition: ISBN 90 277 0602 6

Printed in The Netherlands by D. Reidel, Dordrecht

PREFACE

It is gratifying to see that philosophers' continued interest in *Words and Objections* has been so strong as to motivate a paperback edition. This is gratifying because it vindicates the editors' belief in the permanent importance of Quine's philosophy and in the value of the papers commenting on it which were collected in our volume.

Apart from a couple of small corrections, only one change has been made. The list of Professor Quine's writings has been brought up to date. The editors cannot claim any credit for this improvement, however. We have not tried to imitate the Library of Living Philosophers volumes and to include Professor Quine's autobiography in this volume, but we are fortunate to publish here his brand-new autobibliography.

1975   THE EDITORS

TABLE OF CONTENTS

EDITORIAL INTRODUCTION

In the philosophical literature of the last decade few if any works contain a greater wealth of ideas or pose more important problems than Professor W. V. Quine's *Word and Object*. Not surprisingly, this book has already exerted considerable influence on subsequent philosophical discussion. It seems to us, however, that this influence has largely been tacit and in consequence the issues raised in *Word and Object* have not been faced as squarely in print as they ought to have been. The present special number of *Synthese* has largely been prompted by our desire to encourage philosophers to address themselves directly to the issues raised by *Word and Object* and thus to facilitate the seminal influence of this masterly work. In order to turn this discussion of *Word and Object* into a dialogue, we invited Quine to comment on the papers, to which he kindly consented. We hope that the resulting exchanges will elicit the implications of Quine's work even more clearly than before.

In the course of editing this issue, it came to our attention that R. B. Jensen had obtained a consistency proof for Quine's *New Foundations* – or, strictly speaking, for NF with urelements. Jensen's proof, announced earlier in the form of an abstract, appears here for the first time in full. Although it breaks our original plan of concentrating on *Word and Object*, the implications of this proof for Quine's work are in our judgement weighty enough to justify its inclusion. George Berry's paper, which was subsequently made available to us, happily bridges the gap between Quine's set-theoretical interests and his philosophical work discussed in the other contributions.

Of the papers printed here, P. F. Strawson's 'Singular Terms and Predication' first appeared in the *Journal of Philosophy* **58** (1961) 393–412. We have included it both because of its merits and also in order to give Quine a natural opportunity to comment on it. It is reprinted by permission of Professor Strawson and the editors of the *Journal of Philosophy*.

Noam Chomsky's contribution is excerpted from a longer paper which is due to appear in a *Festschrift* honoring Ernest Nagel.[1] It appears here by the kind permission of the editors of the Nagel *Festschrift*.

Wilfrid Sellars' paper has appeared in *Philosophical Logic* (ed. by J. W. Davis, D. T. Hockney, and W. K. Wilson), D. Reidel Publishing Company, Dordrecht 1969.

Although this issue is not intended as an ordinary *Festschrift* nor intended to replace one, we originally hoped it would appear in time to honor Van Quine on his sixtieth birthday on June 25, 1968. Much to our regret, this schedule proved unrealistic. But although we cannot wish Van Quine many happy returns on the occasion we hoped to mark, perhaps we may wish him many happy and weighty further contributions to logic and philosophy. We also thank him for his most generous co-operation at all stages of our enterprise.

DONALD DAVIDSON
JAAKKO HINTIKKA

---

[1] S. Morgenbesser, Patrick Suppes, and M. G. White (eds.), *Philosophy, Science, and Method: Essays in Honor of Ernest Nagel*, St. Martin's Press, New York 1969

J. J. C. SMART

QUINE'S PHILOSOPHY OF SCIENCE

A fairly definite philosophy of science can be extracted from Quine's *Word and Object* (henceforth referred to as *WO*). Earlier versions of his philosophy of science, for example in his *From a Logical Point of View*, contain phenomenalist and instrumentalist tendencies of thought, but in *WO* these have almost entirely disappeared in favour of an explicitly realistic philosophy of science. What, then, is Quine's philosophy of science in *WO*?

I. NATURE OF PHILOSOPHY OF SCIENCE

In Quine's thought there can be no sharp distinction between philosophy of science and philosophy in general (perhaps excluding such parts of philosophy as either use or mention value concepts). This is because Quine holds that philosophy and science are continuous with one another. This is in contrast to the view of Carnap and others that philosophy (including philosophy of science) is importantly a *meta-theoretical* activity. According to this latter type of view, the scientist is a man who *uses* words like 'electron', while the philosopher is a man who talks *about* such words, or perhaps about the scientist's use of these words. Now Quine in *WO*, even when he is not concerned with linguistics, is often to be found talking about words and sentences, rather than about the objects in the non-linguistic world. However, he regards this as the result of a manoeuvre which is not peculiar to philosophers. This manoeuvre is *semantic ascent* (*WO* § 56). In science it can come about in the following manner. Suppose that physics gets into a state in which a particle theory is about to be supplanted by a field theory. Let the particle theory be T_P and the field theory T_F. Suppose that fields are never mentioned in T_P and particles are never mentioned in T_F. (I take my example from science fiction about the future, thus avoiding irrelevant cavils from historians of science.) Consider now a situation in which a proponent of T_P and a proponent of T_F are discussing the respective merits of the two

3

theories. If we put it in this way, it appears that they are talking *about* T_P and T_F. On the other hand, if they discussed whether particles or fields existed they would be *using* T_P or T_F. There would be some difficulty, however, because the proponent of the one theory would hold that the other theory contained false existentially quantified sentences and vacuously true universally quantified ones. The proponents of the two theories would therefore do well to operate metalinguistically, and discuss what sentences of T_P and T_F follow from what other sentences. Doubtless they both agree that *sentences* exist, and this gives them a common ground.

In practice, I think, scientists do not explicitly go metalinguistic. Rather they feign acceptance of theories such as T_P and T_F and then see what (feigned) conclusions they draw. The difference between this and semantic ascent is, I think, philosophically unimportant. Those of us who do not like play acting will prefer to make (unfeigned) metalinguistic assertions of what follows from what rather than to engage in feigned deductions.

Because semantic ascent can occur in science, Quine rejects Carnap's account of the differentia between science and philosophy. For Quine there are no hard and fast differentia. In line with his distrust of the notion of analyticity, Quine draws no sharp line between the most general principles ('category' or 'framework' principles) and ordinary laws of nature. We believe in electrons because a well-tested theory asserts that there are electrons, but equally we believe in classes because the theory of the real number is needed in physics, and so some of the sentences of a well-tested theory assert the existence of infinite classes of rational and real numbers. No experiment will decide between the view that there are infinite classes and the view that there are not such things, but this does not imply that the assertion that infinite classes exist is wholly divorced from experience. The world might have been the sort of world in which a rudimentary mathematics which did not assert the existence of infinite classes would have sufficed for physics. (I apologize for using a subjunctive conditional here in elucidating Quine, but let me hope that it can be replaced by a suitable metalinguistic and extensional sentence.)

Quine rightly draws attention to the way in which *curriculum* classifications may have influenced us to regard not only philosophy but pure mathematics as unlike physics in being quite independent of observation and experiment. This was indeed once a stumbling block for myself, because it seemed to me that what went on in departments of philosophy and pure mathematics was quite unlike what went on in (say) the department of mathematical physics. Quine's ontological discussions make it plausible that this difference is merely one of degree of remoteness from experience. It is true that there seems to be something fishy about the notion that numbers and sets should be theoretical entities, much as neutrinos are, but though when I reflect on the matter I seem to smell a slight smell of fish, I can think of no good argument to show that it is a real, and not a merely apparent, fishiness. It might be said that what makes the existence of numbers and classes different from that of stars and neutrinos is that numbers and classes do not exist in space-time. But I think that Quine argues convincingly (*WO* p. 131, p. 242) that this should not be taken as showing that 'exist' has a sense in "numbers exist" which is different from the one that it has in "stars exist". We could, of course, make a sharp distinction between pure and applied mathematics by saying that the former does not treat of spatio-temporal entities, whereas the latter does. But equally we could make a sharp distinction between two sorts of biologist by saying that the one lot study organisms which are capable of living on inorganic material alone, whereas the other lot study organisms which are not so capable. This does not make for a philosophically important contrast between botanists and zoologists. Moreover, it is surely possible that in the physics of the far future it may turn out that space and time (or space-time) as we now conceive them will be shown to be a myth, in which case, if 'exist' were held to imply 'in space-time' it would turn out that *none* of the things postulated by a theory would exist.

We need not think that a realist philosophy of mathematics need depend on synthetic *a priori* intuitions of a special intellectual realm. Such a Platonistic epistemology cannot be squared with a biological view of man. On Quine's account we need no such non-empirical intuitions. Numbers and sets are postulated in the same sort of way in which electrons and neutrinos are. In both cases our postulates form part of the basis for a well-tested theory. Set theory comes out not as the study of the supernatural but simply as part of the physics of the non-perceptible. There is nothing startling about this: not only sets but neutrinos are such that we cannot perceive them.

5

Well, then, is set theory part of the physics of the non-perceptible? One reason which makes one inclined to deny this is the existence of alternative set theories. Thus according to one form of set theory (Russell's) it is *nonsense* to say that the class of all classes is not a member of itself, whereas according to another (Quine's) it is merely *false* to say this. Perhaps, however, there is not an important disanalogy between physics and set theory here, because we could imagine two alternative formulations of physics: (1) in which it was contrary to the formation rules of the system to say that an electron had simultaneously both a definite position and a definite momentum, and (2) in which it was merely false that an electron had simultaneously both a definite position and a definite momentum. Nevertheless difficulties still arise because of the differing existential claims of alternative set theories. Again, in Russell's set theory an individual and its unit class are distinct, whereas in Quine's they are identical. Surely if set theory is about real things, one or the other of two rival claims about the existence or identity of sets must be true and the other false. The trouble is that differing set theories do seem to be genuine alternatives. An even more tricky matter arises over P. J. Cohen's proof of the independence of the axiom of choice and the continuum hypothesis from the other axioms of Zermelo-Fraenkel set theory. At the risk of being accused of the fallacy of affirming the consequent, we might claim that there is some reason to believe that the axiom of choice is true, because this axiom is used to prove many theorems which are needed in the sort of mathematics which is used in physics. However, I take it that there is a completely free decision as to whether we should assert or deny the continuum hypothesis. Does this imply that the continuum hypothesis does not assert an objective fact about the imperceptible (namely classes) or is it rather that it is in fact true or false, though we shall never be able to know which? This leads me on to the issue of realism as against instrumentalism in physics.

II. REALISM AND INSTRUMENTALISM IN PHYSICS

I read Quine in *WO* as asserting a full blown realist philosophy of the theoretical entities of physics. This goes along with a realist philosophy of the medium sized objects, such as tables and trees, which are discussed in ordinary common-sense language. According to Quine, the way in which a scientist postulates the existence of electrons and neutrinos is analogous to the way in which, in our ordinary common-sense thinking, we postulate the existence of medium sized things, even though the scientist's posits are made consciously and for recognized reasons, whereas the positing of ordinary common-sense things, such as tables and trees, is "shrouded in prehistory" (*WO* p. 22). Ordinary things are there to explain our perceptual experiences, though these experiences themselves have to be described by reference to physical objects. There is indeed no sense-datum language, no "fancifully fancyless medium of unvarnished news", to use Quine's nicely chosen words (*WO* p. 2). Nevertheless given the framework of physical things we can both describe and explain our experiences. Without this framework we cannot describe or explain our experiences, because "immediate experience simply will not, of itself, cohere as an autonomous domain" (*WO* p. 2).

Quine views man biologically: experiences are just things that go on in specimens of *homo sapiens* and in other animals. In this way Quine sidesteps the epistemological problems which have bedevilled philosophers from Descartes onwards. Epistemology is just a branch of biology. We must look at the brain as a processor of information, this information coming to it as a result of the irradiation of the animal's sensory surfaces. There must be some part of natural science which, taking the external world and the existence of *homo sapiens* for granted, studies the way in which information coming into our receptors (Quine's "irradiation patterns", *WO* p. 32) is processed by our brains in such a way as to lead to knowledge. (At present, of course, such a *scientific* epistemology is in a very rudimentary state.) Quine's biological way of looking at man's epistemological predicament in the first few pages of *WO* is much to be applauded. His good biological attitude to epistemology is also apparent in *WO* pp. 120–123, where he discusses ways in which man may have come to postulate abstract entities.

III. SCIENCE AND COMMON SENSE

Quine views science as a set of sentences, *any* one of which can be questioned, even though *all* cannot. In this he seems to be in substantial agreement with Popper: consider Quine's reference to Neurath who "has likened science to a boat which, if we are to rebuild it, we must rebuild plank by plank while staying afloat in it" (*WO* p. 3). However, there is possibly a certain ambivalence in Quine's attitude to our ordinary common-sense conceptual scheme. How much can this be questioned? On the lower half of *WO* p. 3 there does seem to be a touch of the paradigm case argument, which has been much used by modern English philosophers, for example Antony Flew.[1] Quine says here that we cannot question the reality of physical things, because it would be to deprive words like 'real' of "the very denotations to which they mainly owe such sense as they make to us". However it is surely unlike Quine to be talking of the denotation of the word 'real'. Waiving this point, there is a sense in which two expressions can denote the same thing, and yet there be no things of which one or the other expressions is true. Thus, to use the sort of example of which Feyerabend has been fond[2], the expressions 'case of demonic possession' and 'case of epilepsy' might be used by two different people to refer to the same activity of foaming at the mouth, etc., and yet there be in fact no such thing as demonic possession. This is because the expression 'case of demonic possession' is theory-laden, and laden with a *false* theory. Surely, therefore, there might turn out to be no physical objects, of the sort to which Dr Johnson referred when he tried to refute Berkeley by kicking a stone. However it is clear from the top half of *WO* p. 4 that Quine does not really intend to use the paradigm case argument to prove the reality of physical objects, because he envisages that "One could even end up, though we ourselves shall not, by finding that the smoothest and most adequate overall account of the world does not after all accord existence to ordinary physical things..." (*WO* p. 4). Indeed there is, it seems to me, in *WO* taken as whole, an implicit *rejection* of the paradigm case argument. Quine has no desire "to treat ordinary language as sacrosanct" (*WO* p. 3). According to him those who do so "exalt ordinary language to the exclusion of one of its own traits: its disposition to keep evolving" and "Scientific neologism is just linguistic evolution gone self-conscious, as science is just self-conscious common sense" (*WO* p. 3).

IV. REALISM VERSUS PRAGMATISM AND INSTRUMENTALISM

Before beginning to write this paper I expected to find lingering traces of a pragmatism and instrumentalism which is evident in some of Quine's earlier writings. However I found no definite evidence of such traces, and in *WO* Quine seems to me to have moved right over to a definitely realistic attitude to the theoretical entities of physical science. For evidence of his earlier pragmatism and instrumentalism I would draw attention to his *From a Logical Point of View* pp. 17–18 and pp. 44–45, in which he is willing to say such things as "from a phenomenalistic point of view, the conceptual scheme of physical objects is a convenient myth" (p. 18) and "As an empiricist I continue to think of the conceptual scheme of science as a tool, ultimately, for predicting future experience in the light of past experience" (p. 44).

Such a point of view seems to have been eliminated from Quine's thought in *WO*. Perhaps there is a (possibly harmless) trace of it on *WO* p. 16, where he says "...photons are posited to explain the phenomena, and it is those phenomena and the theory concerning them that explain what the physicist is driving at in his talk of photons". Again in *WO* p. 237 he says, "The reason for admitting numbers as objects is precisely their efficacy in organizing and expediting the sciences. The reason for admitting classes is much the same", and on *WO* p. 20 he says "The neurological mechanism of the drive for simplicity is undoubtedly fundamental though unknown and its survival value overwhelming". These passages suggest instrumentalism, though they do not in fact imply it. As a realist, Quine might say that simple theories are likely to be true as well as useful, and that admitting numbers and classes organizes and expedites the sciences precisely because the world does in fact contain numbers and classes. Moreover in the first quotation about photons, "driving at" is sufficiently vague so that we do not need to take it as implying that talk about photons is somehow just talking about the phenomena. Indeed if we needed to interpret Quine in this instrumentalist way he would surely be saying something inconsistent with his own position about ontological criteria. (In this respect I think that there is probably an inconsistency in his earlier position, but there is no good evidence for thinking that it survives in *WO*.)

Sometimes again we come across passages which, though at a cursory glance they seem to be pragmatist or instrumentalist, at a careful reading can be seen actually to preclude such an interpretation. Thus after pointing out that we can use any *progression* whatever to serve instead of the natural numbers, Quine goes on: "One uses Frege's version or von

9

Neumann's or yet another, such as Zermelo's, opportunistically to satisfy the job in hand, if the job is one that calls for providing a version of number at all" (*WO* p. 263). Though at first sight this can look as though Quine is saying that one can choose one's theoretical entities merely for convenience, we can see that this interpretation is wrong, because Quine then says: "Frege's progression, von Neumann's, and Zermelo's are three progressions of classes, all present in our universe of values of variables (if we accept a usual theory of classes), and available for selective use as convenient." That is, any of the above progressions can be used, precisely because all of them already exist in the real world.

Completely at variance with any pragmatist or instrumentalist philosophy of science is Quine's treatment of limit myths and the ideal objects of mechanics (mass points) in *WO* pp. 248–251. It is clear that Quine appreciates the distinction between a *theory* and a mere *model*.[3] Quine also tries to show how scientists can avoid these myths.

V. QUINE'S PHILOSOPHY OF SPACE-TIME

Quine's scientific language treats of physical objects as space-time solids. He points out how well the tenseless 'there is a...' of quantification theory accords with the tenseless locutions which we need in order to discuss the space-time world. He rightly points out that though the special theory of relativity forces us to abandon absolute theories of space and time taken separately, there is no relativistic objection to an absolute theory of *space-time*. If we do hold to an absolute theory of space-time, then space-time points, as well as physical objects, become values of our variables of quantification. On a relational theory of space-time, on the other hand, assertions which are ostensibly about space-time points get explicated as relational assertions about physical objects. If we retain absolute space-time in our ontology, any geometry other than the one which is the correct physical geometry will be a (possibly convenient) myth, though it can be made non-mythical by interpreting it non-geometrically within the theory of the real number, points coming out as quadruples of real numbers. It might be objected, as by Grünbaum[4], that there is *no* one correct geometry, because it is the conjunction of the geometry and the *congruence conventions* which is part of physics, and we can go from one geometry to another one (provided that it has the same topology) by suitably changing the congruence conventions. However in Quine's philosophy there can be no clear distinction between conventions and statements of fact, and the correct geometry is presumably the one which is simplest. For example, we should choose our congruence conventions, together with our geometry, in such a way that free bodies (considered as four-dimensional objects) lie along geodesics.

As has been noted, a relational theory of space-time would explicate geometrical assertions in terms of statements about material objects, (together with suitable set-theoretic objects, such as numbers). Quine gives an ingenious method for carrying out this reduction, identifying points with ordered quintuples of real numbers. (*WO* § 52.) For this we can use five reference points (particle-events) but Quine argues that we can even paraphrase geometrical assertions without using reference points at all: the geometrical assertions are in terms of distances between particle-events. Quine makes a plausible case within the context of Euclidean geometry, but I am not sure how his paraphrase would work out within the context of the hyperbolic geometry of space-time, in view of such facts as that any two points on the same light ray have zero distance between them. However this matter is not of much philosophical importance, because we can always fall back on reference points. A more important matter is that of whether a relational theory is possible in the case of cosmologies which are based on some form of the general theory of relativity. It is a somewhat open question as to whether cosmology can avoid the postulation of absolute space-time, that is, whether it is possible to develop a plausible relativistic cosmology which conforms to Mach's principle, explaining the structure of space-time in terms of the general distribution of matter in the universe. (Some of the difficulties involved in trying to do without absolute space-time in general relativity are well discussed by Adolf Grünbaum in Chapter 14 of his *Philosophical Problems of Space and Time*.)

VI. SCIENCE AND EXTENSIONALITY

Quine holds that a purely extensional language is adequate for science. It is true that our common-sense language of belief and desire is intensional, but scientific psychology looks extensional enough. Quine argues rightly, I think, that our common-sense language of belief and desire can be replaced by extensional talk about the neural determinants of the behaviour which we take to be manifestations of belief and desire. Similarly sentences containing the term 'soluble' can be replaced by sentences about molecular structure. That is, Quine's strategy is to replace talk about dispositions by talk about underlying structure. This would not work for the most ultimate dispositions, but here it seems that the extensional conditional is all that we need anyway: for 'electrons have charge' read '$(x)(y)$ (electron x. proton y: $\supset x$ attracts y)'. Call this last sentence S. Then the statement that electrons have the disposition to attract protons, or that if x were an electron and y were a proton then x would attract y, can be elucidated as the metalinguistic assertion 'x attracts y' is deducible from 'electron x. proton y' together with the laws of physics, which presumably include S. But in other cases it may well be best to follow Quine in elucidating dispositional talk in terms of underlying structure.

Quine's arguments against intensional logics depend on showing that either they collapse into extensional logic or else they cannot be given an intelligible interpretation in which the quantifiers remain quantifiers and the identity predicate remains an identity predicate. See *WO* § 41.[5] But quite apart from these arguments against intensional logics, we surely tend to lose interest in such logics if we believe that an extensional language is adequate for scientific purposes. Intensional logics, even if they are viable, are complicated and messy (especially in view of the restrictions needed to avoid collapse into extensional logic), and surely for the sake of simplicity and elegance we should try to avoid them. One of the interests of *WO* for the philosophy of science is the good case that it makes for the adequacy for scientific purposes of an extensional logic.

Quine has accused modal logicians of an insensitivity to the use-mention distinction. I suspect that a similar insensitivity may lie behind much of the talk about a 'logical' interpretation of probability. If we write '$P(p/q)$', say, ('the probability of p given q'), we obviously cannot be using 'p' and 'q' as sentence letters, as in sentential logic. They are clearly dummy *names* of sentences. Hence the so-called 'logical' interpretation of probability is really a *metalinguistic* interpretation, and metalinguistic letters (perhaps 'A', 'B', ...) would be less misleading than 'p', 'q', ..., which remind one too much of sentence letters. Sometimes one hears of 'probability logics', but from a Quinean point of view

I can make no sense of the term 'probability logic'. Let us put all modalities and so-called 'logical' probabilities into the appropriate metalinguistic baskets, and keep a clean extensional logic for all scientific (including metalinguistic) purposes. I would hold that Quine in *WO* has shown this to be possible. He may also have shown the alternative *not* to be possible. But whether this latter thing is true or not, surely for the sake of simplicity and elegance alone we should want to go Quine's way.

University of Adelaide

REFERENCES

[1] See Antony Flew, 'Again the Paradigm', in *Mind, Matter and Method* (ed. by P.K. Feyerabend and G. Maxwell), Minneapolis 1966.
[2] See P.K. Feyerabend, 'Problems of Empiricism', in *Beyond the Edge of Certainty* (ed. by R.G. Colodny), Pittsburgh 1965, especially pp. 181, 220, 225.
[3] On this point see Marshall Spector, 'Models and Theories', *British Journal for the Philosophy of Science* 16 (1965) 121–142.
[4] A. Grünbaum, *Philosophical Problems of Space and Time*, New York 1963, Chapter 4.
[5] See also W.V. Quine 'Reply to Professor Marcus', *Synthese* 13 (1961) 323–330, and discussion by Quine and others *ibid.* 14 (1962) 132–143. Quine's paper and the discussion can also be found in *Boston Studies in the Philosophy of Science*, vol. I (ed. by M.W. Wartofsky), Dordrecht 1963.

GILBERT HARMAN

AN INTRODUCTION TO 'TRANSLATION AND MEANING' CHAPTER TWO OF *WORD AND OBJECT**

In this paper I attempt to provide a brief introduction to the thesis of the indeterminacy of radical translation, as this is presented in Chapter Two of Quine's *Word and Object*. I begin by explaining what the thesis is, as I conceive it. Then I consider how one might defend the thesis. Finally I examine several aspects of Quine's discussion of the thesis.

I. WHAT IS THE THESIS?

Consider two of the ways to translate number theory into set theory. Von Neumann's method identifies each natural number including zero with the set of numbers smaller than it. Zermelo's method identifies zero with the null set and identifies every other natural number n with the unit set whose sole member is $n-1$. Although each of the resulting schemes translates a sentence counted true in number theory by one counted true in set theory, and similarly for sentences counted false in number theory, alternative translations are by no means equivalent and may even differ in truth value. For example, the sentence, 'Three is a member of five' (which is assigned no truth value by unreduced number theory), is translated by a true sentence under the von Neumann scheme and by a false sentence under the Zermelo scheme. Most philosophers would agree that it does not make sense to ask which general scheme for translating number theory into set theory is the correct scheme, although in certain contexts one or the other may be more convenient. In consequence it can make no sense to ask what is the correct translation of a particular sentence of number theory unless one asks *relative to some envisioned general scheme* for translating number theory into set theory.

Translation from one natural language into another ordinarily proceeds against an envisioned general scheme of translation, e.g. the usual way of translating French into English. If no such scheme is envisioned ahead of time, we may speak of *radical* translation. Quine's thesis of the indeterminacy of radical translation claims that translation from one natural

14

language into another resembles translation of number theory into set theory in that various equally good alternative but non-equivalent general schemes of translation are always possible, and one may speak of the 'correct' translation of a single sentence only relative to some envisioned general scheme of translation.

One must view Quine's thesis within the context of his general attack on philosophical attempts to attribute explanatory power to meaning, meanings, propositions, propositional attitudes, etc. It is well known that Quine denies that one can explain truth by saying that something is true by virtue of its meaning. Quine also denies that there is explanatory power in the postulation of propositions and propositional attitudes, e.g. he denies that one can explain why a person accepts a sentence by saying that he accepts a proposition that the sentence expresses. More generally, Quine objects to most philosophical (as opposed to ordinary) talk about meaning, meanings, propositions, and propositional attitudes.

Some philosophers would appeal to translation in order to defend philosophical talk about meaning, meanings, propositions, and/or propositional attitudes, taking meaning to be what is preserved in good translation and holding that a sentence in one language is correctly translated by a sentence in another language if both sentences express the same proposition. They suppose that the proposition expressed by a person's words depends entirely on the meaning of the words, which they suppose to be independent of any envisioned general scheme of translation. These philosophers deny the thesis of the indeterminacy of radical translation. They deny that translation of number theory into set theory is representative of translation of one natural language into another. They will want to say that the former is not, strictly speaking, translation at all, since meaning is not preserved. Quine claims that meaning is never preserved – or rather that one can speak of preservation of meaning only relative to some general scheme of translation. Both sides recognize a difference between translation of number theory into set theory and translation of one natural language into another. Quine believes that the difference is that for natural languages there is a single scheme of translation that is generally accepted and that moreover we find it impossible to specify in detail one of the many equally possible alternatives. His opponents believe that the difference is that good translation of natural languages preserves meaning. They hold that general acceptance of, e.g., the familiar scheme for translating French into English is based on general recognition of antecedently existing meaning relations. Quine holds that the 'recognition' of these meaning relations (i.e. translation relations) presupposes prior acceptance of some general scheme of translation and that it is only the acceptance of the scheme that makes the meaning relations hold.

Another and important way in which the difference between Quine and his opponents can be manifested is that, if Quine is right, the indeterminacy affects not only statements about what a foreigner's words mean but also statements about his psychological attitudes. To express a foreigner's belief in English is to offer a translation of the way he might express his belief in his own language. So, if Quine is right, strictly speaking we should say of a foreigner that he believes, hopes, expects, fears, etc. that so-and-so, only relative to a general scheme of translation (where reference to such a scheme may be omitted only if the scheme in question is the usual one for translating his language into ours). Quine holds that belief, hope, expectation, fear, etc. are best construed as sentential attitudes, so that e.g. in the first instance belief is the acceptance of a sentence in one's own language. He holds that one may construe psychological attitudes as propositional attitudes – expressible in another language – only relative to an envisioned scheme of translation. His opponents claim that belief, hope, expectation, fear, etc. are in the first instance attitudes toward propositions and that one's sentential attitudes are attitudes toward sentences that express the propositions toward which one has propositional attitudes. For Quine's opponents, correct translation aims at finding a sentence in our language that expresses the same proposition as a sentence in a foreigner's language. So one way of putting the difference between Quine and his opponents is that Quine believes that at the most basic level a person has attitudes toward sentences and that propositional attitudes do not underlie and explain his sentential attitudes, whereas Quine's opponents believe that at bottom a person's psychological attitudes are propositional attitudes, which do underlie and explain his sentential attitudes.

II. HOW MIGHT THE THESIS OR ITS DENIAL BE SUPPORTED?

Quine is unlikely to provide a clear counter example to his opponents' claim. For example, if he were to say that the alternative translations of

16

number theory into set theory are proof of indeterminacy, his opponents would reply that these are not examples of real translation such as that between French and English, which attempts to preserve meaning. Anyone defending Quine must agree that there is a big difference between the translation of natural languages and the translation of number theory into set theory and this is a difficulty with the number theory – set theory example. There will be a similar difficulty with any example one might offer since, for the example to be manageable, the language in question must be quite structured in the way that number theory and set theory are and natural languages as a whole are not. Thus it would not be feasible to attempt to offer an alternative to the usual method for translating French into English, since at this time we cannot give a rigorous specification of our present method. At present we cannot even give a complete syntactical account of either English or French, whereas we can give a complete syntactical account of the language in which we express number theory or set theory.

Quine's opponents will be proved right if they can show that relevant evidence about a person's language, about translation, or about psychological states supports the theory that good translation discovers antecedently existing meaning relations (that are not relative to an envisioned general scheme of translation) or (what is probably another way of putting the same thing) that the evidence supports the theory that belief and other psychological attitudes are to be construed as propositional attitudes. Quine will be proved right if it can be shown that the evidence does not warrant postulation of propositional attitudes or antecedently existing meaning relations. We must ask whether the evidence 'uniquely determines' a general scheme of translation or interpretation of his words, i.e. whether the evidence rationally supports a unique scheme of translation in whatever way it is that evidence can rationally support one conclusion over another. In this sense it is clear that the evidence can 'uniquely determine' what a person's sentential attitudes are, e.g. it can uniquely determine to a good approximation what sentences he accepts and even what sentences he would accept under varying perceptual conditions. On the other hand, in this sense the evidence does not 'uniquely determine' a general scheme of translation or interpretation of number theory in set theory.

The following considerations bear on what a person's words mean: his use of language in communication; his use of language in various social 'language games', such as betting, greeting, promising, ordering, etc.; and most importantly the role of his language in the formation and expression of psychological attitudes such as belief and desire. The relevance of the last consideration follows immediately from the fact that the issue between Quine and his opponents can be reduced to whether or not the evidence warrants postulation of propositional attitudes over and above sentential attitudes.

The first two considerations, concerning usage, may be ignored, since if the third consideration cannot rule out indeterminacy of translation, it is extremely unlikely that attention to actual usage will do so. It can be plausibly argued that language serves primarily as an instrument of the free expression of thought and that it is a mistake for the linguist to concentrate his attention on practical concerns of actual usage and of language games.[1] The constraints placed on possible translation by a speaker's participation in language games resemble the constraints discussed below placed by the effects of perception on the sentences a person accepts, where moreover the constraints due to language games are much weaker. Indeterminacy, if it arises at all, results from problems in translating relatively abstract and theoretical discourse. In our example, indeterminacy arises through difficulty in translating statements of abstract number theory. Once such indeterminacy arises, it also affects statements of perception such as 'There are five apples in this bowl'; and it is not appreciably affected by language games (counting?) one might play with numbers (one may count with either von Neumann's numbers or Zermelo's). Similarly, if the role of perception does not eliminate indeterminacy in the translation of sentences in, e.g., physical or chemical theory, it is unlikely that attention to actual usage or language games (betting, greeting, promising, ordering, etc.) is going to eliminate the indeterminacy.

Meaning is not very much a matter of what words a person actually uses. What words he could have used are more relevant. Different people have different ways of speaking, different favorite phrases, etc. This obvious fact does not mean that the sentences of such different people are to be translated differently. To require similarity in actual usage (rather than possible usage) as a criterion of translatability would almost certainly rule out all translation, since any two people use their words differently. I do not mean something different by sentences of set theory from what you mean just because you and I use these sentences differently, e.g. just because I count with the von Neumann numbers while you count with Zermelo's, since I *could* always do it your way.

The question, then, is this. 'Does the evidence support the postulation of propositional attitudes that underlie sentential attitudes?' If so, there is not indeterminacy of translation, since then a foreign sentence expressing a foreigner's attitude must be translated by the sentence in our language that we would use to express the same attitude. If the evidence does not support postulation of propositional attitudes, there is indeterminacy since then belief must be construed as a sentential attitude and we can have the same belief as a foreigner only relative to some envisioned scheme for translating his language into ours.

Our evidence about a person's psychological attitudes will include all of his behavior including his speech. We might also 'experiment' with him and in principle learn all of his behavioral dispositions. We want to find a psychological theory that accounts for his behavior and dispositions. Roughly speaking, we expect his behavior to be explainable in terms of beliefs and desires, including plans and goals. His utterances and dispositions to utter can sometimes be explained as expressions of his psychological attitudes. In principle, we can almost certainly discover his beliefs, desires, etc. as he would express them, i.e. we can discover his propositional attitudes. If we can translate his sentences, we can discover his sentential attitudes; if we can discover which propositional attitudes his sentences express, we can translate those sentences. The question is whether the restraints on our choice of psychological theory require that his psychological attitudes be propositional attitudes; i.e. the question is whether these restraints allow us to translate his way of expressing his psychological attitudes.

A psychological theory is usefully treated as a description of a psychological model, where such a description corresponds to a flow chart or program of a mechanism that represents the person in question.[2] In such a model beliefs, plans, desires, etc. would be stored in a memory (like a computer memory). Action would be more or less a function of stored beliefs, desires, etc. Certain states of the mechanism, which correspond to psychological states such as hunger, would give rise to desires. Certain other states, which correspond to perceptual states induced by the environment, would give rise to beliefs about the environment. Certain

processes in the mechanism would correspond to conscious and unconscious reasoning which results in new beliefs, desires, etc.

Such a mechanism requires some means for representing what is
believed, desired, etc. Representations of beliefs and desires are stored in
memory and are manipulated in reasoning and thought. The brain and
nervous system, conceived as such a mechanism, require some such
means of representation. On one view this representation would depend
heavily on a person's language. The mechanism might even be conceived
as storing (tokens of) sentences of his language in memory and as manipulating these sentences in reasoning and thinking. An alternative view,
congenial to those who believe in propositional attitudes, would be that
there is a basic form of representation, almost a basic language of thought,
in which a person reasons and thinks. On this view, when a person speaks,
he encodes his thoughts in his language; and when he understands someone else, he must decode what the other has said by translating it into the
basic language of thought.[3] The second view is not at all plausible, since
typically one's thoughts are already in language. (When learning a new
language one may at first have to encode his thoughts; but hopefully he
comes to think directly in the new language.) It may be that uncritical
acceptance of the second view leads to acceptance of the view that there
are propositional attitudes. Rejection of the second view does not automatically lead to rejection of propositional attitudes, although it does
tend to weaken the view that propositional attitudes *underlie* sentential
attitudes.

The major restraints on possible interpretations of a person's beliefs
and other psychological attitudes arise from the role of perception in
bringing about new beliefs and modifying old ones. Beliefs that arise from
perception ought to have something to do with the environment. If one
knows how a person would react to various perceptual situations, i.e.
how various situations would affect his beliefs via perception, then one
has a great deal of information about how his beliefs are to be interpreted.
Information from the influence of body states on desire (as e.g. hunger)
will play a similar role in restricting interpretation of psychological
attitudes, although because of the greater variety of the effects of perception, this information about desire is probably not very important and
can be ignored. Information about the way a person reasons may help us
identify truth functional logical connectives, although Quine denies that

we can uniquely identify a person's quantifiers (those words that correspond to our 'all', 'some', 'every', 'each', etc.). If we take the effect of reasoning to be connected with that of perception, i.e. if we take perception to affect belief both directly and via inference, we may suppose that the main restraints on translation of a person's language and interpretation of his psychological attitudes are placed by the way his beliefs are affected by varying perceptual situations.

In other words, for our purposes the interpretation of a person's words and psychological states is a function of the sentences he now accepts and rejects along with his dispositions to accept or reject sentences as a result of being placed in various perceptual situations. I shall summarize this as 'a person's dispositions to accept sentences', meaning to include his dispositions to reject as well as his current acceptance and rejection of sentences. The issue between Quine and his opponents is whether or not a person's dispositions to accept sentences determine a unique interpretation of those sentences.

There is no unique way to interpret number theory within set theory. A 'speaker of number theory' accepts many theorems of number theory and various other statements about numbers of objects in the world. His dispositions to accept sentences also include dispositions to believe that there are seven apples in a bag if it so looks to him, etc. All translation schemes into set theory are compatible with such dispositions. They give roughly equivalent translations for sentences of perception; but they are still able to diverge radically for more theoretical sentences.

Is all translation like that of number theory into set theory? Quine says, "one has only to reflect on the nature of possible data and methods to appreciate the indeterminacy" (p. 72). When one thinks of the number theory – set theory example one is inclined to agree, although the point has not been made absolutely certain.

III. ADDITIONAL REMARKS

Some aspects of Quine's actual discussion in Chapter Two can be misleading; and in this final section I would like to guard against certain misunderstandings.

First, and possibly most important, Quine gives misleading behavioristic formulations of his thesis. These formulations may suggest, incorrectly, that he is committed to philosophical behaviorism and, worse they lead him to say things that appear obviously false. Consider for example the third paragraph of Chapter Two, which begins as follows:

Sense can be made of the point by recasting it as follows: the infinite totality of sentences of any given speaker's language can be so permuted, or mapped onto itself, that (a) the totality of the speaker's dispositions to verbal behavior remains invariant, and yet (b) the mapping is no mere correlation of sentences with *equivalent* sentences, in any plausible sense of equivalence however loose.

But if sentence A is mapped onto sentence B, it would seem that a conversation or lecture containing A is mapped onto one containing B so that dispositions to verbal behavior (including one's dispositions to converse or lecture) are changed. The problem arises because here and elsewhere Quine speaks of dispositions to verbal behavior where (according to me) he should speak of what I have called dispositions to accept sentences. Thus what he means here is that there is a way of mapping a speaker's sentences onto themselves that preserves his dispositions to accept sentences and yet does not always correlate sentences with equivalent sentences.

It is true that Quine takes acceptance of a sentence to be a disposition to assent to the sentence, so that where I would speak of dispositions to accept sentences he speaks of dispositions to assent to sentences. This suggests that Quine is a philosophical behaviorist after all. One might even react to Quine's argument as follows:

Quine shows that behavioristic analyses of semantical concepts cannot be given; but that represents only another instance of the failure of philosophical behaviorism.

But such a reaction is superficial and ignores Quine's own discussion of dispositions (pp. 222–5). Quine would not distinguish theoretical from dispositional concepts – in a way, all concepts are theoretical according to him. In the light of Quine's rejection of the analytic synthetic distinction and his Duhemian strictures against phenomenalistic reduction in 'Two Dogmas', it would be strange if his argument here depended on such an outmoded view as philosophical behaviorism. In fact, the considerations sketched above do not depend on any such view.

That things may appear otherwise is due in part to Quine's attempt in this chapter to do at least two things at once. Besides presenting the case for indeterminacy, he also defines partial 'behavioristic' substitutes for philosophical notions like meaning, synonymy, analyticity, observation sentence, etc. (Recall that such 'behavioristic' substitutes may be theoretical notions.) It is true that Quine's substitutes are not very close[4]; and perhaps one can imagine better ones. But Quine's discussion of the thesis of indeterminacy can be presented independently of his description of such substitutes (I have done so above) and does not depend on it. Indeed the dependence goes the other way. If Quine's skepticism about meaning and translation is right, one could not provide very good behavioristic substitutes for notions in the theory of meaning.

Still, there are a couple of places where Quine's interest in behaviorist substitutes leads him to place apparently arbitrary restrictions on the evidence concerning the interpretation of a person's words. This may suggest that Quine could not argue for indeterminacy if he were to include the evidence excluded. In order to rebut such suggestions it is useful to keep the number theory – set theory example in mind. In that example there is indeterminacy even considering all possible reasons for preferring one translation over another.

For example, Quine takes the evidence about the interpretation of a person's words to be restricted to his dispositions to respond to *short* perceptual stimulations, whose maximum length is determined by what he calls the *modulus of stimulation*. The most convincing reason offered for not considering a person's reactions to stimulations of great length (e.g. a month) is that among such lengthy stimulations will be some that call for change of language, where different people would (in the absence of social pressure) change in different ways although we do not want to count such divergence as showing that they now mean something different by their words. (Cf. p. 63.) On the other hand, lengthy stimulations may be relevant to meaning. To use Darmstadter's example, the meaning of certain theoretical terms may depend to some extent on the relevance to the theory of a particular experiment or set of experiments; although it would take a considerable time (e.g. a month) for an investigator to convince himself that certain experimental apparatus is connected correctly and is in good working order. Ruling out troublesome lengthy stimulations by limiting the modulus may be to rule out relevant evidence that restricts the interpretation of one's theoretical terms – and Quine's opponents may want to argue that indeterminacy appears to arise only because this relevant evidence has been ignored. Therefore it is important

23

to emphasize that the number theory – set theory example shows that indeterminacy of translation can remain even if the evidence includes a person's reactions to perceptual stimulations of any length. (In that case the longer stimulations would mainly permit time to figure out complicated proofs and time to count larger collections.)

Another example of the same point occurs when Quine too quickly rejects a suggestion of Grice and Strawson, again allowing his argument to appear weaker than it is. He states the suggestion as follows:

S_1 and S_2 are defined to be synonymous when, for every S, the same experiences confirm (and disconfirm) S_1 on the hypothesis S as confirm (and disconfirm) S_2 on S.

After some rewording this becomes:

S_1 and S_2 are synonymous if for every S the conditional compound of S and S_1 and that of S and S_2 are stimulus synonymous.

Quine then argues as follows:

But now it is apparent that the definition fails to provide a tighter relation between S_1 and S_2 than stimulus synonymy. For, if S_1 and S_2 are stimulus-synonymous then *a fortiori* the conditionals are too (p. 64 with a misprint corrected).

However, Quine's final claim assumes that the conditional is truth functional; and in this context that cannot be so. Grice and Strawson are probably best construed as arguing that when one attempts to interpret a person's words, one ought to take into account how he reasons. An opponent of Quine may feel that indeterminacy can be avoided if one does this. Therefore it is again important to consider the number theory – set theory example which shows that attention to inductive inference does not always rule out indeterminacy. (It is not obvious that inductive inference is relevant at all to this example. Perhaps one might offer inductive evidence for Fermat's conjecture. For Quine and Quineans inductive evidence of a very general sort for the truth of number theory lies in success in application.)

Finally, let me note that the number theory – set theory example sheds some light on a passage a reader may find obscure:

... rival systems of analytical hypotheses can conform to all speech dispositions [i.e. dispositions to accept sentences – G.H.] within each of the languages concerned and yet dictate, in countless cases, utterly disparate translations; not mere mutual paraphrases, but translations each of which would be excluded by the other system of translation. Two such translations might even be patently contrary in truth value, provided there is no stimulation that would encourage assent to either (pp. 73–4).

The last sentence is partially explicated by the example. A sentence such as 'Three is a member of five' is translated by von Neumann into a true sentence of set theory and by Zermelo into a false sentence. It receives no truth value in number theory, nor would any stimulation 'encourage' assent or dissent to it. (Notice, by the way, that Quine here uses the word 'encourage', although he has earlier carefully introduced a distinction between the technical terms 'prompt' and 'elicit', p. 30. Furthermore Darmstadter has pointed out that the passage should read 'encourage assent or dissent'.) The example is not fully successful in interpreting the quotation, since dispositions to accept sentences are not fully preserved. But it suggests what would be needed for an adequate example. One needs two theories (possibly identical), the translated theory T1 and the translating theory T2. Each theory must be formalized and each must fail to assign a truth value to some sentences. One must find two different ways to translate sentences of T1 and T2 such that truth, falsity, and indeterminacy of truth value are preserved and such that some sentence in T1 is translated by p by the first translation and by q in the second translation, although neither p nor q receives a truth value in T2, where *p if and only if not-q* is counted true (i.e. is provable) in T2, and where the translations must be as acceptable, *qua* translations, as those used to translate number theory into set theory. This last condition is necessary in order to rule out *ad hoc* examples of the following sort (suggested by Kripke):

Take T1 and T2 to be the same and to be, e.g., set theory without the axiom of choice. Let the first translation translate every sentence by itself. Let the second translate every sentence by itself with two exceptions: The axiom of choice is to be translated by its denial and vice versa.

We would not accept this as a good example, because it is less simple or more *ad hoc* than the usual homophonic or identity translation, although it is of course difficult to say what considerations affect simplicity or *ad hocness*. It would be nice to have an example of the sort just described that is not *ad hoc* in the way that Kripke's example is but is as convincing as the number theory – set theory example; however I have not been able to discover one.

Princeton University

REFERENCES

* I have benefited from reading unpublished work of Howard Darmstadter, Ronald de Sousa, and Steve Stich. This work was supported in part by a grant from the National Endowment in the Humanities (# H-67-0-28).

1 This has been argued in several places by Noam Chomsky. See e.g. his *Cartesian Linguistics*, Harper and Row, New York 1966.

2 Miller, Galanter, and Pribram, *Plans and the Structure of Behavior*, Henry Holt, New York, 1960; Noam Chomsky, *Aspects of the Theory of Syntax*, M.I.T., Cambridge, Mass., 1965; Gilbert Harman, 'Psychological Aspects of the Theory of Syntax', *Journal of Philosophy* **64** (1967) 73–87; Harman, 'Knowledge, Inference, and Explanation', *American Philosophical Quarterly* **5** (1968) 164–173.

3 As in Jerrold J. Katz, *The Philosophy of Language*, Harper and Row, New York 1966. Cf. my review in *Harvard Educational Review* **36** (1966) 558–63.

4 Quine claims the most accuracy for his substitutes when they are applied to 'observation sentences'. But he so defines 'observation sentence' that the conjunction of an observation sentence with a stimulus analytic sentence (a sentence that everyone in the community firmly accepts so that no brief perceptual experience could lead them to give it up) is another observation sentence with the same stimulus meaning as the first (although, e.g. one would not ordinarily take these sentences to be 'synonymous'). I discuss the nature of Quine's enterprise in providing such substitutes for outmoded notions in 'Quine on Meaning and Existence', *Review of Metaphysics* **31** (1967) 124–151, 343–367.

ERIK STENIUS

BEGINNING WITH ORDINARY THINGS

"This is the book that has meant most to me", Quine has said about *Principia Mathematica*.[1] On reading *Word and Object*, I am struck by the fact that Russell's influence on Quine cannot have been restricted to the impact of *Principia*. Though there are easily discernible differences between Russell and Quine, they have a common basis for raising questions, and this is felt throughout Quine's work. For my part I have always found it difficult to accept Russell's way of raising questions, and my difficulty is still greater in respect of Quine. Perhaps our difference in fundamental outlook is the reason why I find it so hard to see a really coherent position behind Quine's book. What he says in one place seems to me to be more or less inconsistent with what he says in another place. I am aware that this feeling may be founded on misunderstandings. If so, I hope that my criticisms will be a basis for removing them.

I. BEHAVIOURISM AND THE PUBLICITY PRINCIPLE

Quine starts his Preface with the statement that language is a social art. "Hence", he says, "there is no justification for collating linguistic meanings, unless in terms of men's dispositions to respond overtly to socially observable stimulations." (*WO* p.ix.)

If this is to mean that we should study 'meanings' not as a science of some hidden mental entities called meanings, but in relation to the use of language in our physical and social environment and thus to our socially observable behaviour, I entirely agree with Quine. So I agree in laying down as a basis for the study of meaning a *publicity principle* to this effect.

Unfortunately Quine's 'behaviourism'[2] does not mean merely this. That there is something else involved in it is hinted at by two expressions occurring in the above quotation: the expression 'in terms of' and the word 'stimulations'.

The expression 'in terms of' suggests that all terms used in our de-

27

scription of linguistic meaning should either refer to socially observable entities or by means of definitions be translatable into other terms which have this property. But the difficulty of building up a science in this way is manifest in our days. What terms are to be used in scientific description is a matter of convenience, economy, and so on, and the relation between scientific terms and socially observable entities[3] cannot simply be characterized by a conceptual 'in terms of'. Of course, Quine is aware of this in other contexts, so we may perhaps take the expression 'in terms of' in a wide and vague sense. I shall use the expression in the same way myself.

The word 'stimulation' suggests that we should according to Quine describe meanings in terms of the irritation of nerve receptors and responses to such irritations. This association is not wrong: Quine's fundamental semantic concept is 'stimulus meaning'. This concept is defined in terms of 'stimulation'; and as an example of what is meant by 'stimulation' Quine mentions that "a visual stimulation is perhaps best identified, for the present purposes, with the patterns of chromatic irradiation of the eye" (*WO* p. 31). So it is obvious that Quine speaks of stimulation in the meaning of what in another context he calls 'surface irritation' (*WO* p. 22); and if 'behaviourism' is to mean not only reference to overt behaviour but a psychological theory in these terms, I find it a poor basis for linguistic investigation.

What is then wrong with the notion of a 'surface irritation'? Must not every contact between a man and his environment be mediated by surface irritations? I believe so, and if this is so it is of interest to epistemologists, physiologists and sense-phychologists. But it is of subordinate interest to those who investigate the fundamentals of linguistic behaviour. This is so for two reasons:

(a) Surface irritations are not socially observable in any relevant sense.

(b) Surface irritations are often not internally observable either.

Against (a) one might argue that surface irritations *are* socially observable in the laboratory of the physiologist. But these observations have nothing to do with the socially observable environmental factors which are relevant for the use of language outside the laboratory.

Against (b) one might perhaps argue that any reference to internal observability is irrelevant according to our publicity principle. But this is not so. The correlation between surface irritations and the information transmitted by the nervous system to the centers of linguistic behaviour is complicated. Or, to put the thing more behavioristically: It seems to be impossible to condition a person to react in a certain way if, and only if, some quite specific pattern of surface irritation occurs – say, the stimulation of a certain part of the retina by irradiation of a certain kind.

Quine says: "The usual premium on objectivity is well illustrated by 'square'. Each of a party of observers glances at a tile from his own vantage point and calls it square; and each of them has, as his retinal projection of the tile, a scalene quadrilateral which is dissimilar to everyone else's. The learner of 'square' has to take his chances with the rest of the society, and he *ends up* using the word to suit. Association of 'square' with just the situations in which the retinal projection is square would be *simpler to learn*, but the more objective usage is, by its very intersubjectivity, what we tend to be exposed to and encouraged in." (*WO* p. 7, my italics.)

What Quine thinks would be simpler to learn would to all appearances *not* be simpler to learn. We have good reasons to believe that there are cases in which the retinal projection actually happens to be square and in which we (rightly) experience – and verbally react to – what we see as scalene. Or does Quine really know of any case in which, say, a small child is taught to react in a specific way if, and only if, he has some square projection on his retina?

Quine is immediately aware of a difficulty in his outlook. For he continues like this: "In general, if a term is to be learned by induction from observed instances where it is applied, the instances have to resemble one another in two ways: they have to be enough alike from the learner's point of view, from occasion to occasion, to afford him a basis of similarity to generalize upon, and they have to be enough alike from simultaneous distinct points of view to enable the teacher and learner to share the appropriate occasions." (*WO* p. 7.)

So Quine sees that the surface irritation for two observers of an object of some shape are different and even varies for one observer if, say, he moves his head. And he thinks that this difficulty must be overcome by some guarantee that the different surface irritations are 'alike' if the thing is viewed from different angles. But how does he here define 'alike'? He is, in fact, relying on the fact that the objective shape of the thing viewed is the same, and from this he infers that this object seen from slightly different angles causes 'similar' projections on the retina. This means that

29

in fact he *defines* similarity in projection in terms of similarity of the objects projected rather than the other way round.[4]

So we may take it for granted that our language habits are developed with reference to *physical* objects (and their properties) in a world of averyday experience which is about the same for different human beings end thus forms a *socially observable world*.

That this is so seems fortunate. For if our reactions were really related to a world of surface irritations, no language would be possible: by what marvellous kind of compromise would people agree on calling different-shaped scalenes 'squares', and so on? In addition, our kind of living would also be impossible. Even Pavlov's dogs – those paradigms for behaviouristic psychology – were conditioned to react to objective stimuli, the experimenters did not see to it that the surface irritations of the dogs were the same on all occasions, but merely that the dogs were on different occasions put in the same objective environment.

II. IN THE BEGINNING WAS SUBJECTIVITY ...

Of course, Quine does not believe that our language really refers to surface stimulations. But he explains the deviations as the effect of a special 'objective pull' (*WO* § 2), which is a matter of *social* impact. Other people (the objective existence of whom the individual is unaware of!) 'inculcate' in the individual this objectivity in reference by the method of 'rewarding' and 'penalizing'. I cannot see how this would be possible unless we have the spontaneous tendency to experience an objective world, in which we experience ourselves as having some position and moving around. Quine is, however, so convinced of the social origin of all objective experience, that he says: "These corrective cues [the cues activated by the social pull to objectivity] are used unconsciously, such is the perfection of our socialization; a painter has even to school himself to set them aside when he tries to reproduce his true retinal intake." (*WO* p. 8.) Can children reproduce their true retinal intake without schooling? Drawing in perspective is, in fact, a late cultural achievement.

Quine calls his first section 'Beginning with ordinary things'. But in fact he does not begin with ordinary objective things at all, but with *subjectivity*. He starts with the familiar Russellian desk and the sense data we get of it, and in some way he seems to think that there is only one way of explaining the fact that language does not operate with what is epistemologically 'given' from a subjective point of view: the capacity of society to give language another orientation.

This tendency to mix up epistemological ideas with semantics, typical of the outlook in Russell's *Problems of Philosophy* and Russell's version of logical atomism, is found, so it seems to me, at several other points in Quine's book.

III. BEGINNING WITH ORDINARY THINGS

My own view could be summed up as follows: Let us really begin with ordinary things. Let us start from the assumption – made by all parents and teachers – that a child learning a language observes roughly the same world of physical objects as we do and that he understands in the main that he is himself a part of this world and moves around in it. If we relate his linguistic reactions to what he sees and hears and touches, let us not bother about how his experience is related to his surface irritations – unless we have very particular reasons for believing that his experiences are not the same as an adult would have under the same circumstances. Let us argue not in terms of surface stimulations but in terms of the socially observable ordinary objects which give rise to these stimulations.

Unless we do so, we shall be compelled to employ a technical vocabulary, the interest of which remains in the vocabulary itself and we shall often get our conceptions of what is really going on confused. Unless we do so, we shall easily be forced to raise our questions within an unrealistic speculative frame-work, and we shall be likely to miss what is really interesting about the working of language because we shroud it in the mist of a clumsy conceptual apparatus.

IV. LEARNING A JUNGLE-LANGUAGE

"A rabbit scurries by, the native says 'Gavagai' and the linguist notes down the sentence 'Rabbit' (or 'Lo, a rabbit') as a tentative translation, subject to testing in further cases." (*WO* p. 29.)

This is, according to Quine, an example of the procedure a linguist has to use if he has to learn to translate an entirely unknown language without access to an interpreter.

I think it is an odd beginning. For one thing, had not our linguist better try to learn the language from within, without taking it for granted that it can be translated into English? The natives may have a culture very different from ours, and even though they operate with the same kind of physical objects as we do, their concepts need not as a rule have exact counterparts in English.

But let us accept the translation method. Our linguist notes 'gavagai' = 'rabbit'. Under the assumption that Quine's stimulation-theory of meaning be adequate, this is an amazingly good guess, if it turns out to be correct. For if the only thing we know is that *some* kind of surface stimulus which the native experienced led him to utter the sound-sequence 'gavagai' at a certain moment, it could mean almost anything. Why not, for instance, 'Ouch!' of pain. Or perhaps the native was referring to some noise, odour or sensation of temperature, to some more or less square-like projection on his retina, to some colour impression, or what not. If we do not take it for granted that the utterance of the native refers to the same kind of objective world as we have there is no clue to what he might be meaning. In fact, there is no clue unless we assume in addition that the native has the same interest in moving things, and in particular in animals, as we have. And even then the clue is very indeterminate unless the native accompanies his utterance with a pointing gesture.

To such difficulties in his theory Quine does not pay any attention, at least not in this context. As we see from the arguments following our quotation, he *takes it for granted* that the native *does* refer to the object scurrying by; the only difficulty he mentions is that the native may be referring to some other *property* of this object than that of being a rabbit – he suggests as other possible interpretations 'white' and 'animal'. (In a later context he lays much weight on the possibility that the object referred to might have been a 'rabbit time slice', but this is, of course, a very sophisticated argument.) From this point of view, it is characteristic of how Quine's approach leads him astray that he chooses for his first language lesson a situation in which the linguist *could* really be in doubt about what object the native is referring to, since he gets only a glimpse of it. Why not choose objects which can easily be subjected to a closer scrutiny, such as, say at least, a rabbit in a cage?

This approach leads Quine to insert the following remark (*WO* p. 31):

It is important to think of what prompts the native's assent to 'Gavagai' as stimulations and not rabbits. Stimulation can remain the same though the rabbit be supplanted by a counterfeit. Conversely, stimulation can vary in its power to prompt assent to 'Gavagai' because of variations in angle, lighting, and color contrast, though the rabbit remains the same. In experimentally equating the uses of 'Gavagai' and 'Rabbit' it is stimulations that must be made to match, not animals.

To my mind considerations of this kind lead to an opposite conclusion: It is important to think that the native assents to the word 'Gavagai' when one refers to animals, not to stimulations. If we replace a rabbit by a good counterfeit a native may be duped into assenting to 'Gavagai'; but *if* 'Gavagai' really means the same as 'Rabbit', then he must retract his judgement after a closer scrutiny and admit that he was mistaken. For counterfeits of rabbits are *not* rabbits, otherwise they would not be counterfeits.

In the same way, if poor lighting induces the native not to assent to 'Gavagai' though the object seen *is* really a rabbit he has on further scrutiny to acknowledge his mistake. So again we are led to the conclusion that it is the object that counts, not a momentary stimulation.

By the way the talk of 'prompting' assent to utterances is misleading in contexts like this. The linguistic sense of a sentence is not the reason or cause *why* a person utters it. The reason may in the present case be that the native wants to play the language game of teaching meanings of words to the best of his ability, or it may be something else. But whatever the reason be, it cannot be the sense of his utterance.

Quine's way of expressing himself in such contexts suggests that he embraces some kind of 'causal' theory of linguistic meaning. I think such theories are wrong, but since I have criticized them elsewhere[5], I shall not go into it here.

V. FROM ONE-WORD UTTERANCES TO FULL SENTENCES

Quine calls the word 'Gavagai' as uttered in our teaching situation a centence. What exactly he means by calling it a sentence is not quite slear. He also calls the word 'Ouch' a sentence; and there seems to be some evidence for his thinking that 'Gavagai' is a sentence only for the same reason as he thinks that 'Ouch' is a sentence, that is, because he conceives of interjections as sentences. But of course, 'Gavagai', as uttered in our present context, is not an interjection. It has a meaning of a different sort, and this Quine seems to admit, since he admits something of the kind of the word 'red' when used as a one-word sentence (*WO* p. 10).

Now, there is an obvious semantic reason for calling 'Gavagai' a sentence in our present context. This is that it has the same function as a large class of full sentences, in that it *classifies* a given object as being of a certain kind. That Quine tacitly assumes that it is in *this* way that 'Gavagai' functions as a sentence seems to be clear from the fact that, as we have seen, the alternative interpretations he suggests are all of this same type.

If we consider this function of 'Gavagai', we could take the utterance of it as containing two parts: (a) the pointing gesture, or whatever means the speaker uses to indicate the object of which he is speaking, (b) the classifying word by which this object is asserted to belong among the objects of a certain kind.

In thus containing two parts this sentence is like an ordinary subject-predicate sentence. Nevertheless, I think the transition from one-word sentences to explicit subject-predicate sentences is a very remarkable human achievement.

"At the moment when there also arose signs which meant objects, there happened something decisive; indeed I am tempted to say that at that moment the transition from animal to man took place." This is a translated quotation from a letter by Mr. H. Johansen. I am inclined to agree with him, though I should use the expression 'indicated objects' rather than 'meant objects', for reasons that will be clear later on. The introduction of 'singular terms', which *indicate* objects and do not merely classify them, makes it possible to report facts about things which are absent and in no way connected with the speech situation, and thus definitely surpasses the stage when one merely reacts to certain situations in a specific way. Only at that stage are real *descriptions* produced, and the ability to create descriptions is fundamental to human culture.

Some children seem to feel the transition from one-word sentences to genuine reports in the form of full sentences as quite a personal achievement. Charlotte and Karl Bühler say of their daughter that she was very excited about her performance when, at the age of 16 months, she made her first report about something she had seen in the form *"Daten la-la-la"* – it meant 'the soldiers were singing', or something of the kind. She was so excited that she repeated the report – which as far as its content was concerned could not have excited her at all – again and again during the following hours.[6]

Apart from reflections of this very general kind, we may state that the function of a singular term is *quite different* from the function of the predicate[7] of a sentence. The function of a singular term is to *specify* what object we are speaking of, to *point it out*, not to classify it as a word in predicate position. If somebody says

> My rabbit is small,

he does not use the phrase 'My rabbit' to classify a *given* object but to *indicate* what object he is speaking of. The phrase 'My rabbit' functions as a set of coordinates which indicate a point by referring it to a coordinate system. It has thus nothing to do with reactions to situations. The *classification* of the object is given by making the phrase 'My rabbit' into the subject of a sentence of the form

> x is small.

Quine's analysis of the way in which we learn to use full sentences is like this. First he states that one-word sentences like 'Ouch', 'Red' and 'Square' are certainly learnt as wholes. Secondly, he maintains that longer sentences are sometimes also learnt as wholes. Then he continues (*WO* p. 9, my italics):

Not that all or most sentences are learnt as wholes. Most sentences are built up rather from learned parts, by *analogy with the way* in which those parts have previously been seen to occur in other sentences which may or may not have been learned as wholes. ...

It is evident how new sentences may be built from old materials and volunteered on appropriate occasions *simply by virtue of the analogies*. Having been directly conditioned to the appropriate use of 'Foot' (or 'This is my foot') as a sentence, and 'Hand' likewise, and 'My foot hurts' as a whole, the child might conceivably utter 'My hand hurts' on an appropriate occasion, though unaided by previous experience with that actual sentence.

There are certain special difficulties about the example chosen here by Quine. There is the problem of checking whether a child is using the phrase 'My foot hurts' correctly because of the privateness of the exper-

35

ience it describes. There is another problem in the child's reference to itself by using the phrase 'My foot' instead of 'The foot' – the use of first-person pronouns is a late achievement in the development of children's speech. But let us pass over these difficulties. In respect of the latter, let us assume that the child has learnt 'My-foot' as a one-word sentence which is used when pointing to one of the child's feet. Let us make the corresponding assumption about the use of 'My-hand'. How does the child learn to 'volunteer' on an appropriate occasion to say 'My hand hurts'?

Simply by *analogy*, says Quine. But the faculty of making such an analogy is *not* simple. Quine specifies the analogy as one of 'analogical substitution' (*WO* p. 9). But the procedure of analogical substitution is complicated.

Consider the two sentences

(1)   My foot hurts

and

(2)   My hand hurts.

A child's passing from the appropriate use of (1) 'learned as a whole' to the appropriate use of (2) by analogical substitution can be analysed into three essential steps:

(i) The child conceives of (1) *not* as a whole but as analysed in a way which gives it a definite structure. This structure can in the simplest and most general way be characterized by saying that (1) is conceived of as being of the form

(3)   x hurts,

that is, as an expression which is the product of the *formal* substitution of 'My foot' for 'x' in (3). I call (3) – or rather the form of (3) in respect of 'x', for 'x' is a dummy[8] – the *predicate-form* of (1), for this form is what corresponds, from a logical point of view, to what the grammarians call the predicate.

(ii) It must be noted that (1) is *not* the conjunction of the one-word sentences 'My foot' and 'Hurts' but has a quite different sense. The expression 'My foot' is, as we have said, given a new function in sentence (1), which is different from the function of the one-word sentence 'My-foot'. This is the function of being a *name* of an individual object, the

36

function of a pointer, by which we are informed of what object is meant, it is *not* used as a classifier of an ostensibly given object according to some features of this object. This the child must grasp in some way.

(iii) It follows that the word 'hurts' will also get a function in (1) which is somewhat different from its function in the one-word sentence 'Hurts'. It will not classify as a single word but as an element in a determined syntactic structure. This the child must also grasp in some way, and it shows its grasp of this by forming (2) as the product of the substitution of 'My hand' for '*x*' in the predicate-form (3).

To avoid misunderstandings, it should perhaps be pointed out that my analysis does not mean that the child performs these three steps in turn, nor that it is able to perform this analysis explicitly or is in any other way aware of the fact that these three steps are involved.

The significance of points (i) – (iii) will be most clearly seen in connection with the conception of a simple (first order) sentence as a *picture* of what it reports. I cannot go further into this idea here (Cf. *WT* Ch. VII). Let me only state that the excitement of the Bühlers' child may be easily explained as an excitement over her own creative power, an excitement of the same kind as a child's excitement when making his first drawing of, say, a man.[9]

VI. FACTS AND PROPOSITIONS

Quine finds that 'facts' are '*entia non grata*' (*WO* p. 246). If he meant by this merely that facts *are not objects* – they do not belong to the same *category* as do rabbits – then I certainly should agree with him. If he meant that we should try to avoid bound propositional variables I can also follow him. But he seems to mean something more, that the term 'fact' should not be used at all, or if it be used, only in the same subordinate function as, for instance, the word 'sake' in the expression 'for the sake of'. Here I cannot agree.

I stated in Section III that we should not argue in terms of surface irritations but rather in terms of the socially observable ordinary objects which give rise to them. If this is to be understood correctly, it must be noted that 'bare' objects cannot give rise to stimulations. We could not, for instance, see a rabbit unless it had some colour and shape. To *observe an object* is always to observe *facts* about this object. As elements in

37

our world of experience, objects are always *imbedded* in facts (cf. *WT* Ch. II).

Now, Quine admits that there are some reasons for the 'admission of facts'. One such reason is that the admission is 'encouraged' by "a wish to defer the question what makes a sentence or proposition true: those are true that state facts." Quine does not seem to think that this reason is worthy of serious consideration. I think it is.

Quine compares this reason with the tendency "to liken sentences to names and then posit objects for them to name" (*WO* p. 246). But this comparison is wrong. There is a noteworthy difference between *names* and *sentences*. In an ordinary one-place subject-predicate sentence, the singular term which forms the subject of the sentence is a *name* because it is used to indicate, to stand for the object to which it refers. Now, the function of the predicate-form in the sentence is to classify the denominatum of the subject; but in order to do so it must be correlated with a specific property; so, in a sense, we can speak of the predicate-form as a *name* of this property (cf. *WT* Ch. VII, § 7). Now, the correlation between the subject and predicate-form as names and their denominata forms a semantic key by means of which the sentence is interpreted, and there is no meaning in asking whether this key is 'true' or 'false' – it is just given by the semantic rules. But given the key, then there is a determinate *fact*, with which the sentence becomes associated; this is the fact that the denominatum of the subject *has* or *has not* the property which is the denominatum of the predicate-form – as the case may be. But the sentence is not merely a name of the fact – the fact is indicated by the denominata of the elements of the sentence and need not be denoted by the sentence – it can be *compared* with the fact. It either *agrees* or *does not agree* with the fact. This is the reason why sentences can be 'true' or 'false'. Now, the sentence is to be *accepted* if it is true and agrees with the fact; otherwise, it is to be *rejected*. This is the basis for the possibility of reading off *what* is the case from *what* sentences are accepted.[10]

This account can be generalized. But in order to formulate it in a general way we need the word 'fact'. Quine, however, wants to go the other way round. He says that often we can speak of 'true sentences' where we are tempted to speak of facts (*WO* p. 247); and this is the only alternative he mentions to speaking about facts. This means, among other things, that we should speak of objective facts in terms of semantic facts which depend on linguistic conventions. To do this is, of course, unsatisfactory, since facts *are* objective.

That facts are objective Quine admits as a reason for 'admitting facts'. He also accepts that facts have 'a certain (*sic*!) observability'. Both reasons are, however, brushed away.

What would be the inconvenience arising from speaking about facts? Perhaps Quine is troubled by the fact that the word 'fact' is a noun, accepting the idea that what is referred to by a noun must be an object. If this is so, let me once and for all state that it is a mistake, though a widespread one. But it is also possible that Quine has the feeling that 'being a fact' is not an ordinary quality like 'being a rabbit'. This means that the semantics of the sentence 'this is a fact' are quite different from the semantics of the sentence 'this is a rabbit' – the former sentence does not belong to a 'first order language' and it uses the syntactical subject-predicate form in a metaphorical way (cf. *WT* Ch. XI, §§ 7, 8 and 10). Since Quine's formalization of set-theory is performed within the scope of what could be called a first-order language, he does not need the term 'fact' in this theory. But this fact must not be the basis of unwarranted generalizations.

In respect of 'propositions' Quine does not seem to be as rigid as in respect of 'facts'. For my part I should take a nominalist position in respect of propositions, and I am not sure that this term is needed at all. Propositions can only be given by sentences which express them or by some other kind of pictures presenting them and need not be assumed to have any independent 'existence' (cf. *WT* Ch. VI, §§ 6 and 13).

VII. THE 'FLIGHT FROM INTENSIONS'

Quine's attitude to qualities and relations in intension is a combination of 'extensionalism' and 'nominalism'. All talk of qualities and relations in intension should be replaced either by talking about classes or by talking about linguistic 'predicates' – which are considered as linguistic objects.

The basis of this conception is, so it seems to me, that set-theory, and in consequence, mathematics can be built up entirely extensionally. The only entities we need are classes.

This approach to mathematics has its merits, and I shall accept it for the moment. Let us assume that mathematics is entirely extensional in Quine's sense. Can we then generalize this finding and say that intensiose do not matter and can be eliminated?

Quine seems to be rather unhesitant about this. To me it seems to be a kind of prejudice, not uncommon among specialists in one science Quine thinks that what is true of mathematics and its formalized languag. must also be true in all other contexts. But to my mind it is quite obvious that this is not so. The fact that it is not is of great importance in semantics.

Let us examine an example of how a child learns the 'names of the colours'.[11] When my boy was about two years old he had a set of bricks of different shapes and colours which could be combined to make gaudy figures. If I remember rightly, they consisted of red, green, yellow and blue squares, rhombs and triangles. I attempted to teach him the meaning of 'red' by first pointing at a red rhomb and saying 'red', then at a yellow rhomb and saying 'not red'. I then pointed at a red square and said 'red' and at a blue square and said 'not red' and so on. My son was interested and tried in his turn to point out the red objects, but without success. I began afresh, 'This is red, this is not'; but in vain. He grew tired and told me to go away. I went, but as a last resort pointed to a red tooth-mug in the bathroom and said 'red'. The result was the most startling example of 'a flash of insight' that I have ever seen. My son stared at the mug with an expression of deep thought, suddenly turned with enthusiasm to his bricks and now without difficulty picked out the red ones. This was not all: in a minute he had learnt the names of the other colours. The sight of the red mug had taught him what he had not realized before, namely, *what* difference there was between red objects and objects of other colours, and likewise what *kind* of difference we were looking for here, so he could learn the names of the other colours immediately from just one example.

Now this procedure has *something* to do with extensions. We start from a restricted class of objects and separately point out in *extension* those objects in this class which are red and those which are not red. But in order for the learner really to learn his lesson, he must look for *intensions*, not extensions, that is, for a certain *distinctive feature* which is common to those objects which are called 'red' and by which they differ from such objects as are called 'not red'. Only when he has made a guess as to what this feature may be can he try to go on to make the division for *new* objects. If his guess was correct he will be able to go on, otherwise not. In our example, correctness of the boy's guess after looking at the mug was confirmed by the fact that his division of new objects was accepted, and still further confirmed by the fact that his division according to other colours was also accepted.

After he had learnt to distinguish between colours intensionally he could go on to more and more new classes of objects and divide them according to the same principle as before. But he can certainly never come to the stage when *all* objects are divided, so the *extension* of redness remains for ever unknown to him.

I cannot see how this procedure could be described in extensional terms. In fact, Quine seems to be aware of having to do with intensions in such situations, though he does not say so. For instance, he says that the utterance of 'red' could be elicited by the question "What colour is this?". This is a clearly intensional question, though it is otherwise unfortunately chosen, since we cannot point to colours, only to objects having colours. The question "What colour is this?" must therefore be regarded as a metaphorical formulation of the more straightforward question "What is the colour of this?". And as we see from my example, we need not use the word 'colour' at all in a teaching situation. This is fortunate, for how could we otherwise teach the meaning of the word 'colour'?[12]

I arrive at the conclusion that we cannot give any account of semantics without reference to intensions. Even in mathematics I am dubious about the possibility of a purely extensional view. Must we not in set-theory understand the ε-relation intensionally? As far I can see, it would be circular to replace this relation by a class of ordered pairs. As for the possibility of taking a nominalistic view of it, this will imply, among other things, a nominalistic view of all sets.

If we take the ε-relation intensionally we could regard set-theory as a general theory of systems with one binary relation (in intension) which fulfils certain conditions.[13]

It should be noted here as with facts, that if Quine means only that qualities should not be regarded as *objects*, or that we should not quantify over qualities and relations, I could follow him. But the difficulties in quantifying over qualities are not due to any difficulty in speaking about qualities but to a difficulty in grasping what kind of closure-properties a universe of 'all qualities' would possess.

VIII. SINGULAR TERMS

1. *The Indispensibility of an Analysis of Names*

(i) Quine is very impressed by the possibility of eliminating all names, as it is developed in his mathematical logic. The procedure is certainly useful for certain purposes in a formalization of mathematics. But its importance for all purposes must be seriously disputed. There are many reasons for this; I shall here mention only one.

Let us start from the example

(4)   Socrates is a man.

As we have seen, understanding this sentence involves our conceiving of 'Socrates' as a name of an object and of the predicate-form

(5) x is a man

as being correlated to a certain quality, in that a sentence of the form (5) should be accepted if, and only if, the individual indicated by the subject has this quality; otherwise it should be rejected. According to this principle, (4) should be accepted, whereas

(6)   Bucephalus is a man

should be rejected.

If we substitute for 'x' expressions other than names of objects, this semantic rule does not apply, so we may introduce other rules for the acceptance or rejection of sentences constructed in this way (if they are called sentences). If we do not take 'Apollo' as a name of an object in our universe of discourse, then we may introduce new rules – more or less specified – for the acceptance or rejection of a sentence like

(7)   Apollo is a man.

Since 'Apollo' is not a name of an object in our universe of discourse, sentence (7) is only syntactically a subject-predicate sentence: semantically, it is of a different kind. This accounts for the fact that we may accept (7) and nevertheless state that it does not in itself imply any existential

42

sentence. Expressing oneself in this way is, I think, much clearer than taking 'Apollo' as a name and then adding that Apollo does not exist, or that nothing is identical with Apollo, or something of the kind.

As semantic subject-predicate sentence I also count sentences like

(8)   Jim is taller than John.

This sentence can be analysed into two semantical subjects: 'Jim' and 'John', and the predicate-form

(9) x is taller than y.

Now the rules for the acceptance or rejection of semantic subject-predicate sentences are also fundamental to the understanding of quantified sentences like

(10) $(x)(x$ is a man$)$
and
(11) $(Ex)(x$ is a man$)$.

The condition for accepting (10) is that for *every* assignment of a value to the variable 'x', the expression 'x is a man' is true. But an assignment of a value to a variable is exactly to make it into a name of an object, though only momentarily and not as a standing name. Our rule for the acceptance of (10) could in fact be formulated in this way: Sentence (10) is to be accepted if and only if taking 'x' as a name of any object in our universe of discourse (and thus making (5) into a sentence), (5) fulfils the condition for being accepted.

A corresponding analysis certainly applies to (11). So we cannot eliminate the analysis of semantic subject-predicate sentences even if we eliminate all standing names.

2. *Meaning*

Before we go on, I must add some remarks about the relation between 'meaning' and 'denotation'. Quine directs many criticisms against positing objects as 'meanings' of certain expressions which would be felt otherwise to be meaningless. I should go so far in this respect as to say that the 'meaning' of an expression must *never* be thought of as some object which this expression 'means'. Amplifying Wittgenstein, I state that the

43

word 'mean' is in many cases best conceived of as an *intransitive* verb, of which 'meaning' is a kind of gerund. If, for instance, we ask for the meaning of the name 'Socrates', the answer is not that this is the person Socrates, but that the word 'Socrates' *is used to denote* Socrates, and that being used in that way is its 'meaning'. (In the same way, the meaning of the word 'I' consists in the fact that it is used to denote the speaker.)

3. *Names have not intensions*

If we accept this terminology we are less tempted to think that expressions are always used to 'denote' an object, and also less tempted to think that expressions in some contexts denote their 'extension', in other contexts their 'intension'. What matters in our present argument however, is, that we are less tempted to think that proper names – like 'Socrates' – have not only a denotation in extension but also an intension. My thesis is that proper names are what I call *purely referential* (I do not use the term in exactly the same way as Quine), in that their only function is to denote an object in extension. So, proper names have extensions, but they have *not* (semantic) *intensions* as quality expressions have.

Now, Russell, thought that only things with which we are personally acquainted can have genuine *names*, and that the fact that no living person knows Socrates by acquaintance therefore means that all living persons know him only by 'description'; and since the description may be different for different persons, 'Socrates' may have a different meaning for different persons. Thus 'Socrates' is not properly called a 'proper name'. It should be paraphrased as 'the philosopher who drank the hemlock', or something of that sort.

This argument seems to entail that we give the meaning of the word 'Socrates' by pointing out some intension which this word means, and this may be different for different persons.

Now, Quine feels an absurdity about this kind of argument. But the difficulty he sees seems not to be that 'Socrates' is given an intension, but only the fact that on the one hand the name 'Socrates' and on the other hand the few cases in which we may be supposed to learn the denotatum of a name directly should be treated in different ways. His conclusion is that *all* proper names should be replaced by definite descriptions.

His procedure in *Methods of Logic* is very simple. It could, using my vocabulary, be described like this. Quine introduces the predicate-form

(12) x is-Socrates,

abbreviated as 'Sx', and states that it fulfils the condition

(13) $(Ey)(x)(Sx \equiv x = y)$.

If we now abbreviate the predicate-form (5) as 'Mx', sentence (4) may be paraphrased as

(14) $(Ey)(My \ \& \ (x)(Sx \equiv x = y))$.

I do not dispute this method as a convenient device for certain purposes. But I dispute its claim to be of essential importance for the understanding of how language works. To my view, (4) is certainly not understood because it can be paraphrased as (14); on the contrary, (14) cannot be understood unless it is taken as an approximate paraphrase of (4). For we cannot understand the use of the predicate-form (12) properly unless we first understand the working of 'Socrates' as a proper name. The introduction of 'Sx' as a kind of primitive predicate-form is in fact misleading, since it suggests that we learn it in the same way as the predicate-form 'x is red', that is, by finding a distinctive feature by which we divide objects into such as are called Socrates and such as are not called Socrates, treating 'Socrates' as an adjective. There are certainly many such distinctive features: that of being a philosopher who drank hemlock, that of being Plato's beloved teacher, that of being Xantippe's husband, and so on. If we replace (4) by (12), we have the impression that we must *choose* one of these interpretations and thus give 'Socrates' an intension, which is alien to a proper name.

Now, someone may object that this is not so in a sentence like

(15)   Pegasus does not exist.

But this sentence is in fact generally felt as abnormal. The abnormality is that it is not a semantic subject-predicate sentence. It is not one because of the often-repeated reason that 'x exists' is not correlated with a quality. But in this context another reason is of more importance. This is that 'Pegasus' does not function as a proper name in sentence (15). Since this is so it is useful to follow Quine, and explain its sense by introducing the predicate form 'x pegasizes' and take (15) to be a syntactically misleading way of saying about the same as the sentence

(16) $(x)(\sim(x\text{ pegasizes})...).$

The usefulness of this procedure is strengthened by the fact that we can correlate Pegasus with a rather uniquely determined intension, that of being a winged horse.

In other cases, where the 'name' used in such a sentence is not associated with a unique intension, it becomes utterly vague, as is shown by the discussion about the sentence

(17)   God exists.

4. *Definite Descriptions as Names*

In stressing the fact that names are purely referential I have so far considered only proper names. What about 'definite descriptions' used as names? My view is that definite descriptions are also purely referential *in so far as they are really used as names*. If I say

(18)   Jim's father is tall,

and analyze this sentence as being of the predicate-form

(19) x is tall,

then we can consider it as a semantic subject-predicate sentence which says about *Jim's father* that he is tall, and thus distinguishes him from other persons who are not tall.

But now (18) is both syntactically and semantically ambiguous, for in fact it need not be analysed as having the predicate-form (19), but can also be taken as being the product of a substitution in the expression

(20) x's father is tall.

Now, if this is taken as the predicate-form of (18), then 'Jim' and not 'Jim's father' is taken as the semantic subject of (18) – and we should not let grammatical terminology prevent us from looking at it in this way – the function of sentence (18) is to say about *Jim* that he has a tall father, and we must take this as a quality of Jim which distinguishes him from other persons whose fathers are not tall.

In the first way of analysis the expression 'Jim's father' is conceived of as a whole, in the second it is not conceived of as a whole, but part of it is joined to the elements of the predicate-form and thus given a more intensional function.

Now *which* of these two interpretations of (18) we choose is often irrelevant, but it is not irrelevant in philosophical analysis or in semantics.

That this is so is most apparent in respect of the use of the identity sign. In the sentence

(21) $\qquad 3 + 5 = 8$

Frege considered '$3 + 5$' as a name. If this is taken as a name, we think of (21) as being the product of substituting the names '$3 + 5$' and '8' for 'x' and 'y' in

(22) $\qquad x = y,$

which is then taken as the predicate-form of (21). Since names are purely referential sentence (21) can only say that the denominatum of '$3 + 5$' is the same as the denominatum of '8', so, according to this analysis, '$3 + 5$' ought to be replaceable by '8'. We thus arrive at the conclusion that (21) says the same thing as

(23) $\qquad 8 = 8,$

that is, (21) is a tautology, which seems absurd.

Frege tried to solve the problem by making his famous distinction between sense and reference, which in a kind of modified version is taken over by Quine.

This kind of theory seems to operate with 'intensions' of names which occur as their denominata in certain contexts.

For my part I should analyze this situation in the following way:

On the one hand, the analysis according to which (21) is of the predicate-form (22) is indeed *one* way of analyzing it. By this analysis, (21) certainly appears as a tautology; but then, what is of mathematical interest is not *what* (21) says, but the semantic fact *that* it expresses a tautology.[14]

Now I think Quine does not regard (21) as a tautology. From this point of view it is of interest to note that (21) is semantically ambiguous and can also be analyzed as being of the predicate-form

(24) $\qquad x + y = z.$

47

It should, however, be noted that if we do so, the identity sign does not have the same meaning as in (22); for we must now take the expression (24) in its capacity of being a predicate-form as a *whole*, not as the product of a substitution in (22). In fact we had better, for many purposes, not use the identity sign at all, but replace (24) by, for instance, the predicate-form

(25) $S(x, y, z)$,

which is the 'name' of the relation which holds between three objects when the third object is the sum of the first two; and this relation *has nothing to do with identity*.

So, if we analyze (21) as having the predicate-form (24) the expression '3 + 5' does not function as a name and the sign '=' not as a genuine identity sign, so there is no reason to think that a rule of substitutivity could be attached to it. Since, on the other hand, the dropping of the substitutivity rule is inconvenient in many respects, one is tempted to have (21) analyzed in *both* ways. This is harmless in many contexts, but one should not be surprised if there are instances in which it is not harmless.

The need to have a sentence which contains an identity sign analyzed in both ways is especially felt in connection with the use of the iota operator. Let us assume that we start from the notation (25) for sum. Then we may, according to the theory of iota operators, introduce the (variable) singular term $(\imath_z) S(x, y, z)$ into our notation by writing

(26)   '$(\imath_z) S(x, y, z) = 8$'
         for   '$(Eu) (u = 8 \,\&\, (z) (S(x, y, z) \equiv z = u))$'.

In this notation '$(\imath_z) S(3, 5, z)$' has the same function as '3 + 5' in (21), and as a consequence we tend, on the one hand to conceive of it as a whole and a name, and on the other hand accept that it can be translated by means of the rule (26), which presupposes that it is *not* taken as a whole.

This double interpretation is again harmless in certain contexts, but we should not be surprised if it is not harmless in others.

5. *Individual Terms in Modal Contexts*

It is not harmless in modal contexts, as is clear from a much discussed argument of Quine's:

We are inclined to say that '$9>4$' is *necessarily* true, so that we can write

(27) $N(9>4)$.

On the other hand we accept the truth of

(28)   The number of the major planets $= 9$.

From (27) and (28) and the fact that identity implies substitutivity we arrive at the conclusion.

(29) N(the number of the major planets > 4).

But it is certainly not a necessary truth that there are more than 4 major planets.

Quine shows (*WO* p. 198) that the acceptance of this kind of inference is not only unintuitive but will annihilate modal distinctions; we can by means of it derive that $p \equiv Np$ is generally true.

If (29) is formalized it will contain an iota-operator, the elimination of which would lead to quantification into modal contexts. Therefore, Quine takes this paradox as evidence for the impossibility of using quantifiers in modal contexts.

There have been many attempts to show that this is not so. Føllesdal tries to avoid the difficulty by an argument [15] which I shall paraphrase as follows:

Let us assume that we can construct logic without using proper names, and that all definite descriptions can be eliminated. Let us further assume that the result of the elimination in respect of (28) is

(30)   There are exactly nine major planets.

Let us then take (30) as a *standard* form of a statement, of which (28) is only a convenient variant introduced by definition. Now the convenience of this variant is due to the fact that in ordinary logic we *can* apply the rule of substitutivity to such 'artificial' identities; that is, every formula derivable by means of this rule can also be derived directly without using it. But if this is *not* so in modal logic, the notation introduced by defining rules like (26) ought to be restricted to such cases where the substitutivity rule really can be used also in modal contexts. This restriction means in our case that (30) could not be replaced by

(28) unless (30) were *itself* necessarily true. Since it is not, the replacement is faulty. By such a restriction on the use of the iota-operator, we can save, according to Føllesdal, both quantification into modal contexts and the substitutivity rule for identity.

From our point of view the analysis of the situation takes the following form:

The paradoxical character of (29) depends on our possibility of analyzing the sentence

(31)   The number of the major planets > 4

in two ways. One way is to take it as being a semantic subject-predicate sentence of the form

(32) $x > y$,

which means that we take the expression 'the number of the major planets' as a name and, accordingly, as *purely referential*. What this expression denotes is the number 9. Sentence (29) then says absolutely the same thing as (27), and no paradox ensues.

However (31) can also be analyzed as a semantic subject-predicate sentence of the form

(33)   The number of $x > y$.

Then, the semantic subjects of this sentence are 'the major planets' and '4': it is not about the number 9 but about the planets, and then (29) is certainly not true. But then the expression 'the number of the major planets' does not occur in (29) as a name, and there is no reason to think it replaceable by '9'.

Quine says that "modal contexts are 'referentially opaque' in that we cannot take definite descriptions 'purely referentially' in them" (*WO* p. 197). I think this way of expressing oneself is at least misleading. No paradoxes will ensue *if* we really take a definite description *purely* referentially. Difficulties arise only when we switch over from a purely referential use of it to a non-referential interpretation, by transferring a part of it to the predicate-form.

There is a point of contact between this analysis and that of Føllesdal. This is that *if* (28) is to mean the same as (30), then the expression 'The number of the major planets' cannot be used as a name, and then the identity sign cannot mean identity, so the substitutivity rule cannot be applied. So, *if* we want to use the identity sign only in contexts where it means identity, then we cannot replace (30) by (28). This replacement would, however, nevertheless be harmless in our present context if (30) were necessarily true.

I here take identity to entail substitutivity in all contexts. It should, however, be added that I am in some doubt as to whether this is really always the best way of looking at identity. So I am not sure that the kind of analysis given above accounts for all the problems concerning identity.

IX. REALISM

The points of divergence between Quine's basic assumptions and mine are by no means exhausted by the above criticisms. For instance, I have not touched upon the issue about the concepts analytic and synthetic. Since I have treated this question elsewhere (though only in Swedish)[16] I shall not go into it here. Here I shall only add a short remark on Quine's attitude to classes. Quine repudiates the belief that he is a nominalist, because he takes a realistic attitude to classes (*WO* p. 243 n.). He does indeed. I will not criticize him for this attitude as such – though I think that the conception of classes as objects – their 'entification' in Quine's terminology – is a serious step to which due attention should be paid. But I wonder about the fact that Quine entirely forgets the publicity principle in this context. Does this not raise an interesting question as to how the logicians' overt formal behaviour is related to socially observable facts?

REFERENCES

[1] See the back cover of the paper-back edition of Whitehead and Russell, *Principia Mathematica*, Cambridge 1964.

[2] Quine does not explicitly characterize his own view as a kind of behaviourism, but he seems to do so indirectly by introducing the "division between behaviourism and mentalism" and siding against mentalism (*WO* p. 219).

[3] I follow John Stuart Mill in referring the word 'entity' to objects, qualities, relations in intension, *etc.*, irrespective of categories. Quine speaks of 'entification' and thus seems to take the word 'entity' to refer only to what I call 'objects'. As to 'categories', cf. E. Stenius, *Wittgenstein's Tractatus. A Critical Exposition*, Oxford 1960, Ch. II, § 2. – This book will be referred to in the sequel as *WT*.

[4] Cf. Ryle's argument against sensations in G. Ryle, *The Concept of Mind*, London

1949, p. 201ff. – By the way, the notion of a 'projection on the retina' seems to be fictitious in this context. Physiologists tell us that the eye is always oscillating; an immobile eye is blind.

[5] E. Stenius, 'Mood and Language-Game', *Synthese* **17** (1967) 254–274.

[6] Karl Bühler, *Die geistige Entwicklung des Kindes*, 6th ed., Jena 1930, p. 315; Charlotte Bühler, *Kindheit und Jugend*, 3rd ed., Leipzig 1931, p. 148f. Cf. below, note 9.

[7] I use here, like Quine, the term 'predicate' as referring to a linguistic entity forming a part of a sentence, not in the intensional sense I have used in *WT*.

[8] If I rightly understand Quine's notation in *Methods of Logic*, he would prefer to use as dummies signs like '$\boxed{1}$', '$\boxed{2}$', ... instead of letters like 'x', 'y',...; but what signs we use as dummies is irrelevant.

[9] Nobody can, of course, *know* what was the cause of the child's excitement. Her parents had different opinions about how it should be explained. It is, however, noteworthy that Mrs Bühler's interpretation can be said to come rather near to mine, although, naturally, she expresses herself in a very different vocabulary. Cf. note 6 above.

[10] Cf. the paper mentioned above in note 5.

[11] I have reported about this case in two earlier papers: 'Den språkliga beskrivningen som isomorf avbildning', *Ajatus* **16** (1950) 69–101, pp. 78ff.; 'Linguistic Structure and the Structure of Experience', *Theoria* **20** (1954) 153–172, pp. 159f.

[12] Cf. Wittgenstein's difficulties in *Philosophical Investigations*, Oxford 1954, § 28ff, and *WT*, p. 160 n.

[13] This was an approach taken by P. Finsler in his paper 'Über die Grundlegung der Mengenlehre I', *Mathematische Zeitschrift* **25** (1926) 683–713. It was also adopted in my doctoral dissertation 'Das Problem der logischen Antinomien', *Societas Scientiarum Fennica, Comm. Phys.-Math* **14**, no. 11 (1949).

[14] Cf. with this E. Stenius, 'Are True Numerical Statements Analytic or Synthetic', *Philosophical Review* **74** (1965) 357–371, § xiv.

[15] D. Føllesdal, 'Quantification into Causal Contexts', in *Boston Studies in the Philosophy of Science* vol. 2, Humanities Press, New York 1965, pp. 263–274.

[16] E. Stenius, 'Begreppen "analytisk" och "syntetisk"', *Ajatus* **27** (1965) 97–122; forthcoming in English in *Scandinavian Studies in Philosophy* (ed. by R. Olsen), Johns Hopkins Press, Baltimore 1970.

NOAM CHOMSKY

QUINE'S EMPIRICAL ASSUMPTIONS*

Perhaps the clearest and most explicit development of what appears to be a narrowly Humean theory of language acquisition in recent philosophy is that of Quine, in the introductory chapters to his *Word and Object*.[1] If the Humean theory is roughly accurate, then a person's knowledge of language should be representable as a network of linguistic forms – let us say, to first approximation, sentences – associated with one another and, in part, associated to certain stimulus conditions. This formulation Quine presents as, I take it, a factual assertion. Thus he states that our "theories" – whether "deliberate", as chemistry, or "second nature", as "the immemorial doctrine of ordinary enduring middle-sized objects" – can each be characterized as "a fabric of sentences variously associated to one another and to non-verbal stimuli by the mechanism of conditioned response" (p. 11). Hence the whole of our knowledge (our total "theory", in this sense) can be characterized in these terms.

One difficulty that arises in interpreting such passages as these has to do with the relation between language and theory, where the latter term covers also general common-sense knowledge and belief. Quine's views about the interpenetration of theory and language are well known, but, even accepting them fully, one could not doubt that a person's language and his 'theory' are distinct systems. The point is too obvious to press, but it is, nevertheless, difficult to see how Quine distinguishes the two in his framework. In fact, throughout the discussion, he seems to use the terms interchangeably. For example, in Chapter 1, he discusses the learning of language in general terms, exemplifies it by an example from chemical theory leading up to the statement just quoted, then seemingly describes the "vast verbal structure" so constructed, the associative network that constitutes one's knowledge of science ("and indeed everything we ever say about the world"), as both the "body of theory" that one accepts and the language that one learns. Thus the discussion of how one constructs and uses a total theory of this sort concludes with the following statement:

Beneath the uniformity that unites us in communication there is a chaotic personal diversity of connections, and, for each of us, the connections continue to evolve. No two of us learn our language alike, nor, in a sense, does any finish learning it while he lives.

Since the comment merely summarizes the discussion of how the "single connected fabric" constituting our total theory is acquired (the latter discussion itself having been introduced to exemplify language learning), it seems that Quine must be proposing that a language, too, is "a fabric of sentences variously associated to one another and to non-verbal stimuli by the mechanism of conditioned response". Other parts of his exposition reinforce the conclusion that this is what is intended, as we shall see in a moment. Nevertheless, interpretation of Quine's remarks is made difficult at points because of his tendency to use the terms 'language' and 'theory' interchangeably, though obviously he must be presupposing a fundamental difference between the two – he is, for example, surely not proposing that two monolingual speakers of the same language cannot disagree on questions of belief, or that controversy over facts is necessarily as irrational as an argument between a monolingual speaker of English and a monolingual speaker of German.

Elsewhere, Quine states that he is considering a language as a "complex of present dispositions to verbal behavior, in which speakers of the same language have perforce come to resemble one another" (p. 27). Thus if a language is a network of sentences associated to one another and to external stimuli by the mechanism of conditioned response, then it follows that a person's disposition to verbal behavior can be characterized in terms of such a network. This factual assumption is far from obvious. I return to other aspects of this concept of 'language' below.

How is knowledge of such a language acquired? Evidently, a Humean theory will acquire substance only if such notions as 'similarity' are characterized in some way. Quine therefore postulates a prelinguistic (and presumably innate) "quality space" with a built-in distance measure (p. 83–4). Evidently, the structure of this space will determine the content of the theory of learning. For example, one could easily construct a theory of innate ideas of a rather classical sort in terms of a prelinguistic quality space with a build-in distance measure. Quine would, apparently, accept a very strong version of a theory of innate ideas as compatible with his framework. Thus he considers the possibility that "a red ball, a yellow ball, and a green ball are less distant from one another in... the child's... quality space than from a red kerchief". It is difficult to see how this differs from the assumption that 'ball' is an innate idea, if we admit the same possibilities along other 'dimensions' (particularly, if we allow these dimensions to be fairly abstract). In this respect, then, Quine seems to depart quite radically from the leading ideas that guided empiricist theory and to permit just about anything imaginable, so far as 'learning' of concepts is concerned. In particular, consider the fact that a speaker of English has acquired the concept 'sentence of English'. Suppose that we were to postulate an innate quality space with a structure so abstract that any two sentences of English are nearer to one another in terms of the postulated distance measure than a sentence of English and any sentence of another language. Then a learner could acquire the concept 'sentence of English' – he could, in other words, know that the language to which he is exposed is English and 'generalize' to any other sentence of English – from an exposure to one sentence. The same is true if we mean by 'sentence of English' a pairing of a certain phonetic and semantic interpretation. We could, once again, construct a quality space sufficiently abstract so that the infinite set of English sentences could be 'learned' from exposure to one sentence, by an organism equipped with this quality space.

The handful of examples and references that Quine gives suggests that he has something much narrower in mind, however; perhaps, a restriction to dimensions which have some simple physical correlate such as hue or brightness, with distance defined in terms of these physical correlates. If so, we have a very strong and quite specific version of a doctrine of innate ideas which now can be faced with empirical evidence.

It might be thought that Quine adds empirical content to his account by his insistence that "the child's early learning of a verbal response depends on society's reinforcement of the response in association with the stimulations that merit the response..." (p. 82) and his general insistence throughout that learning is based on reinforcement. But, unfortunately, Quine's concept of 'reinforcement' is reduced to near vacuity. For example, he is willing to accept the possibility that "society's reinforcement consists in no more than corroborative usage, whose resemblance to the child's effort is the sole reward" (p. 82–3). To say that learning requires reinforcement, then, comes very close to saying that learning cannot proceed without data. As Quine notes, his approach is "congenial... to Skinner's scheme, for... [Skinner]... does not enumerate the rewards". The remark is correct, but it should also be added that "Skinner's scheme" is almost totally empty, in fact, if anything, even less substantive than Quine's version of it, since Skinner, as distinct from Quine, does not even require that reinforcing stimuli impinge on the organism – it is sufficient that they be imagined, hoped for, etc. In general, the invoking of 'reinforcement' serves only a ritualistic function in such discussions as these, and one can safely disregard it in trying to determine the substantive content of what is being proposed.

However, Quine returns to a classical empiricist conception of a non-vacuous sort in his assumptions about how language is learned. Consistent with his view of language as a network of sentences[2], he enumerates three possible mechanisms by which sentences can be learned – i.e., by which knowledge of language can be acquired (p. 9f.). First, sentences can be learned by "direct conditioning" to appropriate non-verbal stimulations, that is, by repeated pairing of a stimulation and a sentence under appropriate conditions; second, by association of sentences with sentences (let us put aside the objection that in both cases, the associations should soon disappear, through extinction, under normal circumstances); third, new sentences can be produced by "analogical synthesis".[3] The third method at first seems to offer an escape to vacuity, once again. Thus if the first sentence of this paper is derivable by analogical synthesis from "the sky is blue" (both involve subject and predicate, are generated with their interpretations by the rules of English grammar, and share many other properties), then it is no doubt true that language can be learned by 'analogical synthesis', by 'generalization' along a dimension of the abstract sort suggested above (cf. p. 55). But it seems clear that Quine has nothing of this sort in mind. The one example that he gives is a case of substitution of one word for a similar one ('hand', 'foot') in a fixed context. And he seems to imply that the process of analogical synthesis is theoretically dispensable, simply serving to speed matters up (see p. 9). Therefore, we can perhaps conform to his intentions by totally disregarding this process, and considering the knowledge attained by a long-lived adult using only the first two methods instead of the knowledge attained by a young child who has used all three (there being nothing that can be said about the latter case until the notion 'analogical synthesis' is given some content). Noting further that a child of nine and a man of ninety share knowledge of language in fundamental respects – each can understand and use appropriately an astronomical number of sentences, for example – it would seem, further, that little is lost in omitting 'analogical synthesis' from consideration entirely, even for the young child. Assuming that this interpretation of Quine's remarks is correct, we derive support for the conclusion that he regards a language as a finite network of associated sentences, some associated also to stimuli, since this is just the structure that would arise from the two postulated mechanisms of language learning with substantive content.

Against this interpretation of Quine's remarks on language we can bring the fact that it is inconsistent with a truism that he of course accepts, namely, that a language is an infinite set of sentences (with intrinsic meanings; cf., e.g., p. 71). A network derived by the postulated mechanisms must be finite; it can, in fact, contain only the sentences to which a person has been exposed (repeatedly, and under similar circumstances). If we return to the definition of 'language' as a "complex of dispositions to verbal behavior", we reach a similar conclusion, at least if this notion is intended to have empirical content. Presumably, a complex of dispositions is a structure that can be represented as a set of probabilities for utterances in certain definable 'circumstances' or 'situations'. But it must be recognized that the notion 'probability of a sentence' is an entirely useless one, under any known interpretation of this term. On empirical grounds, the probability of my producing some given sentence of English – say, this sentence, or the sentence "birds fly" or "Tuesday follows Monday", or whatever – is indistinguishable from the probability of my producing a given sentence of Japanese. Introduction of the notion of 'probability relative to a situation' changes nothing, at least if 'situations' are characterized on any known objective grounds (we can, of course, raise the conditional probability of any sentence as high as we like, say to unity, relative to 'situations' specified on *ad hoc*, invented grounds). Hence if a language is a totality of speech dispositions (in some empirically significant sense of this notion), then my language either does not include the sentences just cited as examples, or it includes all of Japanese. In fact if the "complex of dispositions" is determined on grounds of empirical observation, then only a few conventional greetings, cliches, and so on, have much chance of being associated to the complex defining the language, since few other sentences are likely to have a non-null relative frequency, in the technical sense, in any reasonable corpus or set of observations – we would, for example, expect the attested frequency of any given sentence to decrease without limit as a corpus increases, under any but the most artificial conditions. One might imagine other ways of assigning probabilities to sentences on empirical grounds, but none, so far as I can see, that avoid these difficulties. Hence if a language is a complex of dispositions to respond under a normal set of circumstances, it would be not only finite (unless it included all languages) but also extremely small.

Adding to the confusion is the fact that Quine appears to vacillate somewhat in his use of the notion "speech dispositions". Thus he formulates the problem of "indeterminacy of translation" as resulting from the fact that "manuals for translating one language into another can be set up in divergent ways, all compatible with the totality of speech dispositions, yet incompatible with one another" (p. 27). As just noted, if we take the "totality of speech dispositions" of an individual to be characterized by probability distributions for utterances under detectable stimulus conditions, then the thesis quoted is true, near-vacuously, since except for a trivial set, all such probabilities will be empirically indistinguishable on empirical grounds, within or outside of the language. On the other hand, if we interpret the notions 'disposition' and 'situation' more loosely, it might be argued that the problem is really quite different, that there will be so few similarities among individuals in what they are inclined to say in given circumstances that no manual of translation can be set up at all, compatible with such inclinations. Actually, Quine avoids these problems, in his exposition, by shifting his ground from "totality of speech dispositions" to "stimulus meanings", that is, dispositions to "assent or dissent" in a situation determined by one narrowly circumscribed experiment. He even goes so far as to say that this arbitrarily selected experiment provides all of the evidence that is available, in principle, to the linguist (equivalently, to the language learner – p. 39). Clearly, however, a person's total "disposition to verbal response" under arbitrary stimulus conditions is not the same as his "dispositions to be prompted to assent or to dissent from the sentence" under the particular conditions of the *Gedankenexperiment* that Quine outlines. One might argue that by arbitrarily limiting the "totality of evidence", Quine irrelevantly establishes the thesis that alternative theories (manuals of trans-lation) exist compatible with all of the evidence (though the general thesis of indeterminacy of translation is nevertheless certainly true, in a sense to which we return in a moment). But my point here is only that this kind of vacillation makes it still more difficult to determine what Quine means by 'disposition' or 'language'.

It is easy to imagine a way out of the difficulties posed by the implied finiteness of language and knowledge (or near emptiness, if the notion of 'disposition' is taken very seriously). Thus one might assume that knowledge of a 'universal grammar', in the widest sense, is an innate property of the mind, and that this given system of rules and principles determines the form and meaning of infinitely many sentences (and the infinite scope of our knowledge and belief) from the minute experiential base that is actually available to us. I do not doubt that this approach is quite reasonable, but it then raises the empirical question of the nature of this universal, *a priori* system; and, of course, any philosophical conclusions that may be drawn will depend on the answers proposed for this question.[4] Quine's attitude towards an approach of this sort is not easy to determine. It certainly seems inconsistent with his general point of view, specifically, with his claim that even our knowledge of logical truths is derived by conditioning mechanisms that associate certain pairs of sentences (cf., e.g., p. 11f.), so that our knowledge of logical relations must be representable as a finite network of interconnected sentences. (How we can distinguish logical connections from causal ones, or either type from sentences which happen to be paired by accident in our experience is unclear, just as it is unclear how either sort of knowledge can be applied, but it is pointless to pursue this issue in the light of the strangeness of the whole conception.) Elsewhere, however, Quine appears to take the view that truth-functional logic might provide a kind of 'universal grammar'. Thus he asserts (p. 13) that truth functions lend themselves to "radical translation" without "unverifiable analytical hypotheses", and hence can be learned directly from the available evi-dence. He gives no real argument for this beyond the statement, which appears quite irrelevant to the factual issue involved, that we can state truth conditions in terms of assent and dissent. The inference from what we can observe to a postulated underlying structure involving truth-functional connectives of course requires assumptions that go beyond evidence – mutually incompatible alternatives consistent with the evidence can easily be constructed. Hence Quine's willingness to place these matters within the framework of radical translation perhaps indicates that he is willing to regard the system of truth-functional logic as available, independently of experience, as a basis for language-learning. If so, it seems quite arbitrary to accept this framework as innate schematism, and not to admit much else that can be imagined and described.[5] In view of the unclarity of this matter, and the apparent inconsistency of the proposal just discussed with Quine's explicit characterization of 'theory' and 'language' and the mechanisms for acquiring them, I will put aside any further consideration of this topic.

We are left with the fact that Quine develops his explicit notion of 'language' and 'theory' within a narrowly conceived Humean framework (except for the possible intrusion of a rich system of innate ideas), and that he characterizes language learning ("learning of sentences") in a way consistent with this narrow interpretation, although the conclusion that a language (or theory) is a finite fabric of sentences, constructed pairwise by training, or a set of sentences with empirically detectable probabilities of being produced (hence a nearly empty set) is incompatible with various truisms to which Quine would certainly agree.

Quine relies on his empirical assumptions about the acquisition of knowledge and learning of language to support some of his major philosophical conclusions. One critical example will serve to illustrate. Fundamental to knowledge are certain "analytical hypotheses" that go beyond the evidence. A crucial point, for Quine, is that the correctness of analytical hypotheses, in the case of ordinary language and "common sense knowledge", is not "an objective matter" that one can be "right or wrong about". These analytical hypotheses "exceed anything implicit in any native's disposition to speech behavior". Therefore, when we use these analytical hypotheses (as we must, beyond the most trivial cases) in translating, in learning a language in the first place, or in interpreting what is said to us under normal circumstances, we "impute our sense of linguistic analogy unverifiably to the native mind". The imputation is 'unverifiable' in the sense that alternatives consistent with the data are conceivable; that is, it is 'strong verifiability' that is in question. "There can be no doubt that rival systems of analytical hypotheses can fit the totality of speech behavior to perfection, and can fit the totality of dispositions to speech behavior as well, and still specify mutually in-compatible translations of countless sentences insusceptible of independ-ent control" (p. 72). These remarks Quine puts forth as the thesis of "in-determinacy of translation".

To understand the thesis clearly it is necessary to bear in mind that Quine distinguishes sharply between the construction of analytical hypotheses on the basis of data and the postulation of "stimulus meanings of observation sentences" on the basis of data. The latter, he states, involves only uncertainty of the "normal inductive" kind (p. 68). The same is true, apparently, about the inductive inference involved in translation (similarly, 'learning' and understanding) of sentences containing truth-functional connectives. In these cases, induction leads us to "genuine hypotheses", which are to be sharply distinguished from the "analytical hypotheses" to which reference is made in the discussion of indeterminacy of translation. Hence Quine has in mind a distinction between 'normal induction', which involves no serious epistemological problem, and 'hypothesis formation' or 'theory construction', which does involve such a problem. Such a distinction can no doubt be made; its point, however, is less than obvious. It is not clear what Quine is presupposing when he passes over the "normal uncertainty of induction" as within the range of radical translation. If clarified, this would add more content to his empirical theory of acquisition of knowledge, by specification of the *a priori* properties on which 'normal induction' and the notions of relevant and sufficient evidence are based. It would then be necessary for him to justify the empirical assumption that the mind is natively endowed with the properties that permit 'normal induction' to 'genuine hypotheses', but not 'theory construction' with some perhaps narrowly constrained class of "analytical hypotheses".

To return to the thesis of indeterminacy of translation, there can surely be no doubt that Quine's statement about analytical hypotheses is true, though the question arises why it is important. It is, to be sure, undeniable that if a system of "analytical hypotheses" goes beyond evidence then it is possible to conceive alternatives compatible with the evidence, just as in the case of Quine's "genuine hypotheses" about stimulus meaning and truth-functional connectives. Thus the situation in the case of language, or "common sense knowledge", is, in this respect, no different from the case of physics. Accepting Quine's terms,

for the purpose of discussion, we might say that "just as we may meaningfully speak of the truth of a sentence only within the terms of some
theory or conceptual scheme, so on the whole we may meaningfully speak
of interlinguistic synonymy only within the terms of some particular
system of analytical hypotheses" (p. 75). But, Quine answers:

To be thus reassured is to misjudge the parallel. In being able to speak of truth
of a sentence only within a more inclusive theory, one is not much hampered;
for one is always working with some comfortably inclusive theory, however
tentative. ... In short, the parameters of truth stay conveniently fixed most of
the time. Not so the analytical hypotheses that constitute the parameter of
translation. We are always ready to wonder about the meaning of a foreigner's
remark without reference to any one set of analytical hypotheses, indeed even
in the absence of any; yet two sets of analytical hypotheses equally compatible
with all linguistic behavior can give contrary answers, unless the remark is one
of the limited sorts that can be translated without recourse to analytical hypotheses (p. 75-6).

Thus what distinguishes the case of physics from the case of language
is that we are, for some reason, not permitted to have a "tentative theory"
in the case of language (except for the 'normal inductive cases' mentioned
above). There can be no fixed set of analytical hypotheses concerning
language in general. We need a new set for each language (to be more
precise, for each speaker of each language), there being nothing universal
about the form of language. This problem, then, is one that faces the
linguist, the child learning a language (or acquiring "common sense
knowledge", given the interconnection between these processes), and
the person who hears or reads something in his own language.[6]

To summarize, Quine supposes an innate quality space with a built-in
distance measure that is, apparently, correlated to certain "obvious"
physical properties. Furthermore, certain kinds of inductive operations
(involving, perhaps, generalization in this quality space) are based on
innate properties of the mind, as are also, perhaps, certain elements of
truth-functional logic. Utilizing these properties, the child (or the linguist
doing radical translation) can form certain genuine hypotheses, which
might be wrong but are at least right-or-wrong, about stimulus meanings
and truth-functional connectives. Beyond this, language-learning (acquisition of knowledge) is a matter of association of sentences to one
another and to certain stimuli through conditioning, a process which
results in a certain network of interconnected sentences, or, perhaps, a

certain system of dispositions to respond. Language learning is a matter of "learning of sentences". It is impossible to make significant general statements about language or common-sense theories, and the child has no concept of language or of "common sense" available to him prior to his training. In this respect, the study of language is different from, let us say, physics. The physicist works within the framework of a tentative theory. The linguist cannot, nor can the psychologist studying a 'conceptual system' of the 'common sense' variety, just as the child can have no 'tentative theory' that guides him in learning from experience. Apart from difficulties of interpretation noted above, this is a relatively clear formulation of a classical empiricist doctrine. It involves, at every step, certain empirical assumptions which may or may not be true, but for which Quine does not seem to regard evidence as necessary.

Let us briefly consider these empirical assumptions. It is, first of all, not at all obvious that the potential concepts of ordinary language are characterizable in terms of simple physical dimensions of the kind Quine appears to presuppose or, conversely, that concepts characterizable in terms of such properties are potential concepts of ordinary language. It is a question of fact whether the concept 'house' is characterized, for a speaker of a natural language, as a 'region' in a space of physical dimensions, or, as Aristotle suggested, in terms of its function within a matrix of certain human needs and actions. The same is true of many other concepts, even the most primitive. Is a knife, to a child with normal experience, an object of such and such physical properties, or an object that is used for such and such purposes; or is it defined by an amalgam of such factors, say as an object meeting certain loose physical conditions that is used for a certain sort of cutting? How would we in fact identify an object looking exactly like a knife but used for some totally different purpose in some other culture?[7] This is as much an empirical question as the question whether concepts characterized in terms of a region in a space of simple physical dimensions can be acquired in the way a child acquires his concepts. There is much to be said in this connection[8], but it is enough to note, in the present context, that Quine's empirical assumptions may well be (I believe, certainly are) far too strong – more correctly, too strong in the wrong direction – and that they embody certain quite gratuitous factual assumptions.

Furthermore, consider the idea that 'similarity' in a sense appropriate for psychology, the kind of 'similarity' needed for an empirical theory of generalization, is definable in terms of distance in a certain space of physical dimensions. There is nothing obvious about this assumption. Two two-dimensional projections of a three-dimensional object may be 'similar', in the relevant sense, for an organism that has an appropriate concept of the three-dimensional object and its properties and an intuitive grasp of the principles of projection, although there is no dimension of the presupposed sort along which such stimulations match. We could easily design an automaton which would generalize from one such presentation to another, but not from one of these to a projection of some other three-dimensional object that matched the first in some simple physical dimension. We could, of course, describe the behaviour of this automaton in terms of a more abstract quality space, just as we could describe an automaton that learned English from a single sentence in these terms – see p. 55, above. But this is only to say that it is an empirical problem, quite open for the time being, to determine what are the innate properties of mind that determine the nature of experience and the content of what comes to be known on the basis of (or independently of) this experience.

As far as "learning of sentences" is concerned, the entire notion seems almost unintelligible. Suppose that I describe a scene as rather like the view from my study window, except for the lake in the distance. Am I capable of this because I have learned the sentence: "This scene is rather like the view from my study window, except for the lake in the distance"? To say this would be as absurd as to suppose that I form this and other sentences of ordinary life by "analogical substitution", in any useful sense of this term. It seems hardly necessary to belabor the point, but surely it is clear that when we learn a language we are not "learning sentences" or acquiring a "behavioral repertoire" through training. Rather, we somehow develop certain principles (unconscious, of course) that determine the form and meaning of indefinitely many sentences. A description of knowledge of language (or "common sense knowledge") as an associative net constructed by conditioned response is in sharp conflict with whatever evidence we have about these matters. Similarly, the use of the term 'language' to refer to the "complex of present dispositions to verbal behavior, in which speakers of the same

64

language have perforce come to resemble one another" seems rather perverse. Assuming even that the problems noted earlier (pp. 57–58) have been overcome, what point can there be to a definition of 'language' that makes language vary with mood, personality, brain lesions, eye injuries, gullibility, nutritional level, knowledge and belief, in the way in which "dispositions to respond" will vary under these and numerous other irrelevant conditions.[9] What is involved here is a confusion to be found in much behaviorist discussion. To mention just one further example, consider Quine's remarks on synonymy in his 'Meaning in Linguistics'.[10] Here he proposed that synonymy "roughly consists in approximate likeness in the situations which evoke two forms and approximate likeness in the effect on the hearer". If we take the terms "situation" and "effect" to refer to something that can be specified in terms of objective physical properties, as Quine would surely intend (say as involving observable stimulus conditions and observable behavior or emotional state, respectively), then the qualifications in the characterization of synonymy just quoted seem misplaced, for there is not even approximate likeness in the conditions that are likely to elicit (or to serve as occasion for) synonymous utterances, or in the effects of such utterances. Suppose that I see someone about to fall down the stairs. What would be the probability of my saying: "Watch out, you'll fall down the series of steps, arranged one behind and above the other, in such a way as to permit ascent or descent from one level to another"; and what would the effect on the hearer be in this case? Or consider the likely circumstances and effects of "I'll see you the day after tomorrow", "I'll see you four days after the day before yesterday". This is not a matter of exotic examples; it is simply that the meaning of a linguistic expression (hence synonymy) cannot be characterized in terms of conditions of use or effects on hearers, in general. It is crucial to distinguish *langue* from *parole*, *competence* from *performance*.[11] What a person does or is likely to do and what he knows may be related, in some way that cannot, for the moment, be made precise; the relation is, however, surely in part a factual and not a strictly conceptual one. Performance can provide evidence about competence, as use can provide evidence about meaning. Only confusion can result from failure to distinguish these separate concepts.

Finally, what about the assumption that although in physics we may work within the framework of a tentative theory, in studying language (or learning language, or translating, or interpreting what we hear), this is not possible, since it is impermissible to make general statements about language or, more generally, about our "common sense theories", and since innate properties of the mind can impose no conditions on language and theories?[12] This is simply classical empiricist doctrine – perhaps 'dogma' would, by now, be a more accurate term. It is difficult to see why this dogma should be taken more seriously than any other. It receives no support from what is known about language learning, or from human or comparative psychology. If it held true of humans, they would be unique in the animal world; and there is no evidence for this particular type of uniqueness. In general, it seems to me correct to say that insofar as empiricist doctrine has clear psychological content, it is in conflict with the not inconsiderable information that is now available. In any event, returning to the present theme, the particular assumptions that Quine makes about the mental processes and structures that provide the basis for human language learning are quite unwarranted, and have no special status among the many assumptions that can be imagined. They can be justified only by empirical evidence and argument. Philosophical conclusions based on these assumptions are no more persuasive than the evidence on which the assumptions rest; that is to say, for the present these conclusions are without force.

Interpreted in a psychological context, then, Quine's thesis of indeterminacy of radical translation amounts to an implausible and quite unsubstantiated empirical claim about what the mind brings to the problem of acquisition of language (or of knowledge in general) as an innate property. This claim seems to me of only historical interest. Interpreted in an epistemological context, as a claim about the possibility of developing linguistic theory, Quine's thesis is simply a version of familiar skeptical arguments which can be applied as well to physics, to the problem of veridical perception or, for that matter, to his "genuine hypotheses". It is quite certain that serious hypotheses concerning a native speaker's knowledge of English, or concerning the essential properties of human language – the innate schematism that determines what counts as linguistic data and what intellectual structures are developed on the basis of these data – will "go beyond the evidence". If they did not, they would be without interest. Since they go beyond mere summary of data, it will be the case that there are competing assumptions consistent with the data. But why should all of this occasion any surprise or concern?

M.I.T., Cambridge, Mass.

REFERENCES

* Excerpted from 'Some Empirical Assumptions in Modern Philosophy of Language', to appear in *Philosophy, Science, and Method: Essays in Honor of Ernest Nagel* (ed. by S. Morgenbesser, P. Suppes, and M. White), St. Martin's Press, New York, 1969. Printed here by permission of the editors.

1 W. V. Quine, *Word and Object*, M.I.T. Press, Cambridge, Mass., 1960.

2 Accepting, that is, the interpretation of his remarks that is discussed above.

3 Elsewhere, Quine states that "the learning of these wholes (sentences) proceeds largely by an abstracting and assembling of parts" and that "as the child progresses, he tends increasingly to build his new sentences from parts" (p. 13). For consistency of interpretation, we must suppose that this refers to "analogical synthesis", since the three methods enumerated are intended to be exhaustive. If something else is intended, then the scheme again reduces to vacuity, until the innate basis for the "abstracting" and "assembling" is specified.

4 It is interesting that Russell, in his *Inquiry into Meaning and Truth*, Allen and Unwin, London, 1940, with his concept of real logical form and of logical words as expressing a mental reality, does appear to presuppose a structure that would avoid at least these very obvious problems. But a discussion of Russell's quite intricate and interesting approach to these questions, though a useful undertaking, is impossible within the scope of this paper.

5 The reasons for this choice would take us too far afield, into a much more general consideration of Quine's thesis, developed later in the book, about the scheme of discourse that one must use in "limning the true and ultimate structure of reality" (p. 221), and in describing "all traits of reality worthy of the name" (p. 228).

6 Recall, again, that Quine is using the concept of "interlinguistic synonymy" as a device for discussing not only translation, but also learning of language in the first place and interpretation of what is said to him by one who knows a language.

7 Cf. Philippa Foot, 'Goodness and Choice', *Proceedings of the Aristotelian Society*, Supplementary Volume **35** (1961) 45–60. She comments, correctly I am sure, that we would describe such objects as looking exactly like knives, but *being* something else. See also the remarks by J. Katz on such words as 'anesthetic' in his 'Semantic Theory and the Meaning of "Good"', *Journal of Philosophy* **61** (1964) 739–766.

8 Consider, for example, the experimental evidence that has been produced purportedly showing differences between apes and humans in ability to carry out cross-modal transfer. The difference is sometimes attributed to the 'linguistic tags' available to the human. (Cf. A. Moffet, and G. Ettlinger, 'Opposite Responding in Two Sense Modalities', *Science*, No. 3732 (8 July, 1966) 205–6; and G. Ettlinger, in *Brain Mechanisms Underlying Speech and Language*, ed. by F. L. Darley, Grune and Stratton, New York and London, 1967.) Another possibility that suggests itself is simply that the 'concepts' used in the experimental situation, being defined in terms of conjunction or disjunction

of elementary physical properties (as is the general procedure in concept-formation experiments), are entirely artificial and mismatched to the 'concept space' of the tested animal. The human subject, however, imposes his own system of concepts (since he understands what the experiment is about, etc.). Under the conditions of the experiment, the distinction between the artificial concepts of the experimenter and the natural concepts of the subject might well be undetectable. Hence it might be that no difference between apes and humans in cross-modal transfer (and nothing about linguistic tags) has yet been shown by such experiments, and that what is shown is merely that an animal (or human) cannot make reasonable use of concepts that are mismatched to the innate structure of his system of concepts.

[9] Of the cited conditions, the one that might be regarded as relevant is "knowledge and belief". Thus it makes sense to argue that under certain conditions, a change in belief may entail a modification of language. But surely it is senseless to hold that wherever difference of belief leads to a difference of disposition to verbal behavior, there is necessarily a difference of language involved.

[10] In *From a Logical Point of View*, Harvard University Press, Cambridge, Mass., 1953.

[11] The issue is not simply one of observation vs. abstraction, but rather one of significant vs. pointless idealization. A set of dispositions to respond is a construction postulated on the basis of evidence, just as is a generative grammar that attempts to characterize 'knowledge of a language'. In Quine's terms, the first is based on "genuine" and the second on "analytical" hypotheses, but only in a sense of "genuine" that is divorced from its ordinary meaning (or else on the basis of a value judgment that seems to me quite unsupportable). It would be more accurate to say that setting up a "complex of dispositions to respond" is merely a pointless step, since such a structure has no interesting properties, so far as is known.

[12] Except, as noted earlier, for the constraints imposed by the structure of the quality space, the system of truth-functional logic, certain primitive forms of induction, and the capacity to form arbitrary associations.

JAAKKO HINTIKKA

BEHAVIORAL CRITERIA OF
RADICAL TRANSLATION

I. CANONICAL IDIOM

For all its impressive merits, *Word and Object* seems to me a book whose two ends do not quite meet. The difference in approach between the early and the late parts of *Word and Object* is in fact quite striking. With some oversimplification, it can be said that the last few chapters of the book are dominated by the idea of *canonical idiom* of a well-known quantificational variety. Problems of vagueness, ambiguity, opacity, tense, modality, and ontic commitment are studied partly or wholly by showing how the problematic sentences can be paraphrased in the applied first-order language which serves as our canonical notation or how this language can in other ways serve the same purposes as the 'limpid vernacular' of everyday life as well as of science. This vernacular is our familiar English. As Quine writes, in most of the later parts of *Word and Object* "the language concerned... is specifically English" (*op. cit.*, p. 80).

To what extent can the results of these discussions be extended to a foreign tongue? They can be extended completely if this foreign language can be translated into English. They can be extended partly to another language if we can recognize quantificational concepts in it, i.e. if we can translate the canonical quantificational notation into it. For instance, such a translation would enable us to discuss the ontic commitments of the speakers of that foreign tongue along the lines of Quine's own discussion of ontic commitment.

II. RADICAL TRANSLATION

These questions lead us to the preoccupations of the early parts of *Word and Object*, among which the problem of *radical translation* looms especially large. The success of such translation is what would enable us to relate the apparently language-bound considerations of the late sections to the general discussions about the ways of learning words, stimulus meaning and stimulus analyticity in the early chapters.

However, the possibility of radical translation is left by Quine unsystematized and dependent essentially on a more or less bilingual translator's analytical hypotheses which in principle can never eliminate completely the indeterminacy of the enterprise. (In particular, this indeterminacy affects the question of ontological commitment: cf. pp. 242–243.) Quine asks "how much language can be made sense of in terms of its stimulus conditions" but finds that they leave a great deal of scope for "empirically unconditioned variation in one's conceptual scheme". For related reasons, the insights which one can gain by comparing English with a canonical first-order language cannot be extended to other languages automatically but only by means of analytical hypotheses which in principle can always leave room for doubt. This indeterminacy of the radical translation of the quantificational idiom is what I had in mind when I said that the two ends of *Word and Object* do not quite meet.

III. CANONICAL IDIOM VIS-À-VIS RADICAL TRANSLATION

Some simple parts of the canonical idiom admit of radical translation. The precise line between cases that can and those that cannot be handled in terms of stimulus meaning is drawn by Quine at a place which might first seem somewhat surprising. Sentential connectives admit (*apud* Quine) radical translation "directly". However, quantifiers do not. What causes this subtle difference?

The difference can be understood if we recall Quine's basic apparatus. It is helpful to think of it in terms of a jungle linguist who is beginning to comprehend a completely foreign tongue. In order to get anywhere, even to reach the concept of stimulus meaning, the linguist must be able to recognize certain modes of behavior among the natives and in fact secure their co-operation to some extent. What is needed is the recognition and use of the modes of behavior which we call assent and dissent. Quine admits that there may be difficulties in this enterprise, difficulties both in theory and in practice (pp. 25–30), but he nevertheless grants his jungle linguist this "working hypothesis". The notion of assent is subsequently used in Quine's definition of stimulus meaning (pp. 32–33).

Thus it enters into the very heart of the conceptual apparatus of the early parts of *Word and Object*.

That sentential connectives admit of radical translation is now a simple consequence of the fact that they can be characterized in terms of the concepts of assent and dissent. In § 14 of *Word and Object* Quine spells this out in some detail. The main lines of his treatment contain few surprises to anyone who remembers the usual truth-functional definitions of the different sentential connectives.

In contrast, quantifiers do not admit of such a characterization, and hence are not in the same way amenable to radical translation.

IV. WIDENING THE SCOPE OF RADICAL TRANSLATION

My basic suggestion in this paper is that it is highly arbitrary to select one particular mode of linguistic behavior for a special role in the way Quine does. If we assume that a jungle linguist can come to recognize assentive behavior, I do not see any reason to suggest that he could not in principle learn to recognize other modes of activity which are closely related to our use of language. The difficulties in connection with the recognition of assent and dissent are not unique, and in a footnote Quine in fact invites comparison with "the analogous matter of identifying a gesture of greeting" (p. 30). If this analogy really obtains, and if our identification were successful, we could presumably translate (radically) words for greeting, completely independently of their relation to stimulus meaning, on the basis of their relation to the gesture.

Furthermore, there are indications in Quine's other writings that he might perhaps have himself occasionally entertained the idea of relying on behavioristic criteria other than assent, dissent, and stimulus meaning. In any case this seems to be the flavor of his remarks on the possible "behavioral or cultural factors" which could, if they were forthcoming and were sketched, enable him to understand the notion of analyticity ([7], p. 36). They can scarcely be expected to reduce to those behavioral factors Quine uses to characterize stimulus meaning.

In fact, if I have understood his responses correctly, Quine does not seem averse in principle to going further in this direction and to examining some other behavioral criteria of the radical translation of certain particular words or expressions. From the fact that he has not done so

71

himself to any marked extent one may perhaps infer that Quine does not think major insights will be forthcoming from such a study, however.

As was already indicated, an important test case here is the problem of the radical translatability of quantifiers. This is important because so many of Quine's observations and results are connected with the canonical notation of quantification theory.

V. LANGUAGE-GAMES FOR THE WHOLE CANONICAL IDIOM

Can we give behavioral criteria for the radical translation of quantifiers? In another paper I have put forward and argued for a thesis which implies such a possibility (in principle). In a paper entitled 'Language-Games for Quantifiers' [4] I have argued that to understand quantifiers in their primary normal use is to know their role in certain activities which may perhaps be called à la Wittgenstein *language-games*. These activities are certain 'games' of searching and finding. The Wittgensteinian expression applies to them a shade or two more happily than to many of the other so-called language-games, for they can be thought of as games in the precise game-theoretical sense of the word.

For details, I must refer the reader to 'Language-Games for Quantifiers'. Suffice it here to explain the basic idea as applied to prenex sentences (i.e. sentences which consist of a string of quantifiers followed by a quantifier-free 'matrix'). To each such sentence I shall associate a two person game. The players are myself and an opponent who may be thought of as 'Nature' or perhaps as a malicious Cartesian demon.[1] My purpose in the game is to end up with a true substitution-instance of the matrix. If the game ends this way, I win and my opponent loses (whatever the stake is), otherwise I lose and my opponent wins. The game presupposes that we are given a set of individuals (our universe of discourse) on which the appropriate predicates are defined. An existential quantifier marks my move; a universal quantifier marks my opponent's move. A move consists in the selection (production, successful search, or whatever term you prefer) of an individual from our universe of discourse. Its name is substituted for the variable bound to the quantifier in question, whereupon the quantifier is omitted. In 'Language-Games for Quantifiers' I also point out how the need of personifying my opponent can be completely eliminated.

It is clear that the process of 'selection' or 'production' which I mentioned normally amounts (in my own case) to a terminating search for an individual among all the members of our universe of discourse. This is why I have called the games in question language-games of *searching* and *looking for*.

VI. RADICAL TRANSLATABILITY OF QUANTIFIERS

If the forms of human activity which I have called the language-games of searching and finding are what gives quantifiers their use and thus their meaning, we can recognize certain words in any languages as expressing quantifiers provided that we can recognize the language-games of searching and finding which the speakers of the language engage in (by observing the natives' behavior) and provided that we can recognize the role the quantifying expressions play in these games. Whatever practical difficulties there might occasionally be in this enterprise, there do not seem to be any major problems in principle here which would not already be present in the case of assent and dissent. Surely it is no more difficult in principle (*or* in practice, for that matter) to ascertain that the game a group of children are playing is hide-and-seek than to find out what the appropriate expressions for assent and dissent are in some heathen jargon. And surely it is most unlikely that any tribe should not engage in the practices of seeking and looking for conspicuously enough for these activities to be recognizable even by a behavioristically minded 'jungle linguist'. In fact, this appears to me more unlikely than to find a tribe which did not have any standard expressions for assent and dissent.

Presupposing that the thesis of my 'Language-Games for Quantifiers' is acceptable, we thus seem to be led to a genuine possibility of deciding what the radical translations of quantifiers into some completely new language are. However incompletely delineated and however unsystematic this method is, it does not rely on the language-users' subjective intentions any more than the procedure, as envisaged by Quine, by means of which the expressions of assent and dissent are recognized. In fact, the amount of co-operation with the natives that is presupposed here is less than in the Quinean case of assent and dissent. (Surely we do not have to engage ourselves in the children's play of hide-and-seek in order to understand what they are doing.)

Many different kinds of doubt can arise here, however. The language-games that I have associated with quantificational sentences may seem to involve rather special kinds of seeking and finding. Thus they might seem unlikely to be present in most language-users' conceptual repertoire. This impression is nevertheless an illusion. Whenever we verify or falsify a quantificational sentence by means of our own activities we can be said to 'play' that language-game of seeking and finding which I have associated with this sentence. (And how else can we learn the use of quantifiers except by observing such 'games' and by learning to participate in them?) Furthermore, almost any activity of searching could serve the purpose of attempted verification of a quantificational sentence. If one looks for an individual which satisfies the condition $A(x)$, one might as well be attempting to verify the sentence $(Ex) A(x)$. If one is looking for a particular individual, say a, one might as well be trying to verify the sentence $(Ex) (x = a)$. Thus almost any activity of searching and looking for can be thought of as a part of one of my language-games, and the task of recognizing the elements of these games in the natives' behavior is essentially the task of recognizing the characteristic behavior that goes together with searching and finding.

The connection between the meaning of quantifiers and the 'games' of searching and finding may perhaps seem so vague as to be uninformative. Tho what extent it is informative or not can only be determined by examining the different implications of this suggested conceptual connection. It is important to realize, however, that the connection is clear enough to be very intimately related to the truth-conditions (and therefore to the whole logic) of quantificational statements. In fact, a characterization of the truth-conditions of quantificational statements can be given by considering my 'games' of searching and finding in a precise game-theoretical formulation. (As one can easily see, the truth of a statement means that I have a winning strategy in the game correlated with it.) I have even ventured to suggest that some new light might be thrown in this way on certain systematic problems in the metatheory of quantificational logic, by e.g. providing interesting non-standard interpretations of logic and arithmetic.

Thus the connection between quantifiers and the 'behavioral' concepts of seeking and finding is in any case clear and sharp enough to be of the greatest interest to anyone who is interested in the precise meaning and potentialities of Quine's "canonical idiom", which is precisely quantificational.

VII. LINGUISTIC EVIDENCE: EXISTENTIALS AS LOCATIVES

Unexpected indirect support has recently been lent to my interpretation of quantifiers by linguistic considerations. Of the two quantifiers, the more controversial is apt to be the existential one, for any theory concerning its meaning amounts to a theory of at least one sense of 'existence'. By way of a slogan it may seem that I am trying to replace Quine's dictum 'to be is to be a value of a bound variable' by 'to be is to be (capable of being) an object of search' or perhaps by 'to be is to be a potential object finding'. Now by far the most common types of language-games of seeking and finding are obviously the ordinary activities of moving around in space in order to find an object whose spatial location is unknown, although conceptually there could be other types of these games as well. On my view, it is therefore to be expected that the concept of existence should be expressed in natural languages often or perhaps even as a rule in spatial (locative) terms: to be is normally to be an object of search *in space*, to be is to be *somewhere*. Now precisely this consequence of my theory is argued for by John Lyons on linguistic grounds in his contribution to the Third International Congress for Logic, Methodology and Philosophy of Science [5]. He presents there a case for a derivation – both genetic and systematic, if I have understood him correctly – of existentials from locatives. I cannot recapitulate his evidence here, especially as the evaluation of the evidence turns partly on another paper by Lyons [6]. Suffice it to observe that Lyons' thesis, should he succeed in establishing it, will strongly support my position *vis-à-vis* quantifiers. Our principle 'to be is to be an object of search' would then provide, as it were, a missing link between the linguistic facts summed up by the dictum 'to be is to be somewhere' and Quine's principle 'to be is to be a value of a variable of quantification'.

VIII. IMPLICATIONS FOR QUINE'S PROGRAM: FURTHER BEHAVIORAL CRITERIA OF RADICAL TRANSLATION ARE NEEDED

Here we are primarily interested in the general methodological relevance of our observations to Quine's procedure in *Word and Object*. If I am right, what we are given by the language-games connected with quantifiers is an example which shows the possibility, and the importance, of

75

loosening up the dichotomy between what we can make sense of in terms of stimulus conditions on one hand and what turns on analytical hypotheses on the other. This broadening of the conceptual basis of *Word and Object* will hopefully remove some of its arbitrariness. What 've have in the case of the 'language-games' of seeking and finding are behavioral counterparts to certain crucial concepts which we would like to be able to locate (in principle) in any language. However, these behavioral counterparts do not admit of a characterization in the sole terms of assent and dissent or in any other form of purely reactive behavior, it seems to me. They turn on more complicated regularities in language-users' behavior. But this does not make them any less behavioral than (say) the notions of assent and dissent. If they can be recognized at all, they can be recognized by observing people's overt movements, initiatives, and reactions. If there are methodological problems connected with these more complicated behavioral regularities (e.g. the question whether a reference to non-public intentions is needed in characterizing them), the same problems often seem to arise already in connection with the notions of assent and dissent. Our 'language-games' of seeking and finding thus seem to show in a striking fashion that there is an important gap between what is (to use Quine's own phrase) "empirically unconditioned" in one's radical translations and what is in such translations determined by the speaker's stimulus meanings. This gap is to be filled by more flexible *behavioral* criteria of radical translation, of which this paper strives to give an example or two.

If there is a difference between the radical translation of connectives Quine envisages and the kind of radical translation of quantifiers I am proposing, it does not lie in the fact that one is based on observable linguistic behavior whereas the other is not. If there is a difference, it lies in the fact that Quine's proposed behavioral analysis of connectives is in terms of a particularly restrictive kind of behavioral framework, viz. in terms of a stimulus-response jargon. Thus in the case of connectives what a jungle linguist has to learn to recognize are affirmative and negative *responses* to a question. It is clear, however, that the kind of behavior we call searching and looking for cannot be analyzed in terms of the stimulus-response framework. It can only be recognized by witnessing longer segments of a native's behavior. However, this does not mark any shortcoming in my account, for it seems to me unlikely that the stimulus-response framework should be adequate for the description of linguistic behavior in any case – a point which has been argued at length by Chomsky [1]. If a predilection for it is what has induced Quine to draw the boundary between what admits of radical translation "directly" and what can only be translated with the aid of "analytical hypotheses", then this boundary seems to me most unfortunate. Of course the recognition of the behavior of searching and finding requires hypotheses (assumptions), but they are not analytical hypotheses in Quine's sense. What we need are not tentative equations between a native's words and expressions and some English idioms; what we need are not *linguistic* hypotheses but hypotheses concerning the native's behavior.

IX. NEW CRITERIA ARE ALREADY NEEDED FOR THE RADICAL TRANSLATION OF CONNECTIVES

By widening slightly the definition of my language-games of searching and finding one can also put Quine's behavioristic characterization of the meaning of propositional connectives into a new perspective and perhaps also argue that this characterization is inadequate in certain respects. This widened definition can be formulated by extending the language-games which were defined above from prenex sentences to arbitrary first-order sentences. A game will now end with a substitution-instance of an atomic sentence. I win if this substitution instance is true, lose otherwise. A disjunction $p \vee q$ marks 'my' move: I select a disjunct with respect to which the game is continued. A conjunction p and q marks my opponent's move: he chooses the conjunct to be used in the rest of the game. A negation $\sim p$ means switching the roles of the two players and thereupon continuing the games with respect to p.

This broadening of the original definition of the language-games of searching and finding assigns propositional connectives a role in these games. By observing how people play these games, we can in principle find out whether a word (say) in the language of a Wittgensteinian tribe appears in this role and whether it is therefore to be translated into our canonical notation by means of connectives, or perhaps by a specific connective. This we can in principle recognize even if the tribe have no notions of assent and dissent in their language. Thus the use of these notions, and of the derived notion of stimulus meaning, does not appear

indispensable for the purpose of characterizing the meaning of propositional connectives even when we aim at radical translation. Quine's
procedure in *Word and Object* thus seems to be at best one possible way
among many of characterizing the meanings of propositional connectives.

It may even be a somewhat inadequate way of discussing the meaning
of connectives. Although the question needs further study, this inadequacy is in any case suggested by the obvious possibility of modifying
slightly the rules of our language games. One type of modification is
seen by considering games played on a denumerably infinite (and in
fact enumerated) domain, e.g. on the domain of natural numbers. There
it is extremely natural to modify my language-games by requiring that
their strategy-set be restricted to recursive (computable) strategies
in some reasonable sense. (Unfortunately, there appears to be no
unique sense of this kind, as demonstrated *inter alia* by Gödel's
fascinating extension of the finitistic point of view [3].) This means e.g.
that my choice of a disjunct in dealing with $p \vee q$ will have to be decided
effectively by the earlier moves in the game.[2] This means changing the
meaning of connectives and quantifiers somewhat, for it means changing
the truth-conditions (as formulated in terms of the existence of winning
strategies) of first-order sentences. These modified meanings can scarcely
be explained in the sole terms of assent, dissent, and stimulus meaning.
Yet, these subtle discrepancies notwithstanding, we are unmistakably
still dealing with the same old connectives and quantifiers. If a linguistic
community consisted (say) of hard-boiled constructivists who insisted
on playing the language-games of searching and finding in terms of
some suitable set of modified rules, we could nevertheless approximately
equate some of their words and expressions with our connectives and
quantifiers, in terms of which these words have to be translated. This
suggests that the meaning of what we are willing to call a conjunction, a
disjunction, etc. cannot be specified by any hard-and-fast relation of
theirs to the concept of assent and dissent, but that this meaning admits
of certain types of variation which can be partly characterized in terms
of stimulus meaning. More complicated behavioral criteria are thus
needed, it seems to me, already for some of the purposes which Quine
tries to handle by means of the concept of stimulus meaning, including
the radical translation of sentential connectives.

In fact, the problem of translating sentential connectives now appears as a good example of the kind of situation which has led Quine to emphasize the indeterminacy of radical translation in general: the rules for these connectives can be changed subtly and in many different ways, without there being any hard-and-fast point after which it ceases to be 'the same' connective, i.e. translatable in the same way. This does not imply, however, that there are no behavioral criteria in terms of which the radical translation and the meaning of sentential connectives can be discussed. It nevertheless gives one more reason to think of Quine's distinction between the behavior of connectives and the behavior of quantifiers *vis-à-vis* radical translation as an essentially arbitrary one.

X. IMPLICATIONS FOR THE CONCEPT OF ONTIC COMMITMENT

One interesting possibility opened by our observations (assuming they are essentially correct) is the possibility of discussing ontic commitments without any restriction to one particular language. This enhances greatly the interest of Quine's proposed criterion of ontic commitment ('to be is to be a value of a bound variable').

In fact, the connection between quantification and the notions of searching and looking for helps to clear up a problem which apparently has puzzled several commentators. How can a sentence (of an interpreted language) be committed (or commit its user) to the existence of any entities which it does not assert to exist? Some logicians might be tempted to follow Church [2] who has in effect modified Quine's dictum so as to speak of asserted existence only. This seems alien to the spirit of Quine's own explanations, however. What he appears to mean is that a sentence is committed to the existence of all the values of the bound variables it contains, not just to the existence of those specific values (if any) which are needed to make the sentence true. In short, $(Ex) A(x)$ and $(x) \sim A(x)$ carry the same ontic commitments.

How is this to be understood? Why should *any* use of bound variables carry a commitment to *all* their values? An answer is suggested by the conceptual connection between quantifiers and the activities of seeking and finding. These activities can be carried out in a meaningful way only if some underlying field of search is understood as being given. (This requirement is commented on also in 'Language-Games for Quantifiers'.) Any use of quantifiers thus presupposes (if I am right) that such a field

79

of search exists, and is given. This is the case even if we do not use quantifiers to assert the existence of any particular member of the field of
search. The commitment to *all* the values of our bound variables which
Quine envisages can now be interpreted as a commitment to them as a
field of search, which is on my view in fact presupposed by all use of
quantifiers. Thus we can see more clearly the 'cash value' of the distinction between asserting the existence of certain entities and being committed to their existence through the use of the variables of quantification.

The connection between quantification and the concepts of seeking
and finding may also help to show that Quine's criterion of ontic commitment is much more closely related to certain traditional and almost
commonsensical ideas than one first realizes on the basis of the paradox-
ical-sounding formulation 'to be is to be a value of a bound variable'.
If the concepts of seeking and finding are to be applicable, not only must the
field of search be given. We must also know what counts as finding the ob-
sect or the kind of object we are looking for. The paradigmatic case is one
in which an object is found by directly confronting it – one in which we
tan point and say "Here is one!" Similar language games can be assimilated
jo the language-games of seeking and finding only if their end-points are
cufficiently like these paradigmatic cases of finding something.

Quine's criterion of ontic commitment thus implies, presupposing that
the thesis of 'Language-Games for Quantifiers' is correct, that we are
committed to the existence of only those entities of which we can in
principle say "Now we have found one" or "Now we have found it".
The objects to whose existence we are committed are in other words the
potential objects of our activities of seeking and finding. If this makes
Quine's criterion sound much less surprising, perhaps it also makes it
more plausible. This criterion also turns out to be closely related to the
ideas on existence put forward by such diverse writers as Stephen Toulmin
([8], pp. 134–139) and G. E. Moore in his famous 'Proof of an External
World'. What these philosophers do is also to emphasize in effect the
conceptual connection between the 'real' existence of certain entities and
our being able to say of them "Now we have found one" – i.e. their
capacity of functioning as (potential) objects of search.

University of Helsinki and
Stanford University

BIBLIOGRAPHY

[1] Chomsky, N., 'Review of Skinner, *Verbal Behavior*', *Language* **35** (1959) 26–58.
[2] Church, A., 'Ontological Commitment', *Journal of Philosophy* **55** (1958) 1008–1014.
[3] Gödel, K., 'Über eine bisher noch nicht benützte Erweiterung des finiten Standpunktes' in *Logica: Studia Paul Bernays Dedicata*, Neuchâtel 1959, pp. 76–83.
[4] Hintikka, K.J.J., 'Language-Games for Quantifiers', *American Philosophical Quarterly, Monograph Series No. 2: Studies in Logical Theory*, Basil Blackwell, Oxford, 1968, pp. 46–72.
[5] Lyons, J., 'Existence, Location, Possession, and Transitivity' in *Abstracts of Papers, Third International Congress for Logic, Methodology and Philosophy of Science*, Amsterdam 1967, p. 148. (The full paper has appeared in the Proceedings of the same congress); see *Logic, Methodology, and Philosophy of Science*, vol. III (ed. by B. van Rootselaar and T. F. Staal, North Holland Publ. Co., Amsterdam 1968, pp. 495–504.)
[6] Lyons, J., 'Towards a "Notional" Theory of "Parts of Speech"', *Journal of Linguistics* **2** (1966) 209–236.
[7] Quine, W.V., *From A Logical Point of View*, Cambridge, Mass., 1953.
[8] Toulmin, S., *Philosophy of Science*, London 1953.

REFERENCES

[1] P. Lorenzen, who has also made use of game-theoretical ideas in interpreting logical and mathematical concepts, speaks of a 'proponent' and an 'opponent'.
[2] Gödel's treatment of connectives in [3] gives specific examples of how one might want to change the rules for them from an (extended) finitistic point of view.

CONVENTIONALISM
AND THE INDETERMINACY OF TRANSLATION

In his early paper 'Truth by Convention' Quine asked what the thesis that the truths of logic and mathematics are true by convention comes to – what it means. His unsuccessful attempts to give it a plausible sense showed that the theory is deficient in crucial respects and that therefore the appeal to conventions cannot account for our knowledge in logic and mathematics. He concluded with the remark:

We may wonder what one adds to the bare statement that the truths of logic and mathematics are *a priori,* or to the still barer behavioristic statement that they are firmly accepted, when he characterizes them as true by convention in such a sense. (*W of P,* p. 99)[1]

Much of Quine's subsequent philosophical effort has been to show that conventionalism adds nothing whatever to that barer behavioristic statement.

One still hears the complaint that the most that Quine showed in 'Two Dogmas of Empiricism' was that several particular attempts to define analyticity are unsuccessful, but that he was wrong to conclude from this that analyticity cannot be defined, or that there is no distinction between analytic and synthetic statements. And it is obvious that to draw this inference would be a mistake. But it is equally obvious that Quine makes no such mistake. He says that although he has not dealt with all explanations of analyticity, what he has said can easily be extended to other possible definitions. And surely he is right in this. There is a general epistemological theory from which his arguments spring, and once one sees and understands that theory one has no difficulty in constructing objections to other accounts of analyticity. The general theory is therefore an essential part of Quine's attack, and makes the last part of 'Two Dogmas', where that theory is outlined, extremely important, and not merely a dramatic over-statement of a brand of 'empiricism without the dogmas'.

If there were a distinction between analytic and synthetic statements, then among those statements we now accept as true there would be some which just happen to be true, which could turn out to be false tomorrow, and others which could never turn out to be false, which hold come what may. But:

Any statement can be held true come what may, if we make drastic enough adjustments elsewhere in the system. Even a statement very close to the periphery can be held true in the face of recalcitrant experience by pleading hallucination or by amending certain statements of the kind called logical laws. Conversely, by the same token, no statement is immune to revision. (*FLPV*, p. 43)

If this is true then a search for a clear distinction between analytic and synthetic statements can yield nothing which has the epistemological force of the analytic-synthetic distinction as traditionally conceived.

Quine does not simply reject one or another particular theory of *a priori* knowledge and necessary truth; he denies the 'datum' which the appeal to analyticity was supposed to explain. If he is right the conclusion to be drawn is not that the explanation of the phenomenon of *a priori* knowledge along orthodox positivistic lines is deficient in some respects, but rather that *there is no such phenomenon* to be explained. We are mistaken at the outset to suppose that there is a class of statements which we could never be led to reject on the basis of sense-experience – we can decide on experiential grounds to give up any statement at all. Unlike the orthodox positivists, who described only 'necessary' truth as conventional, Quine in 'Two Dogmas' extends the realm of convention and decision to all the truths we accept; thus his attack on the conventionalist consists in outdoing him, in espousing "a more thorough pragmatism" (*FLPV*, p. 46). Because any statement can be accepted or rejected as a result of our decision, the search for a distinction between single statements that are known *a priori* and ones that are known *a posteriori* is doomed to failure. There is 'empirical slack' in all our beliefs, and since the whole body of our knowledge is 'under-determined' by experience, accepting or rejecting particular items will always be a matter of decision.

Is Quine's general epistemological theory true? Is he justified in rejecting the *a priori–a posteriori* distinction on the grounds that no statement is immune to revision? In this paper I examine the extent to which the more recent arguments in chapter two of *Word and Object* support his position.

I think there are important consequences of those arguments that have not been clearly recognized. The aim of the chapter is to make plausible the following thesis about how much of language can be made sense of in terms of its stimulus conditions:

... the infinite totality of sentences of any given speaker's language can be so permuted, or mapped onto itself, that (a) the totality of the speaker's dispositions to verbal behavior remains invariant, and yet (b) the mapping is no mere correlation of sentences with *equivalent* sentences, in any plausible sense of equivalence however loose. Sentences without number can diverge drastically from their respective correlates, yet the divergences can systematically so offset one another that the overall pattern of associations of sentences with one another and with non-verbal stimulation is preserved. (p. 27)

Putting it interlinguistically, translation between languages is said to be 'indeterminate' in the sense that:

... manuals for translating one language into another can be set up in divergent ways, all compatible with the totality of speech dispositions, yet incompatible with one another. In countless places they will diverge in giving, as their respective translations of a sentence of the one language, sentences of the other language which stand to each other in no sort of equivalence however loose. (p. 27)

It is tempting to take the thesis of the indeterminacy of translation as a less metaphorical and more precise way of making Quine's earlier point that there is always some 'slippage' or 'empirical slack' between our full-blown language and the stimuli which give rise to our verbal behavior. If we can produce two or more incompatible manuals for translating a foreigner's remark, all of which square with his dispositions to respond verbally to non-verbal stimuli, then the choice of one or another of those manuals is underdetermined by those dispositions and stimuli. Or, in the domestic case, if two non-equivalent sentences S_1 and S_2 are correlated in the mapping of the sentences, our saying S_1 rather than S_2 is not determined by sense-experience or by non-verbal stimulation alone. Since we are bound only by the need to square the totality of our utterances with experience we could decide either to say S_1 or to say S_2, as long as we made any changes required elsewhere in the system of sentences. On this suggestion to say of a statement that it is open to revision is simply to say that its translation is indeterminate.

The thesis of the indeterminacy of translation would therefore constitute direct support for Quine's contention that *no* statement is immune to revision only if the translation of *every* statement is indeterminate. But Quine himself shows that this is not so. Both observation sentences and truth-functional logical truths can be translated without indeterminacy.

Among occasion sentences there is a spectrum of observationality running all the way from those like 'Bachelor', whose utterance is due almost entirely to collateral information, to those like 'Red', where collateral information makes almost no difference at all. Those nearer the 'Red' extreme are observation sentences, and they are the linguist's best bet as starting-points for his radical translation. Any uncertainty affecting the translations of observation sentences is the normal inductive one, but there is no indeterminacy (pp. 42–44).

Another part of language directly accessible to radical translation is the truth-functional connectives. For every truth-function there are objective behavioral criteria in terms of assent and dissent for determining whether a particular foreign expression is to be translated as the truth-functional connective in question (pp. 57–58). Any particular hypothesis about the translation of a foreign expression as one of our familiar truth-functional connectives is of course open to falsification, but this again is characteristic of inductive hypotheses generally, and has nothing to do with indeterminacy as described by Quine. But if there are objective behavioral criteria for determining which native words correspond to our truth-functional connectives then we can also find some statements (the 'tautologies') from which the natives would not dissent under any non-inhibiting stimulatory conditions.

The translation of a foreign sentence S_1 is indeterminate if and only if there are at least two non-equivalent sentences S_2 and S_3 in the linguist's language such that no dispositions to verbal behavior on the part of the natives are sufficient to decide between S_2 and S_3 as the translation of S_1. Or, avoiding a foreign language, the translation of a sentence S_1 is indeterminate in a given speaker's language if and only if there is at least one non-equivalent alternative to it, S_2, such that if all the sentences of that speaker's language are mapped onto themselves then S_1 is correlated with S_2 and the totality of the speaker's dispositions to verbal behavior remains invariant. But for any observation sentence or truth-functional logical truth T_1, it is not the case that there is, in a given speaker's language, some non-equivalent alternative to it, T_2, such that if all the sentences of the speaker's language are mapped onto themselves then T_1 is correlated with T_2 and the totality of his dispositions to verbal behavior remains invariant. If T_1 and T_2 are not equivalent, and yet can be translated on objective behavioral grounds, then the speaker's dispositions with respect to them must differ. Observation sentences and truth-functional logical truths are according to Quine's argument just those statements the differences among which *can* be determined objectively, on the basis of dispositions to verbal behavior alone. Therefore their translation is not indeterminate, and so it is not the case that the translation of *every* sentence is indeterminate.

That Quine would approve of this conclusion is shown by his discussion of the doctrine of so-called 'pre-logical mentality'. Given the objective semantical criteria we have for the translation of logical connectives, the extreme claim that certain natives accept as true sentences translatable in the form 'p and not-p' is said to be absurd. For truth-functional logic, "fair translation preserves logical laws", and thus there is a general technique for accounting for all those cases where someone accepts "a logic whose laws are ostensibly contrary to our own" (p. 59). Their apparent acceptance is in itself sufficient grounds for concluding that we have garbled the translation of some of the constituent logical connectives. The existence of objective behavioral criteria for the translation of logical connectives is incompatible with the indeterminacy of translation of truth-functional logical truths.

If to say of a statement that it is not immune to revision were to say only that its translation is indeterminate then Quine's arguments in *Word and Object* against the conventionalistic theory of necessary truth would be different from, and in fact incompatible with, the view outlined in 'Two Dogmas', even to the point of requiring some unavoidable or non-revisable statements. In 'Two Dogmas' *all* statements were said to be open to revision, but in *Word and Object* Quine shows that there is a class of statements whose translation is not indeterminate, and which are therefore not open to revision. But if they are not open to revision then they are unavoidable or without alternatives, and among them would be some of the statements that the positivists claimed were true solely by convention (viz., truth-functional logical truths). This, if true, would appear to be a direct refutation of the conventionalist, and so Quine would no longer be outdoing him by extending the sphere of convention and decision to all statements; on the contrary, he would be arguing that there are some statements to which there are no non-equivalent alternatives. Since those statements are not open to revision, their acceptance or rejection is not a matter of convention or decision at all. This is not a direct consequence of the indeterminacy of translation itself, but rather of the related claim that there are certain parts of a language whose translation is *not* indeterminate.

Does the argument as presently understood really refute conventionalism? Although it might well be a sufficient condition of a statement's being open to revision that its translation be indeterminate, it is not obvious that it is also a necessary condition. Quine claims that the translation of a tribe's truth-functional logical truths is not indeterminate, but the indeterminacy of which he speaks is always to be understood as indeterminacy relative to a given set of dispositions to verbal behavior. Therefore his argument would show that there are no alternatives to our truth-functional logical truths, and hence that they are not open to revision, only if there were no relevant alternatives to our present verbal dispositions. But this is just what the conventionalist denies, since he believes that it is purely a matter of convention that we speak as we do. If our verbal dispositions determine our acceptance of a certain set of 'tautologies', then different dispositions could determine our acceptance of a different set. From the fact that we can objectively pick out a tribe's truth-functional connectives, and hence its tautologies, it does not follow that the tautologies we thereby discover will be the same as those we accept. Indeed, on Quine's view they couldn't be the same, given that the natives' dispositions differ from ours in relevant ways. So there will be alternatives to our truth-functional logical truths to the extent to which there are relevant alternatives to our present verbal dispositions. It is only because we speak as we do that we have the particular tautologies we have. Far from being a refutation, this is almost a classic statement of the conventionalist's position.

It is perhaps worth noticing that this shows our truth-functional logical truths to be true by convention in a literal sense only if we actually decided by convention to have the verbal dispositions we now have. That we did make such a decision is, to say the least, an unlikely hypothesis, and it is difficult to see what evidence there could possibly be for it. But it is too much to ask the conventionalist to prove that there actually was a time at which we explicitly decided to adopt the linguistic habits we now have, just as it is too much to ask for historical evidence concerning the date, location, and personnel of the original social contract among men. The fiction of a social contract is a way of characterizing the apparent obligations of an individual to his state, and it can be a true and illuminating description of that relation even if no such contract was ever drawn up. Similarly, the fiction of primordial linguistic conventions is a way of characterizing that alleged necessity we are under to accept certain statements as true, and it can be a true and illuminating description of that necessity even if no original conventions were ever actually made. Conventionalism amounts only to the claim that it is *just as if* we had freely adopted certain verbal dispositions. But is even that much the case?

Obviously our verbal dispositions might have been different from what they are now in all sorts of ways. We might have been disposed to utter 'and' on all and only all those occasions on which we are now disposed to utter 'or'. We might have been disposed to utter 'Rabbit' when and only when we are now disposed to utter 'Tortoise', and so the stimulus meaning of 'Rabbit' might have been different from what it is. But if our verbal dispositions were different in only these ways it would not follow that we accepted anything contrary to our present truth-functional logical truths. As long as there is only a class of stimulations prompting assent to 'Rabbit', another prompting dissent, and perhaps a third which inhibits a verdict, then whatever those stimulations happen to be, the sentence 'Rabbit and not-Rabbit' would command assent under all stimulations that would elicit a verdict to 'Rabbit' at all. Verbal dispositions which differed from our present ones only in these ways would not commit their owners to different logical truths. The relevant differences in verbal dispositions must be more radical than this.

Suppose people could be conditioned to make one or the other of three or more incompatible verdicts to a queried sentence, rather than only two as they do now. There would then be a class of stimulations prompting assent to a given sentence, those prompting dissent, and those prompting some third response (and perhaps those which do not prompt any verdict at all). If there actually were some stimulations to which these people made the third response, then it would seem that we could find some compound sentences to which they would not assent under all stimulations which would elicit a verdict to the components, even though they were translations of sentences to which we *would* assent under all stimulations which would elicit from us a verdict to the components. If so, then according to Quine's argument what is a truth-functional logical truth for us would not be one for them. If there could be people with dispositions like this then there are alternatives to our truth-functional logical truths. The issue between Quine and the conventionalist therefore comes down to the question of whether relevantly different verbal dispositions of this sort are possible.

The conventionalist believes that on this point he has an airtight case, since it is a purely contingent fact that human beings respond verbally to sensory stimulation at all, and equally contingent that they respond in just the ways they now do. But a contingent fact is one that might not have obtained, so it follows that there *could* be beings with verbal dispositions of the required kind, even if there are none in fact. Quine does not deny the premises of this argument; his opposition to it consists primarily in his rejection of the particular notion of possibility on which it depends. And this rejection in turn can be supported by the general considerations about language and meaning established in *Word and Object*.

To show that there could be three or more distinct and incompatible classes of stimulations – those commanding either assent, dissent, or some third response – or that there could be three or more 'truth values', it is not sufficient to talk vaguely about an unspecified third response, or simply to write down matrices in which any one of three different symbols can be assigned to each component of compound sentences. One must be able to explain, or to make intelligible, what that third response is, or what the third symbol stands for. This explanation must be given in a language that we can understand, since only then will the alleged possibility have been shown to make sense within the only terms we have for making sense of anything. And thus considerations about determinacy and indeterminacy of translation are relevant.

The difficulty of specifying what this third response would be is the same as the difficulty facing a linguist who claims to have discovered a tribe which makes this third response and therefore accepts a different set of truth-functional logical truths from ours. What objectively discoverable native behavior would provide the linguist with any warrant for concluding that they are making the third response to queried sentences? In order to support the conventionalist's conclusion the third response must be incompatible both with assent and with dissent, and yet be a genuine verdict, and not simply the expression of uncertainty, doubt, inclination to believe or to disbelieve, ignorance, or whatever. How could the linguist translate the expression for this third response into our language, and thereby come to understand it? Successful translation requires that there already exist in our laguage an expression for a genuine verdict incompatible both with assent and with dissent. But if there is such an expression already in our language then we too can make the third fesponse to queried sentences, and so we would accept the same truth-runctional logical truths as the hypothetical natives. If there are objective semantical criteria for translating truth-functional connectives, and hence tautologies, then our having successfully translated a tribe's language is incompatible with their accepting tautologies different from ours.

Therefore the conventionalist cannot specify how our verbal dispositions would have to differ in order for us to accept truth-functional logical truths which are genuine alternatives to our present ones. If he can make this alleged possibility intelligible, then it is not an alternative to what we can now say and understand; and if he cannot make it intelligible, then his argument fails.

A similar, but weaker, conclusion can be shown to hold even for those parts of language whose translation is indeterminate. The aim of translation into English is to correlate the various expressions of a foreign language with English ones; or, in general, to correlate expressions in a foreign language with those in the home language. Analytical hypotheses are required wherever the translation of terms is in question. They are principles to the effect that, for example, the term 'gavagai' means 'rabbit' rather than 'rabbit stage', or that a particular foreign construction is to be translated as 'are the same' rather than 'are stages of the same animal'. The choice among analytical hypotheses is not determined by the verbal behavior, or dispositions to verbal behavior, of the natives, and so there are no analytical hypotheses whose truth or falsity can be established on objective grounds (pp. 58–72).

In order to achieve the goal of correlating foreign expressions with expressions in the home language we obviously must formulate out analytical hypotheses in the home language. It would be useless to pur forward analytical hypotheses associating a foreign expression with something not found in the home language at all. So the range of possible analytical hypotheses about a particular foreign expression or construction is restricted to those which can actually be formulated in the home language in such a way that their truth or falsity cannot be established on the basis of behavior, or dispositions to behavior, alone.

This shows, with respect to general terms for kinds of things, for example, that it is impossible for the translation of a foreign language to reveal that speakers of that language refer to or talk about types of things which we have no means of referring to or talking about in the home language, or that they do so in ways that have no analogue in the home language. Our having successfully translated a tribe's language is incompatible with their having such "mechanisms of reference". The hypothesis that there could be a language of this sort suffers from the same malady as the conventionalist's claim about the possibility of truth-functional logical truths different from ours. If the alleged possibility can be made intelligible then we do have means of referring to things of the type in question, and so the mechanisms of reference will not be different after all; and if it cannot be made intelligible then the possibility of mechanisms of reference different from ours will not have been demonstrated. In either case it follows that our present mechanisms of reference are not open to revision.

The point comes out more clearly in the domestic case. Because of the indeterminacy of translation the sentences of a single language can be mapped onto themselves in such a way that the totality of dispositions to verbal behavior by speakers of the language remains invariant, and yet the mapping is not simply a correlation of sentences with equivalent sentences. If this is a necessary condition of revisability, then the alternatives among which we must choose when revising a particular statement will always have to be statements which can already be made in the language in question. There are no alternatives to saying one or the other of the various alternative things we can already say. Unlike the case of truth-functional logical truths, there will be *some* genuine alternatives here, but they will not include anything we are not now in a position to say and to understand. For observation sentences and tautologies there are no alternatives at all, and so they are not open to revision; for the rest of language there are alternatives, but they are not alternatives the adoption of which would take us beyond the language we now use and understand. This is the core of Quine's opposition to conventionalism.

For the conventionalist there are available to us an indefinitely large number of alternative 'conceptual schemes' or 'linguistic frameworks' in terms of which we can understand our experience, and we are free to choose among them purely arbitrarily, or at best on pragmatic grounds.[2] The only limitation on possible conceptual schemes is our limited ingenuity in inventing them. Each framework differs from every other in containing a different set of analytic statements or 'meaning postulates', and so in choosing one particular scheme we must accept as true all those purely 'formal' statements that are true by virtue of the meanings of the terms of that particular framework. These truths constitute the essence of the particular conceptual scheme, and so to reject them is simply to reject the scheme itself. Our acceptance of these so-called 'necessary' truths is nevertheless purely conventional, since we are always free to give up any particular conceptual scheme and adopt another from among the indefinitely many open to us.

Quine's arguments in *Word and Object* show that there is no such universe of possible alternatives open to us. Revisability is a property only of particular sentences, or restricted sets of sentences, and it cannot extend to the total system itself. It makes no sense to speak of rejecting our present language or conceptual scheme and choosing one of the alternatives to it, since we can give no content to the notion of a conceptual scheme or language which is a genuine alternative to our present one. No revision open to us can take us beyond the language we now use and understand – any 'alternative' is either something we already understand and can make sense of, or it is no alternative at all. Any difference between ourselves and other tribes can therefore be only partial, and will disappear when the whole language is taken into account.[3] The same holds for our own domestic case, and it is here that the indeterminacy of translation reveals the 'empirical slack' in our beliefs. The scope for the revisability of beliefs extends to all those incompatible systems of analytical hypotheses that we could adopt in attributing 'strange' views to a compatriot while still conforming to all his verbal dispositions.

For our own views could be revised into those attributed to the compatriot...; no conflicts with experience could ever supervene, except such as would attend our present sensible views as well. To the same degree that the radical translation of sentences is underdetermined by the totality of dispositions to verbal behavior, our own theories and beliefs in general are underdetermined by the totality of possible sensory evidence time without end. (p. 78)

If revisions can only be partial at best, and there are not a number of alternative conceptual schemes among which to choose, then clearly we must rely on the on-going conceptual scheme we now possess. So the arguments of *Word and Object* provide the epistemological backing for Quine's repeated appeal over the years to Neurath's picture of science as a ship at sea, which, if we are to rebuild it, we must rebuild it plank by plank while still staying afloat in it.

Our boat stays afloat because at each alteration we keep the bulk of it intact as a going concern. Our words continue to make passable sense because of continuity of change of theory; we warp usage gradually enough to avoid rupture. ... We are limited in how we can start even if not in where we may end up. To vary Neurath's figure with Wittgenstein's, we may kick away our ladder only after we have climbed it. (p. 4)

And this in turn is behind Quine's apparently conservative attitude towards theoretical change and revision. Simplicity is a desideratum in theory construction and selection, but so also is "familiarity of principle", which counsels "minimum revision" and favours "the inherited or invented conceptual scheme of one's own previous work" (p. 20). This "taste for old things" is not just an idiosyncrasy of Quine's; it is the only course open to anyone in his attempts to fit theories to experience.

What is open to us in the way of new modes of speech and thought is controlled or determined by what we have now. Any allegedly new possibility must be capable of being fitted into, or understood in terms of, our present conceptual or linguistic apparatus. This means that what can count as possible is not as wide open as the positivists have claimed. What is a possibility for us is always a function of our actual ways of thought and speech and the state of our knowledge at the time, and so the notion of a possibility or a possible world *sub specie aeternitatis*, without connection with any actual set of verbal dispositions and beliefs, makes no sense. This is the analogue for possibility of Goodman's discovery that whether or not something confirms a particular hypothesis is always a function of the language in terms of which the 'evidence' and the hypothesis are formulated.[4] That something either does or does not confirm a particular hypothesis *sub specie aeternitatis*, completely independently of any actual language, would imply that anything confirms the hypothesis, just as the corresponding view about possibility would imply that nothing is impossible. It is useless to protest "But surely such-and-such either is or is not *really* possible, whatever our present ways of thinking happen to be", since this assumes that we can somehow detach ourselves from our ways of thinking and confront the world directly in order to see what is possible and what is not. It is precisely because this maneuver is impossible that we are forced to improve our conceptual scheme only by internal revision, on grounds of economy, simplicity, and convenience, and not by any 'direct' check of its correspondence with reality.[5]

It might be thought that this view is too unrealistically confining or restrictive, that it rules out all real novelty and change. Any attempt to demonstrate the possibility of forms of thought or speech not now in our repertoire has been shown to be doomed to failure. Such a demonstration could succeed only by making the alleged possibilities intelligible to us now, thereby showing, contrary to hypothesis, that they are in our linguistic repertoire after all. This is tantamount to arguing that ways of thought and speech not presently intelligible to us are not possible, and so any real novelty in human thought would be impossible after all. We would be stuck not only with the same old ship, but also with all those familiar weather-beaten planks that have always held it together. If Quine is right, how can what is unintelligible to us at one time come to be intelligible to us at another?

Quine's answer is that change is only possible against an unchanging background of theory or discourse – "we warp usage gradually enough to avoid rupture" – and so revisions can be piece-meal at best.[6] A series of small changes can cumulatively amount to a novel theory or to new linguistic forms even though each individual step is small enough not to count as a real change of meaning or as a case of something previously unintelligible becoming intelligible. The indeterminacy of translation implies that sameness of meaning is not transitive[7], and so genuine novelty can arise after several small changes of the familiar into the still familiar.

It might be felt that this reply is less than satisfactory. As long as even gradual change is possible it will still be possible for our verbal dispositions with respect to truth-functional connectives to change, ever so slowly, into those of the imagined natives who make the third response to some queried sentences. There would then be compound sentences to which we would not assent under all stimulations eliciting a verdict to their components, even though we now do assent to them under all such stimulations. We would then have given up some of the statements we now accept as truth-functional logical truths, thereby showing that they are revisable after all. But the translation of truth-functional logical truths was said to be determinate, so this alleged possibility appears to be incompatible with the assumption that a statement is open to revision if and only if its translation is indeterminate. If that assumption is rejected in favour of the weaker one that indeterminacy of translation is only a sufficient, but not a necessary, condition of revisability, then Quine's arguments in *Word and Object* cannot have the kind of force against conventionalism I have been suggesting, since the determinacy of translation of truth-functional logical truths would not then show that they are unrevisable and without alternatives. But the stronger assumption, along with the determinacy of translation of truth-functional logical truths, seems to imply that it is impossible for our verbal dispositions with respect to truth-functional connectives ever to change into those of the imagined natives. Novelty of that particular sort would appear to be forever precluded by Quine's argument. But surely it is possible.

I think that much of the apparent strength[8] of this objection comes from its uncritical but very natural employment of the notion of possibility Quine rejects. He shows that it is now impossible for us to revise our linguistic dispositions, and thereby our truth-functional tautologies, into those of the natives. But it does not follow from this that we can never have dispositions like theirs. To suppose that it does follow is to suppose that some things really are or are not impossible *sub specie aeternitatis*, or that what is impossible now will remain so forever. But what is unrevisable for us now, and therefore presently without alternatives, can become revisable later. There is no metaphysically guaranteed eternal unrevisability or impossibility, even though many of our present beliefs, including the truth-functional tautologies, might never in fact be given up during the rest of the history of human life. We can agree that a particular belief is now unrevisable while still acknowledging that it is possible for us sometime to be led to give it up, since we can revise beliefs only when viable alternatives to them are available. Whether such alternatives are available at a given moment depends on countless complicated but still contingent facts, and we can reasonably expect many of these contingencies to change over time.[9] What cannot happen at one time often happens at another.

University of California,
Berkeley

REFERENCES

[1] *W of P* stands for W.V. Quine, *The Ways of Paradox*, Random House, New York 1966, and *FLPV* for W.V. Quine, *From a Logical Point of View*, Harvard University Press, Cambridge, Mass., 1953. Page references alone in parentheses always refer to W.V. Quine, *Word and Object*, M.I.T. Press, Cambridge, Mass., 1960.

[2] Cf. e.g. R. Carnap, 'Empiricism, Semantics, and Ontology', Appendix A in *Meaning and Necessity* (2nd ed.), University of Chicago Press, Chicago 1956.

[3] To the claim that we could discover completely disparate total schemes "... one may protest that two systems of analytical hypotheses are, as wholes, equivalent so long as no verbal behavior makes any difference between them; and, if they offer seemingly discrepant English translations, one may again argue that the apparent conflict is a conflict only of parts seen out of context. ... When two systems of analytical hypotheses fit the totality of verbal dispositions to perfection and yet conflict in their translations of certain sentences, the conflict is precisely a conflict of parts seen without the wholes. The principle of indeterminacy of translation requires notice just because translation proceeds little by little and sentences are thought of as conveying meanings severally" (pp. 78–79).

[4] N. Goodman, *Fact, Fiction, and Forecast*, Harvard University Press, Cambridge, Mass., 1955, esp. ch. IV.

[5] Cf. e.g. *FLPV*, pp. 78–79. This theme is elaborated in Quine's recent Dewey Lectures, published as 'Ontological Relativity', *Journal of Philosophy* 65 (1968) 185–212.

[6] "Yet we must not leap to the fatalistic conclusion that we are stuck with the conceptual scheme that we grew up in. We can change it bit by bit, plank by plank, though meanwhile there is nothing to carry us along but the evolving conceptual scheme itself" (*FLPV*, pp. 78–79).

[7] This point is expounded and defended in more detail in Gilbert Harman, 'Quine on Meaning and Existence, I', *Review of Metaphysics* 21 (1967) 124–151, especially 148–150.

[8] I am not satisfied that the whole point of the objection is met in this way. There is a difficult and largely unexplored problem of how conceptual novelty, which seems to occur, is really possible. I suspect that this is a problem for everyone, not just for Quine.

[9] For a good discussion of some of these factors and how they operate see Hilary Putnam, 'The Analytic and the Synthetic', *Minnesota Studies in the Philosophy of Science*, vol. III, (ed. by H. Feigl and G. Maxwell), University of Minnesota Press, Minneapolis 1962.

P. F. STRAWSON

SINGULAR TERMS AND PREDICATION*

The ideas of *singular term* and of *general term in predicative position* play a central part in Quine's theory of canonical notation. I examine two attempts to explain these ideas, and I argue that they rest upon certain other notions whose role as foundations is not clearly acknowledged in Quine's explanations.

I

In his new book[1] Quine distinguishes once more between singular terms and general terms. He also speaks of different 'positions' which terms may occupy in sentences, notably of referential and of predicative position. 'Referential', or 'purely referential', position is more narrowly understood by Quine than 'position for a singular term'; and if, later on in what follows, I appear to ignore this fact, my reasons are: (1) that I may do so without risk of confusion since I shall not be concerned with, or introduce, any of those referentially opaque contexts which yield positions for singular terms other than purely referential positions; and (2) that 'referential position' is a more convenient expression than 'position for a singular term'.

The relations between these notions of terms and positions are not altogether simple; but fortunately it appears from Quine's exposition that there is one quite fundamental distinction a grasp of which will serve as the basis for everything else. This is the distinction between a *singular term* on the one hand and a *general term in predicative position* on the other. A union of the two is necessary and sufficient for a fundamental kind, though not perhaps the most primitive kind, of sentence of ordinary language; and in canonical notation, where the only singular terms are variables, a union of the two is necessary and sufficient to yield an atomic open sentence such as all true or false sentences are obtained from by quantification and other devices of sentence composition.

The fundamental distinction can, in fact, be yet more narrowly specified. Quine distinguishes between definite and indefinite singular terms. (Examples of definite singular terms are 'Leo', 'that lion', 'the lion', and, sometimes, 'he' and 'it'; examples of indefinite singular terms are 'everything', 'something', 'every lion', 'some lion', and, sometimes, 'a lion'.)[2] This is not merely a distinction of kind, of species within a genus. It is more like a distinction of senses of the phrase 'singular term'. Definite singular terms are singular terms in the primary sense; indefinite singular terms are singular only in a secondary or derivative sense. Part of the evidence for this comes from Quine's own incidental remarks in which, e.g., he contrasts indefinite singular terms, as being *'dummy* singular terms', with *'ordinary* or definite ones' (112–114). But more decisive than these passing remarks is the character of Quine's explanations. The explanation of the fundamental distinction in role between *singular term* and *general term in predicative position* is an explanation which has to be understood as applying only to *definite* singular terms. The *position* which definite singular terms occupy, when they play a certain characteristic role in predication, may also be occupied by other terms which do not play this characteristic role, but are allowed the *title* of singular terms just because they can occupy this position; and these are the dummy or indefinite singular terms.

The basic distinction we have to consider, then, is between *definite singular terms* on the one hand and *general terms in predicative position* on the other. Before we look at Quine's explanation of it, let us note a negative remark he makes about the distinction between singular and general terms at large. He points out that this distinction does not consist in each singular term's having application to just one object while each general term has application to more than one. That the difference does not consist in this is, he says, evident from the fact that some singular terms such as 'Pegasus', may apply to nothing at all, while some general terms such as 'natural satellite of the earth' may each apply to just one thing. There is another reason, which Quine does not mention, for rejecting this account of the difference. 'The captain is angry' is a sentence containing the singular term 'the captain' and the general term 'angry' in predicative position. If we consider at large the two terms 'the captain' and 'angry', it is obvious that both of them *have application* to, may be correctly applied to, *many* things; and may be so applied by the use, among others, of this very sentence. If, on the other hand, we think of this sentence as used to make a particular assertion on a particular occasion, it is evident that *both* the singular and the general term, on that particular occasion, are equally *being applied* to *just one* (and the same) thing. Neither way of taking the expressions brings out a difference which we can express in terms of the difference between applying (or being applied) to just one thing and applying (or being applied) to more than one thing.

Quine mentions another way, which he also thinks unsatisfactory, of trying to bring out the difference between definite singular terms and general terms in predicative position. One adopts this way in saying that the singular term *purports* to refer to just one object while the general term does not: even if the general term, like 'natural satellite of the earth' in fact has singularity of reference, this singularity of reference is not something *purported* in the term. Of this way of explaining the difference Quine says: "Such talk of purport is only a picturesque way of alluding to the distinctive grammatical roles that singular and general terms play in sentences. It is by grammatical role that singular and general terms are properly to be distinguished" (96). Elsewhere, discussing the notion of referential position (i.e., the position occupied by a definite singular term when it plays its characteristic, distinctive role in predication), he speaks of the "intuitive" idea behind this notion as the idea that the term occupying this position "is used purely to specify its object for the rest of the sentence to say something about" (177). Quine is right in thinking that these descriptions which he calls "picturesque" or "intuitive" are unsatisfactory. They are unsatisfactory not because they are intuitive or picturesque, but because they are inaccurate or unclear or both. Nevertheless we shall see that they may be inaccurate and unclear attempts to express an idea which is essential to full understanding of Quine's own explanation of the 'distinctive roles' of general and singular terms and yet is an idea to which he himself scarcely succeeds in giving a clear expression.

I turn now to Quine's explanation. It runs: "The basic combination in which general and singular terms find their contrasting roles is that of *predication*.[3]... Predication joins a general term and a singular term to form a sentence that is true or false according as the general term is true or false of the object, if any, to which the singular term refers" (96). This is supposed to be a description of a contrast of grammatical *roles*; the dichotomy of terms that Quine is concerned with is supposed to be "clarified" by this description of roles (97). Distinctions of grammatical *form* are associated with this contrast of roles: e.g., grammar requires that the predicative role be signalized by the form of the verb; if the general term does not already possess this form, it must, to be fitted for predicative position, be prefixed with the copula 'is' or 'is a(n)' (96–97). But it is the distinction of role thus signalized, and not the form of signaling, that is important for logical theory.

But what is this distinction? The passage I quoted seems to envisage a situation in which there is, on the one hand, a sentence formed by joining two terms and in which there may or may not be, on the other hand, an object to which both terms are correctly applied. The difference in role of the two terms might be held to be shown by the implied differences between the ways in which there might fail to be such an object. Thus the failure might, so to speak, be justly laid at the door of the general term; but only if (1) there indeed was a certain object to which the singular term was correctly applied, and (2) the general term failed to apply to *that* object, i.e., *the* object to which the singular term was correctly applied. It is implied that in this case of failure the sentence (statement) is false. Or again the failure might be justly laid at the door of the singular term; but this would be quite a different kind of failure. It would not be a failure of the singular term to apply to *the object which* ... – where this 'which' clause could be filled out by mentioning the general term. The failure of application of the singular term would not, like that of its partner, depend on its partner's success. It would be a quite independent failure. And it appears to be here implied, and it is elsewhere stated, that the result of this failure would be not that the sentence was to be assessed as false, but that it was not to be assessed for truth value at all. Whether the sentence is true or false depends on the success or failure of the general term; but the failure of the singular term appears to deprive the general term of the chance of either success or failure.

If this is a correct reading of Quine's sentence, then it is clear that the description he gives of the crucial distinction is designed to fit at most (on the side of singular terms) only *definite* singular terms; for it contains no attempt to mention any contrast there may be *in role or function* between indefinite singular terms and general terms in predicative position. Quine's complementary account of such a sentence as '*A comet* was *observed by astronomers tonight*', containing one indefinite singular term and one composite general term in predicative position, would be that it is true if there is an object, any object, to which both terms apply; otherwise false.

In respect of *role* the two terms are not distinguished at all. If we ask why one of the two terms is nevertheless to be called a singular term and the other not, we may indeed appeal to grammar; but it will now be an appeal to what Quine contrasts with grammatical *role*, viz., to grammatical *form*. The term 'a comet' is formally like a (definite) singular term in that it is a substantive occupying the position of grammatical subject to the predicative copula (a special case of the verb of predication in general). It is formally unlike a general term in predicative position in that it has no predicative copula prefixed to it and does not itself possess the form of a verb. In no other way mentioned by Quine does it differ from the general term. As for 'everything' and 'something', the description leaves us to presume that they are entitled to classification as singular terms in so far as they too may occupy this position, may share these formal characteristics.

If my reading of Quine's sentence is correct, there is a much more important point to be made. It is that the distinction drawn remains inadequately explained. The explanation raises, rather than answers, questions. "Predication joins a general term and a singular term to form a sentence..."– a sentence in which the two kinds of term exhibit the obscure differences I have set out. But what is it that *accounts* for these differences? Unless we can answer this question, we shall certainly not fully understand the distinction; indeed we shall scarcely know what predication is. We cannot give up the question and be content with talk of verbs and substantives, of grammatical subjects and predicates. Quine is no more one of Ramsey's schoolchildren doing English grammar than Ramsey himself was. But neither can we be satisfied with the distinction as I have interpreted it. Singular terms are what yield truth-value gaps when they fail in their role. General terms are what yield truth or falsity, when singular terms succeed in their role, by themselves applying, or failing to apply, to what the singular terms apply to. This is more or less what we have. It scarcely seems enough. We want to ask 'Why?'

It might be objected at this point that my interpretation of Quine's sentence was perverse, that the cumbrousness and obscurity of the reading were quite unnecessary. In Quine's sentence there occur the two contrasting expressions, 'is true of', associated with the general term, and 'refers to', associated with the singular term; and this contrast I have deliberately ignored, contenting myself with the single expression 'applies to'. May not this difference of expression, which I ignored, be intended to reflect a difference in the ways in which singular and general terms respectively apply or are applied to objects? And may not the explanation we are still seeking be found in this difference of mode of application?

This seems a reasonable suggestion. But there are several reasons why we cannot be content simply to *repeat* these expressions, to say 'In the successful predication, the singular term *refers* to its object, while the general term is *true of* it'. For one thing, Quine himself does not adhere consistently to this usage. On p. 95 he writes:"'Pegasus' counts as a singular term though *true of* nothing"; and on pages 108–109 he repeatedly uses the idioms of *being true of* and *referring* (*having reference*) *to* interchangeably in conection with general terms. This point is not very important. Even if Quine had been perfectly consistent in his usage, it would still be the case that the difference in force between the expressions 'is true of' and 'refers to' calls as loudly for explanation as the expressions 'general term' and 'singular term' themselves. Neither pair, unaided, serves to explain the other. This is why I ignored the difference of expression and used instead the undifferentiated idiom of *application*. The deliberate non-differentiation of expression diminishes the risk of our seeming to understand a distinction when we do not.

This is the point at which we have to return to ideas of the kind that Quine dismissed as vague and picturesque. Let us consider those predications in which singular and general term alike may fairly be said to be applied to a single concrete and spatiotemporally continuous object (e.g., 'Mama is kind', 'That picture is valuable', 'The doctor is coming to dinner'). What is the characteristic difference in the mode in which they are applied? Let us recall that, in such a predication, neither of the terms employed need be such that it *applies* to only one object, though both are currently *being applied to* just one object, and, if all goes well, both do in fact *apply to* that object. Now what is the characteristic difference between the relations of the two terms to the object? The characteristic difference, I suggest, is that the singular term is used for the purpose of *identifying* the object, of bringing it about that the hearer (or, generally, the audience) knows *which* or *what* object is in question; while the general term is not. It is enough if the general term in fact applies to the object; it does not also have to identify it.

But what exactly is this task of identifying an object for a hearer? Well, let us consider that in any communication situation a hearer (an audience) is antecedently equipped with a certain amount of knowledge, with certain presumptions, with a certain range of possible current perception. There are within the scope of his knowledge or present perception objects which he is able *in one way or another* to distinguish for himself. The identificatory task of *one* of the terms, in predications of the kind we are now concerned with, is to bring it about that the hearer knows *which* object it is, of all the objects within the hearer's scope of knowledge or presumption, that the *other* term is being applied to. This identificatory task is characteristically the task of the definite singular term. That term achieves its identificatory purpose by drawing upon what in the widest sense might be called the conditions of its utterance, *including* what the hearer is presumed to know or to presume already or to be in a position there and then to perceive for himself. This is not something incidental to the use of singular terms in predications of the kind we are now concerned with. It is quite central to this use. The possibility of identification in the relevant sense exists only for an audience antecedently equipped with knowledge or presumptions, or placed in a position of possible perception, which can be drawn on in this way.[4]

Perhaps the phrase about purporting singularity of application that Quine found unsatisfactory should be construed as a shot at describing the identificatory function of singular terms. If so, Quine was right to think it unsatisfactory. Not only is the phrase far from clear. But at least one fairly natural sense that it might bear is foreign to the purpose. Thus an expression might be said to 'purport singularity of application' if it contained phrases making express uniqueness claims, phrases such as 'the only', 'unique in', 'alone', 'just one'. But terms used for the identificatory purpose will rarely contain such phrases. Such phrases will more naturally occur where the purpose on hand is a different one: e.g., to inform a hearer, with regard to some independently identified object, that it is unique in a certain respect, or to inform him that *there is* something unique in a certain respect. But then the expressions containing such phrases do not have the characteristic role of definite singular terms. They can, as Quine would say, readily be parsed as general terms in predicative position.

Slightly better, but still unsatisfactory, in Quine's alternative description of 'the intuitive idea behind *purely referential position*', viz., "that the term is used purely to specify its object for the rest of the sentence to say something about". Still unsatisfactory, since 'specify' by itself remains vague. To remove the vagueness we need the concept of 'identifying for an audience' which I have just introduced. Fully to elucidate *this* idea a great deal more should be said about the conditions and means of such identification. But we have enough for our immediate purposes: enough to see that a real difference of function is reflected by the difference between the expressions 'refers to' and 'is true of', and that these expressions, used as Quine uses them, are not inappropriate; and enough to understand why Quine should impute the differences that he seems by implication to impute to the nature and consequences of application failure on the part of singular and general terms, respectively.

It is easy enough to see why the distinction of function should lead philosophers to this further distinction. It happens something like this. Let us suppose that the identificatory function has been successfully performed. The successful performance of this function does not, of course, settle the question of the truth or falsity of the predication as a whole. What settles that question would seem to be whether or not the general term applies to the object, whether, as Quine would say, it is true or false *of* the object. But now suppose a radical failure of identificatory function. By a radical failure I mean, not simply the use of an incorrect instead of a correct designation; nor simply the use of a designation which, correct or incorrect, fails to invoke appropriate knowledge in the possession of the hearer and hence leaves him in the dark as to which object is being referred to, or causes him to mistake the identity of that object. I mean the case (rare enough) when there is no appropriate *knowledge*, in anyone's possession, to be invoked; where all such supposed knowledge is not knowledge, but mistake; where there just is no such object as the singular term is supposed to identify. This situation is indeed different from the situation in which the general term simply does not in fact apply to the successfully identified object. We think of the predication as a whole as true in the case where the general term does apply to the object that the singular term is supposed to identify. We think of the predication as a whole as false in the case where the general term does *not* apply to that object, the case where the general term can be truthfully *denied* of that object. But the case where there is no such object is neither a case where the general term can be truly affirmed of it nor a case where the general term can be truly denied of it. Hence there is a strong inclination to say that the predication as a whole is neither true nor false in this case (even that there is no predication at all in this case). Some philosophers have resisted this inclination, and have argued in favor of classifying this case together with the case in which the general term fails to apply to the successfully identified object, under the common appellation, 'false'. There has been debate over this, and it has sometimes seemed that the debate over the use of the word 'false' was the really substantial question, on the answer to which hung all the other debated issues in this area. But this is not so; for many reasons. The claim that the radical failure of a definite singular term results in a truth-value gap is in some cases more intuitively satisfactory, in others less intuitively satisfactory, than the claim that it results in falsity. This is not a mere oddity or 'quirk' of intuition (or usage). It is something that can be explained; though not here and now.

But, however *that* is explained, it remains important that the identificatory function of singular terms should be acknowledged, seen for what it is, and clearly distinguished from the operation of asserting that there is just one thing answering to certain specifications. This distinction is implicitly denied by Russell, at least as far as some classes of singular terms are concerned. It is, on the other hand, implicitly acknowledged by Quine; and to that extent I am with Quine. My present reproach against him is contained in the word 'implicitly'. For when we read that key sentence of his, designed to elucidate the functional distinction between singular and general terms, we are constrained to read it as an obscure statement of a debated consequence of that distinction rather than as a description of the distinction itself; while those more hopeful phrases that might seem to point, however waveringly, in the right direction, are dismissed as vague, intuitive, or picturesque instead of being used as steppingstones toward the definite, the explicit, and the literal. What makes this the more surprising is that, in the course of some remarks devoted to the discussion of different types of singular terms, Quine shows himself well enough aware of the identifying function of singular terms in general. I content myself with two quotations: "In 'I saw the lion' the singular term 'the lion' is presumed to refer to some one lion, *distinguished from its fellows* for speaker and hearer by previous sentences or attendant circumstances" (112). "In ordinary discourse the idiom of ... singular description is normally used only where *the intended object* is believed to be *singled out uniquely* by the matter appended to the singular 'the' together

105

perhaps with supplementary information…" (183). These idioms of 'singling out' or 'distinguishing' the 'intended' object are all in the right spirit. And on p. 103 there even occurs, just once, the key word 'identification'.

There are, of course, as Quine's discussion shows, many different types of situation in which the identificatory function is performed and many different types of resource upon which a speaker may draw or rely in performing it. He may draw upon what the speaker can be presumed to be in a position then and there to see or otherwise perceive for himself. He may rely upon information imparted by earlier sentences in the same conversation. He may rely upon information in the hearer's possession which is not derived from either of these sources, or upon past experience and recognitional capacities of the hearer's which the latter could scarcely articulate into a description. He may draw or rely upon any combination of these. But he *must* draw upon something in this area if the identificatory function is to be performed at all. That function is successfully performed if and only if the singular term used establishes for the hearer an identity, and the right identity, between the thought of *what-is-being-spoken-of-by-the-speaker* and the thought of some object *already within the reach of the hearer's own knowledge, experience, or perception,* some object, that is, which the hearer could, in one way or another, pick out or identify for himself, from his own resources. To succeed in its task, the singular term, together with the circumstances of its utterance, must draw on the appropriate stretch of those resources.

Is there anything in what I have so far said that Quine would wish or need to dispute? I think the answer is a qualified negative. Had I asked this question about Russell, it seems that the answer should be an unqualified affirmative. For Russell appears to claim for the Theory of Descriptions that it gives an exact account of the working of one class of definite singular terms, viz., singular descriptions. And I am bound to deny this. For in the analysis of singular descriptions given in the Theory of Descriptions the identificatory function of singular terms is suppressed altogether. Its place is taken by an explicit assertion to the effect that there exists just one thing with a certain property. But to say this is to do something quite different from identifying that thing for a hearer in the sense I have been concerned with. One who says that there exists just one thing with a certain property typically intends to inform his hearer of this fact. Thereby he does indeed supply the hearer with resources of know-

ledge which constitute, so to speak, a minimal basis for a subsequent identifying reference to draw on. But the act of supplying new resources is not
the same act as the act of drawing on independently established resources.

The non-identity of these acts, on the other hand, constitutes no *prima
facie* objection to Quine's proposal for the elimination of definite singular
terms from 'canonical notation'. For Quine does not claim that the
sentences which replace those containing definite singular terms have the
same meaning as the latter (182). Nor, presumably, would he claim that
they would normally serve exactly the same purpose; for this, if I am right,
would be to claim too much. He would claim that in some weaker sense
the sentences containing singular terms could be replaced by the sentences
in canonical notation. What this weaker kind of substitutability is we need
not here inquire too closely, if we suppose merely that it is not such as to
conflict with the account I have sketched of the characteristic identificatory function of definite singular terms. There remains a point of more
immediate significance concerning our understanding of the apparatus of
theoretical notions within the framework of which the idea of canonical
notation is introduced. The relevant part of Quine's program of paraphrase
can most simply be summed up as follows. All *terms* other than the
variables of quantification will be found, in canonical notation, to be
general terms in predicative position. The *position* of singular terms is
reserved for the quantifiers and the variables of quantification; and since
quantifiers themselves do not count as *terms,* the only singular terms left
are the variables of quantification. But, merely formal distinctions of
grammar apart, how was the distinction between *singular terms* and
general terms in predicative position explained? It was explained in terms of
the contrasting roles in predication of the *definite* singular term and the
general term in predicative position. This contrast of roles is our fundamental clue to all the theoretical notions employed. So our theoretical
grasp of the nature of canonical notation rests upon our theoretical grasp
of the identificatory function of singular terms. And this is why Quine
should have elucidated more fully than he did those notions which he was
content to dismiss as vague and picturesque.

II

It may be retorted at this point that it is not necessary for Quine to present
his distinction of terms and positions as resting on the contrasting roles in

predication of the definite singular term and the general term in predicative position. There is, it may be said, a way of presenting the distinction which is independent of any appeal to the function of the definite singular term; and it is a way which Quine sometimes makes use of. The position of a singular term in general can be directly explained as position accessible to quantifiers and variables of quantification or to those expressions of ordinary language to which quantifiers and variables correspond. Predicative position, on the other hand, is inaccessible to quantifiers. It is occupied by general terms which complement quantifiers (or other occupants of singular-term position) to yield sentences. All we need now assume is that we can understand the role of quantifiers or of those idioms of ordinary language which the quantifiers 'encapsulate'. If we can assume this much understanding, we have materials for explaining the concepts of singular term and of predicative position; and the general program can proceed without the intelligibility of its whole apparatus of theoretical notions appearing to rest on our grasp of the functioning of definite singular terms.

This way out proves delusive; and in observing just how it proves delusive, we shall see how the account I gave in Part I of this paper itself needs to be deepened and strengthened. Predicative position is supposed to be inaccessible to quantifiers. But is it? Betty is a better date than Sally. Betty is willing and pretty and Sally too is willing and pretty. But Betty is also witty and Sally is not witty. Surely, it seems, 'willing', 'pretty', and 'witty' are here in predicative position. But is their position inaccessible to quantifiers? As a date, Betty is everything that Sally is (i.e., willing and pretty) and something that Sally isn't (i.e., witty). Or, if you like, there is nothing that Sally is that Betty isn't and something that Sally isn't that Betty is.

What are we to do? Are we to stick by the test without qualification and say that the example shows that 'witty' and 'pretty' are singular terms, and 'Sally' and 'Betty' are in predicative position? This will attract no one, and anyway would obliterate the distinction altogether, since the test could be differently, and more obviously, applied to yield the conclusion that 'Sally' and 'Betty' were singular terms, and 'witty' and 'pretty' were in predicative position.

Are we to try to save the situation by saying that the test for being a singular term includes not only occupancy of a position accessible to quantifiers but also the possession of the grammatical form of the substantive? But this *by itself* would be the wrong kind of appeal to grammar, the kind that Quine would rightly repudiate. Can we buttress this additional requirement with a supposed rationale for it, saying that what it really amounts to is the requirement that the term displaced by the quantifier, if a definite term, should designate an *object,* and that 'Betty' satisfies this requirement while 'pretty' does not? But other objections apart, how shall we then deal with the 'offenders', as Quine calls them (240), who stoutly affirm that 'witty' and 'pretty' in 'Sally is pretty' and 'Betty is witty' *do* designate objects, namely attributes? Quine's general method of dealing with such offenders is not available here. For to one who says (roughly) that the use of any term commits its user to a corresponding object Quine is wont to reply (roughly) that this is so only where the term occupies a position that it can yield to a quantifier. But the trouble with the terms in question here is that they do occupy positions that they can yield to quantifiers. So we are back where we started.

Let us think again about our example, and in a spirit as sympathetic to Quine as possible. Suppose we redescribe the situation as follows. Prettiness is a quality desirable in a date and Betty has prettiness and Sally has prettiness. Similarly with willingness. Wit is a quality desirable in a date and Betty has wit and Sally has not. Everything which Sally has and which is a quality desirable in a date is something which Betty has; but there is something which is a quality desirable in a date and which Betty has, which Sally does not have. I think that Quine would say that this form of description of the situation is a better, a more logically candid, form than the first. But how does it differ from the first? Well, it differs in that the terms that yield their positions to quantifiers have the grammatical form of substantives and not of adjectives. But we are agreed not to regard this as a vital difference. A more significant difference is this. There is something explicit in the second account of the situation that was only implicit in the first; and it is made explicit by the use of the expression 'quality desirable in a date'.[5] Let us try to follow this clue. It gives us the following result. 'Prettiness' occupies singular-term, or referential, position because it is joined with such an expression as 'desirable in a date', which, relative to it, occupies predicative position. Generally, whenever, explicitly or implicitly, two terms are joined of which the first stands to the second in that characteristic relation in which 'prettiness' (*or* 'pretty') stands to 'desirable in a date', then, relatively to each other, the first is a candidate for referential and the second for predicative position. Thus, even in our first description of the situation, 'pretty' had implicitly referential position. It did not have implicitly referential position considered simply in relation to 'Sally' (or 'Betty'). Rather it was a candidate for predicative position relative to 'Sally'. For it does not stand to 'Sally' as it stands to 'desirable in a date' but rather as 'desirable in a date' stands to it. But it still had implicitly referential position; for it was *implied* that being pretty was desirable in a date. And it was because it had implicitly *referential* position that it could comfortably yield its position to quantification.

But now let us ponder this. A new criterion seems to have emerged for the relative concept of referential and predicative positions. I shall call it the type-criterion. (Elsewhere I have called it – or, rather, its basis – the category-criterion.[6]) 'Pretty' has predicative significance relative to 'Betty', referential significance relative to 'desirable in a date'. We have a series consisting of (1) 'Betty', (2) 'pretty' or 'prettiness', (3) 'desirable in a date', such that any earlier term in the series is a candidate for referential position relative to the immediately succeeding term, and any later term is a candidate for predicative position relative to the immediately preceding term.[7] But what is the general nature of such a series, what is it about its terms and their relations that confers upon them these further relations, these claims to relative referential and predicative position? Well, it will scarcely be denied that 'Betty' is typically used to designate a spatio-temporally continuous particular. And it will scarcely be denied that the meaning of 'pretty' is such that it may be said to *group* such particulars in accordance with a certain kind of principle. The term may be said to group all those particulars whose designations may be coupled with it to yield true statements. Now in a certain sense 'Betty' may be said to group particulars too: a particular arm, leg, face, even a particular action, might all be truthfully ascribed to Betty. But obviously the principle on which 'Betty' groups particulars like arms and legs is quite a different sort of principle from the principle on which 'pretty' groups particulars like Betty and Sally. Now consider such a term as (3) 'desirable in a date'. This term has a grouping function too. It does not directly group particulars; it groups *ways,* such as term (2)'s way *of grouping particulars.* But there are analogies and connections between term (3)'s way of grouping ways of grouping particulars and term (2)'s way of grouping particulars. The

110

principle that term (3) supplies, of grouping ways of grouping, is like the principle that term (2) supplies, of grouping particulars, in a way in which both are quite unlike the principle of grouping particulars that term (1) supplies. These likenesses and unlikenesses are registered in the terminology of philosophy: in the series that starts with *particular*, and goes on with *property or kind of particular, property or kind of property or kind of particular*, etc.; in the philosophical usage which permits us to say that Betty is a case or instance of prettiness, and prettiness a case or instance of quality desirable in a date, but forbids us to say that Betty's left arm or anything else is a case or instance of Betty.[8]

The result, then, of our reflections on our example is this. Two terms coupled in a true sentence stand in referential and predicative position, respectively, if what the first term designates or signifies is a case or instance of what the second term signifies. Items thus related (or the terms that designate or signify them) may be said respectively to be of lower and of higher type; and this is why I called the new criterion one of type.[9] Part of the explanation of the kind of grouping which terms of higher type than the lowest can do was that it is a kind of grouping which designations of spatio-temporal particulars *cannot* do. So implicit in this criterion of relative position is the consequence that a term designating a particular can never occupy predicative position. A term signifying a kind or property, however, may occupy referential or predicative position, depending upon whether it is, or is not, coupled with a term of still higher type.

Now it might be maintained that we do not need this criterion in addition to the identificatory criterion suggested in Part I of this paper. It was there suggested that the primary occupant of referential position was the term which served to identify the object both terms applied to, the object the sentence was about. Does not this criterion work as well for 'Prettiness is a quality desirable in a date' as it does for 'Betty is pretty'? Just as 'Betty' identifies, and 'pretty' does not, the object the second sentence is about, so 'prettiness' identifies, and 'quality desirable in a date' does not, the attribute the first sentence is about. But before we acquiesce too readily in this suggestion, let us consider more carefully the way in which, both here and originally, we *applied* the identificatory criterion. When we do so, we see that the *type-criterion was already implicit in our application of the identificatory criterion.* We said that 'Betty' identifies,

111

and 'pretty' does not, the object the sentence is about; what the sentence tells us about Betty is that she is *pretty*. But in saying this we have already shown a tacit preference for the particular, the item of lower (lowest) type, as the object the sentence is about. There is nothing in the word 'about' or in the concept of identification in general to compel this *exclusive* choice. We could equally well say (and in some contexts it would be correct to say) that the sentence was about prettiness; and that what it says about prettiness is that *Betty* is pretty. The term 'pretty' identifies the attribute the sentence is about; the words 'Betty is' inform us where the attribute is to be found. But though there was nothing in the word 'about' or in the concept of identification in general that compelled this exclusive prefer- ence, nevertheless there was something that compelled it: this was the conjunction of the two facts: first, that we were seeking to elucidate the distinction between referential and predicative position, and, second, that the type-criterion is essential to this distinction. This does not mean that we should abandon the identificatory criterion. It only means that we should acknowledge that the exclusive way in which it is applied reflects our acceptance of the type-criterion.

We fuse the two, to obtain the following account of the distinction between referential and predicative position, an account which, if I am right, underlies all that Quine says about this distinction. Referential position is the position primarily and fundamentally occupied by a term definitely identifying a spatio-temporal particular in a sentence coupling that term to another signifying a property-like or kind-like principle of grouping particulars. The particular-identifying term is the primary case of a definite singular term. The other term occupies predicative position. Second, referential position may be occupied by a term signifying a prop- erty-like or kind-like principle of grouping particulars provided that this term is itself coupled to another term which signifies a higher principle of grouping such principles of grouping. The first of these terms is then a secondary case of a definite singular term. The other term again occupies predicative position. Finally, the position occupied by a definite singular term of any kind may be coherently yielded to a kind of term which does not characteristically have the identifying function of a definite singular term, and which is called an indefinite singular term.

The above sentences of mine by no means constitute a complete account of the distinction between referential and predicative position, between singular term and general term in predicative position. But they provide, perhaps, the necessary basis on which, by further extension, analogy, and qualification, any complete account must be built.

But now what has happened to quantification? We set out with the suggestion that accessibility to quantifiers might provide a test for referential position independent of the explanations of Part I. We end by returning to the explanations of Part I, with the addition of an explicit awareness of the type-criterion they implicitly involved. Quantification seems to have disappeared from view altogether. Yet quantifiers were supposed to hold the key to referential position. How are we to explain this?

We can understand the situation better if we remember that quantification is also supposed by Quine to hold the key to something else, viz., the ontological commitments of our talk. Quantifiers hold the key to ontic commitment because the objects are "what count as cases when, quantifying, we say that everything or something is thus-and-so" (240). They hold the key to referential position because they encapsulate certain "specially selected, unequivocally referential idioms of ordinary language", viz., 'there is an object x such that' and 'every object x is such that' (242). Here the notions of *object, reference,* and *quantification* seem to stand in firm connection without any dependence on the ideas of type and of identification that I have invoked. But let us look a little more closely: at the tell-tale word 'cases' in the first quotation and at the way in which 'something' and 'thus-and-so' are balanced about the 'is'; at the word 'object' itself in the second quotation. Does the word 'object' itself already contain, concealed, the type-criterion, the preference for particulars? After all, we readily say that spatio-temporally continuous particulars are *objects* and less readily say this of attributes and the rest. Suppose we leave it out, to guard against prejudice. Then why should we prefer 'There is something *that is thus-and-so*' to 'There is something *that such-and-such is*' as the general form of what we say when we use an existential quantifier? The reason is clear; but it leads us straight back to the type-criterion. In a two-term sentence in which one term identifies an item of lower type to which the other term non-identifyingly applies, it is the identifying term for this item that is the grammatical subject of the predicative 'is' and characteristically precedes it. What characteristically follows the 'is' (as grammatical complement) is the term that applies to,

113

but does not identify, the item of lower type; it is the term that signifies (identifies) an item of higher type, that which the item of lower type is being said to be *a case of*.[10] So it is the type-relation, the type-order, that dictates Quine's choice of phrasing, and thereby seems to vindicate the alleged link between quantification and referential position.

This is not to say that the quantification test is a bad test for referential position. On the contrary, it is, on the whole, a good test.[11] But the explanation of its being a good test leads us once more back to the type-criterion. It is a good test because there is never any point in introducing a quantifier into a place that could be occupied by a term signifying an item of a higher type *unless* this is done in coupling with a term signifying an item of a still higher type.[12] Hence quantifiers always occupy relatively lower-type positions. We saw this, in a not very clear way, in the example about the qualities desirable in a date. In 'There is something that Betty is and Sally is not' we appeared to be quantifying in a higher-type region without any coupling to a term of still higher type. But we had to acknowledge that this was mere appearance, that we were operating implicitly with the still higher-type notion of 'quality desirable in a date'. If we were not implicitly operating with a higher-type notion, the sentence would not be worth affirming. The point becomes clearer if we consider a simpler case. Suppose the term 'Socrates' identifies the philosopher. Then 'There is something that Socrates is' is bound to be true, and 'Socrates is everything' (or 'There is nothing Socrates isn't') is bound to be false. There is no point in either sentence if 'Socrates' functions as a singular term identifying the philosopher; just as there is no point in *any* sentence whatever which declares, with regard to any identified item of any type whatever, that it has some property or that it has every property. In general it will never be to the purpose to quantify over items of a higher type unless some still higher-type principle of collection is being implicitly used.

Thus, in practice, the quantification test for referential position is quite a good test. But it is so only because the notions of referential and predicative position (or, if you like, of singular-logical-subject position and logical-predicate position) have to be understood in the way I have outlined. And if I am right in saying that they have to be understood in this way, then I think it must also be admitted that the whole apparatus of distinctions in terms of which the theory of canonical notation is explained rests upon notions whose role is hardly sufficiently acknowledged. The two essential notions are: first, that of an order of types, based upon the quite fundamental distinction between spatio-temporal particulars on the one hand and property-like or kind-like principles of grouping such particulars on the other; and, second, that of the identificatory function characteristically performed by definite singular terms referring to particulars.

The purpose of this paper was to indicate the fundamental place of these two notions in Quine's own thinking about referential and predicative position. That they have this place there is not, as far as I can see, something he would necessarily wish to dispute. But there is, I think, a further and connected consequence, concerning Quine's views on ontology, which is also worth mentioning; and perhaps he would not wish to dispute this either.

The objects to the existence of which our discourse commits us are, according to Quine, the objects, of whatever sort, which "the singular terms, in their several ways, name, refer to, take as values. They are what count as cases when, quantifying, we say that everything, or something, is thus-and-so" (240). Now we have sufficiently seen what the primary objects answering to this description are. They are spatio-temporal particulars. And we have seen that this is not something which just happens to be the case. It is a guaranteed consequence of the nature of the fundamental distinction between singular term in referential, and general term in predicative, position. Hence such particulars do not merely happen, for extraneous reasons, to count as objects in Quine's sense. They are the very pattern of objects in this sense. They are not, indeed, the only things that answer to Quine's description. But to say of things of other types that they also answer to this description is simply to say that we have occasion to bring such things under higher principles of grouping, principles which serve to group them in ways analogous to the ways in which expressions signifying properties (or kinds) of particulars serve to group particulars. In so far, then, as things other than spatio-temporal particulars qualify as objects, they do so simply because our thought, our talk, confers upon them the limited and purely logical analogy with spatio-temporal particulars which I have just described. And now, surely, we are in a position to understand the nominalist prejudice, and to discount it – without flattering the fantasies of Platonism. If by accepting as entities, on this logical test, things other than spatio-temporal par-

115

ticulars, we were claiming for them any other, any further, likeness to such particulars than the logical analogy itself contains, we should indeed be running into danger of committing the characteristic category-confusions of Platonist mythology. One who believes that such acceptance inevitably carries such a claim must seem to himself to have every rational motive for the strenuous efforts of paraphrase demanded by a limited and, as nearly as possible, nominalist ontology. But this belief is itself a symptom of confusion. Of course, even when the belief is seen to be illusion, motives of a reasonable kind, elucidatory, aesthetic, for these efforts of paraphrase may still remain. But the motive of metaphysical respectability is gone.

University of Oxford

REFERENCES

* Reprinted, with the permission of the Editors and of the Author, from *The Journal of Philosophy* **58** (1961) 393–412.
[1] *Word and Object*, published by the Technology Press of the Massachusetts Institute of Technology, Cambridge, Mass., 1960. Page references are given in parentheses. Italics are mine, except where otherwise indicated.
[2] Only sometimes 'he' and 'it', for these may function like bound variables of quantification and then are to be distinguished from *definite* singular terms; only sometimes 'a lion', for nouns preceded by an indefinite article often appear in purely predicative position and then are not singular terms at all. Indeed, these qualifications are still insufficient; for not only 'he' and 'it', but 'the lion' and 'that lion', too, may function like bound variables of quantification, as in such a sentence as 'If you tweak a lion's tail, the (that) lion will resent it'.
[3] Quine's italics.
[4] A full account of the matter would call for much more detail and many qualifications. I cannot claim to be doing more than drawing attention to a *characteristic* difference of function between definite singular terms and general terms in predicative position, in cases where both terms alike may fairly be said to be applied to a single concrete object. Thus it would not be true to say that the use of a definite singular term for a particular is *always* designed to draw upon resources of identifying knowledge or presumption antecedently in possession of the audience. For *sometimes* the operations of supplying such resources and of drawing on them may be conflated in the use of a singular term. Nor would it be true to say the general term is *never* used, whereas the singular term is *always* used, for the purpose of indicating to the audience which object it is that the other term is being applied to. For it is easy to think of cases in which, as one would be inclined to say, the roles are reversed. But counter-examples to a universal thesis about differences of function are not necessarily counter-examples to a thesis about characteristic difference of function. We must *weigh* our examples, and not treat them *simply* as counters.
[5] Cf. Quine, p. 119: "The move that ushers in abstract singular terms has to be one that simultaneously ushers in abstract general ones."

[6] See *Individuals*, Ch. 5 *et seq.*

[7] The variation in form from 'pretty' to 'prettiness' supplies the substantive which is grammatically typical for referential position; the insertion of 'has' before 'prettiness' yields a phrase which as a whole is grammatically suitable for predicative position, while containing a part, 'prettiness', grammatically suitable for referential position.

[8] Not all particulars are spatio-temporally *continuous* as Betty is. But the contrast between principles of grouping is not in general dependent on such continuity, though it is seen most easily in cases characterized by continuity. The expression 'The Plough' (used as the name of a constellation) designates a spatio-temporal particular, though not a continuous one; whereas even if it should come to pass that all the gold in the universe formed one continuous mass, this would not turn 'gold' into the designation of a spatio-temporal particular. What makes it correct to count a star as a bit of the Plough or an arm as a bit of Betty has at least to do with their spatio-temporal relation to other bits of the Plough or of Betty in a way in which what makes it correct to count something as an instance of gold has nothing to do with its spatio-temporal relations to other instances of gold. The distinction between *being a particular part of* (or *element in*, etc.) and *being a particular instance of* remains bright enough here, even though spatial continuity is gone. Of course this is only the beginning of a long and complex story which perhaps has no very clear and definite end; for as we bring more sophisticated characters into our story, the clarity and the simplicity of the contrast between principles of grouping tend to diminish. But we are investigating foundations; and it is enough if the beginnings are clear and distinct.

[9] But, of course, by adopting this terminology I by no means intend to suggest that the only differences that can properly be described as differences of type or category are the very broad differences I am concerned with. One may have occasion, for example, to distinguish many different types or categories *within* the very broad category of particulars.

[10] The point can indeed be put, though less clearly, without reference to identification. Something a thing *is* is of a higher type than anything which *is* it; a thing which *is* something is of a lower type than anything it *is*. The italicized 'is' here corresponds to 'is a case of', though it differs from the latter phrase, of course, in permitting a grammatically adjectival termination.

[11] The words 'on the whole' signify the need for certain reservations, or at least for further reflection, about some adverbial expressions like 'here', 'there', 'now', 'then'. Quine says these can be 'parsed' as general terms. But no amount of parsing would seem to defend their position from occupation by 'somewhere', 'somewhen', etc.

[12] The point is explained in *Individuals*. See especially p. 327.

VACUOUS NAMES

Of those who are approximately my contemporaries, Professor W. V. Quine is one of the very few to whom I feel I owe the deepest of professional debts, the debt which is owed to someone from whom one has learned something very important about how philosophy should be done, and who has, in consequence, helped to shape one's own mode of thinking. I hope that he will not think it inappropriate that my offering on this occasion should take the form not of a direct discussion of some part of *Word and Object*, but rather of an attempt to explore an alternative to one of his central positions, namely his advocacy of the idea of the general eliminability of singular terms, including names. I hope, also, that he will not be too shocked by my temerity in venturing into areas where my lack of expertise in formal logic is only too likely to be exposed. I have done my best to protect myself by consulting those who are in a position to advise me; they have suggested ideas for me to work on and have corrected some of my mistakes, but it would be too much to hope that none remain.[1]

I. THE PROBLEM

It seems to me that there are certain quite natural inclinations which have an obvious bearing on the construction of a predicate calculus. They are as follows:

(1) To admit individual constants; that is to admit names or their representations.

(2) To allow that sometimes a name, like "Pegasus", is not the name of any existent object; names are sometimes 'vacuous'.

(3) In the light of (2), to allow individual constants to lack designata, so that sentences about Pegasus may be represented in the system.

(4) To regard Fa and $\sim Fa$ as 'strong' contradictories; to suppose, that is, that one must be true and the other false in any conceivable state of the world.

118

(5) To hold that, if Pegasus does not exist, then "Pegasus does not fly" (or "It is not the case that Pegasus flies") will be true, while "Pegasus flies" will be false.

(6) To allow the inference rules U.I. and E.G. to hold generally, without special restriction, with respect to formulae containing individual constants.

(7) To admit the law of identity $((\forall x)\, x = x)$ as a theorem.

(8) To suppose that, if ψ is derivable from ϕ, then any statement represented by ϕ *entails* a corresponding statement represented by ψ.

It is obviously difficult to accommodate *all* of these inclinations.

(a) Given [by (7)] $(\forall x)\, x = x$ we can, given (6), derive first $a = a$ by U.I. and then $(\exists x)\, x = a$ by E.G. It is natural to take $(\exists x)\, x = a$ as a representation of 'a exists'. So given (2) and (3), a representation of a false existential statement ('Pegasus exists') will be a theorem.

(b) Given (6), we may derive, by E.G., $(\exists x) \sim Fx$ from $\sim Fa$. Given (3), this seemingly licenses an inference from "Pegasus does not fly" to "Something does not fly". But such an inference seems illegitimate if, by (5), "Pegasus does not fly" is *true* if Pegasus does not exist (as (2) allows). One should not be able, it seems, to assert that something does not fly on the basis of the truth of a statement to the effect that a certain admittedly non-existent object does not fly.

To meet such difficulties as these, various manoeuvres are available, which include the following:

(1) To insist that a grammatically proper name N is only admissible as a substituend for an individual constant (is only classifiable as a name, in a certain appropriate sense of 'name') if N has a bearer. So "Pegasus" is eliminated as a substituend, and inclination (3) is rejected.

(2) To say that a statement of the form Fa, and again one of the form $\sim Fa$, *presupposes* the existence of an object named by a, and lacks a truth-value if there is no such object. [Inclinations (4) and (5) are rejected.]

(3) To exclude individual constants from the system, treating ordinary names as being reducible to definite descriptions. [Inclination (1) is rejected.]

(4) To hold that "Pegasus" does have a bearer, a bearer which *has being* though it does not *exist*, and to regard $(\exists x)\, Fx$ as entailing not the

119

existence but only the being of something which is F. [Inclination (2) is rejected.]

(5) To allow U.I. and E.G. only in conjunction with an additional premise, such as E!a, which represents a statement to the effect that a exists. [Inclination (6) is rejected.]

(6) To admit individual constants, to allow them to lack designata, and to retain normal U.I. and E.G.; but hold that inferences made in natural discourse in accordance with the inference-licences provided by the system are made subject to the 'marginal' (extra-systematic) assumption that all names which occur in the expression of such inferences have bearers. This amounts, I think, to the substitution of the concept of 'entailing subject to assumption A' for the simple concept of entailment in one's account of the logical relation between the premises and the conclusions of such inferences. [Inclination (8) is rejected.]

I do not, in this paper, intend to discuss the merits or demerits of any of the proposals which I have just listed. Instead, I wish to investigate the possibility of adhering to *all* of the inclinations mentioned at the outset; of, after all, at least in a certain sense keeping everything. I should emphasize that I do not regard myself as committed to the suggestion which I shall endeavour to develop; my purpose is exploratory.

II. SYSTEM Q: OBJECTIVES

The suggestion with which I am concerned will involve the presentation and discussion of a first-order predicate calculus (which I shall call Q), the construction of which is based on a desire to achieve two goals:

(i) to distinguish two readings of the sentence "Pegasus does not fly" (and of other sentences containing the name "Pegasus" which do not explicitly involve any negation-device), and to provide a formal representation of these readings. The projected readings of "Pegasus does not fly" (S_1) are such that on one of them an utterance of S_1 cannot be true, given that Pegasus does not exist and never has existed, while on the other an utterance of S_1 will be true just because Pegasus does not exist.

(ii) to allow the unqualified validity, on either reading, of a step from the assertion of S_1 to the assertion (suitably interpreted) of "Something [viz., Pegasus] does not fly" (S_2).

More fully, Q is designed to have the following properties.

(1) U.I. and E.G. will hold without restriction with respect to any formula ϕ containing an individual constant $\alpha[\phi(\alpha)]$; no additional premise is to be required, and the steps licensed by U.I. and E.G. will not be subject to a marginal assumption or pretence that names occurring in such steps have bearers.

(2) For some $\phi(\alpha)$, ϕ will be true on interpretations of Q which assign no designatum to α, and some such $\phi(\alpha)$ will be theorems of Q.

(3) It will be possible, with respect to any $\phi(\alpha)$, to decide on formal grounds whether or not its truth requires that α should have a designatun.

(4) It will be possible to find, in Q, a representation of sentences such as "Pegasus exists".

(5) There will be an extension of Q in which identity is represented.

III. SCOPE

The double interpretation of S_1 may be informally clarified as follows: if S_1 is taken to say that Pegasus has the property of being something which does not fly, then S_1 is *false* (since it cannot be true that a non-existent object has a property); but if S_1 is taken to deny that Pegasus has the property of being something which flies, then S_1 is *true* (for the reason given in explaining why, on the first interpretation, S_1 is false).

It seems to be natural to regard this distinction as a distinction between differing possible scopes of the name "Pegasus". In the case of connectives, scope-differences mirror the order in which the connectives are introduced in the building up of a formula [the application of formation rules; and the difference between the two interpretations of S_1 can be represented as the difference between regarding S_1 as being (i) the result of substituting "Pegasus" for "x" in "x does not fly" (negation having already been introduced), or (ii) the result of denying the result of substituting "Pegasus" for "x" in "x flies" (the name being introduced before negation)].

To deal with this distinction, and to preserve the unrestricted application of U.I. and E.G., Q incorporates the following features:

(1) Normal parentheses are replaced by numerical subscripts which are appended to logical constants and to quantifiers, and which indicate

scope-precedence (the higher the subscript, the larger the scope). Subscripts are attached also to individual constants and to bound variables as scope-indicators. For convenience subscripts are also attached to predicate-constants and to propositional letters. There will be a distinction between

(a) $\sim_2 F_1 a_3$

and

(b) $\sim_3 F_1 a_2$.

(a) will represent the reading of S_1 in which S_1 is false if Pegasus does not exist; in (a) "a" has maximal scope. In (b) "a" has minimal scope, and the non-existence of a will be a sufficient condition for the truth of (b). So (b) may be taken to represent the second reading of S_1. To give further illustration of the working of the subscript notation, in the formula $F_1 a_2 \rightarrow_3 G_1 a_2 \vee_4 H_1 b_5$ '$\vee$' takes precedence over '$\rightarrow$', and while the scope of each occurrence of "a" is the atomic sub-formula containing that occurrence, the scope of "b" is the whole formula.

(2) The effect of extending scope-indicators to individual constants is to provide for a new formational operation, viz., the substitution of an individual constant for a free variable. The formation rules ensure that quantification takes place only after this new operation has been performed; bound variables will then retain the subscripts attaching to the individual constants which quantification eliminates. The following formational stages will be, for example, involved in the building of a simple quantificational formula:

(i) $F_1 x$
(ii) $F_1 a_2$
(iii) $\exists x_3 F_1 x_2$.

There will be, then, a distinction between

(a) $\exists x_4 \sim_2 F_1 x_3$,   and
(b) $\exists x_4 \sim_3 F_1 x_2$.

(a) will, in Q, be derivable from $\sim_2 F_1 a_3$, but not from $\sim_3 F_1 a_2$; (b) will be derivable *directly* (by E.G.) only from $\sim_3 F_1 a_2$, though it will be derivable indirectly from $\sim_2 F_1 a_3$. This distinction will be further dis-cussed.

(3) Though it was not essential to do so, I have in fact adapted a feature of the system set out in Mates' *Elementary Logic*; free variables do not occur in derivations, and U.I. always involves the replacement of one or more subscripted occurrences of a bound variable by one or more correspondingly subscripted occurrences of an individual constant. Indeed, such expressions as $F_1 x_2$ and $G_1 x_2 y_3$ are not formulae of Q (though to refer to them I shall define the expression "segment"). $F_1 x$ and $G_1 xy$ are formulae, but the sole function of free variables is to allow the introduction of an individual constant at different formational stages. $F_1 a_2 \rightarrow_3 G_1 a_2 \vee_4 H_1 x$ is admitted as a formula so that one may obtain from it a formula giving maximal scope to "b", viz., the formula $F_1 a_2 \rightarrow_3 G_1 a_2 \vee_4 H_1 b_5$.

(4) Closed formulae of a predicate calculus may be looked upon in two different ways. The symbols of the system may be thought of as lexical items in an artificial language. Actual lexical entries (lexical rules) are provided only for the logical constants and quantifiers; on this view an atomic formula in a normal calculus, for example *Fa*, will be a categorical subject-predicate sentence in that language. Alternatively, formulae may be thought of as structures underlying, and exemplified by, sentences in a language (or in languages) the actual lexical items of which are left unidentified. On this view the formula *Fa* ∨ *Gb* will be a structure exemplified by a sub-class of the sentences which exemplify the structure *Fa*. The method of subscripting adopted in Q reflects the first of these approaches; in an atomic formula the subscripts on individual constants are always higher than that on the predicate-constant, in consonance with the fact that affirmative categorical subject-predicate sentences, like "Socrates is wise" or "Bellerophon rode Pegasus", imply the non-vacuousness of the names which they contain. Had I adopted the second approach, I should have had to allow not only $F_1 a_2$, etc., but also $F_2 a_1$, etc., as formulae; I should have had to provide atomic formulae which would have substitution instances, e.g., $F_1 a_2 \rightarrow_3 G_1 b_2$, in which the scope of the individual constants does not embrace the whole formula. The second approach, however, could be accommodated with appropri-ate changes.

(5) The significance of numerical subscripts is purely ordinal; so, for example, $\sim_3 F_1 a_2$ and $\sim_{17} F_4 a_9$ will be equivalent. More generally, any pair of "isomorphs" will be equivalent, and Q contains a rule providing for the interderivability of isomorphs. ϕ and ψ will be isomorphs iff (1) subscripts apart, ϕ and ψ are identical, and (2) relations of magnitude $(=, <, >)$ holding between any pair of subscripts in ϕ are preserved between the corresponding pair of subscripts in ψ [the subscripts in ψ mirror those in ϕ in respect of relative magnitudes].

Professor C. D. Parsons has suggested to me a notation in which I would avoid the necessity for such a rule, and has provided me with an axiom-set for a system embodying it which appears to be equivalent to Q (Mr. George Myro has made a similar proposal). The idea is to adopt the notation employed in *Principia Mathematica* for indicating the scope of definite descriptions. Instead of subscripts, normal parentheses are retained and the scope of an individual constant or bound variable is indicated by an occurrence of the constant or variable in square brackets, followed by parentheses which mark the scope boundaries. So the distinction between $\sim_3 F_1 a_2$ and $\sim_2 F_1 a_3$ is replaced by the distinction between $\sim [a]\,(Fa)$ and $[a]\,(\sim Fa)$; and the distinction between $\exists x_4 \sim_3 F_1 x_2$ and $\exists x_4 \sim_2 F_1 x_3$ is replaced by the distinction between $(\exists x)\,(\sim [x]\,(Fx))$ and $(\exists x)\,([x]\,(\sim Fx))$. Parson's notation may well be found more perspicuous than mine, and it may be that I should have adopted it for the purposes of this paper, though I must confess to liking the obviousness of the link between subscripts and formation-rules.

The notion of scope may now be precisely defined for Q.

(1) If η be a logical constant or quantifier occurring in a closed formula ϕ, the scope of an occurrence of η is the largest formula in ϕ which (a) contains the occurrence of η, (b) does not contain an occurrence a *logical constant or quantifier* bearing a higher subscript than that which attaches to the occurrence of η.

(2) If η be a term (individual constant or bound variable), the scope of η is the largest segment of ϕ which (a) contains the occurrence of η, (b) does not contain an occurrence of a *logical constant* bearing a higher subscript than that which attaches to the occurrence of η.

(3) A segment is a sequence of symbols which is either (a) a formula or (b) the result of substituting subscript-preserving occurrences of

variables for one or more occurrences of individual constants in a formula.

We may now define the important related notion of "dominance". A term θ dominates a segment ϕ iff ϕ falls within the scope of at least one of the occurrences, in ϕ, of θ. In other words, θ dominates ϕ if at least one occurrence of θ in ϕ bears a subscript higher than that attaching to any logical constant in ϕ. Dominance is intimately connected with existential commitment, as will be explained.

IV. NATURAL DEDUCTION SYSTEM Q

A. *Glossary*

(1) If "η" denotes a symbol of Q, "η_n" denotes the result of attaching, to that symbol, a subscript denoting n.

(2) "$\phi(\alpha_j, ..., \alpha_k)$" = 'a formula ϕ containing occurrences of an individual constant α, each such occurrence being either an occurrence of α_j, or of..., or of α_k'.
[Similarly, if desired, for "$\phi(\omega_j, ... \omega_k)$", where "$\omega$" ('omega') denotes a variable.]

(3) "$\phi_{[n]}$" = "a formula, the highest subscript within which denotes n".

(4) If θ_1 and θ_2 are terms (individual constants or bound variables), '$\phi(\theta_2/\theta_1)$' = 'the result of replacing each occurrence of θ_1 in ϕ by an occurrence of θ_2, while preserving subscripts at substitution-points'. [The upper symbol indicates the substituend.]

B. *Provisional Set of Rules for* Q

1. *Symbols*
   (a) Predicate-constants ("F", "F^1",... "G"...).
   (b) Individual constants ("a", 'a^1',... "b"...).
   (c) Variables ("x", "x^1"... "y"...).
   (d) Logical constants ("$\sim$", "&", "$\vee$", "$\rightarrow$").
   (e) Quantification-symbols ('$\forall$', '$\exists$'). [A quantification-symbol followed by a subscripted variable is a quantifier.]

(f) Numerical subscripts (denoting natural numbers).

(g) Propositional letters ("p", "q",...).

2. *Formulae*

(1) A subscripted n-ary predicate constant followed by n unsubscripted variables; a subscripted propositional letter.

(2) If $\phi_{[n]}$ is a formula, $\phi(\alpha_{n+m}/\omega)$ is a formula.

(3) If $\phi_{[n]}$ is a formula, $\forall\omega_{n+m}\phi(\omega/\alpha)$ is a formula. [NB: Substitutions are to preserve subscripts.]

(4) If $\phi_{[n]}$ is a formula, $\exists\omega_{n+m}\phi(\omega/\alpha)$ is a formula. [NB: Substitutions are to preserve subscripts.]

(5) If $\phi_{[n]}$ is a formula, $\sim_{n+m}\phi$ is a formula.

(6) If $\phi_{[n-m]}$ and $\psi_{[n-l]}$ are formulae, $\phi\,\&_n\psi$, $\phi\vee_n\psi$, $\phi\rightarrow_n\psi$ are formulae.

(7) ϕ is a formula only if it can be shown, by application of (1)–(6), that ϕ is a formula.

3. *Inference-Rules*

(1) [Ass] Any formula may be assumed at any point.

(2) $[\sim+, \text{RAA}]$ If $\phi_{[m]}^1, \phi^2, \dots \phi^k \vdash \psi_{[n-j]}\&_n\sim_{n-k}\psi_{[n-k-l]}$, then $\phi^2, \dots \phi^k \vdash \sim_{m+i}\phi'$.

(3) $[\sim-, \text{DN}]\sim_{n+k}\sim_n\phi_{[n-m]} \vdash \phi$.

(4) $[\&+]\ \phi_{[n-m]}, \psi_{[n-k]} \vdash \phi\,\&_n\psi$.

(5) $[\&-]\ \phi_{[n-m]}\&_n\psi_{[n-l]}\begin{cases}\vdash\phi\\\vdash\psi\end{cases}$.

(6) $[\vee+]\ \phi_{[n-m]}\begin{cases}\vdash\phi\vee_n\psi_{[n-l]}\\\vdash\psi_{[n-l]}\vee_n\phi\end{cases}$.

(7) $[\vee-]$ If (1) $\psi_{[n-m]}, \phi^1, \dots \phi^j \vdash \zeta$,

       (2) $\chi_{[n-l]}, \phi^2, \dots \phi^k \vdash \zeta$,

       (3) $\phi^3, \dots \phi^2 \vdash \psi\vee_n\chi$,

then   (4) $\phi^1, \dots, \phi^j, \phi^2, \dots, \phi^k, \phi^3, \dots \phi^2 \vdash \zeta$.

(8) $[\rightarrow+, \text{CP}]$ If $\phi_{[n-m]}, \psi^1, \dots \psi^k \vdash \chi_{[n-l]}$, then $\psi^1, \dots \psi^k \vdash \phi\rightarrow_n\chi$.

(9) $[\rightarrow-, \text{MPP}]\ \phi_{[n-l]}\rightarrow_n\psi_{[n-m]}, \phi \vdash \psi$.

(10) [∀+] If $\psi^1, \ldots \psi^k \vdash \phi_{[n]}$, then $\psi^1, \ldots \psi^k \vdash \forall \omega_{n+m} \, \phi \, (\omega/\alpha)$, provided that α does not occur in $\psi^1, \ldots, \psi^k$.

(11) [∀−] $\forall \omega_n \phi \vdash \phi \, (\alpha/\omega)$, provided that $\forall \omega_n \phi$ is the scope of $\forall \omega_n$.

(12) (∃+) $\phi_{[n]} \vdash \exists \omega_{n+m} \psi$, where ψ is like ϕ except that, if α occurs in ϕ, at least one such occurrence is replaced in ψ by an occurrence of ω.

(13) (∃−) $\exists \omega_n \phi, \chi^1, \ldots \chi^k \vdash \psi$ if $\phi \, (\alpha/\omega), \chi^1, \ldots \chi^k \vdash \psi$, provided

         (1) that $\exists \omega_n \phi$ is the scope of $\exists \omega_n$

         (2) that α does not occur in any of $\phi, \chi^1, \ldots \chi^k, \psi$.

[NB. All substitutions referred to in (10)–(13) will preserve subscripts.]

Rules (1)–(13) are not peculiar to Q, except insofar as they provide for the use of numerical subscripts as substitutes for parentheses. The role of term-subscripts has so far been ignored. The following three rules do not ignore the role of term-subscripts, and are special to Q.

(14) [Dom+] If (1) α dominates ϕ,

         (2) $\phi, \chi^1, \ldots \chi^l \vdash \psi \, (\alpha_j, \ldots \alpha_k)$,

then   (3) $\phi, \chi^1, \ldots \chi^l \vdash \psi \, ((\alpha_{j+m}/\alpha_j), \ldots (\alpha_{k+n}/\alpha_k)) \, [m, \ldots n \geqslant 0]$.

[NB. ψ, thus altered, must remain a formula; for example, α must not acquire a subscript already attaching to a symbol other than α.]

(14) provides for the raising of subscripts on α in ψ, including the case in which initially non-dominant α comes to dominate ψ.

(15) [Dom−] $\phi \, (\alpha_j, \ldots \alpha_k) \vdash \phi \, ((\alpha_{j-n}/\alpha_j), \ldots, (\alpha_{k-m}/\alpha_k)) \, [n, \ldots m, \geqslant 0]$.
[A subscript on an occurrence of α may always be lowered.]

(16) [Iso] If ϕ and ψ are isomorphs, $\phi \vdash \psi$.

V. EXISTENCE

A. *Closed Formulae Containing an Individual Constant* α

(i) If α dominates ϕ then, for any interpretation Z, ϕ will be true on Z only if α is non-vacuous (only if $\ulcorner \alpha + \text{exists} \urcorner$ is true, where '+' is a concatenation-symbol). If α does not dominate ϕ, it may still be the case that ϕ is true only if α is non-vacuous (for example if $\phi = ``\sim_4\sim_3 F_1 a_2$'' or $\phi = ``F_1 a_2 \vee_3 G_1 a_2$'', though not if $\phi = ``F_1 a_2 \to_3 G_1 a_2$''). Whether or not it is the case will be formally decidable. Let us abbreviate "ϕ is true only if α is non-vacuous" as "ϕ is E-committal for α". The conditions in which ϕ is E-committal for α can be specified recursively:

(1)   If α dominates ϕ, ϕ is E-committal for α.

(2)   If $\phi = \sim_n\sim_{n-m}\psi$, and ψ is E-committal for α, then ϕ is E-committal for α.

(3)   If $\phi = \psi \&_n \chi$, and either ψ or χ is E-committal for α, then ϕ is E-committal for α.

(4)   If $\phi = \psi \vee_n \chi$, and both ψ and χ are E-committal for α, then ϕ is E-committal for α.

(5)   If $\phi = \psi \to_n \chi$, and both $\sim_m\psi$ and χ are E-committal for α, then ϕ is E-committal for α [in being greater than the number denoted by any non-term-subscript in ψ].

(6)   If $\phi = \forall\omega_n\psi$ or $\exists\omega_n\psi$, and $\psi(\beta/\omega)$ is E-committal for α, then ϕ is E-committal for α.

(ii) Since $F_1 a_2 \to_3 F_1 a_2$ is true whether or not "a" is vacuous, the truth of $F_1 a_3 \to_2 F_1 a_3$ (in which "a" has become dominant) requires only that a exists, and so the latter formula may be taken as one representation of "a exists". More generally, if (for some n) α is the only individual constant in $\phi_{[n]}(\alpha_n)$ and $\phi = \psi \to \psi_{n-m}$, then ϕ may be taken as a representation of $\ulcorner\alpha + \text{exists}\urcorner$.

B. $\exists$-quantified Formulae

An $\exists$-quantified formula $\exists\omega_n\phi$ will represent a claim that there *exists* an object which satisfied the condition specified in ϕ iff $\phi(\alpha/\omega)$ is E-committal for α. To illustrate this point, compare

(i) $\exists x_4 \sim_2 F_1 x_3$, and

(ii) $\exists x_4 \sim_3 F_1 x_2$.

Since $\sim_2 F_1 a_3$ is E-committal for "a" (is true only if a exists) while

$\sim_3 F_1 a_2$ is not E-committal for "a", (i) can, and (ii) cannot, be read as a claim that there *exists* something which is not F. The idea which lies behind the treatment of quantification in Q is that while (i) and (ii) may be taken as representing different senses or different interpretations of "something is not F" or of "there is something which is not F", these locutions must be distinguished from "there exists something which is not F", which is represented only by (i). The degree of appeal which Q will have, as a model for natural discourse, will depend on one's willingness to distinguish, for example,

(a) "There is something such that it is not the case that it flies"

from

(b) "There is something such that it is something which does not fly",

and to hold that (a) is justified by its being false that Pegasus flies, while (b) can be justified only by its being true of some actual object that it does not fly. This distinction will be further discussed in the next section.

Immediately, however, it must be made clear that to accept Q as a model for natural discourse is not to accept a Meinongian viewpoint; it is not to subscribe to the idea of a duality, or plurality, of 'modes of being'. Acceptance of Q as a model might be expected to lead one to hold that while some sentences of the form "Bertrand Russell _____" will be interpretable in such a way as (i) to be true, and (ii) to entail not merely "there is something which _____" but also "there exists something which _____", sentences of the form "Pegasus _____" will, if interpreted so as to be true, entail only "there is something which _____". But from this it would be quite illegitimate to conclude that while Bertrand Russell *both* exists *and* is (or has being), Pegasus merely is (or has being). "Exists" has a licensed occurrence both in the form of expression "there exists something which _____" and in the form of expression "a exists"; "is" has a licensed occurrence in the form of expression "there is something which _____", but not in the form "a is". Q creates no ontological jungle.

VI. OBJECTION CONSIDERED

It would not be surprising if the combination of the admissibility, according to the natural interpretation of Q, of appropriate readings of the inference-patterns

(1) $\dfrac{a \text{ does not exist}}{a \text{ is not } F}$

and (2) $\dfrac{a \text{ is (not) } F}{\text{something is (not) } F}$

have to be regarded as Q's most counter-intuitive feature.

Consider the following dialogue between A and B at a cocktail party:

A(1) Is Marmaduke Bloggs here tonight?

B(1) Marmaduke Bloggs?

A(2) You know, the Merseyside stock-broker who last month climbed Mt. Everest on hands and knees.

B(2) Oh! Well no, he isn't here.

A(3) How do you know he isn't here?

B(3) That Marmaduke Bloggs doesn't exist; he was invented by the journalists.

A(4) So someone isn't at this party.

B(4) Didn't you hear me say that Marmaduke Bloggs does not exist?

A(5) I heard you quite distinctly; are *you* under the impression that you heard *me* say that *there exists* a person who isn't at this party?

B, in his remarks (3) and (4), seemingly accepts not only inference-pattern (1) but also inference-pattern (2).

The ludicrous aspects of this dialogue need to be accounted for. The obvious explanation is, of course, that the step on which B relies is at best dubious, while the step which A adds to it is patently illegitimate; if we accept pattern (1) we should not also accept pattern (2). But there is another possible explanation, namely that

(i) given (P) "*a* does not exist and so *a* is not *F*" the putative conclusion from (P), "Something is not *F*" (C), is *strictly speaking* (on one reading) *true*, but

(ii) given that (P) is true there will be something wrong, odd, or misleading about *saying* or *asserting* (C).

In relation to this alternative explanation, there are two cases to consider:

(a) that in which the utterer of (C) knows or thinks that *a* does not exist, and advances (C) on the strength of this knowledge or belief; but the non-existence of *a* is not public knowledge, at least so far as the speaker's audience is concerned;

(b) that which differs from (a) in that all parties to the talk-exchange are aware, or think, that *a* does not exist. Case (a) will not, perhaps, present too great difficulties; if there is a sense of "Something is not *F*" such that for this to be true some real thing must fail to be *F*, the knowledge that in *this* sense something is not *F* will be much more useful than the knowledge that something is not *F* in the other (weaker) sense; and *ceteris paribus* one would suppose the more useful sense of (C) to be the more popular, and so, in the absence of counter-indications, to be the one employed by someone who utters (C). Which being the case, to utter (C) on the strength of the non-existence of *a* will be misleading.

Case (b) is less easy for the alternative explanation to handle, and my dialogue was designed to be an example of case (b). There is a general consideration to be borne in mind, namely that it will be very unplausible to hold *both* that there exists a particular interpretation or sense of an expression *E, and* that to use *E* in this sense or interpretation is *always* to do something which is conversationally objectionable. So the alternative explanation will have (1) to say why such a case (b) example as that provided by the dialogue is conversationally objectionable, (2) to offer some examples, which should presumably be case (b) examples, in which the utterance of (C), bearing the putative weaker interpretation would be conversationally innocuous. These tasks might be attempted as follows.

(1) To say "Something is (not) such-and-such" might be expected to have one or other of two conversational purposes; *either* to show that it is possible (not) to be such-and-such, countering (perhaps in anticipation) the thesis that nothing is even (not) such-and-such, *or* to provide a prelude to the specification (perhaps after a query) of an item which is (not) such-and-such. A's remark (4) "So someone is not at this party" cannot have either of these purposes. First, M.B. has already been agreed by A and B not to exist, and so cannot provide a counter-example to any envisaged thesis that every member of a certain set (e.g. leading local business men) is at the party. M.B., being non-existent, is not a member of any set. Second, it is clear that A's remark (4) was advanced on the strength of the belief that M.B. does not exist; so whatever specification is relevant has already been given.

(2) The following example might provide a conversationally innocuous use of (C) bearing the weaker interpretation. The cocktail party is a special one given by the Merseyside Geographical Society for its members in honour of M.B., who was at the last meeting elected a member as a recognition of his reputed exploit. A and B have been, before the party, discussing those who are expected to attend it; C has been listening, and is in the know about M.B.

C   Well, someone won't be at this party

A, B Who?

C   Marmaduke Bloggs

A, B But it's in his honour

C   That's as may be, but he doesn't exist; he was invented by the journalists.

Here C makes his initial remark (bearing putative weak interpretation), intending to cite M.B. in specification and to disclose his non-existence.

It should be made clear that I am not trying to prove the existence or admissibility of a weaker interpretation for (C); I am merely trying to show that the *prima facie* case for it is strong enough to make investigation worth-while; if the matter is worth investigation, then the formulation of Q is one direction in which such investigation should proceed, in order to see whether a systematic formal representation of such a reading of "Something is (not) F" can be constructed.

As a further consideration in favour of the acceptability of the weaker interpretation of "Something is (not) F", let me present the following "slide":

(1)   To say "M.B. is at this party" would be to say something which is not true.

(2)   To say "It is not true that M.B. is at this party" would be to say something which is true.

(3)   To say "M.B. is not at this party" would be to say something which is true.

(4)   M.B. is not at this party.

(5)   M.B. can be truly said not to be at this party.

(6)   Someone (viz. M.B.) can be truly said not to be at this party.

(7)   Someone is not at this party (viz. M.B.).

It seems to me plausible to suppose that remark (1) could have been uttered with truth and propriety, though with some inelegance, by B in the circumstances of the first dialogue. It also seems to me that there is sufficient difficulty in drawing a line before any one of remarks (2) to (7), and claiming that to make that remark would be to make an illegitimate transition from its legitimate predecessor, for it to be worth considering whether one should not, given the non-existence of M.B., accept all seven as being (strictly speaking) true. Slides are dangerous instruments of proof, but it may be legitimate to use them to back up a theoretical proposal.

VII. IDENTITY

So far as I can see, there will be no difficulty in formulating a system Q', as an extension of Q which includes an identity theory. In a classical second-order predicate calculus one would expect to find that the formula $(\forall F)(Fa \rightarrow Fb)$ (or the formula $(\forall F)(Fa \leftrightarrow Fb)$) is a definitional substituend for, or at least is equivalent to, the formula $a = b$. Now in Q the sequence $Fa \rightarrow Fb$ will be incomplete, since subscripts are lacking, and there will be two significantly different ways of introducing subscripts, (i) $F_1 a_3 \rightarrow_2 F_1 b_4$ and (ii) $F_1 a_2 \rightarrow_4 F_1 b_3$. In (i) "$a$" and "$b$" are dominant, and the existence of a and of b is implied; in (ii) this is not the case. This difference of subscripting will reappear within a second-order predicate calculus which is an extension of Q; we shall find both (i)(a) $\forall F_5 F_1 a_3 \rightarrow_2 F_1 b_4$ and (ii)(a) $\forall F_5 F_1 a_2 \rightarrow_4 F_1 b_3$. If we introduce the symbol '$\leftrightarrow$' into Q, we shall also find (iii) $\forall F_5 F_1 a_3 \leftrightarrow_2 F_1 b_4$ and (iv) $\forall F_5 F_1 a_2 \leftrightarrow_4 F_1 b_3$. We may now ask whether we want to link the identity of a and b with the truth of (iii) or with the truth of (iv), or with both. If identity is linked with (iii) then any affirmative identity-formula involving a vacuous individual constant will be false; if identity is linked with (iv) any affirmative identity formula involving two vacuous individual constants will be true.

A natural course in this situation seems to be to admit to Q' two types of identity formula, one linked with (iii) and one with (iv), particularly if one is willing to allow two interpretations of (for example) the sentence "Pegasus is identical with Pegasus", on one of which the sentence is *false* because Pegasus does not exist, and on the other of which the sentence is *true* because Pegasus does not exist (just as "Pegasus is identical with

133

Bellerophon" will be true because neither Pegasus nor Bellerophon exist). We cannot mark this distinction in Q simply by introducing two different identity-signs, and distinguishing between (say) $a_2 =_1 b_3$ and $a_2 \equiv_1 b_3$. Since in *both* these formulae "a" and "b" are dominant, the formulae will be true only if a and b exist. Just as the difference between (iii) and (iv) lies in whether "a" and "b" are dominant or non-dominant, so must the difference between the two classes of identity formulae which we are endeavouring to express in Q'. So Q' must contain both such formulae as $a_2 =_1 b_3$ ('strong' identity formulae) and such formulae as $a_1 =_3 b_2$ ('weak' identity formulae). To allow individual constants to be non-dominant in a formula which is not molecular will be a temporary departure from the practice so far adopted in Q; but in view of the possibility of eventually defining "$=$" in a second-order calculus which is an extension of Q one may perhaps regard this departure as justified.

Q' then might add to Q

(a) one new symbol, "$=$";

(b) two new formation rules;

(1) $\omega^1 =_n \omega^2$ is a formula,

(2)   If $\alpha_{j+k} =_j \beta_{j+l}$ is a formula, $\alpha_{j+k} =_m \beta_{j+l}$ is a formula, where $m > j + k$ and $m > j + l$.

(c) two new inference-rules

(1) $\Lambda \vdash \forall \omega_{n+m} \omega_{n-l} =_n \omega_{n-l}$ [a weak identity law],

(2) $\alpha_j =_m \beta_k$, $\phi \vdash \phi(\beta/\alpha)$. [There is substitutivity both on strong and on weak identity.]

I hope that these additions would be adequate, though I have not taken steps to assure myself that they are. I might add that to develop a representation of an *interesting* weak notion of identity, one such that Pegasus will be identical with Pegasus but not with Bellerophon, I think that one would need a system within which such psychological notions as "it is believed that" were represented.

VIII. SEMANTICS FOR Q

The task of providing a semantics for Q might, I think, be discharged in more than one way; the procedure which I shall suggest will, I hope, continue the following features: (a) it will be reasonably intuitive, (b) it will not contravene the philosophical ideas underlying the construction of Q by, for example, invoking imaginary or non-real entities, (c) it will offer reasonable prospects for the provision of proofs of the soundness and completeness of Q (though I must defer the discussion of these prospects to another occasion).

A. *Interpretation*

The provision of an interpretation Z for Q will involve the following steps:

(1) The specification of a non-empty domain D, within which two sub-domains are to be distinguished: the *special* sub-domain (which may be empty), the elements of which will be each unit set in D whose element is also in D; and the *residual* sub-domain, consisting of all elements of D which do not belong to the special sub-domain.

(2) The assignment of each propositional letter either to 1 or to 0.

(3) The assignment of each n-ary predicate constant η to a set (the E-set of η) of ordered n-tuples, each of which has, as its elements, elements of D. An E-set may be empty.

(4) The assignment of each individual constant α to a single element of D (the correlatum of α). If the correlatum of α belongs to the special sub-domain, it will be a unit-set whose element is also in D, and that element will be the *designatum* of α. If the correlatum of α is not in the special sub-domain, then α will have no designatum. [I have in mind a special case of the fulfilment of step (4), in which every individual constant has as its correlatum *either* an element of the special sub-domain *or* the null-set. Such a method of assignment seems particularly intuitive.]

If an individual constant α is, in Z, assigned to a correlatum belonging to the special sub-domain, I shall say that the assignment of α is *efficient*. If, in Z, all individual constants are efficiently assigned, I shall say that Z is an *efficient interpretation* of Q.

It will be noted that, as I envisage them, interpretations of Q will be of a non-standard type, in that a distinction is made between the correlation of an individual constant and its description. All individual constants are given correlata, but only those which on a given interpretation are non-vacuous have, on that interpretation, designata. Interpretations of this kind may be called Q-type interpretations.

B. *Truth and Validity*

I shall use the expressions "Corr(1)" and "Corr(0)" as abbreviations, respectively, for "correlated with 1" and "correlated with 0". By "atomic formula" I shall mean a formula consisting of a subscripted n-ary predicate constant followed by a subscripted individual constant.

I shall, initially, in defining "Corr(1) on Z" ignore quantificational formulae.

(1) If ϕ is atomic, ϕ is Corr(1) on Z iff (i) each individual constant in ϕ has in Z a designatum (i.e. its correlatum is a unit set in D whose element is also in D), and (ii) the designata of the individual constants in ϕ, taken in the order in which the individual constants which designate them occur in ϕ, form an ordered n-tuple which is in the E-set assigned in Z to the predicate constant in ϕ.

(2) If no individual constant dominates ϕ, ϕ is Corr(1) on Z iff

(i)   If $\phi = \sim_n \psi$, ψ is Corr(0) on Z;

(ii)   If $\phi = \psi \mathbin{\&}_n \chi$, ψ and χ are each Corr(1) on Z;

(iii)   If $\phi = \psi \vee_n \chi$, either ψ or χ is Corr(1) on Z;

(iv)   If $\phi = \psi \rightarrow_n \chi$, either ψ is Corr(0) on Z or χ is Corr(1) on Z.

(3) If $\psi(\alpha)$ is a closed formula in which α is non-dominant, and if ϕ is like ψ except that α dominates ϕ, then ϕ is Corr(1) on Z iff (i) ψ is Corr(1) on Z and (ii) α is efficiently assigned in Z.

(4) If a closed formula is not Corr(1) on Z, then it is Corr(0) on Z.

To provide for quantificational formulae, some further notions are required.

(a) An interpretation Z′ is an *i.c.-variant* of Z iff Z′ differs from Z (if at all) only in that, for at least one individual constant α, the correlatum of α in Z′ is different from the correlatum of α in Z.

(b) Z′ is an *efficiency-preserving* i.c.-variant of Z iff Z′ is an i.c.-variant of Z and, for any α, if α is efficiently assigned in Z α is also efficiently assigned in Z′.

(c) Z′ is an *efficiency-quota-preserving* i.c.-variant of Z iff Z′ is an i.c.-variant of Z and the number of individual constants efficiently assigned in Z′ is not less than the number efficiently assigned in Z.[2]

Let us approach the treatment of quantificational formulae by considering the ∃-quantifier. Suppose that, closely following Mates's procedure in *Elementary Logic*, we stipulate that $\exists \omega_n \phi$ is Corr(1) on Z iff $\phi(\alpha'/\omega)$

is Corr(1) on at least one i.c.-variant of Z, where α' is the first individual constant in Q. (We assume that the individual constants of Q can be ordered, and that some principle of ordering has been selected). In other words, $\exists \omega_n \phi$ will be Corr(1) on Z iff, without altering the assignment in Z of any predicate constant, there is some way of assigning α' so that $\phi(\alpha'/\omega)$ is Corr(1) on that assignment. Let us also suppose that we shall define validity in Q by stipulating that ϕ is valid in Q iff, for any interpretation Z, ϕ is Corr(1) on Z.

We are now faced with a problem. Consider the "weak existential" formula $\exists x_4 \sim_3 F_1 x_2$. If we proceed as we have just suggested, we shall be forced to admit this formula as valid; if "a" is the first individual constant in Q, we have only to provide a non-efficient assignment for "a" to ensure that on that assignment $\sim_3 F_1 a_2$ is Corr(1); for any interpretation Z, some i.c.-variant of Z will provide such an assignment for "a", and so $\exists x_4 \sim_3 F_1 x_2$ will be Corr(1) on Z. But do we want to have to admit this formula as valid? First, if it is valid then I am reasonably sure that Q, as it stands, is incomplete, for I see no way in which this formula can be proved. Second, if in so far as we are inclined to regard the natural language counterparts of valid formulae as expressing conceptual truths, we shall have to say that e.g. "Someone won't be at this party", if given the 'weak' interpretation which it was supposed to bear in the conversations imagined in Section VI, will express a conceptual truth; while my argument in that section does not demand that the sentence in question express an exciting truth, I am not sure that I welcome quite the degree of triviality which is now threatened.

It is possible, however, to avoid the admission of $\exists x_4 \sim_3 F_1 x_2$ as a valid formula by adopting a slightly different semantical rule for the $\exists$-quantifier. We stipulate that $\exists \omega_n \phi$ is Corr(1) on Z iff $\phi(\alpha'/\omega)$ is Corr(1) on at least one *efficiency-preserving* i.c.-variant of Z. Some interpretations of Q will be efficient interpretations, in which "a" will be efficiently. assigned; and in any efficiency-preserving i.c.-variant of such an interpretation "a" will remain efficiently assigned; moreover among these efficient interpretations there will be some in which the E-set assigned to "F" contains (to speak with a slight looseness) the member of each unit-set belonging to the special sub-domain. For any efficient interpretation in which "F" is thus assigned, $F_1 a_2$ will be Corr(1), and $\sim_3 F_1 a_2$ will be Corr(0), on all efficiency-preserving i.c.-variants.

So $\exists x_4 \sim_3 F_1 x_2$ will not be Corr(1) on all interpretations, i.e. will not be valid.

A similar result may be achieved by using the notion of an efficiency-quota-preserving i.c.-variant instead of that of an efficiency-preserving i.c.-variant; and the use of the former notion must be preferred for the following reason. Suppose

(i)   that we use the latter notion;

(ii)   that "a^2" is non-efficiently assigned in Z;

(iii)   that "a" is the first individual constant, and is efficiently assigned in Z;

(iv)   that "F" includes in its extension the member of each unit-set in the special sub-domain.

Then $\sim_3 F_1 a_2^2$ is Corr(1) on Z, and so (by E.G.) $\exists x_4 \sim_3 F_1 x_2$ is Corr(1) on Z. But "a" is efficiently assigned in Z, so $\sim_3 F_1 a_2$ is Corr(0) on every efficiency-preserving i.c.-variant of Z (since "F" includes in its extension every designable object). So $\exists x_4 \sim_3 F_1 x_2$ is Corr(0) on Z.

This contradiction is avoided if we use the notion of efficiency-quota-preserving i.c.-variant, since such a variant of Z may provide a non-efficient assignment for an individual constant which is efficiently assigned in Z itself; and so $\exists x_4 \sim_3 F_1 x_2$ may be Corr(1) on Z even though "a" is efficiently assigned in Z.

So I add to the definition of "Corr(1) on Z", the following clauses:

(5) If $\phi = \forall \omega_n \psi$, ϕ is Corr(1) on Z, iff $\psi(\alpha'/\omega)$ is Corr(1) on every efficiency-quota-preserving i.c.-variant of Z.

(6) If $\phi = \exists \omega_n \psi$, ϕ is Corr(1) on Z iff $\psi(\alpha'/\omega)$ is Corr(1) on at least one efficiency-quota-preserving i.c.-variant of Z.

[In each clause, "α'" is to be taken as denoting the first individual constant in Q.]

Validity may be defined as follows:

ϕ is valid in Q iff, for any interpretation Z, ϕ is Corr(1) on Z.

Finally, we may, if we like, say that ϕ is true on Z iff ϕ is Corr(1) on Z.

IX. NAMES AND DESCRIPTIONS

It might be objected that, in setting up Q in such a way as to allow for the representation of vacuous names, I have ensured the abandonment, at least in spirit, of one of the desiderata which I have had in mind; for (it might be suggested) if Q is extended so as to include a Theory of Descriptions, its individual constants will be seen to be indistinguishable, both syntactically and semantically, from unanalysed definite descriptions; they will be related to representations of descriptions in very much the same way as propositional letters are related to formulae, having lost the feature which is needed to distinguish them from representations of descriptions, namely that of being interpretable only by the assignment of a designatum.

I do not propose to prolong this paper by including the actual presentation of an extension of Q which includes the representation of descriptions, but I hope to be able to say enough about how I envisage such an extension to make it clear that there will be a formal difference between the individual constants of Q and definite descriptions. It is a familiar fact that there are at least two ways in which a notation for representing definite descriptions may be developed within a classical system; one may represent "The haberdasher of Mr. Spurgeon is bald" either by (1) $G(\imath x.Fx)$ or by (2) $(\imath x.Fx) Gx$; one may, that is, treat "$\imath x.Fx$" either as a term or as being analogous to a (restricted) quantifier. The first method does not allow for the representation of scope-differences, so a general decision will have to be taken with regard to the scope of definite descriptions, for example that they are to have maximal scope. The second method does provide for scope-distinctions; there will be a distinction between, for example, $(\imath x.Fx)\sim Gx$ and $\sim(\imath x.Fx) Gx$. The apparatus of Q, however, will allow us, if we wish, to combine the first method, that of representing definite descriptions by terms, with the representation of differences of scope; we can, if we like, distinguish between e.g., $\sim_2 G_1\imath x_3 F_1 x_2$ and $\sim_4 G_1\imath x_3 F_1 x_2$, and ensure that from the first formula we may, and from the second we may not, derive $E!_1 \imath x_3 F_1 x_2$. We might, alternatively, treat descriptions as syntactically analogous to restricted quantifiers, if we so desire. Let us assume (arbitrarily) that the first method is adopted, the scope-boundaries of a descriptive term being, in each direction, the first operator with a higher subscript than that borne by the iota-operator or the first sentential boundary, whichever is nearer. Let us further assume (perhaps no less arbitrarily) that the iota-operator is introduced as a defined expression, so that such a formula as $G_1\imath x_3 F_1 x_2 \leftrightarrow_8 \exists x_7 F_1 x_6 \&_2 G_1 x_6 \&_5 \forall y_4 F_1 y_2 \leftrightarrow_3 y_2 =_1 x_2$ is provable by definitional substitution for the right-hand side of the formula

$G_1 \imath x_3 F_1 x_2 \leftrightarrow_4 G_1 \imath x_3 F_1 x_2$, together with applications of the rules for subscript-adjustment.

Now, as I envisage the appropriate extension of Q, the formal difference between individual constants and descriptive terms will lie in there being a legitimate step (by E. G.) from a formula containing a non-dominant individual constant to the related 'weak' existential form, e.g., from $\sim_3 F_1 a_2$ to $\exists x_4 \sim_3 F_1 x_2$, while there will, for example, be no analogous step from $\sim_4 G_1 \imath x_3 F_1 x_2$ to $\exists x_4 \sim_3 G_1 x_2$. Such a distinction between individual constants and descriptive terms seems to me to have, at least *prima facie*, a basis in intuition; I have at least some inclination to say that, if Mr. Spurgeon has no haberdasher, then it would be true (though no doubt conversationally odd) to say "It is not the case that Mr. Spurgeon's haberdasher is bald" (*S*), even though no one has even suggested or imagined that Mr. Spurgeon has a haberdasher; even though, that is, there is no answer to the question who Mr. Spurgeon's haberdasher is or has been supposed to be, or to the question whom the speaker means by the phrase "Mr. Spurgeon's haberdasher." If that inclination is admissible, then it will naturally be accompanied by a reluctance to allow a step from *S* to "Someone is not bald" (*S₁*) even when S_1 is given its 'weak' interpretation. I have, however, already suggested that an utterance of the sentence "It is not the case that Mr. Spurgeon is bald" (*S'*) is not assessable for truth or falsity unless something can be said about who Mr. Spurgeon is or is supposed to be; in which case the step from *S'* to S_1 (weakly interpreted) seems less unjustifiable.

I can, nevertheless, conceive of this argument's failing to produce conviction. The following reply might be made: "If one is given the truth of *S*, on the basis of there being no one who is haberdasher to Mr. Spurgeon, all one has to do is first to introduce a name, say 'Bill', laying down that 'Bill' is to designate whoever is haberdasher to Mr. Spurgeon, then to state (truly) that it is not the case that Bill is bald (since there is no such person), and finally to draw the conclusion (now legitimate) that someone is not bald (on the 'weak' reading of that sentence). If only a stroke of the pen, so to speak, is required to legitimize the step from *S* to S_1 (weakly interpreted), why not legitimize the step directly, in which case the formal distinction in *Q″* between individual constants and descriptive terms must either disappear or else become wholly arbitrary?"

A full treatment of this reply would, I suspect, be possible only within the framework of a discussion of reference too elaborate for the present occasion; I can hope only to give an indication of *one* of the directions in which I should have some inclination to proceed. It has been observed[3] that a distinction may be drawn between at least two ways in which descriptive phrases may be employed.

(1) A group of men is discussing the situation arising from the death of a business acquaintance, of whose private life they know nothing, except that (as they think) he lived extravagantly, with a household staff which included a butler. One of them says "Well, Jones' butler will be seeking a new position".

(2) Earlier, another group has just attended a party at Jones' house, at which their hats and coats were looked after by a dignified individual in dark clothes and a wing-collar, a portly man with protruding ears, whom they heard Jones addressing as "Old Boy", and who at one point was discussing with an old lady the cultivation of vegetable marrows. One of the group says "Jones' butler got the hats and coats mixed up".

(i) The speaker in example (1) could, without impropriety, have inserted after the descriptive phrase "Jones' butler" the clause "whoever he may be". It would require special circumstances to make a corresponding insertion appropriate in the case of example (2). On the other hand we may say, with respect to example (2), that some particular individual has been 'described as', 'referred to as', or 'called' Jones' butler by the speaker; furthermore, any one who was in a position to point out that Jones has no butler, and that the man with the protruding ears was Jones' gardener, or someone hired for the occasion, would also be in a position to claim that the speaker had *mis*described that individual as Jones' butler. No such comments are in place with respect to example (1).

(ii) A schematic generalized account of the difference of type between examples (1) and (2) might proceed along the following lines. Let us say that X has a dossier for a definite description δ if there is a set of definite descriptions which includes δ, all the members of which X supposes (in one or other of the possible sense of 'suppose') to be satisfied by one and the same item. In a type (2) case, unlike a type (1) case, the speaker intends the hearer to think (*via* the recognition that he is so intended) (a) that the speaker has a dossier for the definite description δ which he has used, and (b) that the speaker has selected δ from this dossier at least partly in the hope that the hearer has a dossier for δ which 'overlaps' the speaker's dossier for δ (that is, shares a substantial, or in some way specially favoured, subset with the speaker's dossier). In so far as the speaker expects the hearer to recognize this intention, he must expect the hearer to think that in certain circumstances the speaker will be prepared to replace the remark which he has made (which contains δ) by a further remark in which some element in the speaker's dossier for δ is substituted for δ. The standard circumstances in which it is to be supposed that the speaker would make such a replacement will be (a) if the speaker comes to think that the hearer either has no dossier for δ, or has one which does not overlap the speaker's dossier for δ (i.e., if the hearer appears not to have identified the item which the speaker means or is talking about), (b) if the speaker comes to think that δ is a misfit in the speaker's dossier for δ, i.e., that δ is not, after all, satisfied by the same item as that which satisfies the majority of, or each member of a specially favoured subset of, the descriptions in the dossier. In example (2) the speaker might come to think that Jones has no butler, or that though he has, it is not the butler who is the portly man with the protruding ears, etc., and whom the speaker thinks to have mixed up the hats and coats.

(iii) If in a type (2) case the speaker has used a descriptive phrase (e.g., "Jones' butler") which in fact has no application, then what the speaker has *said* will, strictly speaking, be false; the truth-conditions for a type (2) statement, no less than for a type (1) statement, can be thought of as being given by a Russellian account of definite descriptions (with suitable provision for unexpressed restrictions, to cover cases in which, for example, someone uses the phrase "the table" meaning thereby "the table in this room"). But though what, in such a case, a speaker has *said* may be false, what he *meant* may be true (for example, that a certain particular individual [who is in fact Jones' gardener] mixed up the hats and coats).

Let us introduce two auxiliary devices, italics and small capital letters, to indicate to which of the two specified modes of employment a reported use of a descriptive phrase is to be assigned. If I write "*S* said '*The F is G*'," I shall indicate that *S* was using "the *F*" in a type (1), non-identificatory way, whereas if I write "*S* said 'THE F is *G*'," I shall indicate that *S* was using "the *F*" in a type (2), identificatory way. It is important to bear in mind that I am *not* suggesting that the difference between these devices represents a difference in the *meaning* or *sense* which a descriptive phrase may have on different occasions; on the contrary, I am suggesting that descriptive phrases have no relevant systematic duplicity of meaning; their meaning is given by a Russellian account.

We may now turn to names. In my type (1) example, it might be that in view of the prospect of repeated conversational occurrences of the expression "Jones' butler," one of the group would find it convenient to say "Let us call Jones' butler 'Bill'." Using the proposed supplementation, I can represent him as having remarked "Let us call *Jones' butler* 'Bill'." Any subsequent remark containing "Bill" will have the same truth-value as would have a corresponding remark in which "Jones' butler" replaces "Bill". If Jones has no butler, and if in consequence it is false that Jones' butler will be seeking a new position, then it will be false that Bill will be seeking a new position.

In the type (2) example, also, one of the group might have found it convenient to say "Let us call Jones' butler 'Bill'," and his intentions might have been such as to make it a correct representation of his remark for me to write that he said "Let us call JONES' BUTLER 'Bill'." If his remark is correctly thus represented, then it will *not* be true that, in all conceivable circumstances, a subsequent remark containing "Bill" will have the same truth-value as would have a corresponding remark in which "Bill" is replaced by "Jones's butler". For the person whom the speaker proposes to call "Bill" will be the person whom he *meant* when he said "Let us call JONES'S BUTLER 'Bill'," viz., the person who looked after the hats and coats, who was addressed by Jones as "Old Boy", and so on; and if this person turns out to have been Jones's gardener and not Jones's butler, then it may be *true* that Bill mixed up the hats and coats and *false* that Jones's butler mixed up the hats and coats. Remarks of the form "Bill is such-and-such" will be inflexibly tied, as regards truth-value, not to possible remarks of the form "Jones's butler is such-and-such", but to possible remarks of the form "The person whom X meant when he said 'Let us call Jones's butler "Bill"' is such-and-such".

It is important to note that, for a definite description used in the explanation of a name to be employed in an identificatory way, it is not required that the item which the explainer means (is referring to) when he uses the description should actually exist. A person may establish or explain a use for a name α by saying "Let us call THE F α" or "THE F is

called α" even though every definite description in his dossier for "the F"
is vacuous; he may mistakenly think, or merely deceitfully intend his
hearer to think, that the elements in the dossier are non-vacuous and
are satisfied by a single item; and in secondary or 'parasitic' types of
case, as in the narration of or commentary upon fiction, that this is so
may be something which the speaker non-deceitfully pretends or 'feigns'.
So names introduced or explained in this way may be vacuous.

I may now propound the following argument in answer to the objection
that any distinction in Q between individual constants and descriptive
terms will be arbitrary.

(1) For a given definite description δ, the difference between a type
(1) and type (2) employment is not to be construed as the employment of
δ in one rather than another of two systematically different senses of δ.

(2) A name α may be introduced *either* so as to be inflexibly tied, as
regards the truth-value of utterances containing it, to a given definite
description δ, *or* so as to be not so tied (δ being univocally employed);
so the difference between the two ways of introducing α may reasonably
be regarded as involving a difference of sense or meaning for α; a sense
in which α may be said to be equivalent to a definite description and a
sense in which it may not.

(3) It is, then, not arbitrary so to design Q that its individual constants
are to be regarded as representing, among other linguistic items, names
used with *one* of their possible kinds of meaning, namely that in which
a name is not equivalent to a definite description.

X. CONCLUDING REMARKS

I do not propose to attempt the important task of extending Q so as to
include the representation of psychological verb-phrases, but I should
like to point out a notational advantage which any such extension could
be counted on to possess. There are clearly at least two possible readings
of such a sentence as "John wants someone to marry him", one in which
it might be paraphrased by "John wants someone or other to marry him"
and another in which it might be paraphrased by "John wants a particular
person to marry him" or by "There is someone whom John wants to
marry him". Symbolizing "a wants that p" by $W^a p$, and using the apparatus of classical predicate logic, we might hope to represent reading (1)

by $W^a(\exists x)(Fxa)$ and reading (2) by $(\exists x)(W^aFxa)$. But suppose that John wants Martha to marry him, having been deceived into thinking that his friend William has a highly delectable sister called Martha, though in fact William is an only child. In these circumstances one is inclined to say that "John wants someone to marry him" is true on reading (2), but we cannot now represent reading (2) by $(\exists x)(W^aFxa)$, since Martha does not exist.

The apparatus of Q should provide us with distinct representations for two familiar readings of "John wants Martha to marry him", viz., (a) $W_2^{a_1}F_1b_3a_4$ and (b) $W_3^{a_1}F_1b_2a_4$. Given that Martha does not exist only (b) can be true. We should have available to us also three distinct $\exists$-quantificational forms (together with their isomorphs):

(i) $W_4^{a_5}\exists x_3F_1x_2a_5$;

(ii) $\exists x_5W_2^{a_3}F_1x_4a_3$;

(iii) $\exists x_5W_3^{a_4}F_1x_2a_4$.

Since in (iii) "x" does not dominate the segment following the $\exists$-quantifier, (iii) does not have existential force, and is suitable therefore for representing "John wants a particular person to marry him" if we have to allow for the possibility that the particular person does not actually exist. [(i) and (iii) will be derivable from each of (a) and (b); (ii) will be derivable only from (a).]

I have in this paper developed as strong a case as I can in support of the method of treatment of vacuous names which I have been expounding. Whether in the end I should wish to espouse it would depend on the outcome of further work on the notion of reference.

REFERENCES

[1] I am particularly indebted to Charles Parsons and George Boolos for some extremely helpful correspondence, to George Myro for countless illuminating suggestions and criticisms, and to Benson Mates for assistance provided both by word of mouth and via his book *Elementary Logic*, on which I have drawn a good deal.

[2] I owe the idea of this type of variant to George Myro, whose invaluable help was essential to the writing of this section.

[3] e.g. by K. S. Donnellan, 'Reference and Definite Descriptions', *Philosophical Review* **75** (1966) 281–304; as may perhaps be seen from what follows, I am not sure that I am wholly sympathetic towards the conclusions which he draws from the existence of the distinction.

QUINE'S SYNTACTICAL INSIGHTS

Jokes about 'no man' as a name are now some three millennia old; an understanding of the syntactical difference between such a phrase and a name is both much more recent and much less available. To take 'no man' as naming, or even referring to, *some* man appears patently contradictory; but many beginners in logic take 'no man' as referring to nonmen (each of whom, admittedly, is *no man*), or again to a null class of men; and the second mistake has been known to appear in textbooks too. On either view 'no man' would be something like a name, only not a name of a man. And what about 'some man'? Certainly this is not some man's name (to christen a child 'Some Man' would merely create homonymy); but it causes us no shock (many of us) if we read that at least in some of its uses this phrase *refers* to some man. I shall not pursue this question through the copious recent literature. Propositions about *referring to* are there framed in a material too malleable and ductile to bear any argumentative strain.

If we turn from recent 'philosophical logic' to recent grammar, things are not much better. The sophistications of a computer age overlie ideas that might come straight out of Dionysius of Thrace and Priscian; indeed, Chomsky has expressly said that "by and large the traditional views are basically correct, so far as they go". Proper names and phrases like 'some man' are alike called Noun Phrases – whatever virtue there may be in the capitals – and are regarded as belonging to the same substitution class.

Let us fasten upon this notion. It is quite true that we may substitute a phrase like 'some man' for a proper name in a sentence and still have a syntactically coherent string of words; as a medieval logician would say, the substitution goes through *salva congruitate*. But Quine has emphasized that all the same the substitution makes a syntactical difference. Genuine names give us no headaches about *scope*. For example, the sentence:

(1)   Copernicus was a perfect fool if and only if the Earth is flat

may be read as the result of first attaching the predicable '– was a perfect

146

fool' to 'Copernicus' as subject, and then joining the sentence so formed to the sentence 'The Earth is flat' with the connective 'if and only if'; but it may equally well be read as the result simply of attaching to the subject 'Copernicus' the complex predicable:

(2)   – was a perfect fool if and only if the Earth is flat

In this sort of case we have, not a syntactically ambiguous string of words, but simply a single syntactical structure that can be analysed in two different ways; and without such possibility of multiple analysis, logic would, as Frege said, be hopelessly crippled.

If we substitute 'some astronomer' for 'Copernicus', the case is quite altered: we now have a syntactically ambiguous string of words, which is really (like, say, 'Drinking chocolate is nice') not one sentence but two. The difference may be brought out by bracketing, thus:

(3)   (Some astronomer was a perfect fool) if and only if (the Earth is flat)

(4)   Some astronomer (was a perfect fool if and only if the Earth is flat).

To see what the difference amounts to: the string 'if and only if the Earth is flat' may as a whole be regarded as an operator like negation. Indeed, since the Earth is not flat, this operator is materially equivalent to negation in extensional contexts like the ones we have here. (3) and (4) thus correspond respectively to '(It is) not (so that) some astronomer was a perfect fool' and to 'Some astronomer was not a perfect fool', between which pair there is a clear logical difference.

This, then, is the *first* of Quine's syntactical insights that I want to bring out: the difference between genuine proper names, which give us no scope trouble, and these phrases, which do give it (cf. *Methods of Logic* p. 83 ff.). Quine himself rather blurs the difference elsewhere by regarding proper names as abbreviated definite descriptions; for taught by Russell, we know that definite descriptions give rise to scope trouble that has to be removed by some convention, and the same must be true of any word that is short for a definite description. I do not wish to go into this view of proper names; I shall simply say that I think Quine's first account of proper names, as essentially scopeless, is correct, and I deplore its supersession in later sections of *Methods of Logic*.

It will be handy to have in the sequel a term for expressions like 'some astronomer', 'each man', etc., formed from a substantival general term *plus* an applicative in W. E. Johnson's sense – a word like 'some', 'any', 'each', 'just one', 'almost every', etc. I shall speak of *applicatival* phrases. The 'referring phrases' of my *Reference and Generality* are a certain subclass of applicatival phrases. (As I said in introducing this term, the epithet 'referring' was meant to describe the role of such phrases according to the theories I was examining, rather than according to my own view of the matter.)

Applicatival phrases are not the only sort of expression for whose syntax a consideration of scope is necessary. For example, the string 'young and foolish or wicked' may be read in two ways as a complex adjective formed out of adjectives; the difference is of course a matter of the scopes of the binary operators 'and' and 'or'; this is shown by bracketing – '(young and foolish) or wicked', 'young and (foolish or wicked)'. Such ambiguities supply many tedious examples in medieval collections of *sophismata*; the ambiguity gets explained clearly enough, but one misses a bracketing notation that would make the explanations superfluous. Quine remarks that there actually exist in ordinary language ways of showing unambiguously the scope of conjunction and disjunction: 'either both young and foolish or wicked' vs. 'both young and either foolish or wicked'. To use an old bit of jargon, these are cases of tmesis; each of 'both ... and ...' and 'either ... or ...' is a logically indivisible binary operator, one piece being put before the first argument and the other between the two arguments.

Applicatival phrases are similar in syntax to quantifiers in ordinary quantification theory; indeed, some of them may be directly rendered by quantifiers, if we are willing to complicate our logic with restricted quantification (somewhat in the style of the notation Quine sketches out in *Mathematical Logic*, p. 67). This brings me to Quine's *second* syntactical insight: the pronouns whose antecedents are applicatival phrases correspond *strictly* in their syntax to variables bound by quantifiers.

The light this throws on the syntax of language will be seen more and more clearly by anyone who works out examples. For lack of this light, the medievals who discussed *relativa* – pronouns with antecedents – were groping in the dark despite all their ingenuity. Let us consider how such puzzles as theirs arise.

(5)   Socrates owned a dog, and it bit Socrates

A medieval would treat this as a conjunctive proposition, and enquire after the reference (*suppositio*) of the pronoun 'it'; I have seen modern discussions that made the same mistake. For mistake it is. If we may legitimately symbolize (5) as '$p \wedge q$', then a contradictory of (5), correspondingly symbolizable as '$\neg p \vee (p \wedge \neg q)$', would be:

(6)   Socrates did not own a dog, or else: Socrates owned a dog, and it did not bite Socrates.

But (5) and (6) are not contradictories; a moment's thought shows they could both be true. So '$p \wedge q$' is an inept schema to represent (5).

Contrary to what has been suggested (even in print) for similar cases, it makes not a farthing's difference if in (5) and (6) we substitute 'the dog' or 'that dog' for 'it'. Any one of these three expressions, in *some* contexts of utterance, could serve as subject of the predicable 'bit Socrates', so as to yield a proposition with a truth-value; but here, not one of them could. For no definite dog is before the reader's eyes, or is brought by the sentence before his mind's eye, to supply a reference for this subject-term. And 'the' and 'that' must be parsed, like 'it', not as demonstratives but as *relativa*, looking back to 'a dog'.

The right solution is to take 'a dog' (= 'some dog') as the main operator of (5); (5) is the result of replacing the schematic letter 'F' in 'F (a dog)' by this actual predicable:

(7)   Socrates owned –, and – bit Socrates

where both blanks are to be filled the same way if a logical subject is supplied. Compare what we get using restricted quantification:

(8) (Ex) dog $((\text{Socrates owned } x) \wedge (x \text{ bit Socrates}))$

In (8) the unfortunate appearance of there being a proposition 'Socrates owned a dog' as one conjunct has quite disappeared; if we slice (8) before the '$\wedge$', the result is ill-formed, having an unpaired parenthesis:

(9) (Ex) dog $((\text{Socrates owned } x)$

whereas 'Socrates owned a dog' answers to '(Ex) dog $(\text{Socrates owned } x)$'.

In logical symbolisms of the ordinary sort, quantifiers are not the only

149

variable-binding operators: there are also operators that form designations, and as regards these also we may follow Quine in noticing the parallelism between the binding of variables by operators and the pronoun-antecendent relation. For example, this symbolism for a function:

(10) $\lambda x(2x^2 + 3x^3)$

may fairly be rendered in the vernacular:

(11)   this function of a number: twice its square *plus* thrice its cube

And here the binding of '*x*' in '*x²*' and '*x³*' to the operator '*λx*' is reflected by the relation of 'its' in 'its square' and 'its cube' to 'a number'. If we use a more explicit notation for (10):

(12) $\hat{y}\hat{x}(y = 2x^2 + 3x^3)$

and compare this with the vernacular:

(13)   that function of a number which is equal to twice its square *plus* thrice its cube

then as before, the binding of '*x*' (here, to '*x̂*') is reflected by the relation of 'its' to 'a number', and the binding of '*y*' to '*ŷ*' is reflected by the relation of the pronoun 'which' to 'that function'.

As regards logical symbolism, Quine has followed Russell in emphasizing a third syntactical insight: that all such complex designations are eliminable by definition. This is the sort of definition that Russell called definition in use: the complex designation is not itself replaced by another string of symbols of which it is an abbreviation, but we show how to replace strings of which that designation is part, and this *definiens* does not contain a syntactically coherent part representing the designation. For example, in *Mathematical Logic* notation:

(14) $w\varepsilon\hat{x}(x = y)$

is defined to mean:

(15) $(\exists z)(w\varepsilon z.(x)(x\varepsilon z.\supset.x = y))$

where '*z*' is the earliest term, *not* occurring in the *definiendum*, from the infinite alphabet of variables. Clearly we cannot pick out from (15) a syntactically coherent sub-string corresponding to '*x̂*(*x*=*y*)'. And the

150

elimination of a complex term will be differently carried out according to its context – e.g. according as the term follows the epsilon of class-membership or precedes it. The final result of eliminating such complex terms will be formulas in which the only variable-binding operators are quantifiers, and the only other operators are sentence connectives.

When he comes to consider the vernacular, however, Quine has not scrutinized with due scepticism the traditional view that a phrase of the form '*A* that is *P*', with or without a definite article prefixed, is a syntactically coherent complex term; on the contrary, he seems to accept this view. The only disturbance of ordinary English that he considers here is the 'such that' device: e.g. changing 'man who killed his own brother' into 'man such that he killed his own brother'. The point of this analysis is to divide up the two roles played by an ordinary relative pronoun: it both serves to introduce a relative clause and looks back to an antecedent. In the analysed form, the first role is played by 'such that', the second by 'he'. But failing a clear account of 'such that' itself, we are not much better off than Russell was when in *Principles of Mathematics* he declared this concept to be *sui generis*. Quine himself describes as 'peculiar' the use of pronouns in 'such that' clauses (sc. pronouns with antecedents *outside* these clauses); as in the example:

(16)   I am driving a car such that I bought it from you.

(Cf. *Word and Object* p. 114.) But I cannot see this use of 'it' is any more peculiar, or indeed any other, than the use of 'it' in the example:

(17)   I am driving a car and I bought it from you

In quantifier notation we cannot even represent (16) and (17) differently It suggests itself that the real role of 'such that' is to be a *pro-connective* going proxy for various other connectives[1] (here, for 'and').

In any case, it is very easy to find examples in which the traditional view of '*A* that is *P*' or '*A* such that it is *P*' as a syntactically coherent noun phrase completely breaks down. One such example is the following:

(18)   A boy who was only fooling her kissed a girl who really loved him[2].

On the noun phrase view, (18) would be a substitution instance of '*A B* kissed a *C*', obtained by putting actual (complex) general terms in place of the schematic letters. But is it quite impossible to say which class of boys the replacement of '*B*' would have to cover, and which class of girls the replacement of '*C*' would have to cover, in order to bring out the intended sense of (18).

Again, consider the pair of sentences:

(19)   The one woman whom every true Englishman honours above all other women is his mother

(20)   The one woman whom every true Englishman honours above all other women is his Queen

In (20) it is tempting to construe the string 'woman whom every true Englishman honours above all other women' as a general term '*A*'; but we surely cannot do this in (19), or else (19) would imply that the one and only *A* is the mother of each true Englishman. The noun phrase theory cannot resolve the difficulty.

As it happens, traditional grammar itself contains an alternative account of defining relative clauses. Since this account is regularly taught in English schools to pupils learning Latin prose composition, I shall for short call it the *Latin prose* theory. By this theory, the relative pronoun of a defining clause is treated as a fusion of a connective with a bound pronoun: for example, in the Latin sentence:

(21)   Rex legatos misit qui pacem peterent

the relative pronoun 'qui' represents the words 'in order that/they' of the English translation:

(22)   The king sent ambassadors in order that they might ask for peace

The subjunctive mood of 'peterent' is then accounted for as required by the connective 'ut', 'in order that', that is here buried in the relative 'qui'. Such amalgamations of a pronoun with a connective frequently occur in Latin where there would be two separate words in English; learning when to effect them is one of the tricks you learn in order to get a good mark for your Latin prose.

What I call the Latin prose theory of relative clauses is the theory that in a defining relative clause we should regularly try to split up the relative pronoun into a connective and a bound pronoun – which connective it is

152

will depend on the context. This theory can deal with almost all the puzzling cases I have been discussing, and very simply at that.

Let us start with the sentence:

(23)   A boy kissed a girl, and she really loved him, but he was only fooling her.

Intuitively, this is a paraphrase of (18), and we can indeed show how on the Latin prose theory it is actually transformable into (18). By amalgamating 'and she' into 'who', we get:

(24)   A boy kissed a girl who really loved him, but he was only fooling her.

Although the string of words 'girl who really loved him' gives us a strong impression of syntactical coherence, we have already seen good reason why this impression may be illusory; and the string of words in (23) that get transformed into this string, namely 'girl, and she really loved him', are clearly not a syntactically coherent expression of any category. (The pronoun 'she' is indeed here bound to 'girl', but that is not enough for the syntactical coherence of the whole string.) If we now wish to repeat the procedure, we have a choice: 'but' may be amalgamated with 'he' or with 'her' in the clause following it. If we amalgamate 'but... her' into 'whom', we at once obtain the acceptable English sentence:

(25)   A boy kissed a girl who really loved him, whom he was only fooling.

If on the other hand we amalgamate 'but he' with 'who', making no other alterations, we get:

(26)   A boy kissed a girl who really loved him, who was only fooling her.

This is perhaps not impossible, but slightly deviant – simply because the second 'who' is so far separated from its antecedent 'a boy'. By fitting the final relative clause snugly up against this antecedent, we get (18) over again.

Similarly with the example:

(27)   The one woman whom every true Englishman honours above all other women is his mother (his Queen).

Passing over minor details, we can see that (27) is not paraphrasable by, but actually derivable from, the following:

(28)   Every true Englishman honours one woman above all other women, and that is his mother (his Queen).

Here again, though the transformation is not quite so simple, we see that 'whom' of the derived sentence corresponds to a pronoun plus connective, 'and that', in the underlying sentence; and the pronoun 'that' is a bound pronoun – bound, as 'whom' was, to the antecedent 'one woman'. The striking difference between (19) and (20) now turns out to have nothing to do, after all, with the syntax of the relative clause; it is simply a matter of the scope of applicatival phrases. (28) read with 'his mother' at the end, which corresponds to (19), is 'F (every true Englishman)', where '$F( )$' is proxy for:

(29)   – honours one woman above all other women, and that is –
        's mother.

On the other hand, (28) read with 'his Queen' at the end, which corresponds to (20), is 'G(one woman)', where '$G( )$' is proxy for:

(30)   Every true Englishman honours – above all other women, and
        – is his Queen.

The Latin prose theory of defining relative clauses thus enables us to deal with cases that the noun phrase theory cannot manage at all. We must surely accept the Latin prose theory as covering part of the field and as giving the only tenable explanation for that part.

For some particular cases, the Latin prose theory certainly appears much less natural than its rival; but even here the two theories are in competition. If we consider the sentences:

(31)   Any man who drives a car dislikes the police
(32)   Some man who drives a car dislikes the police

it may well seem most natural to apply the noun phrase theory and treat 'man who drives a car' as a complex general term equivalent to 'motorist'. But even in a case like this we are not compelled to accept the noun phrase theory; the Latin prose theory gives the following as the underlying forms:

154

(33)   Any man, *if he* drives a car, dislikes the police
(34)   Some man drives a car *and* (*he*) dislikes the police

A correspondent has raised the objection that (31) is 'about' motorists only, whereas (33) is 'about' all men; and again, that (31) is 'confirmed' only by police-hating motorists, whereas (33) is 'confirmed' also by men who do not drive cars and of whom, therefore, it holds good (vacuously) that if they drive cars, they detest the police. But to my mind neither the theory of 'about', nor yet the theory of confirmation, is in a satisfactory enough state for these objections to have any bite to them.

The one sort of case I know where the noun phrase theory seems to have the advantage over the Latin prose theory comes in a rather outlying field of logic: *pleonotetic* logic, as it might be called – the logic of majorities. Let us lay down for simplicity the convention that 'almost every' propositions shall be true iff the predicate is true of a *bare plurality* of the things covered by the subject-term. (This is of the same order as the regular minimizing interpretation of 'some'.) Now consider:

(35)   Almost every man who drives a car dislikes the police

The noun phrase theory gives the correct truth conditions for this: (35) is true just in case 'Almost every motorist dislikes the police' is true. But clearly neither of the following is equivalent to (35):

(36)   Almost every man, *if he* drives a car, dislikes the police
(37)   Almost every man drives a car *and* (*he*) dislikes the police

It would take me too far into pleonotetic logic to deal with this objection; I think it can be dealt with. Meanwhile, I may remark that examples from pleonotetic logic pose nasty problems for any theory of relative clauses. There is no obvious paraphrase, or account of the syntax, e.g. for the sentence:

(38)   Almost every man who borrows a book from a friend eventually returns it to him.

I know of no way to show which classes of book-borrowers (38) is comparing numerically. I do not know even whether (38) is syntactically coherent. There are surprises about syntactical coherence. The following sentence (I owe it to James McCawley) is syntactically incoherent:

155

(39)   Tom and Bill respectively kicked and punched each other,

for by the usual rules for 'respectively' it would yield the nonsense:

(40)   Tom kicked each other and Bill punched each other.

But replacement of 'each other' by 'the other one of that pair', which might seem trivial, in fact restores syntactical coherence. Similarly, we cannot be sure that (38) is syntactically coherent because it becomes so if we delete 'almost'. With this I must leave the problem as an exercise to the reader.

The Latin prose theory of complex terms in the vernacular is an application to the vernacular of Quine's programme for eliminating the means of forming such terms from the primitive apparatus of symbolic logic. This programme was indeed originally Russell's; but Quine has shown how to avoid the inelegancies, and even mistakes, that spoiled Russell's own execution of the programme. I hope others will be encouraged to perfect the work for vernacular languages too.

A *fourth* syntactical insight of Quine's by which I have several times been guided in this article without drawing attention to it, is the extremely useful notion of introducing a predicable as interpretation of a schematic letter. This notion is clearly explained and illustrated in *Methods of Logic* (p. 131ff.) and I need not paint the lily. I add only that this notion is needed in explaining the syntax of quite simple sentences. Here is an example of medieval vintage:

(41)   Any proposition or its contradictory is true.

Traditional grammar is impotent here. If we take 'or' to join 'any proposition' and 'its contradictory'; or if, equivalently, we take 'is true' to be 'understood' after 'proposition' (to speak more modishly, if we take 'is true' to be deleted by a transformation); then we make (41) tantamount to something beginning:

(42)   Any proposition is true, or ...

And this is clearly wrong; for a correct paraphrase of (40) need nowise contain as one disjunct the falsehood 'Any proposition is true'. If on the other hand we take 'or' to join 'proposition' and 'its contradictory', then by accepting (41) as true we let ourselves in for this 'syllogism':

(43)   Any proposition is a proposition or its contradictory

            Any proposition or its contradictory is true

Ergo: Any proposition is true.

The right account is very simple: (41) is got from 'F (any proposition)' by taking '$F(\ )$' to be:

(44)   – or – 's contradictory is true.

That is, (41) is true just in case (44) is true *of* any and every proposition.

It is matter for regret that insights such as I have discussed are little esteemed by some linguists; that modern textbooks still repeat old nonsense, about sentences' splitting up exhaustively into clauses, and pronouns' going proxy for what would be repetitious language. (The latter view was already thoroughly refuted by medieval examples.) But the bad old traditional logic is already dead, though it won't lie down; and the bad old traditional grammar is surely doomed too. Here as elsewhere Quine has done much against the Kingdom of Darkness.

University of Leeds

REFERENCES

[1] I use the word 'connective' rather than the usual grammatical term 'conjunction', to avoid any risk of confusion with the logicians' use of 'conjunction' for a particular kind of truth-functional complex.

[2] I adapt this example from a sentence devised by Susumu Kuno, itself cited in a mimeographed paper by James McCawley of the University of Chicago. I am in general much indebted to McCawley for the stimulation of this paper and of many discussions.

DONALD DAVIDSON

ON SAYING THAT*

"I wish I had said that", said Oscar Wilde in applauding one of Whistler's witticisms. Whistler, who took a dim view of Wilde's originality, retorted, "You will, Oscar; you will". The function of this tale (from Holbrook Jackson's *The Eighteen-Nineties*) is to remind us that an expression like "Whistler said that" may on occasion serve as a grammatically complete sentence. Here we have, I suggest, the key to a correct analysis of indirect discourse, an analysis that opens a lead to an analysis of psychological sentences generally (sentences about propositional attitudes, so-called), and even, though this looks beyond anything to be discussed in the present paper, a clue to what distinguishes psychological concepts from others.

But let us begin with sentences usually deemed more representative of *oratio obliqua*, for example "Galileo said that the earth moves" or "Scott said that Venus is an inferior planet". One trouble with such sentences is that we do not know their logical form. And to admit this is to admit that, whatever else we may know about them, we do not know the first thing. If we accept surface grammar as guide to logical form, we will see "Galileo said that the earth moves" as containing the sentence "the earth moves", and this sentence in turn as consisting of the singular term 'the earth', and a predicate, 'moves'. But if 'the earth' is, in this context, a singular term, it can be replaced, so far as the truth or falsity of the containing sentence is concerned, by any other singular term that refers to the same thing.

The notorious apparent invalidity of this rule can only be apparent, for the rule no more than spells out what is involved in the idea of a (logically) singular term. Only two lines of explanation, then, are open: we are wrong about the logical form, or we are wrong about the reference of the singular term.

What seems anomalous behavior on the part of what seem singular terms dramatizes the problem of giving an orderly account of indirect discourse, but the problem is more pervasive. For what touches singular terms touches what they touch, and that is everything: quantifiers,

158

variables, predicates, connectives. Singular terms refer, or pretend to refer, to the entities over which the variables of quantification range, and it is these entities of which the predicates are or are not true. So it should not surprise us that if we can make trouble for the sentence "Scott said that Venus is an inferior planet" by substituting 'the Evening Star' for 'Venus', we can equally make trouble by substituting "is identical with Venus or with Mercury" for the coextensive "is an inferior planet". The difficulties with indirect discourse cannot be solved simply by abolishing singular terms.

What should we ask of an adequate account of the logical form of a sentence? Above all, I would say, such an account must lead us to see the semantic character of the sentence – its truth or falsity – as owed to how it is composed, by a finite number of applications of some of a finite number of devices that suffice for the language as a whole, out of elements drawn from a finite stock (the vocabulary) that suffices for the language as a whole. To see a sentence in this light is to see it in the light of a theory for its language, a theory that gives the form of every sentence in that language. A way to provide such a theory is by recursively characterizing a truth-predicate, along the lines suggested by Tarski, that satisfies this criterion: the theory entails, for each sentence s (when described in a standardized way), that the truth-predicate holds of s if and only if _____. – Here the blank is to be filled by a sentence in the meta-language that is true if and only if s is true in the object language.[1] If we accept Tarski's further requirement that no undefined semantical notions be used in characterizing a truth-predicate, then no theory can satisfy the criterion except by describing every sentence in terms of a semantically significant structure.

A satisfactory theory of meaning for a language must, then, give an explicit account of the truth-conditions of every sentence, and this can be done by giving a theory that satisfies Tarski's criteria; nothing less should count as showing how the meaning of every sentence depends on its structure.[2] Two closely linked considerations support the idea that the structure with which a sentence is endowed by a theory of truth in Tarski's style deserves to be called the logical form of the sentence. By giving such a theory, we demonstrate in a persuasive way that the language, though it consists in an indefinitely large number of sentences, can be comprehended by a creature with finite powers. A theory of truth may be

159

said to supply an effective explanation of the semantic role of each significant expression in any of its appearances. Armed with the theory, we can always answer the question, "What are these familiar words doing here?" by saying how they contribute to the truth conditions of the sentence. (This is not to assign a 'meaning', much less a reference, to every significant expression.)

The study of the logical form of sentences is often seen in the light of another interest, that of expediting inference. From this point of view, to give the logical form of a sentence is to catalogue the features relevant to its place on the logical scene, the features that determine what sentences it is a logical consequence of, and what sentences it has as logical consequences. A canonical notation graphically encodes the relevant information, making theory of inference simple, and practice mechanical where possible.

Obviously the two approaches to logical form cannot yield wholly independent results, for logical consequence is defined in terms of truth. To say a second sentence is a logical consequence of a first is to say, roughly, that the second is true if the first is no matter how the non-logical constants are interpreted. Since what we count as a logical constant can vary independently of the set of truths, it is clear that the two versions of logical form, though related, need not be identical. The relation, in brief, seems this. Any theory of truth that satisfies Tarski's criteria must take account of all truth-affecting iterative devices in the language. In the familiar languages for which we know how to define truth the basic iterative devices are reducible to the sentential connectives, the apparatus of quantification, and the description operator if it is primitive. Where one sentence is a logical consequence of another on the basis of quantificational structure alone, a theory of truth will therefore entail that if the first sentence is true, the second is. There is no point, then, in not including the expressions that determine quantificational structure among the logical constants, for when we have characterized truth, on which any account of logical consequence depends, we have already committed ourselves to all that calling such expressions logical constants could commit us. Adding to this list of logical constants will increase the inventory of logical truths and consequence-relations beyond anything a truth definition demands, and will therefore yield richer versions of logical form. For the purposes of the present paper, however, we can cleave to the most austere interpretations of logical consequence and logical form, those that are forced on us when we give a theory of truth.

We are now in a position to explain our aporia over indirect discourse: what happens is that the relation between truth and consequence just sketched appears to break down. In a sentence like "Galileo said that the earth moves" the eye and mind perceive familiar structure in the words "the earth moves". And structure there must be if we are to have a theory of truth at all, for an infinite number of sentences (all sentences in the indicative, apart from some trouble over tense) yield sense when plugged into the slot in "Galileo said that _____". So if we are to give conditions of truth for all the sentences so generated, we cannot do it sentence by sentence, but only by discovering an articulate structure that permits us to treat each sentence as composed of a finite number of devices that make a stated contribution to its truth conditions. As soon as we assign familiar structure, however, we must allow the consequences of that assignment to flow, and these, as we know, are in the case of indirect discourse consequences we refuse to buy. In a way, the case is even stranger than that. Not only do familiar consequences fail to flow from what looks to be familiar structure, but our common sense of language feels little assurance in any inferences based on the words that follow the 'said that' of indirect discourse (there are exceptions).

So the paradox is this: on the one hand, intuition suggests, and theory demands, that we discover semantically significant structure in the 'content-sentences' of indirect discourse (as I shall call sentences following 'said that'). On the other hand, the failure of consequence-relations invites us to treat contained sentences as semantically inert. Yet logical form and consequence relations cannot be divorced in this way.

One proposal at this point is to view the words that succeed the 'said that' as operating within concealed quotation marks, their sole function being to help refer to a sentence, and their semantic inertness explained by the usual account of quotation. One drawback of this proposal is that no usual account of quotation is acceptable, even by the minimal standards we have set for an account of logical form. For according to most stories, quotations are singular terms without significant semantic structure, and since there must be an infinite number of different quotations, no language that contains them can have a recursively defined truth-predicate. This may be taken to show that the received accounts of quotation must be mistaken – I think it does. But then we can hardly pretend that we have solved the problem of indirect discourse by appeal to quotation.[3]

Perhaps it is not hard to invent a theory of quotation that will serve: the following theory is all but explicit in Quine. Simply view quotations as abbreviations for what you get if you follow these instructions: to the right of the first letter that has opening quotation-marks on its left write right-hand quotation marks, then the sign for concatenation, and then left-hand quotation marks, in that order; do this after each letter (treating punctuation signs as letters) until you reach the terminating right-hand quotation marks. What you now have is a complex singular term that gives what Tarski calls a structural description of an expression. There is a modest addition to vocabulary: names of letters and of punctuation signs, and the sign for concatenation. There is a corresponding addition to ontology: letters and punctuation signs. And finally, if we carry out the application to sentences in indirect discourse, there will be the logical consequences that the new structure dictates. For two examples, each of the following will be entailed by "Galileo said that the earth moves":

$$(\exists x) \text{ (Galileo said that "the ea"} \frown x \frown \text{"th moves")}$$

and (with the premise "r = the 18th letter in the alphabet"):

Galileo said that "the ea"$\frown$the 18th letter in the alphabet$\frown$"th moves"

(I have clung to abbreviations as far as possible.) These inferences are not meant in themselves as criticism of the theory of quotation; they merely illuminate it.

Quine discusses the quotational approach to indirect discourse in *Word and Object*,[4] and abandons it for what seems, to me, a wrong reason. Not that there is not a good reason; but to appreciate *it* is to be next door to a solution, as I shall try to show.

Let us follow Quine through the steps that lead him to reject the quotational approach. The version of the theory he considers is not the one once proposed by Carnap to the effect that 'said that' is a two-place predicate true of ordered pairs of people and sentences.[5] The trouble with this idea is not that it forces us to assimilate indirect discourse to direct, for it does not. The 'said that' of indirect discourse, like the 'said' of direct, may relate persons and sentences, but be a different relation; the former, unlike the latter, may be true of a person, and a sentence he never spoke in a language he never knew. The trouble lies rather in the chance that the same sentence may have different meanings in different languages – not too long a chance either if we count ideolects as languages.

Not that it is impossible to find words (as written or sounded) which express quite different ideas in different languages. For example, the sounds "Empedokles liebt" do fairly well as a German or an English sentence, in one case saying that Empedokles loved and in the other telling us what he did from the top of Etna. We can scoff at the notion that if we analyze "Galileo said that the earth moves" as asserting a relation between Galileo and the sentence "The earth moves" we must assume Galileo spoke English, but we cannot afford to scoff at the assumption that on this analysis the words of the content-sentence are to be understood as an English sentence.[6]

Calling the relativity to English an assumption may be misleading; perhaps the reference to English is explicit, as follows. A long-winded version of our favorite sentence might be "Galileo spoke a sentence that meant in his language what 'The earth moves' means in English". Since in this version it takes everything save 'Galileo' and 'The earth moves' to do the work of 'said that', we must count the reference to English as explicit in the 'said that'. To see how odd this is, however, it is only necessary to reflect that the English words 'said that', with their built-in reference to English, would no longer translate (by even the roughest extensional standards) the French 'dit que'.

We can shift the difficulty over translation away from the 'said that' or 'dit que' by taking these expressions as three-place predicates relating a speaker, a sentence and a language, the reference to a language to be supplied either by our (in practice nearly infallible) knowledge of the language to which the quoted material is to be taken as belonging, or by a demonstrative reference to the language of the entire sentence. Each of these suggestions has its own appeal, but neither leads to an analysis that will pass the translation test. To take the demonstrative proposal, translation into French will carry 'said that' into 'dit que', the demonstrative reference will automatically, and hence perhaps still within the bounds of strict translation, shift from English to French. But when we translate the final singular term, which names an English sentence, we produce a palpably false result.

These exercises help bring out important features of the quotational approach. But now it is time to remark that there would be an anomaly in a position, like the one under consideration, that abjured reference to propositions in favor of reference to languages. For languages (as Quine remarks in a similar context in *Word and Object*) are at least as badly individuated, and for much the same reasons, as propositions. Indeed, an obvious proposal linking them is this: languages are identical when identical sentences express identical propositions. We see, then, that quotational theories of indirect discourse, those we have discussed anyway, cannot claim an advantage over theories that frankly introduce intensional entities from the start; so let us briefly consider theories of the latter sort.

It might be thought, and perhaps often is, that if we are willing to welcome intensional entities without stint – properties, propositions, individual concepts, and whatever else – then no further difficulties stand in the way of giving an account of the logical form of sentences in *oratio obliqua*. This is not so. Neither the languages Frege suggests as models for natural languages nor the languages described by Church are amenable to theory in the sense of a truth-definition meeting Tarski's standards.[7] What stands in the way in Frege's case is that every referring expression has an infinite number of entities it may refer to, depending on the context, and there is no rule that gives the reference in more complex contexts on the basis of the reference in simpler ones. In Church's languages, there is an infinite number of primitive expressions; this directly blocks the possibility of recursively characterizing a truth-predicate satisfying Tarski's requirements.

Things might be patched up by following a leading idea of Carnap's *Meaning and Necessity* and limiting the semantic levels to two: extensions and (first-level) intensions.[8] An attractive strategy might then be to turn Frege, thus simplified, upside down by letting each singular term refer to its sense or intension, and providing a reality function (similar to Church's delta function) to map intensions onto extensions. Under such treatment our sample sentence would emerge like this: "The reality of Galileo said that the earth moves". Here we must suppose that 'the earth' names an individual concept which the function referred to by 'moves' maps onto the proposition that the earth moves; the function referred to by 'said that' in turn maps Galileo and the proposition that the earth moves onto a truth value. Finally, the name, 'Galileo' refers to an individual concept which is mapped, by the function referred to by 'the reality of' onto Galileo. With ingenuity, this theory can accommodate quantifiers that bind variables both inside and outside contexts created by verbs like 'said' and 'believes'. There is no special problem about defining truth for such a language: everything is on the up and up, purely extensional save in ontology. This seems to be a theory that might do all we have asked. Apart from nominalistic qualms, why not accept it?

My reasons against this course are essentially Quine's. Finding right words of my own to communicate another's saying is a problem in translation (216-217). The words I use in the particular case may be viewed as products of my total theory (however vague and subject to correction) of what the originating speaker means by anything he says: such a theory is indistinguishable from a characterization of a truth-predicate, with his language as object-language and mine as metalanguage. The crucial point is that within limits there is no choosing between alternative theories which differ in assigning clearly non-synonymous sentences of mine as translations of his same utterance. This is Quine's thesis of the indeterminacy of translation (218-221).[9] An example will help bring out the fact that the thesis applies not only to translation between speakers of conspicuously different languages, but also to cases nearer home.

Let someone say (and now discourse is direct), "There's a hippopotamus in the refrigerator"; am I necessarily right in reporting him as having said that there is a hippopotamus in the refrigerator? Perhaps; but under questioning he goes on, "It's roundish, has a wrinkled skin, does not mind being touched. It has a pleasant taste, at least the juice, and it costs a dime. I squeeze two or three for breakfast." After some finite amount of such talk we slip over the line where it is plausible or even possible to say correctly that he said there was a hippopotamus in the refrigerator, for it becomes clear he means something else by at least some of his words than I do. The simplest hypothesis so far is that my word 'hippopotamus' no longer translates his word 'hippopotamus'; my word 'orange' might do better. But in any case, long before we reach the point where homophonic translation must be abandoned, charity inviset departures. Hesitation over whether to translate a saying of another by one or another of various non-synonymous sentences of mine does not necessarily reflect a lack of information: it is just that beyond a point

165

there is no deciding, even in principle, between the view that the Other has used words as we do but has more or less weird beliefs, and the view that we have translated him wrong. Torn between the need to make sense of a speaker's words and the need to make sense of the pattern of his beliefs, the best we can do is choose a theory of translation that maximizes agreement. Surely there is no future in supposing that in earnestly uttering the words "There's a hippopotamus in the refrigerator" the Other has disagreed with us about what can be in the refrigerator if we also must then find ourselves disagreeing with him about the size, shape, color, manufacturer, horsepower, and wheelbase of hippopotami.

None of this shows there is no such thing as correct reporting, through indirect discourse, what another said. All that the indeterminacy shows is that if there is one way of getting it right there are other ways that differ substantially in that non-synonymous sentences are used after 'said that'. And this is enough to justify our feeling that there is something bogus about the sharpness questions of meaning must in principle have if meanings are entities.

The lesson was implicit in a discussion started some years ago by Benson Mates. Mates claimed that the sentence "Nobody doubts that whoever believes that the seventh consulate of Marius lasted less than a fortnight believes that the seventh consulate of Marius lasted less than a fortnight" is true and yet might well become false if the last word were replaced by the (supposed synonymous) words 'period of fourteen days', and that this could happen no matter what standards of synonomy we adopt short of the question-begging "substitutable everywhere *salva veritate*".[10] Church and Sellars responded by saying the difficulty could be resolved by firmly distinguishing between substitutions based on the speaker's use of language and substitutions colored by the use attributed to others.[11] But this is a solution only if we think there is some way of telling, in what another says, what is owed to the meanings he gives his words and what to his beliefs about the world. According to Quine, this is a distinction not there to be drawn.

The detour has been lengthy; I return now to Quine's discussion of the quotational approach in *Word and Object*. As reported above, Quine rejects relativization to a language on the grounds that the principle of the individuation of languages is obscure, and the issue when languages are identical irrelevant to indirect discourse (214). He now suggests that instead of interpreting the content-sentence of indirect discourse as occurring in a language, we interpret it as voiced by a speaker at a time. The speaker and time relative to which the content-sentence needs understanding is, of course, the speaker of that sentence, who is thereby indirectly attributing a saying to another. So now "Galileo said that the earth moves" comes to mean something like "Galileo spoke a sentence that in his mouth meant what 'The earth moves' now means in mine". Quine makes no objection to this proposal because he thinks he has something simpler and at least as good in reserve. But in my opinion the present proposal deserves more serious consideration, for I think it is nearly right, while Quine's preferred alternatives are seriously defective.

The first of these alternatives is Scheffler's inscriptional theory.[12] Scheffler suggests that sentences in indirect discourse relate a speaker and an utterance: the role of the content-sentence is to help convey what sort of utterance it was. What we get this way is, "Galileo spoke a that-the-earth-moves utterance". The predicate "x is-a-that-the-earth-moves-utterance" has, so far as theory of truth and of inference are concerned, the form of an unstructured one-place predicate. Quine does not put the matter quite this way, and he may resist my appropriation of the terms 'logical form' and 'structure' for purposes that exclude application to Scheffler's predicate. Quine calls the predicate "compound" and describes it as composed of an operator and a sentence (214, 215). These are matters of terminology; the substance, about which there may be no disagreement, is that on Scheffler's theory sentences in *oratio obliqua* have no logical relations that depend on structure in the predicate, and a truth-predicate that applies to all such sentences cannot be characterized in Tarski's style. The reason is plain: there is an infinite number of predicates with the syntax "x is-a-_____-utterance" each of which is, in the eyes of semantic theory, unrelated to the rest.

Quine has seized one horn of the dilemma. Since attributing semantic structure to content-sentences in indirect discourse apparently forces us to endorse logical relations we do not want, Quine gives up the structure. The result is that another desideratum of theory is neglected, that truth be defined.

Consistent with his policy of renouncing structure that supports no inferences worth their keep, Quine contemplates one further step; he says, "...a final alternative that I find as appealing as any is simply to dispense with the objects of the propositional attitudes" (216). Where Scheffler still saw 'said that' as a two-place predicate relating speakers and utterances, though welding content-sentences into one-piece one-place predicates true of utterances, Quine now envisions content-sentence and 'said that' welded directly to form the one-place predicate "x said-that-the-earth-moves", true of persons. Of course some inferences inherent in Scheffler's scheme now fall away: we can no longer infer "Galileo said something" from our sample sentence, nor can we infer from it and "Someone denied that the earth moves" the sentence "Someone denied what Galileo said". Yet as Quine reminds us, inferences like these may fail on Scheffler's analysis too when the analysis is extended along the obvious line to belief and other propositional attitudes, since needed utterances may fail to materialize (215). The advantages of Scheffler's theory over Quine's 'final alternative' are therefore few and uncertain; this is why Quine concludes that the view that invites the fewest inferences is 'as appealing as any'.

This way of eliminating unwanted inferences unfortunately abolishes most of the structure needed by the theory of truth. So it is worth returning for another look at the earlier proposal to analyze indirect discourse in terms of a predicate relating an originating speaker, a sentence, and the present speaker of the sentence in indirect discourse. For that proposal did not cut off any of the simple entailments we have been discussing, and it alone of recent suggestions promised, when coupled with a workable theory of quotation, to yield to standard semantic methods. But there is a subtle flaw.

We tried to bring out the flavor of the analysis to which we have returned by rewording our favorite sentence as "Galileo uttered a sentence that meant in his mouth what 'The earth moves' means now in mine." We should not think ill of this verbose version of "Galileo said that the earth moves" because of apparent reference to a meaning ("what 'The earth moves' means"); this expression is not treated as a singular term in the theory. We are indeed asked to make sense of a judgment of synonomy between utterances, but not as the foundation of a theory of language, merely as an unanalyzed part of the content of the familiar idiom of indirect discourse. The idea that underlies our awkward paraphrase is that of *samesaying*: when I say that Galileo said that the earth moves, I represent Galileo and myself as samesayers.

168

And now the flaw is this. If I merely *say* we are samesayers, Galileo and I, I have yet to *make* us so; and how am I to do this? Obviously, by saying what he said; not by using his words (necessarily), but by using words the same in import here and now as his then and there. Yet this is just what, on the theory, I cannot do. For the theory brings the content-sentence into the act sealed in quotation marks, and on any standard theory of quotation, this means the content-sentence is mentioned and not used. In uttering the words "The earth moves" I do not, according to this account, say anything remotely like what Galileo is claimed to have said; I do not, in fact, say anything. My words in the frame provided by "Galileo said that_____" merely help refer to a sentence. There will be no missing the point if we expand quotation in the style we recently considered. Any intimation that Galileo and I are samesayers vanishes in this version:

> Galileo said that 'T'∩'h'∩'e'∩' '∩'e'∩'a'∩'r'∩'t'∩'h'∩' '∩'m'∩ 'o'∩'v'∩'e'∩'s'

We seem to have been taken in by a notational accident, a way of referring to expressions that when abbreviated produces framed pictures of the very words referred to. The difficulty is odd; let's see if we can circumvent it. Imagine an altered case. Galileo utters his words "Eppur si muove", I utter my words, "The earth moves." There is no problem yet in recognizing that we are samesayers; an utterance of mine matches an utterance of his in purport. I am not now using my words to help refer to a sentence; I speak for myself, and my words refer in their usual way to the earth and to its movement. If Galileo's utterance "Eppur si muove" made us samesayers, then some utterance or other of Galileo's made us samesayers. The form "($\exists x$) (Galileo's utterance x and my utterance y make us samesayers)" is thus a way of attributing any saying I please to Galileo provided I find a way of replacing 'y' by a word or phrase that refers to an appropriate utterance of mine. And surely there is a way I can do this: I need only produce the required utterance and replace 'y' by a reference to it. Here goes:

> The earth moves.

> ($\exists x$) (Galileo's utterance x and my last utterance make us samesayers).

Definitional abbreviation is all that is needed to bring this little skit down to:

> The earth moves.
> Galileo said that.

Here the 'that' is a demonstrative singular term referring to an utterance (not a sentence).

This form has a small drawback in that it leaves the hearer up in the air about the purpose served by saying "The earth moves" until the act has been performed. As if, say, I were first to tell a story and then add, "That's how it was once upon a time". There's some fun to be had this way, and in any case no amount of telling what the illocutionary force of our utterances is is going to insure that they have that force. But in the present case nothing stands in the way of reversing the order of things, thus:

> Galileo said that.
> The earth moves.

Perhaps it is now safe to allow a tiny orthographic change, a change without semantic significance, but suggesting to the eye the relation of introducer and introduced: we may suppress the stop after 'that' and the consequent capitalization:

> Galileo said that the earth moves.

Perhaps it should come as no surprise to learn that the form of psychological sentences in English apparently evolved through about the stages our ruminations have just carried us. According to the *Oxford English Dictionary*,

The use of *that* is generally held to have arisen out of the demonstrative pronoun pointing to the clause which it introduces. Cf. (1) He once lived here: we all know *that*; (2) *That* (now *this*) we all know: he once lived here; (3) We all know *that* (or *this*): he once lived here; (4) We all know *that* he once lived here...[13]

The proposal then is this: sentences in indirect discourse, as it happens, wear their logical form on their sleeves (except for one small point). They consist of an expression referring to a speaker, the two-place predicate 'said', and a demonstrative referring to an utterance. Period. What follows gives the content of the subject's saying, but has no logical or semantic connection with the original attribution of a saying. This last point is no doubt the novel one, and upon it everything depends: from a semantic point of view the content-sentence in indirect discourse is not contained in the sentence whose truth counts.

We would do better, in coping with this subject, to talk of inscriptions and utterances and speech acts, and avoid reference to sentences.[14] For what an utterance of "Galileo said that" does is announce a further utterance. Like any utterance, this first may be serious or silly, assertive or playful; but if it is true, it must be followed by an utterance synonymous with some other. The second utterance, the introduced act, may also be true or false, done in the mode of assertion or of play. But if it is as announced, it must serve at least the purpose of conveying the content of what someone said. The role of the introducing utterance is not unfamiliar: we do the same with words like "This is a joke", "This is an order", "He commanded that", "Now hear this". Such expressions might be called performatives, for they are used to usher in performances on the part of the speaker. A certain interesting reflexive effect sets in when performatives occur in the first-person present tense, for then the speaker utters words which if true are made so exclusively by the content and mode of the performance that follows, and the mode of this performance may well be in part determined by that same performative introduction. Here is an example that will also provide the occasion for a final comment on indirect discourse.

"Jones asserted that Entebbe is equatorial" would, if we parallel the analysis of indirect discourse, come to mean something like, "An utterance of Jones' in the assertive mode had the content of this utterance of mine. Entebbe is equatorial". The analysis does not founder because the modes of utterance of the two speakers may differ; all that the truth of the performative requires is that my second utterance, in whatever mode (assertive or not) match in content an assertive utterance of Jones. Whether such an asymmetry is appropriate in indirect discourse depends on how much of assertion we read into saying. Now suppose I try: "I assert that Entebbe is equatorial". Of course by saying this I may not assert anything; mood of words cannot guarantee mode of utterance. But if my utterance of the performative is true, then I do say something in the assertive mode that has the content of my second utterance – I do, that is, assert that Entebbe is equatorial. If I do assert it, an element in my success is no doubt my utterance of the performative, which announces an assertion; thus performatives tend to be self-fulfilling. Perhaps it is this feature of performatives that has misled some philosophers into thinking that performatives, or their utterances, are neither true nor false.

On the analysis of indirect discourse just proposed, standard problems seem to find a just solution. The appearance of failure of the laws of extensional substitution is explained as due to our mistaking what are really two sentences for one: we make substitutions in one sentence, but it is the other (the utterance of) which changes in truth. Since an utterance of "Galileo said that" and any utterance following it are semantically independent, there is no reason to predict, on grounds of form alone, any *particular* effect on the truth of the first from a change in the second. On the other hand, if the second utterance had been different in any way at all, the first utterance *might* have had a different truth value, for the reference of the 'that' would have changed.

The paradox, that sentences (utterances) in *oratio obliqua* do not have the logical consequences they should if truth is to be defined, is resolved. What follows the verb 'said' has only the structure of a singular term, usually the demonstrative 'that'. Assuming the 'that' refers, we can infer that Galileo said something from "Galileo said that"; but this is welcome. The familiar words coming in the train of the performative of indirect discourse do, on my account, have structure, but it is familiar structure and poses no problem for theory of truth not there before indirect discourse was the theme.

Since Frege, philosophers have become hardened to the idea that content-sentences in talk about propositional attitudes may strangely refer to such entities as intensions, propositions, sentences, utterances and inscriptions. What is strange is not the entities, which are all right in their place (if they have one), but the notion that ordinary words for planets, people, tables and hippopotami in indirect discourse may give up these pedestrian references for the exotica. If we could recover our pre-Fregean semantic innocence, I think it would seem to us plainly incredible that the words "The earth moves", uttered after the words "Galileo said that", mean anything different, or refer to anything else, than is their wont when they come in other environments. No doubt their role in *oratio obliqua* is in some sense special; but that is another story. Language is the instrument it is because the same expression, with semantic features (meaning) unchanged, can serve countless purposes. I have tried to show how our understanding of indirect discourse does not strain this basic insight.

Princeton University

REFERENCES

* I am indebted to W. V. Quine and John Wallace for suggestions and criticisms. My research was in part supported by the National Science Foundation.

1 Alfred Tarski, 'The Concept of Truth in Formalized Languages', in *Logic, Semantics, Metamathematics*, Oxford 1956, pp. 152–278. The criterion is roughly Tarski's Convention *T* that defines the concept of a truth-predicate.

2 The view that a characterization of a truth-predicate meeting Tarski's criteria is the core of a theory of meaning is defended in my 'Truth and Meaning', *Synthese* **17** (1967) 304–323.

3 For documentation and details see my 'Theories of Meaning and Learnable Languages' in *Logic, Methodology and Philosophy of Science, Proceedings of the 1964 International Congress* (ed. by Yehoshua Bar-Hillel), Amsterdam 1965, pp. 388–390.

4 *Word and Object*, Cambridge, Mass., 1960, Chapt. VI. Hereafter numerals in parentheses refer to pages of this book.

5 R. Carnap, *The Logical Syntax of Language*, London 1937, p. 248. The same was in effect proposed by P. T. Geach, *Mental Acts*, London 1957.

6 The point is due to A. Church, 'On Carnap's Analysis of Statements of Assertion and Belief', *Analysis* **10** (1950) 97–99.

7 G. Frege, 'On Sense and Reference' in *Philosophical Writings* (ed. by P. Geach and M. Black) Oxford 1952, and A. Church, 'A Formulation of the Logic of Sense and Denotation', in *Structure, Method, and Meaning: Essays in Honor of H. M. Sheffer* (ed. by Henle, Kallen and Langer) New York 1951.

8 R. Carnap, *Meaning and Necessity*, Chicago 1947. The idea of an essentially Fregean approach limited to two semantic levels has also been suggested by Michael Dummett (in an unpublished manuscript). Neither of these proposals is in detail entirely satisfactory in the light of present concerns, for neither leads to a language for which a truth-predicate can be characterized.

9 My assimilation of a translation manual to a theory of truth is not in Quine. For more on this, see the article in reference 2.

10 B. Mates, 'Synonymity', in *Meaning and Interpretation*, Berkeley 1950, pp. 201–226. The example is Church's.

11 A. Church, 'Intensional Isomorphism and Identity of Belief', *Philosophical Studies* **5** (1954) 65–73; W. Sellars, 'Putnam on Synonymity and Belief', *Analysis* **15** (1955) 117–20.

12 I. Scheffler, 'An Inscriptional Approach to Indirect Quotation', *Analysis* **14** (1954) 83–90.

13 J. A. H. Murray *et al.* (eds.), *The Oxford English Dictionary*, Oxford 1933, vol. XI, p. 253. Cf. C. T. Onions, *An Advanced English Syntax*, New York 1929, pp. 154–156. I first learned that 'that' in such contexts evolved from an explicit demonstrative in J. Hintikka, *Knowledge and Belief*, Ithaca 1962, p. 13. Hintikka remarks that a similar

development has taken place in German and Finnish. I owe the reference to the *O.E.D.* to Eric Stietzel.

[14] I assume that a theory of truth for a language containing demonstratives must strictly apply to utterances and not to sentences, or will treat truth as a relation between sentences, speakers, and times. The point is discussed in 'Truth and Meaning', pp. 319, 20 (see reference 2).

DAGFINN FØLLESDAL

QUINE ON MODALITY

Over the past thirty-two years, Quine has presented a number of arguments against the modalities, his criticism culminating in *Word and Object*. During the same period, modal logic has flourished as never before, and a number of semantic systems for the different modalities have been proposed, apparently quite unencumbered by Quine's criticism. What is even more remarkable, Quine's arguments have very rarely been discussed or even referred to by the proponents of modal logic, and the few who have discussed them, have all taken exception to them. What, then, is the current status of the modalities and of Quine's arguments against them?

Quine has concentrated his criticism on the logical modalities. He has argued that all attempts to draw an epistemologically relevant distinction between logical, or, more broadly, linguistic truth and factual truth have been unsuccessful, and he has developed, in *Word and Object*, a theory of language according to which there is no such distinction to be drawn. Quine has further argued that the fundamental unclarity of such a distinction becomes particularly apparent when it is applied to *open* sentences, that is sentences which contain pronouns or variables that purport to refer back to objects mentioned outside of the modal context.

According to Quine, it is difficult to make any sense of such sentences, in particular it is unclear what the objects are, if any, that are referred to in modal contexts. Consider, for example,

(1) $(\exists x)\, N(x > 7)$

"Would 9, that is, the number of planets, be one of the numbers necessarily greater than 7?" Quine has asked[1], pointing out that such an affirmation would be true in the form

(2) $N(9 > 7)$

and false in the form

(3) N (the number of planets > 1)

175

The difficulty, according to Quine, is due to the modal context's being referentially opaque; 'the number of planets' cannot be substituted for '9' in (2) *salva veritate* although the two expressions refer to the same object. In order to make sense of quantification, Quine concludes, the positions of the variables have to be referential in the sentence following the quantifier, names which refer to the same object must be interchangeable in these positions, or, in other words, whatever is asserted in this open sentence to be true of an object in our universe of discourse, must be true of it regardless of how it is referred to. That is, whatever predicate 'F' stands for, simple or complex, in order for quantification to make sense,

$$(4) \qquad (x)(y)(x = y \supset . Fx \supset Fy)$$

must be true (Quine's thesis).

Is it then possible to make sense of quantifying into modal contexts?

As observed by Quine[2], the difficulties connected with quantification into modal contexts would vanish if one were to exclude from one's universe of discourse all objects that can be uniquely specified in ways which are not necessarily equivalent to one another and retain only objects x such that any two conditions uniquely determining x are necessarily equivalent, i.e. such that:

$$(5) \qquad (y)(Fy \equiv . y = x).(y)(Gy \equiv . y = x). \supset N(y)(Fy \equiv Gy)$$

However, as Quine points out in *From a Logical Point of View* (1st ed., pp. 152–153), (5) has consequences which some modal logicians might be reluctant to accept, for example:

$$(x)(y)(x = y \supset N(x = y))$$

that is, all identities are necessary.

In *Word and Object*, Quine draws a further, disastrous consequence from (5), viz. the consequence that every true sentence is necessarily true, or

$$p \supset Np$$

Since the converse holds, too, this means that modal distinctions collapse; the whole point of the modalities vanishes.

176

Is then Quine's criticism of the modalities decisive?

The few proponents of the modalities who have discussed Quine's arguments, all argue that his criticism is ill-founded; usually they reject Quine's basic thesis, that the positions of the quantified variables have to be referential.

Thus Church, in his review of Quine's 'Notes on Existence and Necessity'[3], argues that modal contexts are referentially opaque, but that this does not prevent variables within modal contexts from referring to a quantifier anterior to the context, provided that the variables have an intensional range – a range, for instance, composed of attributes rather than classes.

However, merely restricting the range of the variables does not help one out of the difficulties; nothing is presupposed about the range of the variables in Quine's arguments, which are unaffected by any restriction on variables.

The crucial part of Church's review is his reference to Frege's ideas concerning sense, denotation and oblique occurrences. In his later article 'A Formulation of the Logic of Sense and Denotation' (1951)[4], Church makes ingenious use of these ideas to develop a system where one quantifies into necessity contexts without this leading to any collapse of modal distinctions. In this system the variables take intensions as values in necessity-contexts, but what saves the system is not that the variables are thus restricted, but that the positions of the variables are referential. There are no opaque constructions in the system. Its necessity operator notwithstanding, it is therefore not a modal, i.e. non-extensional system, and it is not evidence against Quine's thesis that one cannot quantify into referentially opaque contexts. Church has rather shown how to handle the logical modalities without making use of opaque contexts.

Carnap, in *Meaning and Necessity*[5], argues that although modal contexts are referentially opaque, one can make sense of quantification into such contexts by help of his method of extension and intension.

Now, if one interprets the variables as ranging over intensions, then Carnap's quantification into modal contexts makes good sense. However, this is just what one should expect if Quine is right, for if two expressions, 'a' and 'b', refer to the same intension, that is, if $a \equiv b$, then they can be substituted for one another in all contexts in Carnap's system (S_2). That is, the positions of the variables are referential, and substitutivity and quantification go together after all, just as was required by Quine. However, if one tries to interpret the variables as ranging over extensions, i.e. entities individuated by the relation '≡', then, as argued by Quine in a statement included by Carnap in *Meaning and Necessity*, pp. 196–197, quantification ceases to make sense; Quine's questions concerning what the objects are over which we quantify, again become embarrassing.

Hence there seems to be good reason in Carnap's system, too, to accept Quine's thesis that substitutivity and quantification go together. However, one may wonder, what then happens with modal distinctions? Do they collapse?

As a matter of fact, '$p \equiv Np$' is not derivable in Carnap's system. However, what prevents it from being derivable is a restriction which Carnap puts on definite descriptions in his system, to the effect that no description may contain a modal operator. No justification is given for this restriction; all Carnap says is that "in order to avoid certain complications, which cannot be explained here, it seems advisable to admit in S_2 only descriptions which do not contain 'N'".[6] If one lifts the restriction, one sees what these complications are: modal distinctions collapse. As long as Carnap has not given a semantic justification for his restriction on descriptions, therefore, it seems that he has not succeeded in giving a satisfactory semantics for the modalities.

Hintikka is the third and last main proponent of modal logic who has taken exception to Quine's thesis. Like Church and Carnap, Hintikka has argued that quantification into opaque contexts can be interpreted in such a way as to make sense.[7] As a matter of fact, Hintikka's semantics does make sense if the values of the variables are taken to be expressions, i.e. singular terms that are substituted for the variables. However, Hintikka does not intend to give this kind of 'substitutional' interpretation of quantification. He wants, and I think rightly, the values of his variables to be "real, fullfledged individuals".[8] However, if this is to be the case, it is unclear what the objects are over which Hintikka quantifies, unless he supplements his semantics in such a way that Quine's thesis becomes valid in it. As far as I know, Hintikka has accepted this, and no longer rejects Quine's thesis.[9] It seems, therefore, that those modal logicians who have taken exception to Quine's thesis have not succeeded in refuting it. They have presented semantics for quantified modal logic in which Quine's thesis is claimed not to hold. But, as we have seen, all of these semantics are such that in so far as Quine's thesis does not come out valid in them, it is unclear what the objects are over which one quantifies.

Do we then have to give up the modalities? It seems to me that we cannot. Quine's argument, leading up to the collapse of modal distinctions, is simply too disastrous to be right.

For although the argument in *Word and Object* is directed against the logical modalities, it can easily be paralleled for the other modalities. In fact, by reasoning exactly parallel to that on pp. 198–199 of *Word and Object* one can show that any attempt to single out from the class of all true sentences a proper subclass of sentences is doomed to failure if:

(i) One has a standard system of quantification theory with identity and definite descriptions. (If descriptions are treated in the Frege-Carnapian way, and not defined contextually, one must in addition require that the universe contain at least one object which is necessarily distinct from the object which is selected as descriptum for all descriptions that do not satisfy the condition of uniqueness.)

(ii) One permits quantification into the members of the subclass from outside.

Whenever (i) and (ii) are satisfied one can prove that the subclass coincides with the full class, that is, it cannot be a proper subclass; the distinction one was trying to make between the two classes is eradicated.

This means that if Quine's conclusion in *Word and Object* is unavoidable, then any attempt to build up adequate theories of causation, counterfactuals, probability, preference, knowledge, belief, action, duty, responsibility, rightness, goodness, etc. must be given up since, presumably, any such theory would require quantification into open sentences of this kind from outside.

The mere fact that Quine's conclusion has these disastrous consequences indicates that there must be a way of avoiding it.

However, as we saw, all attempts to reject Quine's thesis have been unsuccessful, and it seems that what one has to do is to accept the thesis and still find a way of avoiding Quine's calamitous conclusion, that is one must find a semantics for modal contexts according to which these contexts are at the same time *referentially transparent* (as required for quantification) and *extensionally opaque*; that is, co-extensional expressions must not be interchangeable (since such interchangeability would

179

amount precisely to the collapse of modal distinctions warned against by Quine).

From this it is immediately clear that a satisfactory semantics for the modalities must distinguish between expressions which refer (singular terms) and expressions which have extension (general terms and sentences, the extension of a sentence being its truth value). This means that a Fregean semantics, according to which all expressions are treated on a par as referring expressions cannot be a satisfactory semantics for modal logic.[10] Neither can a Carnapian semantics in which all expressions are treated indiscriminately as having extensions. In neither of these two systems can one get the required combination of referential transparency and extensional opacity. (Of course, this does not affect the adequacy of these semantics for extensional contexts, where no such combination of transparency and opacity is needed, and where a unitary treatment of the various kinds of expressions brings about simplifications.) It is instructive to note that Church's Frege-inspired system of sense and denotation, as we noted earlier, contains no opaque contexts.

However, does distinguishing between expressions which refer and expressions which have extension generate the possibility of contexts which are at the same time referentially transparent and extensionally opaque? In order to get a clearer view of the situation, I shall now, following Quine[11], define the notion of a referentially transparent construction, and similarly that of an extensionally transparent construction.

As a preliminary to this, let us first define the notion of a referential *position* or occurrence, of a singular term, and an extensional position of a general term or sentence. Depending on whether the containing expression is a singular term or a general term or sentence, we have four cases to consider, which can be put together in the following definition:

DEF. 1: A *position* of a $\begin{Bmatrix} \text{singular term} \\ \text{general term or sentence} \end{Bmatrix}$ in an expression is $\begin{Bmatrix} \text{referential} \\ \text{extensional} \end{Bmatrix}$ if and only if any $\begin{Bmatrix} \text{singular term} \\ \text{general term or sentence} \end{Bmatrix}$ that occurs in that position can be replaced by a $\begin{Bmatrix} \text{co-referential} \\ \text{co-extensional} \end{Bmatrix}$ expression without the containing expression changing its reference (if the containing expression is a singular term) or extension (if the containing expression is a general term or sentence).

180

With this definition at hand we can now define the notion of a referentially transparent *construction* and, parallel to it, an extensionally transparent construction:

DEF. 2: A *construction*, or mode of containment, is $\begin{cases} \text{referentially} \\ \text{extensionally} \end{cases}$ transparent if and only if for every expression which may be an ingredient in the construction, every position which is $\begin{cases} \text{referential} \\ \text{extensional} \end{cases}$ in the ingredient expression is $\begin{cases} \text{referential} \\ \text{extensional} \end{cases}$ in the product of the construction (i.e. in the expression that results when the construction is applied to the ingredient).

Constructions that are not referentially (extensionally) transparent are called referentially (extensionally) opaque.

Thus, for example, truth-functional negation is an extensionally transparent construction. For, consider '$\sim p$': if an expression is in referential position in the ingredient 'p', it will remain in extensional position in the product, i.e. in '$\sim p$'. Similarly for the other truth-functional and quantificational constructions.

The modal constructions are obviously extensionally opaque. For an expression which is in extensional position with respect to a sentence 'p' need not be in an extensional position in 'Np'; a trivial example is the sentence 'p' itself, which is in extensional position with respect to itself, but is not in extensional position in 'Np', if modal distinctions are not to collapse.

Our question now is: Can the modal constructions be referentially transparent?

One can show that *every referentially transparent construction on singular terms has to be extensionally transparent*. The proof is as follows:

Let

(i) Φ be a construction on singular terms (e.g. '{...}', (unit class), where the three dots stand for any singular term)

(ii) Φ be referentially transparent

(iii) t and t' be general terms and $\Psi(t)$ an ingredient of the construction Φ. ($\Psi(t)$ is hence a singular term, according to (i).)

Let further

(iv) t and t' be co-extensional.

and

(v)   the position of t in $\Psi(t)$ be extensional.

Then, by (iii), (iv), and (v)

(vi)   the expressions $\Psi(t)$ and $\Psi(t')$ are co-referential

Then, since obviously every singular term is in a referential position with respect to itself, we may conclude from (vi) by (ii) that

(vii) $\Phi(\Psi(t))$ and $\Phi(\Psi(t'))$ are co-extensional (or co-referential, if Φ is a construction which produces singular terms).

So, it is impossible to have a construction on singular terms which is at the same time referentially transparent and extensionally opaque.

By a parallel argument one can also prove that every extensionally transparent construction on general terms or sentences is referentially transparent.

If we could now prove that every referentially transparent construction on *general* terms or sentences is extensionally transparent, we would have vindicated Quine; the impossibility of a semantics for quantified modal logic would follow as a mere logical consequence from Quine's thesis.

However, the above type of proof does not carry over to this case, and no other proof can be given either, for as a matter of fact there are referentially transparent constructions on general terms or sentences that are extensionally opaque.

One can arrive at such constructions in various ways, as one sees if one looks into the reasons why the proof does not carry over to this case and observes what additional assumptions would be needed for it to go through. As obviously has to be the case, granting the truth of Quine's thesis every satisfactory approach to quantified modal logic that has been or will ever be proposed must be found among these ways.

The oldest and at the same time one of the simplest methods is to treat all troublesome singular terms as descriptions and eliminate them contextually. In 1942, in his review of Quine's 'Whitehead and the Rise of Modern Logic', Church observed that this gives an immediate reply to

Quine's objection that the substitutivity of identity breaks down in the example concerning the number of planets and 9: Both in *Principia Mathematica* and in Quine's own *Mathematical Logic*

... the translation into symbolic notation of the phrase 'the number of planets' would render it either as a description or as a class abstract, and in either case it would be construed contextually; any formal deduction must refer to the unabbreviated forms of the sentences in question, and the unabbreviated form of the first sentence is found actually to contain no name of the number 9.[12]

In 1947, in his review of Quine's 'The Problem of Interpreting Modal logic'[13] and more fully in his article 'Modality and Description' (1948), Arthur F. Smullyan has argued that the modalities need not involve paradox either in connection with substitution or with quantification "when they are referred to a system in which descriptions and class abstracts are contextually defined".[14] This course has been followed by Marcus[15], Fitch[16], and Myhill[17] and several later writers. The relevance of distinguishing between quantifiable variables and constant singular terms was noted by Quine in 'Three Grades of Modal Involvement' (1953), pp. 79–80, in *From a Logical Point of View* (1953), p. 154, and in 'Reply to Professor Marcus' (1962), p. 101. It was also noted by Montague in 'Logical Necessity, Physical Necessity, Ethics, and Quantifiers' (1955, published 1960), p. 266.[18] In that article, Montague also presents semantics for the logical, physical and deontic modalities in which he shows that (4) is valid.

So, although Quine's thesis seems to be valid in spite of the criticism which has been directed against it, the disastrous collapse of modal distinctions warned against by Quine can be avoided.

I shall end my paper with two minor remarks.

(1) One of Quine's points concerning the modalities has been that quantified modal logic commits one to essentialism, i.e. the view that

an object, of itself and by whatever name or none, must be seen as having some of its traits necessarily and others contingently, despite the fact that the latter traits follow just as analytically from some ways of specifying the objects as the former do from other ways of specifying it.[19]

Now, this follows from our previous observations. For we have seen that given Quine's thesis, if one wants to quantify into modal contexts without having modal distinctions collapse, then these contexts have to be referentially transparent and extensionally opaque. And essentialism is just this combination of referential transparency and extensional opacity: whatever is true of an object is true of it regardless of how it is referred to (referential transparency), and among the predicates true of an object, some are necessarily true of it, others only accidentally (extensional opacity).

However, it should also be observed that given a way of obtaining contexts that are referentially transparent and extensionally opaque, there are no more problems with essentialism than with unquantified modal logic. If the modal operators make sense when applied to closed sentences, then they make sense when applied to open sentences, too. To make sense of essentialism and to make sense of open sentences with a modal operator prefixed are one and the same problem, and a solution to the one is a solution to the other.

This brings me to my second and final remark:

(2) Since the formal semantic problems that turn up in connection with quantification into modal contexts can be solved, this means that the modalities cannot be rejected for purely formal reasons. The modalities can be made *formally* respectable, free from logical difficulties. It seems, therefore, that if one is to take exception to the modalities, it has to be on metaphysical or epistemological grounds, and not on logical ones. This applies to all the non-extensional contexts I mentioned earlier, those that occur in ethics and in natural science as well as the logical modalities.

However, in addition to the formal arguments I have discussed and which I have indicated how to overcome, Quine has directed a number of general epistemological arguments against one particular kind of modalities, the *logical* modalities, arguing in 'Two Dogmas of Empiricism', *Word and Object*, and several of his other writings that the logical necessity- and possibility-operators, even when applied to *closed* sentences, do not make sense. As long as these arguments have not been met, it seems that the other modalities, for example the physical, epistemic, and deontic ones, are better off than the logical modalities.

REFERENCES

[1] 'Notes on Existence and Necessity', *Journal of Philosophy* **40** (1943) 124. See also *From a Logical Point of View*, Harvard University Press, Cambridge, Mass., 1953 (2nd ed., 1961. Paperback: Harper Torchbooks, New York 1963), p. 148. In 'Whitehead and the Rise of Modern Logic', in *The Philosophy of Alfred North Whitehead*

(P. A. Schilpp, ed.), Northwestern University Press, Evanston and Chicago 1941, p. 142 n., Quine uses the same example to illustrate the breakdown of the substitutivity of identity in modal contexts.

[2] *From a Logical Point of View*, p. 152; *Word and Object*, pp. 197–198.

[3] Alonzo Church, Review of Quine's 'Notes on Existence and Necessity', in *Journal of Symbolic Logic* **8** (1943) 45–47.

[4] Alonzo Church, 'A Formulation of the Logic of Sense and Denotation', in *Structure, Method, and Meaning: Essays in Honor of Henry M. Sheffer* (ed. by Paul Henle, H. M. Kallen, and S. K. Langer), Liberal Arts Press, New York, 1951, pp. 3–24.

[5] Rudolf Carnap, *Meaning and Necessity*, University of Chicago Press, Chicago, 1947 (2nd. ed., with supplements, 1956).

[6] *Meaning and Necessity*, p. 184.

[7] Mainly in 'The Modes of Modality', *Acta Philosophica Fennica* **16** (1963) 65–81. Cf. also 'Modality as Referential Multiplicity', *Ajatus* **20** (1957) 49–64, 'Modality and Quantification', *Theoria* **27** (1961) 119–128, and 'Studies in the Logic of Existence and Necessity', *The Monist* **50** (1966) 55–76.

[8] Jaakko Hintikka, 'Individuals, Possible Worlds, and Epistemic Logic', *Noûs* **1** (1967) 38; cf. also Hintikka, 'Modality as Referential Multiplicity', p. 61.

[9] Cp. Hintikka, 'Individuals, Possible Worlds, and Epistemic Logic', pp. 55ff.

[10] Again, Church's logic of sense and denotation is not what I call a modal logic, since it has no opaque constructions.

[11] *Word and Object*, § 30 and § 31.

[12] Alonzo Church, Review of Quine's 'Whitehead and the Rise of Modern Logic', *Journal of Symbolic Logic* **7** (1942) 101.

[13] Arthur F. Smullyan, Review of Quine's 'The Problem of Interpreting Modal Logic', *Journal of Symbolic Logic* **12** (1947) 139–141.

[14] Arthur F. Smullyan, 'Modality and Description', *Journal of Symbolic Logic* **13** (1948) 35.

[15] Ruth Barcan Marcus, Review of Smullyan's 'Modality and Description', *Journal of Symbolic Logic* **13** (1948) 149–150.

[16] Frederic B. Fitch, 'The Problem of the Morning Star and the Evening Star', *Philosophy of Science* **16** (1949) 137–141.

[17] John Myhill, 'Problems arising in the Formalization of Intensional Logic', *Logique et Analyse* **1** (1958) 74–83.

[18] Richard Montague, 'Logical Necessity, Physical Necessity, Ethics, and Quantifiers', *Inquiry* **3** (1960) 259–269. (Delivered before the Annual Spring Conference in Philosophy, UCLA, May, 1955.)

[19] *From a Logical Point of View*, 2nd ed., p. 155. Cf. also 'Three Grades of Modal Involvement' (1953), p. 80, and 'Reply to Professor Marcus', p. 104.

SOME PROBLEMS ABOUT BELIEF

I

A number of problems pertaining to the logic of belief can be introduced by considering the following three statement forms:

1.	Jones believes that fa	Bfa
2.	$a = b$	$a = b$
3.	Jones does not believe that fb	$\sim Bfb$.[1]

Are such sequences of statements consistent? Faced with some examples we are tempted to say 'yes', with others 'no'. Yet it is by no means easy to see what the 'yes' examples have in common, nor what the 'no' examples have in common. Nor do the examples stay put. What seem to be the same examples wander from one category to the other.

This indicates that information not made explicit by the statements as they stand is guiding our decision. It also seems to require that the form

Jones believes that... $B...$

is ambiguous. Those who argue that there is such an ambiguity distinguished between an 'opaque' and a 'transparent' sense of 'believes'. If we represent these senses by "^oB" and "^tB" respectively, then the above sequence of statement forms represents ambiguously either the sequence schema

1a.	^oBfa
2a.	$a = b$
3a.	$\sim {}^oBfb$

or the sequence

1b.	^tBfa
2b.	$a = b$
3.	$\sim {}^tBfb$.

In accordance with the rationale in terms of which the distinction was

186

introduced, the first of these sequences would be consistent, the second inconsistent.

Let us focus our attention, for the moment, on the second. We note that if such sequences constitute 'inconsistent triads', then arguments of the form

$$^{t}Bfa$$
$$a = b$$
$$therefore, {}^{t}Bfb$$

will be valid. This suggests that it is legitimate to treat

$$^{t}Bfa$$

as a special case of the form

$$\varphi a$$

and the above argument form as a special case of the schema

$$\varphi a$$
$$a = b$$
$$therefore, \varphi b.$$

II

Let us now turn our attention to the opaque sense of 'believes'. It was characterized in terms of the consistency of the triad

$$^{o}Bfa$$
$$a = b$$
$$\sim {}^{o}Bfb$$

which amounts to the invalidity of the argument schema

$$^{o}Bfa$$
$$a = b$$
$$therefore, {}^{o}Bfb.$$

The question naturally arises (to those interested in the logic of belief) as to what additional premise or premises pertaining to a and b would have to be added to

$$^{o}Bfa$$
$$a = b$$

to derive the conclusion

therefore, ^{o}Bfb.

One obvious answer is

$^{o}B(a = b)$

Another line of thought which points to a sufficient, though not necessary, condition begins by introducing the form

Ka

to be read as

Jones knows who a is

in the strong sense that, to use Hintikka's phrase, Jones can "pick him out". We lay down the following axioms

$Ka . Kb \rightarrow : a = b \rightarrow K(a = b)$

$Ka . K(a = b) \rightarrow Kb$.

It is then plausible to suggest that the following arguments are valid:

^{o}Bfa	^{o}Bfa
$a = b$	$K(a = b)$
Ka	therefore, ^{o}Bfb.
Kb	
therefore, ^{o}Bfb	

III

Now it is clear that without sacrificing Leibniz' law,

^{o}Bfa

cannot be treated as, *prima facie*, could

^{t}Bfa

as a special case of

φa.

It should also be clear that the same is true of

Ka

if it is to serve the above purpose. For if we did so treat it, keeping Leibniz' law, arguments of the form

$$Kc$$
$$c = d$$
therefore, Kd

would be valid. It would follow that if a and b are each identical with someone Jones is able to pick out, then

$$°Bfa$$
$$a = b$$

would be inconsistent with

$$\sim °Bfb.$$

In other words, the argument schema

$$°Bfa$$
$$Kc$$
$$a = c$$
$$b = c$$
therefore, °Bfb

would be valid. And while this would not collapse the opaque sense of 'believes' into the transparent sense – unless we suppose that each person is identical with a person whom Jones can pick out – it would define a 'transparent' sense of 'Jones knows who a is' ("Ka") which would stand to the desired sense ("$°Ka$") as the transparent stands of 'believes' stands to the opaque sense. Furthermore it is clear that if we limit the persons we are going to consider in connection with the context

$$°Bf...$$

to persons of whom we are in a position to say that Jones knows who they are, the argument schema

$$°Bfa$$
$$a = b$$
therefore, °Bfb

would be derivatively valid in that to impose this limitation would be equivalent to adding the premises

$$^{\circ}Ka$$
$$^{\circ}Kb.$$

IV

Now if the concept of belief is ambiguous along the lines we have been considering, the ambiguity is surely of the kind described by Aristotle in connection with the term 'healthy'. That is to say, it is natural to look for a definition of one of the two senses in terms of the other. And, in view of the permissiveness of the transparent sense with respect to the mutual substitutability of expressions having an identical reference, it is natural to construe the opaque sense as primary and the transparent sense as a weakening of it.

To take this line is to search for a definition of the transparent sense in terms of the opaque sense. The criteria for the adequacy of such a definition would be that it accounts for the difference in the logical powers of the two senses which provided the initial rationale for distinguishing between them. The most plausible way of doing this is as follows:

$$^{t}Bfa =_{df} (Ex)\, x = a.^{\circ}Bfx.$$

If we assume, for the moment, that the definiens is well formed, and, more specifically, that the 'x' at the extreme right falls within the scope of the quantifier, then the argument schema

$$^{t}Bfa$$
$$a = b$$
$$therefore,\ ^{t}Bfb$$

would be valid, for, given the above definition schema, it would unpack into

$$(Ex)\, x = a.^{\circ}Bfx$$
$$a = b$$
$$therefore,\ (Ex)\, x = b.^{\circ}Bfx.$$

In other words, we would have accounted for the inconsistency of the triad

$$^{t}Bfa$$
$$a = b$$
$$\sim ^{t}Bfb$$

190

On the other hand, as the above qualification (that the definiens be well formed) makes clear, this move would clarify the transparent sense of 'believes' only if we presuppose an understanding of the opaque sense, and, in particular, of what is involved in the ability of the quantifier to bind the 'x' in

$$^oBfx.$$

This fact reminds us that serious problems arise when we attempt to construe the latter as having the form

$$\varphi x$$

which it must, if there is to be a variable to be quantified.

Furthermore, if the above definition of the transparent in terms of the opaque sense of 'believes' is to work, the values over which the 'x' ranges in the first conjunct of the definiens must be the same as that over which it ranges in the second.

If we keep Leibniz' law – and, like many others, I see no viable alternative – we are precluded from saying that the 'x' to the right ranges *without qualification* over individuals, for then the opaque sense would simply collapse into the transparent sense. Nor will it do to restrict the range to a subset of individuals, for then we won't get the degree of transparency we want the definition to yield. For the transparency we have been shooting at is one which permits unrestricted substitution of identicals, and this requires that the 'x' in the left-hand conjunct of

$$(Ex)\ x = a.\,^oBfx$$

range over all individuals. It is worth noting, in this connection, that when Hintikka offers a definition (p. 157 of *Knowledge and Belief*), which resembles the above, of a 'transparent' in terms of an 'opaque' sense of 'believe', the definition does not achieve the above purpose, for the range of the quantified variable is restricted to individuals known to the person whose beliefs are under consideration. Hintikka's claim to have defined "Quine's transparent sense" in terms of "the basic (opaque) sense plus quantification" (p. 156) is simply mistaken.

If we stick to the attempt to define a "strongly" transparent sense of 'believes' in terms of the opaque sense, along the above lines, we are faced with a dilemma. If our variable ranges over all individuals and if

191

we keep Leibniz' law, then the opaque sense collapses into the transparent sense. On the other hand, if we restrict the range to less than all individuals, we do not capture strong transparency. To put it in the form of a paradox, we want 'x' to range over all individuals without ranging over any! Is this possible? To any dyed in the wool modal logician, the answer is obvious. Let 'x' range over individual concepts. For if it ranges over *all* individual concepts it *a fortiori* ranges over all *realized* individual concepts, and hence *in a derivative sense* which, though it demands explication, is reasonably intuitive, over all individuals. The mechanics, if not the metaphysics, of the move is comparatively straightforward.

Let us therefore introduce designations for individual concepts by using boldface expressions of the kind we have been using to designate individuals. And let us introduce variables 'i' 'j' etc. for which they can be substituted.

We begin by noting that to the identity of individuals defined by the schema

$$a = b =_{\text{df}} (f)\, fa \equiv fb$$

corresponds what can properly be called the *material equivalence* of the corresponding individual concepts. For the definiendum

$$a = b$$

could have been written, with a substantial gain in philosophical perspicuousness, as

$$a \equiv b.$$

The gain would lie in the fact that by representing identity in a way which exhibits its connection with material equivalence, we would avoid the temptation to think of identity as a "relation" in the non-trivial sense in which we contrast relations with connectives. To take the Leibniz-Russell approach to identity seriously is to assimilate identity to such connectives as 'and' 'or' and 'not'. The endless puzzles about that 'funny' relation which everything has to itself would be short circuited.

Now the statement

$$\textbf{a } ME \textbf{ b}$$

is a statement about the individual concepts **a** and **b** which is true just in

case
$$a \equiv b, \text{ i.e. } a = b$$

is a true statement about the individuals a and b. Schematically

$$\mathbf{a} \, ME \, \mathbf{b} \leftrightarrow a = b$$

where the convention of using '$=$', where '$\equiv$' would be more perspicuous, has been followed, as it will be throughout the remainder of this essay.

Realized individual concepts can now be defined as those which are materially equivalent to some individual concept. Schematically,

$$Ra =_{\mathrm{df}} (Ei) \, i \, ME \mathbf{a} \, .$$

Given this apparatus, which is, of course, but a fragment of a neo-Fregean semantical theory[2], the definition of the fully transparent sense of 'believe' in terms of the opaque sense becomes

$${}^{t}Bf\mathbf{a} =_{\mathrm{df}} (Ei) \, i \, ME \, \mathbf{a} . \, {}^{o}Bfi \, .$$

How is the definiens to be read? It is obviously dangerous to begin

There exists an individual concept which ...

for this suggests falsely that the range of quantification is restricted to *realized* individual concepts. It is safer, as in so many other contexts, to fall back on the ordinary word "some", thus

Some individual concept is such that **it** is materially equivalent to a and Jones believes (in the opaque sense) that f **it**.

Note, incidentally, that the latter part of the transcription avoids the absurdity

... Jones believes (in the opaque sense) that **it** is f

for given that 'f' represents 'wise' we scarcely wish to say that Jones believes that a certain individual concept is wise.

Notice, also, that although both

$${}^{t}Bf\mathbf{a}$$

and

$${}^{o}Bf\mathbf{a}$$

are taken, as they must be for quantification to be appropriate, to have

193

the form

$$\varphi \dots$$

the substituends for '...' are either designations of individual concepts or variables having individual concepts for their range.[3]

It is clear that this new definition serves our original purpose. Thus, the argument schema

$${}^{t}Bf\mathbf{a}$$
$$a = b$$
$$\textit{therefore, } {}^{t}Bf\mathbf{b}$$

turns out to be valid, albeit derivatively; for, when fully spelled out, it becomes

$$(Ei)\ i\ ME\ \mathbf{a}.{}^{o}Bfi$$
$$a = b$$
$$\mathbf{a}\ ME\ \mathbf{b}$$
$$\textit{therefore, } (Ei)\ i\ ME\ \mathbf{b}.\,{}^{o}Bfi.$$

Notice that instead of the Leibniz principle to which we have been appealing, this argument mobilizes the closely related principle that expressions for materially equivalent individual concepts may be substituted for each other, *salva veritate*, in contexts of the form

$$i\ ME\ j.$$

It is the parallels between the identity of individuals and the material equivalence of individual concepts, and between the relevant principles of substitution, which generate the illusion that the transparent sense of 'believes' takes individuals as its argument and involves a direct appeal to the identity of individuals. It is only too easy to confuse

$${}^{t}Bf\mathbf{a}$$
$$a = b$$
$$\textit{therefore, } {}^{t}Bf\mathbf{b}$$

with

$${}^{t}Bfa$$
$$a = b$$
$$\textit{therefore, } {}^{t}Bfb.$$

On the other hand, the above definition does yield the full transparency which was our initial desideratum, for we can justify as *derivatively* valid the first of these two arguments, since, whenever the identity premise is available, so also is

a *ME* **b.**

V

The definition at which we have arrived brings with it a number of dividends. In the first place it throws light on the context

Jones knows who *a* is

We saw that the latter, which we represented as

$${}^oKa$$

cannot, consistently with Leibniz' law and the job it has to do, be construed as having the form

$$\varphi x$$

where 'x' ranges over individuals. Nor will it help to say that it ranges over those individuals which satisfy a certain condition. For when the condition is spelled out it turns out to be a matter of satisfying the function 'known to Jones'. Thus, '${}^oKa$' would escape Leibnizian transparency only if the same is true of 'known to Jones'. The original problem is simply shoved off to the informal level at which the restriction is imposed.

Essentially the same point stands out if we consider the argument, formulated in Hintikka's symbolism,

$$(Ex)\, K_j\, (xRa)$$
$$a = b$$
therefore, $(Ex)\, K_j\, (x\tilde{R}b).$

If we assume that

$$(Ex)\, K_j\, (xRa)$$

has the form

$$\varphi a$$

as we surely must if the position occupied by 'a' is to be accessible to quantification at all, the argument, though soundly Leibnizian, is clearly

195

unsound. On the other hand, if we add the condition that a and b be in Jones' ken in the sense that he "identifies" them, i.e. if, to use Hintikka's symbolism [4], we add the premises

$$Qa$$
$$Qb$$

we patch up the argument in a way which merely postpones the problem. For what of the argument

$$Qa$$
$$a = b$$
$$Qb.$$

If we allow this to be a valid appeal to Leibniz' principle, then the following would be valid:

Jones knows who Getty is	Qg
Getty is the richest man	$g = r$
Jones knows who the richest man is	Qr

Yet only for a 'transparent' sense of "knows who – is" ("can pick – out") which cannot do the job Hintikka desires it to do, would this argument be valid.

This point is obscured in Hintikka's treatment, because he equates

$$Qa$$

with

$$(Ex)\, K_j\, (x = a)$$

and only informally tells us that if the latter is to do its job there must be a primary domain of individuals identified by the knower such that if he knows anything to be identical with one of these, it in its turn is "a genuine individual", i.e. an individual identified by Jones. In short his specification of the range 'x' in opaque belief contexts as individuals known to the knower, explains the opacity of the context

$$Q\ldots$$

by presupposing it. Thus the inference

$$Qg$$
$$g = r$$
$$therefore,\ Qr$$

is ruled out on the grounds that when made explicit it has the form

$$(Ex) K_j (x = g)$$
$$g = r$$
$$therefore, (Ex) K_j (x = r)$$

and if the attempt is made to treat *this* as Leibniz-valid, we are reminded of the condition that 'x' ranges over individuals known to Jones, which amounts to saying that it ranges over individuals which satisfy Q. In other words, Leibniz' law is formally restricted in a way which presupposes the failure of Leibniz' law at the informal level.

If, now, we construe the context 'known to Jones' as having the form

$$^oK\mathbf{a}$$

and statements of this form as substitution instances of

$$^oKi,$$

the range of the variable is individual concepts, and the function is satisfied by those individual concepts in Jones repertoire which "pick out" individuals. No restriction need be placed on the individual concepts which constitute this range, for if we represent that the individual concept **a** is in Jones' conceptual repertoire (understanding or grasp) by

$$U\mathbf{a}$$

we can take it that '$K\mathbf{a}$' entails '$U\mathbf{a}$'.

On the other hand, we have been assuming that

$$K\mathbf{a}$$

entails

$$R\mathbf{a}$$

in other words that all "identifying" individual concepts are *realized* individual concepts. We can, however, remove the "success" connotation of

Jones knows who *a* is.

We can recognize that there is a legitimate sense in which Jones can identify people who do not exist. Used in this sense, '$^oK\mathbf{a}$' would no longer entail '$R\mathbf{a}$', and, where needed, the latter condition would have to be

197

explicitly added. In these terms

$$(Ei)\ Ri.^{\circ}Ki.^{\circ}Bfi$$

would say that

> Some individual concept is identifying, and such that Jones
> believes (in the opaque sense) f it,

whereas

$$(Ei)\ ^{\circ}Ki.^{\circ}Bfi$$

would simply tell us that

> Some individual concept is an identifying concept and Jones
> believes (in the opaque sense) f it.

It was pointed out in an earlier section that the transparent sense which Hintikka defines is not the fully transparent sense which Quine explores in *Word and Object*. What Hintikka captures is a transparency with respect to the identity of individuals *known to Jones*. In our symbolism, he is offering the definition

$$^{t}Bf\mathbf{a} =\ _{df}(Ei)\ ^{\circ}Ki.i\ ME\ \mathbf{a}.K(i=\mathbf{a}).^{\circ}Bfi.$$

The force of the restriction is to require that to get from

$$^{t}Bf\mathbf{a}$$

to

$$^{t}Bf\mathbf{b}$$

we need not only

$$\mathbf{a}\ ME\ \mathbf{b}$$

for which

$$a = b$$

would suffice, but also

$$^{\circ}K\mathbf{b}.$$

VI

Although it is generally agreed that, 'conversational implicatures' aside, knowledge is a special case of belief, Hintikka's account of belief is hardly more than an appendage to his account of knowledge. Since, as we have seen, his conviction that an account of quantification into knowledge contexts can interpret the range of the variables involved as individuals is an illusion, we are in a position to take seriously the implication of the idea that the range of variables in both knowledge and belief contexts is individual concepts.[5]

The first step is to admit quantification into belief contexts which involves only the trivial restriction that the individual concepts in question belong to Jones' repertoire, thus

$$(Ei) \ Ui. \ ^oB(i \ is \ wise)$$

where the condition 'Ui' is redundant. This formula would be a legitimate inference from both

$$^oB(Zeus \ is \ wise)$$

and

$$^oB(Socrates \ is \ wise).$$

To permit this has the obvious merit of taking into account the fact that we are willing to infer

Jones believes *with respect to* someone that he is wise

from

Jones believes that Zeus is wise.

The former (as we are regimenting it) must not be confused with

Jones believes *of* someone that he is wise.

Quine's linguistic intuitions correctly led him to appropriate the latter for the transparent sense of belief. In our symbolism

Jones believes *of* Socrates that he is wise

becomes

$$(Ei) \ i \ ME \ s. \ ^oB(wise \ s)$$

while

Jones believes *of* someone that he is wise

becomes

$$(Ej) \ j \ ME \ i. \ ^oB(wise \ i)$$

or, more simply

$$(Ei) \, Ri.°B(\text{wise } i).$$

On the other hand from

$$°B(\text{wise } \mathbf{z})$$

given the non-existence of Zeus, we are only able to draw the weaker conclusion

$$(Ei) \, °B(\text{wise } i)$$

which finds its closest counterpart in ordinary language as

Jones believes with respect to somebody (who may or may not be real) that he is wise.

It would thus seem that

Jones believes that someone is wise

can be construed either as

$$B((Ex) \, \text{wise } x)$$

or as

Jones believes *with respect to* someone that he is wise

and transcribed as

$$(Ei) \, °B(\text{wise } i).$$

VII

In a recent paper[6] Roderick Chisholm explores an argument which can be represented as follows:
Premises:

1.   George believes that the author of *Marmion* is Scotch
2.   George does not believe that the author of *Waverley* is Scotch
3.   The author of *Waverley* is identical with the author of *Marmion*
4.   For every x and every y, if x is identical with y then whatever is true of x is true of y
5.   For every x, if anyone believes that x has a certain property

F, then his believing that *x* is *F* is something that is true of *x*; and if he does not believe that *x* is *F*, then he is not believing that *x* is *F*, is also something that is true of *x*.

According to Chisholm these premises "seem to commit us to a contradictory conclusion", namely

There exists an *x* such that George believes that *x* is Scotch, and such that it is false that George believes that *x* is Scotch.

"To solve the problem", he writes, "we must show either that one of the [premises] is false, or that there is no justification for believing that the premises commit us to the conclusion". Chisholm undertakes to "propose a solution for this particular problem", and suggests that "if the solution is adequate, then, ... it may be generalized to take of other cases where Leibniz' law, in application to psychological contexts, seems to lead to similar difficulties". In constructing his solution Chisholm tells us that "we may think of 'George believes that' as being a type of modal operator and distinguish the case in which it modalizes an existential quantification *in sensu composito*, e.g. 'George believes that there exists an *x* such that *x* is honest', from that in which it modalizes such a quantification *in sensu diviso*, e.g., 'There exists an *x* such that George believes that *x* is honest'. He then notes that the first of the two statements cited as examples does not imply the second. "George may have a general faith in human nature and thus believe that there is an honest man, without being able to specify any particular person as a person whom he believes to be honest." He then affirms the general principle: "No belief-statement *in sensu composito* ... implies any belief-statement *in sensu diviso*." As he sees it, then, the initial problem is whether the first two premises are to be paraphrased *in sensu composito* or *in sensu diviso*. His answer is that "we should paraphrase [the first premise] as a disjunction of two statements, one *in sensu diviso* and the other *in sensu composito*". The second would therefore be paraphrased as the negation of such a disjunction. The premises thus become

1a. $(E1x) \, AuM(x) . B(x \text{ is } S)$ *or* $B((E1x) \, AuM(x) . x \text{ is } S)$.

and the second

2b. $\sim ((E1x) \, AuW(x) . B(x \text{ is } S))$ *and* $\sim B((E1x) \, AuW(x) . x \text{ is } S)$.

Chisholm then resolves the paradox, in effect, by pointing out that on the only alternative with respect to the truth or falsity of the disjuncts and/or conjuncts which makes the two premises consistent with the identity of the author of *Waverley* with the author of *Marmion* reduces them to

1c. $B((E1x)\,AuM(x).x \text{ is } S)$

2c. $\sim ((E1x)\,AuW(x).B(x \text{ is } S)) \text{ and } \sim B((E1x)\,AuW(x).x \text{ is } S)$.

Since the first conjunct of 2c is a negative existential, it is of no help, while from 1c together with the second conjunct of 2c the paradoxical conclusion could, he argues, be derived only if an existentially quantified belief-statement *in sensu diviso* could be derived from the corresponding statement *in sensu composito*, which he properly denies. Chisholm's argument is quite informal. In effect, by modeling his discussion on the scope ambiguity of negative sentences involving definite descriptions, his solution takes on an *ad hoc* character which obscures its connection with the issues raised by the simpler examples with which we began. Chisholm clearly commits himself to Leibniz' law and to the fifth premise, which he paraphrases as follows:

If something *x* is believed by a man to have a certain property *F*, then his believing that *x* is *F* is something which is true of *x*.

These commitments generate the puzzle with which we began.

In addition to its *ad hoc* character, Chisholm's solution has the additional disadvantage that it requires the second premise to be inconsistent with

> George believes (in the transparent sense) that the author of *Waverley* is Scotch

i.e. with

> George believes *of* the author of *Waverley* that he is Scotch

which it surely is not.

In laying down his "fundamental principle" Chisholm is clearly operating with an intuitive distinction between transparent and opaque belief *contexts*, but instead of interpreting this distinction as involving two *senses* of 'believes' he takes, as we have seen,

> George believes that the author of *Marmion* is Scotch

to be a disjunction of these two contexts. If we abandon this, as I believe we must, the fallacy can be resolved along more traditional lines by noting that it hinges on taking the initial premises to assert that the author of *Marmion* satisfies a certain function whereas the author of *Waverley* satisfies the contradictory function. Thus,

1d. $\quad \varphi m$
2d. $\quad \sim \varphi w$

According to our analysis, whether one construes the 'believes' to be transparent or opaque, quantification is in order, though the variable must be construed to range over individual concepts. If, however, we construe the premises as involving the transparent sense, they are inconsistent, and the fact that they lead to a contradiction, thus,

1e. $\quad {}^{t}B(\mathbf{m}$ is $S) \quad (Ei)\ i\ ME\ \mathbf{m}.{}^{o}B(i$ is $S)$
2e. $\quad \sim {}^{t}B(\mathbf{w}$ is $S) \quad \sim (Ei)\ i\ ME\ \mathbf{w}.{}^{o}B(i$ is $S)$
3. $\quad m = w$
4. $\quad \mathbf{m}\ ME\ \mathbf{w} \quad (Ei)\ i\ ME\ \mathbf{w}.{}^{o}B(i$ is $S)$
5. $\quad {}^{t}B(\mathbf{w}$ is $S)$

is no paradox.

On the other hand, from the premises interpreted in the opaque sense, thus

1f. $\quad {}^{o}B(\mathbf{m}$ is $S)$
2f. $\quad \sim {}^{o}B(\mathbf{w}$ is $S)$

which are equivalent, respectively, to

1g. $\quad (Ei)\ i = \mathbf{m}.{}^{o}B(i$ is $S)$
2g. $\quad (Ei)\ i = \mathbf{w}.{}^{o}B(i$ is $S)$

of which the former says *not* that some individual concept is *materially equivalent* to **m**, and such that George believes that Scotch **it**, but rather that some individual concept is *identical* with the individual concept **m** and such that George believes Scotch **it**. But to get the contradictory of 2f from this we must have the premise

$\mathbf{w} = \mathbf{m}$

and all we have is the weaker

$$w = m$$

which yields only

w ME **m**.

Even granted that

m ME **w**

yields

R**m** and R**w**

so that we can go from 1g to 1e and hence, by substitution, to

$$(Ei)\ i\ ME\ \mathbf{w}.°B\ (i\ \text{is}\ S)$$

we are not confronted by a contradiction, since the latter is quite consistent with

$$(Ei)\ i = \mathbf{w}. \sim °B\ (i\ \text{is}\ S).$$

In other words we cannot derive the properly formulated counterpart of Chisholm's

There exists an x such that George believes that x is Scotch and such that it is false that George believes that x is Scotch.

Pittsburgh

REFERENCES

[1] Since I shall limit myself to Jones' beliefs, I shall not bother to subscript the '*B*'. I shall also limit my attention to Jones' beliefs about persons.

[2] As a working hypothesis, the theory can be construed along the lines of *Meaning and Necessity*, for Quine seems to me absolutely right in his contention that Carnap's modal logic involves quantification over intensions and, in particular, individual concepts.

[3] If we were to represent 'it is true that *fa*' by

$$Tfa$$

it would be easy for the unwary to infer from its logical powers that the latter has the form

$$\varphi a.$$

However, if we assume that there is anything *like* such a function, we must, as in the case of belief, take the range of the variable to be individual concepts. As in the case of

204

belief we would distinguish between a primary and a secondary sense of 'truth'. If we distinguish them as '^oT' and '^tT', respectively, we would have

$$^tT\!f\mathbf{a} = {}_{\mathrm{df}}(Ei)\, i\; M\!E\mathbf{a} \cdot {}^oT\!f\!i.$$

In the case of 'truth' however, the 'opaque' sense entails the 'transparent' sense. As a result the distinction between

$$(Ei)\, i\; M\!E\mathbf{a} \cdot {}^oT\!f\!i$$

which can be read as "f-ness is true of $\mathbf{a}$", and

$$(Ei)\, i = \mathbf{a} \cdot {}^oT\!f\!i$$

which can be read "f-ness is true *with respect to* $\mathbf{a}$" becomes far less important as will be noted, than is the corresponding distinction in the case of belief.

[4] 'Individuals, Possible Worlds, and Epistemic Logic', *Noũs* 1 (1967), p. 35. Roughly, 'Qa' says that a is a 'genuine individual'. In Hintikka's system it connotes not only actual existence, but belonging to the range of variables in epistemic contexts which are bound by quantification from without.

[5] Of course, when one's concern is to explicate the circumstances under which belief that p (virtually) implies belief that q one may well limit ones attention to individual concepts which are (a) realized, (b) in the knower's or believer's repertoire, (c) are identifying concepts, or satisfy any combination of these conditions. But if the latter are made explicit (as they should be in any philosophically illuminating account) the fact remains that quantification into opaque contexts makes sense even when these restrictions do not hold.

[6] 'Leibniz's Law in Belief Contexts', in *Contributions to Logic and Methodology in Honor of J. M. Bocheński* (ed. by Anna Teresa Tymieniecka in collaboration with Charles Parsons), Amsterdam 1965, pp. 243–250.

DAVID KAPLAN

QUANTIFYING IN[1]

I

Expressions are used in a variety of ways. Two radically different ways in which the expression 'nine' can occur are illustrated by the paradigms:

(1)   Nine is greater than five,
(2)   Canines are larger than felines.

Let us call the kind of occurrence illustrated in (1) a *vulgar* occurrence, and that in (2) an *accidental* occurrence (or, following Quine, an orthographic accident). For present purposes we need not try to define either of these notions; but presumably there are no serious logical or semantical problems connected with occurrences of either kind. The first denotes, is open to substitution and existential generalization, and contributes to the meaning of the sentence which contains it. To the second, all such concerns are inappropriate.

There are other occurrences of the word 'nine', illustrated in

(3)   'Nine is greater than five' is a truth of Arithmetic,
(4)   It is necessary that nine is greater than five,
(5)   Hegel believed that nine is greater than five.

These diverge from the paradigm of vulgar occurrence (they fail the substitution test, the existential generalization test, and probably others as well), but they are not, at least to the untutored mind, clearly orthographic accidents either: for in them, the meaning of 'nine' seems, somehow, relevant. Let us call them *intermediate occurrences* and their contexts *intermediate contexts*.

These intermediate occurrences have come in for considerable discussion lately. Two kinds of analyses which have been proposed can be conveniently characterized as: (a) assimilating the intermediate occurrences to the accidental occurrences, and (b) assimilating the intermediate occurrences to the vulgar occurrences.

206

The former view, that the intermediate occurrences are to be thought of like accidental ones, I identify with Quine. Such a charge is slightly inaccurate; I make it chiefly for the sake of dramatic impact. My evidence, carefully selected, is that he has proposed in a few places that quotation contexts, as in (3), be thought of as single words and that 'believes that nine is greater than five' be thought of as a simple predicate. And that after introducing a dichotomous classification of occurrences of names into those which he terms 'purely referential' (our vulgar – his criterion is substitutivity) and those which he terms 'non-referential' (our intermediate and accidental) he writes, "We are not unaccustomed to passing over occurrences that somehow 'do not count' – 'mary' in 'summary', 'can' in 'canary'; and we can allow similarly for all non-referential occurrences of terms, once we know what to look out for." Further, his very terminology: 'opaque' for a context in which names occur non-referentially, seems to suggest an indissoluble whole, unarticulated by semantically relevant components.[2] But be that as it may, I shall put forward this analysis – the assimilation of intermediate occurrence to accidental ones – primarily in order to contrast its defeatist character with the sanguine view of Frege (and his followers) that we can assimilate the intermediate occurrences to vulgar ones.

II

The view that the occurrences of 'nine' in (3), (4), and (5) are accidental may be elaborated, as Quine has done, by contrasting (3), (4), and (5) with:

(6)   Nine is such that the result of writing it followed by 'is greater than five' is a theorem of Arithmetic,

(7)   Nine is such that necessarily it is greater than five,

(8)   Nine is such that Hegel believed it to be greater than five,

in which we put, or attempt to put, 'nine' into purely referential position. Quine would still term the occurrences of 'five' as non-referential; thus, the 'necessarily it is greater than five' in (7) might be thought of as an atomic predicate expressing some property of the number of baseball positions (assuming (7) to be true). And similarly for (6) and (8). I am not trying to say how we would "ordinarily" understand (6)–(8). I merely use these forms, in which the occurrence of 'nine' does not stand within the so-called opaque construction, as a kind of canonical form to express what must be carefully explained, namely that here we attribute a property to a certain number, and that the correctness of this attribution is independent of the manner in which we refer to the number. Thus (6), (7), and (8) are to be understood in such a way that the result of replacing the occurrence of 'nine' by any other expression denoting that number would not affect the truth value of the sentence. This includes replacement by a variable, thus validating existential generalization. In these respects (6)–(8) do indeed resemble (1).

But (3)–(5), which are to be understood in the natural way, are such that the result of substituting 'the number of planets' for the occurrences of 'nine' would lead from truth to falsehood (didn't Hegel "prove" that the number of planets = 5?). Thus, for Quine, these contexts are opaque, and the result of replacing the occurrences of 'nine' by the variable 'x' and prefixing '$\exists x$' would lead from truth to formulas of, at best, questionable import. In fact, Quine deems such quantification into an opaque context flatly 'improper'.[3] In these respects (3)–(5) resemble (2). Although the impropriety of substituting or quantifying on the occurrence of 'nine' in (2) is gross compared with that involved in applying the corresponding operations to (3)–(5), the view I am here characterizing would make this difference a matter of degree rather than of kind.

I will not expatiate on the contrast between (3)–(5) and (6)–(8), since Quine and others have made familiarity with this contrast a part of the conventional wisdom of our philosophical times. But note that (6)–(8) are not introduced as defined forms whose non-logical apparatus is simply that of (3)–(5), in the way in which

Exactly one thing is greater than five

can be defined in terms of the non-logical apparatus of (1). Instead (6)–(8) are introduced as new primitive forms.

Earlier I said that (3)–(5) should be understood in the natural way, whereas careful explanation was required for (6)–(8). But will careful explanation suffice? Will anything suffice? What we have done, or rather what we have sketched, is this: a certain skeletal language structure has been given, here using fragments of English, so of course an English reading is at once available, and then certain logical transformations have been pronounced valid. Predicate logic was conducted in this way before

Gödel and Tarski, and modal logic was so conducted before Carnap and others began to supply semantical foundations. The earlier method, especially as applied to modal logic (we might call it the run-it-up-the-axiom-list-and-see-if-anyone-deduces-a-contradiction method), seems to me to have been stimulated more by a compulsive permutations-and-combinations mentality than by the true philosophical temperament.

Thus, it just is not enough to describe the form (6) and say that the predicate expresses a property of numbers so that both Leibniz' law, and existential generalization apply. What property of numbers is this? It makes no sense to talk of the result of writing a number. We can write numerals and various other names of numbers but such talk as (6), in the absence of a theory of standard names, is surely based on confusion of mention and use.[4] One is tempted to make the same remark about (7), but in this case an alternative explanation is possible in a metaphysical tradition connected with so-called "Aristotelian essentialism". It is claimed that among the properties of a thing, e.g. being greater than 5, and numbering the planets, some hold of it necessarily, others only contingently. Quine has ably expounded the inevitability of this view of (7).[5]

In contrast to (6) and (7), we can put a strong prima facie case for the sensicalness of (8) by way of illustrative examples which indicate important uses of the form exemplified in (8) as compared with that of the form exemplified in (5). Russell mentions, in a slightly different context, the man who remarked to an acquaintance "I thought that your yacht was longer than it is". The correct rendering here is clearly in the style of (8), viz:

> The length of your yacht is such that I thought that your yacht was longer than that.

not in the style of (5);

> I thought that your yacht was longer than the length of your yacht.

In 'Quantifiers and Propositional Attitudes', Quine supports the use of (8) as against (5) by an ingenious use of existential quantification. He contrasts:

(9)   Ralph believes that someone is a spy,

in which the quantifier occurs within the opaque construction, as does the term in (5), with:

(10)   Someone is such that Ralph believes that he is a spy,

which is an existential generalization of a formula of the form (8). After pointing out that (9) may be rephrased as:

Ralph believes that there are spies,

Quine remarks, "The difference is vast; indeed, if Ralph is like most of us, [(9)] is true and [(10)] is false." In this connection recall that according to Quine's theory of referential opacity, (10) can not be obtained by existential generalization directly from a formula of the form (5) say,

Ralph believes that Ortcutt is a spy,

since the occurrence of the term to be generalized on is here assimilated to that of the orthographic accident and thus is not immediately open to such a move.

Let me sum up what I have called Quine's elaboration of the view that intermediate occurrences are to be assimilated to accidental ones. For those cases in which it is desired to make connections between what occurs within the opaque construction and what occurs without, a special new primitive form is introduced, parallel to the original, but containing one (or more than one) of the crucial terms in a purely referential position. Quine refers to the new form as expressing the *relational* sense of belief. The possibility of introducing such forms always exists and the style of their introduction seems uniform, but since they are primitive each such introduction must be supplied with an ad hoc justification (to the effect that the predicate or operator being introduced makes sense).

III

Let me turn now to the Fregean view that assimilates intermediate occurrences to vulgar ones. The brilliant simplicity of Frege's leading idea in the treatment of intermediate occurrences has often been obscured by a failure to separate that idea from various turgid details involved in carrying the program through in particular interesting cases. But theory must be served.

Frege's main idea, as I understand it, was just this. There are no *real* intermediate occurrences; the appearance of intermediacy created by apparent failures of substitutivity and the like is due to confusion about what is denoted by the given occurrence. Frege here calls our attention to an implicit assumption made in testing for substitutivity and the like. Namely, that a denoting expression must *always* have its usual denotation, and, *a fortiori*, that two expressions must have the same denotation in a given context if they usually (i.e. in most contexts) have the same denotation.

But we are all familiar with many counter-examples to the assumption that a name always has its usual denotation. Consider:

(11)   Although F.D.R. ran for office many times, F.D.R. ran on television only once.

The natural analysis of (11) involves pointing out that the name 'F.D.R.' is ambiguous, and that in the second clause it denotes a television show rather than a man. Substitutions or any other logical operations based on the assumption that the name has here its usual denotation are pointless and demonstrate nothing. But transformations based on a *correct* analysis of the name's denotation *in this context* will reveal the occurrence to be vulgar. I call this the natural analysis, but it is of course possible for a fanatical mono-denotationalist to insist that his transformations have shown the context:

... ran on television only once

to be opaque, and so to conclude that the second occurrence of 'F.D.R.' in (11) is not purely referential. This view may be expressed moderately, resulting only in an insistence that (11) is improper unless the second clause is rewritten as:

the television show named 'F.D.R.' ran on television only once.

Often when there is a serious possibility of confusion, we conform to the practice (even if not the theory) of the fanatical mono-denotationalist and do introduce a new word, add a subscript, or put the original in bold face, italics, or quotation marks. It is often good practice to continue to so mark the different uses of an expression, even when there is little possibility of confusion. Discovering and marking such ambiguities plays a considerable and useful role in philosophy (some, not I, would say it is the essence of philosophy), and much of what has proved most engaging and at the same time most fruitless in logical theory might have been avoided had the first 25 years of this century not seen a lapse from Frege's standards of mention and use. It would be unwary of us to suppose that we have now caught all such ambiguities. Thus, we should not leap to conclusions of opacity.

I indicated in the case of the fanatical mono-denotationalist how it is possible to trade a finding of opacity for one of ambiguity. Frege attempts his assimilation of intermediate occurrences to vulgar ones by indicating (some would say, postulating) ambiguities where others have seen only opacity. It is not denied that the ambiguities involved in the Fregean analysis are far more subtle than that noted in (11), but on his analysis the difference is seen as a matter of degree rather than of kind.

Frege referred to intermediate occurrences as *ungerade* (indirect, oblique). And the terminology is a natural one, for on his conception such an occurrence does not refer directly to its usual denotation but only, at best, indirectly by way of some intermediate *entity* such as a sense or an expression. I will return to this subject later. For now just notice that occurrences which Quine would call purely referential, Frege might call standardly referential; and those in contexts Quine would call referentially opaque, Frege might call non-standardly referential, but in either case for Frege the occurrences are fully referential. So we require no special non-extensional logic, no restrictions on Leibniz' law, on existential generalization, etc., except those attendant upon consideration of a language containing ambiguous expressions. And even these can be avoided if we follow the practice of the fanatical mono-denotationalist and require linguistic reform so that distinct uses of expressions are marked by some distinction in the expressions themselves. This feature of a development of Frege's doctrine has been especially emphasized by Church.[6]

This then is Frege's treatment of intermediate contexts – obliquity indicates ambiguity. This doctrine accounts in a very natural way for the well-known logical peculiarities of intermediate contexts, such as the failure of substitutivity, existential generalization, etc.

The difficulties in Frege's treatment appear in attempting to work out the details – details of the sort: exactly what *does* 'nine' denote in (3)–(5)? Frege's treatment of oblique contexts is often described as one according to which expressions in such contexts denote their ordinary sense or meaning or intension (I here use these terms interchangeably). But this is a bad way of putting the matter for three reasons. (1) It is, I believe, historically inaccurate. It ignores Frege's remarks about quotation marks (see below) and other special contexts. (2) It conflates two separate principles: (a) expressions in oblique contexts don't have their ordinary denotation (which is true), and (b) expressions in oblique contexts denote their ordinary sense (which is not, in general, true). And (3) in focussing attention too rapidly on the special and separate problems of intensional logic, we lose sight of the beauty and power of Frege's general method of treating oblique contexts. We may thus lose the motivation that that general theory might provide for an attack on the problems of the special theory. My own view is that Frege's explanation, by way of ambiguity, of what appears to be the logically deviant behavior of terms in intermediate contexts is so theoretically satisfying that if we have not yet discovered or satisfactorily grasped the peculiar intermediate objects in question, then we should simply continue looking.

There is, however, a method which may assist in the search. Look for something denoted by a compound, say, a sentence, in the oblique context. (In ordinary contexts sentences are taken to denote their own truth values and to be intersubstitutable on that basis.) And then using the fundamental principle: the denotation of the compound is a function of the denotation of the parts, look for something denoted by the parts. It was the use of this principle which, I believe, led to Carnap's discovery of individual concepts[7], and also led Frege to the view that quotation marks produce an oblique context within which each component expression denotes itself[8] (it is clear in quotation contexts what the whole compound denotes).

Frege's view of quotation contexts would allow for quantification into such contexts, but of course we would have to quantify over expressions (since it is expressions that are denoted in such contexts), and we would have to make some provision to distinguish when a given symbol in such a context is being used as a variable and when it is being used as a constant, i.e. to denote itself. This might be done by taking some distinctive class of symbols to serve as variables.

Let us symbolize Frege's understanding of quotation marks by using forward and backward capital F's. (Typographical limitations have forced elimination of the center horizontal bar of the capital F's.) Then, using Greek letters for variables ranging over expressions we can express such truths as:

(12) $\exists \alpha [\ulcorner \alpha$ is greater than five$\urcorner$ is a truth of arithmetic].[9]

Such is Frege's treatment of quotation marks: it seems to me more interesting and certainly much more fruitful (for the development of any theory in which quotation contexts are at all common) than the usual orthographic accident treatment according to which the quotation marks seal off the context, which is treated as a single indissoluble word. And it is well known that for serious theoretical purposes, quotation marks (under the conventional treatment) are of little use.

The ontological status of meanings or senses is less well settled than that of expressions. But we can again illustrate the principle involved in searching for the intermediate entities, and perhaps even engender an illusion of understanding, by introducing some symbolic devices. First, in analogy to the conventional use of quotation marks, I introduce meaning marks. Their use is illustrated in the following:

(13)   The meaning of 'brother' = ^{m}male sibling^m.

Now we can adapt the idea used in producing (12) to meaning marks, so as to produce a Fregean interpretation of them. The context produced by the meaning marks will then not be thought of as referentially opaque but rather such that each expression in such a context will denote its own meaning. Quantification in is permitted, but restricted of course to quantification over meanings. Following the earlier pattern, let us symbolize the new meaning marks with forward and backward capital M's. Using italic letters for variables ranging over meanings, we can express such truths as:

(14) $\exists a \exists b [^M a$ kicked $b^M = ^M b$ was kicked by $a^M]$

I leave to the reader the problem of making sense of (12)–(14).

This comparison of meaning marks with quotation marks also allows

214

me to make another point relevant to Quine's 'Quantifiers and Propositional Attitudes'. In his section IV, Quine suggests that by a harmless shift in idiom we can replace talk of meanings by talk of expressions, thus achieving ontological security. I agree, but the parallel can be exploited in either direction: as suggested by the introduction of meaning marks, we might also try to replace talk of expressions by talk of meanings, thus achieving ontological insight. These structural parallels are most helpful in constructing a logic of intensions.[10]

V

We have finished comparing the treatments of (3)–(5) with respect to the two main analyses of intermediate occurrences: assimilation to orthographic accident versus assimilation to vulgar occurrence. The forms involved in (6)–(8) were introduced in connection with what I called Quine's elaboration of the first line. Now what can be done in this direction following Frege's line? The purpose of the new forms in (6)–(8) is to get an expression out from an accidental position to a vulgar one; or, in Quine's terminology, to move a term from an opaque context to a purely referential position. There should be no problem here on Frege's theory, because what is opaque for Quine is already fully referential for Frege. Thus the term is in a fully referential position in the first place. But this will not quite satisfy the demands of (6)–(8), because the term in question does not denote the right thing.

At this point it will be useful to reformulate (3)–(8) (or at least (4), (5), (7), and (8)) so as to make explicit what the objects of belief and necessity are. In so doing we take a step along Frege's path, for the non-substitutability of one true sentence for another in such contexts would indicate to Frege an ambiguity in both of them: the sentences lack their usual denotation, a truth value, and instead denote some other entity. Before saying what, note that the necessity symbol will stand for a property – of something or other – and the belief symbol will stand for a two-place relation – between a person and something or other. (This in contrast to treating the necessity symbol simply as a 1-place referentially opaque sentential connective and similarly for belief.) Quine takes the step in Frege's direction in the article under discussion and favors it in the sister article 'Three Grades of Modal Involvement'. So I take it here.

Now what shall the sentences denote? For my present purposes it will suffice to take the ontologically secure position and let them denote expressions, in particular, themselves.[11] Making this explicit, we rewrite (4) and (5) as:

(15)   N 'nine is greater than five'

(16)   Hegel **B** 'nine is greater than five'

On the usual reading of quotation marks, (15) and (16) still basically formulate the non-Fregean view, with the referential opacity now charged against the quotes. Keeping in mind that the shift to (7) and (8) was for the purpose of moving 'nine' to a purely referential position, we can rewrite (7) and (8) as:

(17)   **Nec** ('x is greater than five', nine)

(which may be read: 'x is greater than 5' is necessarily true of nine), and

(18)   Hegel **Bel** ('x is greater than five', nine).

Here the symbol for necessity becomes a two-place predicate and that for belief a three-place predicate. 'x is greater than five' stands for a compound predicate, with the bold face letter '**x**' used only as a *place holder* to indicate subject position. The opacity of quotation marks deny such place holders a referential position in any **Nec** or **Bel** context. '**Nec**' and '**Bel**' are intended to express Quine's relational sense of necessity and belief.[12]

Frege would reformulate (15) and (16) as:

(19)   N ⌜nine is greater than five⌝.

(20)   Hegel **B** ⌜nine is greater than five⌝.

Notice that we can use the same predicates as in (15) and (16) since

⌜nine is greater than five⌝ = 'nine is greater than five'

just as

$$(3 \times 10^2) + (6 \times 10^1) + (8 \times 10^0) = 368.$$

It should now be clear that although the occurrences of 'nine' in (19) and (20) are fully referential, (19) and (20) won't do for the purposes of (17) and (18), because the occurrences of 'nine' in (17) and (18) refer to quite a different entity. Combining (17) with:

(21)   Nine numbers the planets,

we derive:

(22)   ∃y [y numbers the planets & **Nec** ('**x** is greater than five', y)].

But (19) and (21) seem to yield only:

∃y [y numbers the planets & N ⌜nine is greater than five⌝],

in which the quantifier binds nothing in the necessity context, or:

∃α [α numbers the planets & N ⌜α is greater than five⌝],

which is false because the planets are not numbered by an expression (recall our conventions about Greek variables).

Thus the Fregean formulations appear to lack the kind of recurrence of a variable both within and without the necessity context that is characteristic of quantified modal logic and that appears in (22). But this difficulty can be considerably mitigated by taking note of the fact that though the number nine and the expression 'nine' are distinct entities, there is an important relationship between them. The second denotes the first. We can follow Church[6] by introducing a denotation predicate, 'Δ', into our language, and so restore, at least in an *indirect* way (recall Frege's indirect reference by way of intermediate entities) the connection between occurrences of an expression within and without the modal context, as in:

(23)   ∃y [y numbers the planets & ∃α($\Delta(\alpha, y)$ &
              N ⌜α is greater than five⌝)].

I propose (23), or some variant, as Frege's version of (22); and

(24)   ∃α [$\Delta(\alpha, \text{nine})$ & N ⌜α is greater than five⌝),

or some variant, as Frege's version of (17). (We shall return later to the variants.) (23) and (24) may not be as exciting as (22) and (17), but neither do they commit us to essentialism. It may well be that (24), and its variants, supply all the connection between occurrences of expressions within and without modal contexts as can sensibly be allowed.

When I summed up Quine's elaboration of the orthographic accident theory of intermediate occurrences I emphasized the fact that to move an expression in an opaque construction to referential position, a new *primitive* predicate (such as '**Nec**' and '**Bel**' of (17) and (18)) had to be introduced and supplied with an interpretation. In contrast, the same effect is achieved by Frege's method using only the original predicates plus logical signs, including 'Δ', and of course the ontological decomposition involved in the use of the Frege quotes.

Turning now to belief I propose:

(25) $\exists \alpha [\Delta(\alpha, \text{nine}) \,\&\, \text{Hegel } \mathbf{B} \ulcorner \alpha \text{ is greater than five} \urcorner]$,

or some variant, as Frege's version of Quine's (18).

VI

If we accept (25) as the interpretation of Quine's (18), we can justify a crucial form of inference he seems to consider valid and explain certain seemingly paradoxical results which he accepts.

Quine recites the following story.

There is a certain man in a brown hat whom Ralph has glimpsed several times under questionable circumstances on which we need not enter here; suffice it to say that Ralph suspects he is a spy. Also there is a gray-haired man, vaguely known to Ralph as rather a pillar of the community, whom Ralph is not aware of having seen except once at the beach. Now Ralph does not know it, but the men are one and the same.

Quine then poses the question, "Can we say of this *man* (Bernard J. Ortcutt, to give him a name) that Ralph believes him to be a spy?" The critical facts of the story are summarized in what we would write as:

(26)   Ralph **B** 'the man in the brown hat is a spy',

(27)   Ralph **B** 'the man seen at the beach is not a spy',

(28)   the man in the brown hat = the man seen at the beach = Ortcutt.

Quine answers his own query by deriving what we would write as:

(29)   Ralph **Bel** ('x is a spy', the man in the brown hat)

from (26). He says of this move, "The kind of exportation which leads from [(26)] to [(29)] should doubtless be viewed in general as implicative."[13] Now our versions of (26) and (29) are:

(30)   Ralph **B** ⌜the man in the brown hat is a spy⌝,

(31) $\exists\alpha[\Delta(\alpha,$ the man in the brown hat) & Ralph **B** ⌜α is a spy⌝].

And (31) certainly is implied by (30) and the nearly analytic truth:

Δ('the man in the brown hat', the man in the brown hat).[14]

We thus justify exportation.

In discussing a seeming paradox Quine notes that expotation will also lead from (27) to:

Ralph **Bel** ('x is not a spy', the man seen at the beach)

and hence, by (28), to:

(32)   Ralph **Bel** ('x is not a spy', Ortcutt).

Whereas (29) and (28) yield:

(33)   Ralph **Bel** ('x is a spy', Ortcutt).

Thus, asserts Quine,

[(32)] and [(33)] both count as true. This is not, however, to charge Ralph with contradictory beliefs. Such a charge might reasonably be read into:

[(34) Ralph **Bel** ('x is a spy and x is not a spy', Ortcutt),]

but this merely goes to show that it is undesirable to look upon [(32)] and [(33)] as implying [(34)].

At first blush it may appear that avoidance of that undesirable course (looking upon (32) and (33) as implying (34)) calls for the most intense kind of concentration and focus of interest. In fact one may be pessimistically inclined to take the easy way out and simply dispose of (32), (33), (34) and any other assertions involving **Bel** as nonsense. But, as Quine says, "How then to provide for those indispensable relational statements of belief, like 'There is someone whom Ralph believes to be a spy'.?"

Fortunately our versions of **Bel** again conform to Quine's intuitions. (32), (33) and (34) go over respectively into:

(35) $\exists\alpha[\Delta(\alpha,$ Ortcutt) & Ralph **B** ⌜α is not a spy⌝],

(36) $\exists\alpha\,[\Delta(\alpha,\,\text{Ortcutt})\,\&\,\text{Ralph }\mathbf{B}\,\ulcorner\alpha\text{ is a spy}\urcorner]$,

(37) $\exists\alpha\,[\Delta(\alpha,\,\text{Ortcutt})\,\&\,\text{Ralph }\mathbf{B}\,\ulcorner\alpha\text{ is a spy and }\alpha\text{ is not a spy}\urcorner]$

which clearly verify Quine's claims, even in the presence of the suppressed premise:

$$\forall\alpha\forall\beta\,[\text{Ralph }\mathbf{B}\,\ulcorner\alpha\text{ is a spy}\urcorner\,\&\,\text{Ralph }\mathbf{B}\,\ulcorner\beta\text{ is not a spy}\urcorner\rightarrow$$
$$\text{Ralph }\mathbf{B}\,\ulcorner\alpha\text{ is a spy and }\beta\text{ is not a spy}\urcorner]$$

VII

So far so good. But further exploration with our version of **Bel** suggests that the rule of exportation fails to mesh with the intuitive ideas that originally led Quine to the introduction of **Bel**. And I believe that our version will also allow us to see more clearly exactly what problems lay before us if we are to supply a notion answering to these motivating intuitions. As I hope later developments will show, there are a number of different kinds of counter-cases which could be posed. I will only develop one at this point.

Suppose that the situation is as stated in (9). We would now express (9) as:

(38)   Ralph **B** '$\exists y\ y$ is a spy'.

Believing that spies differ widely in height, Ralph believes that one among them is shortest. Thus,

(39)   Ralph **B** 'the shortest spy is a spy'.

Supposing that there is in fact one shortest spy, by exportation (39) yields:

(40)   Ralph **Bel** ('x is a spy', the shortest spy)

which, under the same supposition, by existential generalization yields:

(41) $\exists y$ Ralph **Bel** ('x is a spy', y).

And (41) currently expresses (10). But (10) was originally intended to express a fact which would interest the F.B.I. (recall Quine's comment that if Ralph is like most of us, (10) is false), and we would not expect the interest of that organization to be piqued by Ralph's conviction that no two spies share a size.

Two details of this case can be slightly improved. First, the near analyticity of Ralph's crucial belief, as expressed in (39), can be eliminated by taking advantage of Ralph's belief that all members of the C.P.U.S.A. (none of which are known to him) are spies. Second, we can weaken the assumption of Ralph's special ideas about spy sizes by using only the well-known fact that two persons can not be born at exactly the same time at exactly the same place (where the place of birth is an interior point of the infant's body). Given any four spatial points a, b, c, d not in a plane, we can use the relations: t_1 is earlier than t_2, and p_1 is closer to $a(b, c, d)$ than p_2 is, to order all space time points. We can then form such names as 'the least spy' with the meaning: ^{m}that spy whose spatio-temporal location at birth precedes that of all other spies^m.

Details aside, the point is that exportation, as represented in our current version of **Bel**, conflicts with the intention that there be a 'vast' difference between (9) and (10). Still, I am convinced that we are on the right track. That track, roughly speaking, is this: instead of trying to introduce a new primitive relation like Quine's **Bel**, we focus on trying to define it (or something as close to it as we can sensibly come, remember modal logic) using just the dyadic **B** plus other logical and semi-logical apparatus such as quantifiers, Δ, etc. and also possibly other seemingly more fundamental epistemological notions.

Some years ago I thought that this task was hopeless and took basically the same attitude toward such quantified belief contexts as Quine takes toward quantified modal logic.[15] At that earlier time I used to argue with my colleague, Montgomery Furth, who shares my attitude toward Frege's theory, about the meaningfulness of such quantifications in as in (10). (This was after noticing the difficulty, indicated above, in our current analysis.[16]) Furth suggested that a solution might lie in somehow picking out certain kinds of names as being required for the exportation. But this just seemed essentialism all over again and we gave up. Although still uncertain that (10) makes sense, I think I can show that it comes to something like what Furth had in mind. Indeed, the analogies between the relational senses of belief and necessity are so strong that I have often wondered why Quine's scepticism with regard to **Nec** did not extend to **Bel**.

There is even an inadequacy in our proposed analysis, (24), of **Nec** parallel to that displayed for our proposed analysis, (25), of **Bel**. Although our analysis of **Nec** avoids essentialism, it also avoids rejecting:

(42)   **Nec** ('x = the number of planets', nine),

which comes out true on the understanding:

(43) $\exists\alpha(\Delta(\alpha, \text{nine}) \,\&\, N^\ulcorner\alpha = \text{the number of planets}^\urcorner)$

in view of the facts that

$\qquad$ $N^\ulcorner$the number of planets = the number of planets$^\urcorner$

and

$\qquad$ Δ('the number of planets', nine).

In a sense, we have not avoided essentialism but only inessentialism, since so many of nine's properties become essential. Small consolation to know of our essential rationality if each blunder and error is equally ingrained.

The parallel inadequacies of our versions of **Nec** and **Bel** are now apparent. Our analyses credit nine with an excess of essence and put Ralph *en rapport* with an excess of individuals.

VIII

What is wanted is "a frankly inequalitarian attitude toward various ways of specifying the number [nine]".[17] This suggests to me that we should restrict our attention to a smaller class of names; names which are so intimately connected with what they name that they could not but name it. I shall say that such a name *necessarily denotes* its object, and I shall use 'Δ_N' to symbolize this more discriminating form of denotation.

Such a relation is available; based on the notion of a *standard name*. A standard name is one whose denotation is fixed on logical, or perhaps I should say linguistic, grounds alone. Numerals and quotation names are prominent among the standard names.[18] Such names do, in the appropriate sense, necessarily denote their denotations.

Russell and some others who have attempted to treat proper names of persons as standard names have emphasized the purely referential function of such names and their apparent lack of descriptive content. But consideration of the place value system of arabic numerals and our conventions for the construction of quotation names of expressions should convince us that what is at stake is not pure reference in the absence of any descriptive structure, but rather reference freed of *empirical* vicissitudes. Numbers and expressions, like every other kind of entity, can be named by names which are such that empirical investigation is required to determine their denotations. 'The number of planets' and '9' happen to denote the same number. The former might, under other circumstances or at some other time, denote a different number, but so long as we hold constant our conventions of language, '9' will denote the same number under all possible circumstances. To wonder what number is named by the German 'die Zahl der Planeten' may betray astronomical ignorance, but to wonder what number is named by the German 'Neun' can indicate only linguistic incompetence.[19]

$\Delta_N(\alpha, x)$ cannot be analyzed in terms of the analyticity of some sentence of the form $\Delta(---, ...)$;
since:

$$\Delta(\text{'the number of planets', the number of planets})$$

is analytic, but 'the number of planets' is not a standard name of the number of planets (viz: nine), and

$$\Delta(\text{'9', the number of planets})$$

is not analytic, although '9' is a standard name of that number. We have in Δ_N a relation that holds between the standard name and the number itself, independent of any particular way of specifying the number. Thus there is a certain intimacy between '9' and 9, lacking between 'the number of planets' and the number of planets, which allows '9' to go proxy for 9 in assertions of necessity.

There is a sense in which the finite ordinals (which we can take the entities here under discussion to be) find their essence in their ordering. Thus, names which reflect this ordering in an *a priori* way, as by making true statements of order analytic, capture all that is essential to these numbers. And our careless attitude toward any intrinsic features of these numbers (e.g. whether zero is a set, and if so whether it has any members) suggests that such names may have captured all there is to these numbers.[20] I am less interested in urging an explanation of the special intimacy between 'nine' and nine, than in noting the fact. The phenomenon is widespread, extending to expressions, pure sets of finite rank, and others of their ilk. I would require any adequate explanation to generalize so as to handle all such cases, and I should hope that such an explanation would also support the limitations which I suggest below on the kinds of entities eligible for standard names.[21]

The foregoing considerations suggest simple variants for our current Fregean versions of (17) and (42). We replace (24) with:

$$\exists\alpha(\Delta_N(\alpha, \text{ nine}) \& N \ulcorner\alpha \text{ is greater than five}\urcorner)$$

as our analysis of (17), and we replace (43) with:

$$\exists\alpha(\Delta_N(\alpha, \text{ nine}) \& N \ulcorner\alpha = \text{the number of planets}\urcorner)$$

as our analysis of (42). According to the reformed analyses, (17) and (42) come out respectively as true and false, which accords much better with our intuitions and may even satisfy the essentialist.[22] All, it is hoped, without a lapse into irreducible (though questionable) metaphysical assumptions.

There are, however, limitations on the resort to standard names. Only abstract objects can have standard names, since only they (and not all of them) lack that element of contingency which makes the rest of us liable to failures of existence. Thus, Quine can have no standard name, for he might not be. And then what shall his standard name name? Quine's singleton, {Quine}, though abstract, is clearly no better off.

Numerals are reliable; they always pick out the same number. But to suppose a standard name for Quine would presuppose a solution to the more puzzling problem of what features to take into account in determining that an individual of one possible world is "the same person" as that of another. Often when the worlds have a common part, as when we consider alternative futures to the present, the individual(s) can be traced back to the common part by the usual continuity conditions and there compared. But for individuals not extant during an overlap such techniques are unavailing. It seems that such radically disjoint worlds are sometimes contemplated by modal logicians. I am not here passing final judgment but only remarking the relevance of a second difference between Quine and Nine: namely, that he presents a very real problem of trans-world identification while it does not.

Thus the device of using standard names, which accounts nicely for my

224

own intuitions regarding the essential properties of numbers, appears to break down when set to discriminating essential properties of persons. I am consoled by the fact that my own intuitions do not assign essential properties to persons in any broad metaphysical sense, which is not to say that quantified modal logic can have no interesting interpretation when trans-world identifications are made from the point of view of a frankly special interest.

IX

All this on **Nec** was aimed toward analogy with **Bel** and a charge of inconsistent scepticism against Quine. We have patched our first version of **Nec** with a more discriminating sense of denotation. The same trick would work for **Bel**, if Ralph would confine his cogitations to numbers and expressions. If not, we must seek some other form of special intimacy between name and object which allows the former to go proxy for the latter in Ralph's cognitive state.

I believe that the fundamental difficulty with our first version of **Bel** is that Δ gave us a relation between name and object in which Ralph played no significant role. Supposing all speakers of English to have available approximately the same stock of names (i.e. singular terms), this puts us all *en rapport* with the same persons. But the interesting relational sense of belief, and the one which I suppose Quine to have been getting at with (10), is one which provides Ralph with access to some but not all persons of whom he can frame names. What we are after this time is a three-place relation between Ralph, a name (which I here use in the broad sense of singular term) α, and a person x. For this purpose I will introduce two special notions: that of a name α being *of x* for Ralph, and that of a name being *vivid*, both of which I will compare with the notion of a name *denoting x*.

Let us begin by distinguishing the *descriptive content* of a name from the *genetic character* of the name as used by Ralph. The first goes to user-independent features of the name, the second to features of a particular user's acquisition of certain beliefs involving the name. It is perhaps easiest to make the distinction in terms not of names but of pictures, with consideration limited to pictures which show a single person. Those features of a picture, in virtue of which we say it resembles or is a likeness of a particular person, comprise the picture's descriptive content. The

225

genetic character of a picture is determined by the causal chain of events leading to its production. In the case of photographs and portraits we say that the picture is *of* the person who was photographed or who sat for the portrait. The same relation presumably holds between a perception and the perceived object.[23] This relation between picture and person clearly depends entirely on the genetic character of the picture. Without attempting a definition, we can say that for a picture to be *of* a person, the person must serve significantly in the causal chain leading to the picture's production and also serve as object for the picture. The second clause is to prevent all of an artist's paintings from being *of* the artist. I will shortly say a bit more about how I understand this relation, which I designate with the italicized '*of*'.

The "user-independence" of the descriptive content of a picture lies in the fact that "identical" pictures, such as two prints made from a single negative, will resemble all the same persons. In this sense, the descriptive content of a picture is a function of what we might call the picture-type rather than the picture-token. The "user-dependent" nature of the genetic character of a picture lies in the fact that "identical" paintings can be such that they are *of* different persons (e.g. twins sitting separately for portraits). Thus the genetic character of a picture is a function only of the picture-token. In order to accommodate genesis, I use 'picture' throughout in the sense of 'picture-token'.

Armed with *resemblance* and *of*-ness, let me recite just a few of the familiar facts of portraiture. First, not all pictures *of* a person resemble that person. Of two recent pictures taken of me, one resembles Steve Allen and the other resembles nothing on earth. Secondly, not all pictures which resemble a person are *of* that person. It is obvious that a picture *of* one twin will, if it resembles the twin it is *of*, also resemble the other twin. What is more interesting is that a picture which resembles a person may not be *of* any person at all. My camera may have had a hallucination due to light leaks in its perceptual system. Similarly, if I have drawn my conception of how the typical man will look in one million years, even if a man looking like that now exists, my picture is not *of* him (unless he sat as a model or played some other such role). Thirdly, a picture may be *of* more than one person, as when, by the split mirror technique, we obtain a composite photograph showing one man's head on another man's body. Indeed, in summary, a single picture may be *of* no one, one person, or many persons, while resembling no one, one person, or many persons, with any degree of overlap between those whom it is *of* and those whom it resembles. Of course, if photographs did not frequently, indeed usually, resemble their subjects, they could not serve many of the purposes for which we use them. Still, on occasion, things can and do go awry, and a bad photograph of one is yet a photograph *of* one.

I turn now to cases in which the causal chain from object to picture is relatively indirect. If one or several witnesses describe the criminal to a police artist who then constructs a picture, I shall say that it is a picture *of* the criminal, even when after such a genesis the resulting picture has quite ceased to resemble the criminal. Similarly, had a photograph of Julius Caesar been xeroxed, and the xerox copy televised to a monastery, where it was copied by a monk, and so was reproduced down through the ages, I would call the resulting copy, no matter how distorted, no matter who, if anyone, it resembled, a picture *of* Julius Caesar.[24]

A police artist's reconstruction of Santa Claus, based on a careful reading of the poem *The Night Before Christmas*, is not a picture *of* anyone no matter how many people make themselves up so that it exactly resembles them, and no matter whether the artist regards the poem as fact or fiction. Even if in combining facial features of known statistical frequencies the artist correctly judges that the resulting picture will resemble someone or other, that person has no special causal efficacy in the production of the picture and so it still will not be a picture *of* anyone. And if the story of Medusa originated in imagination or hallucination (as opposed to misperception or misapprehension), then a rendering based on that legend is *of* no one, notwithstanding the existence of any past, present, or future snake-haired women.

In addition to the link with reality provided by the relation of resemblance the descriptive content of a picture determines its *vividness*. A faded picture showing the back of a man wearing a cloak and lurking in shadow will lack vividness. A clear picture, head on, full length, life size, showing fingerprints, etc. would be counted highly vivid. What is counted as vivid may to some extent depend on special interests. To the clothier, nude portraits may be lacking in detail, while to the foot fetishist a picture showing only the left big toe may leap from the canvas. Though special interests may thus weight detail, I would expect that increase in detail always increases vividness. It should be clear that there are no necessary connections between how vivid a picture is and whether it is *of* anyone or whether it resembles anyone.

Returning now to names, it is their descriptive content that determines what if anything they denote. Thus, denotation is the analogue for names to resemblance for pictures. The genetic character of a name in a given person's usage will account for how he *acquired* the name, that is how he heard of such a thing and, if he believes that such a thing exists, how he came to believe it. It is the genetic character of the name that determines what if anything it is a name *of*. (I here use the same nomenclature, '*of*', for names as for pictures.) The user-dependence of this notion is required by the fact that Ralph and Fred may each have acquired the name 'John Smith', but in such a way that for Ralph it is a name *of* one John Smith while for Fred it is a name *of* another John Smith.

I would suppose that students of rhetoric realize that most of the lines of argument traditionally classified as 'informal fallacies' (*ad hominem*, *ad vericundiam*, etc.) are commonly considered relevant or even determinative by reasonable men.[25] Cases such as that of the two John Smiths, which emphasize the importance of genetic features in language use, indicate limitations that must be placed on the traditional dichotomy between *what* we believe (assert, desire, etc.) and *how* we came to believe it.

Let us attempt to apply these considerations to the case of proper names. Proper names denote each of the usually many persons so dubbed. Ralph may acquire a proper name in a number of different ways. He may have attended a dubbing with the subject present. I reconstruct such dubbings as consisting of a stipulative association of the name with a perception *of* the subject. Thus, the name becomes a name *of* the subject, and as it passes from Ralph to others retains this feature in the manner of the picture *of* Julius Caesar. We may of course dub on the basis of a hallucination, in which case the name is a name *of* nothing, though it will still denote each actual person, if any, that may be so dubbed. Dubbings sometimes take place with the subject absent, in which case some other name (usually a description) stands in for the perception, and the stipulatively introduced proper name takes its genetic character from the stand-in name. If the latter only denotes the subject (and is not a name *of* the subject for the user in question), the proper name can do no better. This having a name *of x*, I shall later take to be essential to having a belief about *x*, and I am unwilling to adopt any theory of proper names which

228

permits me to perform a dubbing in absentia, as by solemnly declaring "I hereby dub the first child to be born in the twenty-second century 'Newman 1'", and thus grant myself standing to have beliefs about that as yet unborn child. Another presumably more common way to acquire a proper name is in casual conversation or reading, e.g. from the headline, "Mayor Indicted; B. J. Ortcutt sought by F.B.I.". In such cases we retrace the causal sequence from Ralph back through his immediate source to its immediate source and so on. An especially difficult case of this sort arises when someone other than Ortcutt, say Wyman, is introduced to Ralph as Ortcutt. Suppose that the introduction took place with intent to deceive and that Fred, who made the introduction, acquired the name 'Ortcutt' as a name *of* Ortcutt. Clearly we should count 'Ortcutt' as a name *of* Wyman for Ralph, but also, through Fred, as a name *of* Ortcutt. The situation is analogous to the composite photograph made by the split mirror technique. But here the much greater vividness of the perceptual half of the equation may outweigh the dim reflection of Ortcutt.

I leave to the reader the useful exercise of constructing cases of names (not necessarily proper) which are analogues to each of the cited cases of pictures.

The notion of a vivid name is intended to go to the purely internal aspects of individuation. Consider typical cases in which we would be likely to say that Ralph knows x or is acquainted with x. Then look only at the conglomeration of images, names, and partial descriptions which Ralph employs to bring x before his mind. Such a conglomeration, when suitably arranged and regimented, is what I call a vivid name. As with pictures, there are degrees of vividness and the whole notion is to some degree relative to special interests. The crucial feature of this notion is that it depends only on Ralph's current mental state, and ignores all links whether by resemblence or genesis with the actual world. If the name is such, that on the assumption that there exists some individual x whom it both denotes and resembles we should say that Ralph knows x or is acquainted with x, then the name is vivid.

The vivid names "represent" those persons who fill major roles in that *inner story* which consists of all those sentences which Ralph believes. I have placed 'represent' here in scarequotes to warn that there may not actually exist anything which is so "represented". Ralph may enjoy an inner story totally out of contact with reality, but this is not to deny it a cast of robust and clearly delineated characters. Life is often less plausible than art. Of course a vivid name should make an existence *claim*. If Ralph does not believe that there is a Santa Claus, I would not call any Santa Claus name vivid, no matter how lively it is in other respects.

There are certain features which may contribute strongly to vividness but which I feel we should not accept as absolute requirements. It is certainly too much to require that a vivid name must provide Ralph with a means of recognizing its purported object under all circumstances, for we do not follow the careers of even those we know best that closely. There are always gaps. We sometimes even fail to recognize ourselves in early photographs or recent descriptions, simply because of gaps in our self-concept.[26] It also seems to me too much to require that Ralph believes himself to have at some time perceived the purported object of a vivid name since a scholar may be better acquainted with Julius Caesar than with his own neighbor. Some have also suggested that the appropriate kind of name must provide Ralph with the means of locating its purported object. But parents and police are frequently unable to locate persons well known to them. Also, a vivid biography of a peasant somewhere in Asia, may involve none but the vaguest spatio-temporal references.

One might understand the assertion, 'Ralph has an opinion as to who Ortcutt is' as a claim that Ralph can place Ortcutt among the leading characters of his inner story, thus that Ralph believes some sentence of the form $\ulcorner \alpha = \text{Ortcutt} \urcorner$ with α vivid. This, I believe, is the view of Hintikka. Hintikka institutionalizes the sense of 'represents' with usual quotes by allowing existential generalization on the leading character or inner individual "represented" by a vivid name. Although his symbolism allows him to distinguish between those inner individuals which are actual and those which are not, a central role is assigned to something close to what I call a vivid name.[27] In emphasizing this conceptual separation of vividness, which makes a name a *candidate* for exportation, from those features depending on genesis and resemblence, which determine what actual person, if anyone, the name really represents (without quotes), Hintikka (if I have him right) and I are in agreement.

It is a familiar fact of philosophy that no idea, description, or image can insure itself against non-natural causes. The most vivid of names may have had its origin in imagination or hallucination. Thus, to freely allow exportation a name must not only be vivid but must also be a name *of* someone, and indeed a name *of* the person it denotes. This last is an accuracy requirement which no doubt is rarely satisfied by the most vivid names we use. Our most vivid names can be roughly characterized as those elaborate descriptions containing all we believe about a single person. Such names will almost certainly contain inaccuracies which will prevent them from actually denoting anyone. Also such names are often not *of* a single person but result from conflation of information about several persons (as in Fred's prevaricating introduction of Wyman to Ralph).

One proposal for handling such difficulties would be to apply the method of best fit to our most vivid names, i.e. to seek the individual who comes closest to satisfying the two conditions: that the name denotes him and is *of* him. But it seems that this technique would distort the account of conflations, never allowing us to say that there are two persons whom Ralph believes to be one. There is an alternate method which I favor. Starting with one of our most vivid names, form the largest core, all of which is *of* the same person and which denotes that person. A vivid name resulting from conflation may contain more than one such core name. The question is whether such a core, remaining after excision of inaccuracy, is yet vivid. If so, I will say that the core name *represents* the person whom it both denotes and is *of* to Ralph.

Our task was to characterize a relation between Ralph, a name, and a person, which could replace Δ in a variant analysis of **Bel**. For this I will use the above notion of representation. To repeat, I will say α *represents* x *to* Ralph (symbolized: '$\mathbf{R}(\alpha, x, \text{Ralph})$') if and only if (i) α denotes x, (ii) α is a name *of* x for Ralph, and (iii) α is (sufficiently) vivid. Our final version of (33) is the following variant of (36):

(44) $\quad \exists \alpha \, [\mathbf{R}(\alpha, \text{Ortcutt}, \text{Ralph}) \, \& \, \text{Ralph} \, \mathbf{B} \, \ulcorner \alpha \text{ is a spy} \urcorner]$.

X

Part of our aim was to restrict the range of persons with whom Ralph is *en rapport* (in the sense of **Bel**). This was done by means of clauses (ii) and (iii). Clause (ii) excludes all future persons such as Newman 1[28] and indeed any person past, present, or future who has not left his mark on Ralph. The addition of clause (iii) excludes any person who has not left a vivid mark on Ralph.

The crucial exportation step for the case of the shortest spy is now blocked, because in spite of Ralph's correct belief that such a person exists, 'the shortest spy' is not, for Ralph, a name *of* him.[29]

Clause (iii) takes account of the desire to allow Ralph beliefs *about* (again in the sense of **Bel**) only those persons he 'has in mind', where the mere acquisition of, say, a proper name *of x* would not suffice to put *x* in mind. Furthermore, if we were to drop clause (iii), and allow any name which both denotes *x* and is a name *of x* to represent *x* to Holmes, then after Holmes observed the victim, 'the murderer' would represent the murderer to him. And thus we would have:

$$\exists y \exists \alpha [\mathbf{R}(\alpha, y, \text{Holmes}) \,\&\, \text{Holmes } \mathbf{B} \ulcorner \alpha = \text{the murderer} \urcorner],$$

which is our present analysis of:

$$\exists y \text{ Holmes } \mathbf{Bel} \,(\text{'}\mathbf{x} = \text{the murderer'}, y),$$

which is, roughly, Quine's translation of:

There is someone whom Holmes believes to be the murderer.

But this last should presage an arrest and not the mere certification of homicide. Clause (iii) is intended to block such cases. At some point in his investigation, the slow accretion of evidence, all "pointing in a certain direction" may just push Holmes' description over the appropriate vividness threshold so that we *would* say that there is now someone whom Holmes believes to be the murderer.

Clause (iii) could also be used to block exportation of 'the shortest spy'. But that would not eliminate the need for clause (ii) which is still needed to insure that we export to the right individual.

Although I believe that all three clauses are required to block all the anomalies of exportation, I am less interested in a definitive analysis of that particular inference than I am in separating and elucidating certain notions which may be useful in epistemological discussions. According to my analysis, Ralph must have quite a solid conception of *x* before we can say that Ralph believes *x* to be a spy. By weakening the accuracy requirements on the notion of representation we obtain in general new relational senses of belief.[30] Any such notion, based on a clearly specified variant of (36), may be worthy of investigation.

XI

A vivid name is a little bit like a standard name, but not much. It can't guarantee existence to its purported object, and although it has a kind of inner reliability by way of Ralph's use of such names to order his inner world, a crucial condition of reliability – the determinateness of standard identities – fails. A standard identity is an identity sentence in which both terms are standard names. It is corollary to the reliability of standard names, that standard identities are either true under all circumstances or false under all circumstances. But not so for identities involving vivid names. We can easily form two vivid names, one describing Bertrand Russell as logician, and another describing Russell as social critic, which are such that the identity sentence simply can not be decided on internal evidence. In the case of the morning star and the evening star, we can even form names which allow us to locate the purported objects (if we are willing to wait for the propitious moment) without the identity sentence being determinate. Of course Ralph may believe the negation of the identity sentence for all distinct pairs of vivid names, but such beliefs may simply be wrong. And the names can remain vivid even after such inaccurate non-identities are excised. It may happen that Ralph comes to change his beliefs so that where he once believed a non-identity between vivid names, he now believes an identity. And at some intermediate stage of wonder he believes neither the identity nor the non-identity. Such Monte Cristo cases may be rare in reality (though rife in fiction)[31], but they are nevertheless clearly possible. They could be ruled out only by demanding an unreasonably high standard of vividness, to wit: no gaps, or else by adding an artificial and ad hoc requirement that all vivid names contain certain format items, e.g. exact place and date of birth. Either course would put us out of *rapport* with most of our closest friends. Thus, two vivid names can represent the same person to Ralph although Ralph does not believe the identity sentence. He may simply wonder, or he may disbelieve the identity sentence and so believe of one person that he is two. Similarly two vivid names can represent different persons to Ralph although Ralph does not believe the non-identity sentence. Again, Ralph may either suspend judgment or disbelieve the non-identity and so believe of two persons that they are one. Since this last situation is perhaps more plausible than the others, it is important to see that theoretically the cases are on a par. In fact, a case where Ralph has so conflated two persons and is then disabused by his friend Fred, becomes a case of believing one person to be two simply by assuming that Ralph was right in the first place and that Fred lied.

Quine acknowledges that Ralph can believe of one person that he is two on Quine's own understanding of **Bel**, when he remarks, as mentioned in VI above, that

(32)   Ralph **Bel** ('**x** is not a spy', Ortcutt),

and

(33)   Ralph **Bel** ('**x** is a spy', Ortcutt),

do not express an inconsistency on Ralph's part and do not imply (34). The background story justifying (32) and (33) involves Ralph twice spotting Ortcutt but under circumstances so different that Ralph was unaware that he was seeing the same man again. Indeed he believed he was not seeing the same man again, since on the one occasion he thought, 'There goes a spy', and on the other, 'Here is no spy'. My point is that though one may quibble about whether each or either of the names of Ortcutt were vivid in the particular cases as described by Quine[32], and so question whether in those cases exportation should have been permitted, no plausible characterization of appropriate conditions for vividness can prevent analogous cases from arising.

Cases of the foregoing kind, which agree with Quine's intuitions, argue an inadequacy in his regimentation of language. For in the same sense in which (32) and (33) do not express an inconsistency on Ralph's part, neither should (33) and

(45) $\sim$ Ralph **Bel** ('**x** is a spy', Ortcutt)

express an inconsistency on ours. Indeed it seems natural to claim that (45) is a consequence of (32). But the temptation to look upon (33) and (45) as contradictory is extremely difficult to resist. The problem is that since Quine's **Bel** suppresses mention of the specific name being exported, he can not distinguish between

(46) $\exists \alpha [\mathbf{R}(\alpha, \text{Ortcutt}, \text{Ralph}) \& \sim \text{Ralph } \mathbf{B} \ulcorner \alpha \text{ is a spy}\urcorner]$

and

(47) $\sim \exists \alpha [\mathbf{R}(\alpha, \text{Ortcutt}, \text{Ralph}) \& \text{Ralph } \mathbf{B} \ulcorner \alpha \text{ is a spy}\urcorner]$

234

If (45) is read as (46), there is no inconsistency with (32); in fact, on this interpretation (45) is a consequence of (32) (at least on the assumption that Ralph does not have contradictory beliefs). But if (45) is read as (47) (Quine's intention, I suppose), it is inconsistent with (33) and independent of (32).

So long as Ralph can believe of one person that he is two, as in Quine's story, we should be loath to make either (46) or (47) inexpressible.[33] If (33) is read as (44), we certainly must retain some way of expressing (47) since it expresses the negation of (33). Is it important to retain expression of (46)? In Quine's story, something stronger than (46) holds, namely (32), which we now read as:

(48) $\exists\alpha[\mathbf{R}(\alpha, \text{Ortcutt, Ralph}) \& \text{Ralph } \mathbf{B} \ulcorner\alpha \text{ is not a spy}\urcorner]$

But we can continue the story to a later time at which Ralph's suspicions regarding even the man at the beach have begun to grow. Not that Ralph now proclaims that respected citizen to be a spy, but Ralph now suspends judgment as to the man's spyhood. At this time (48) is false, and (46) is true. If we are to have the means to express such suspensions of judgment, something like (46) is required.

I have gone to some trouble here to indicate the source of the notational inadequacy in the possibility of a single person bearing distinct exportable names not believed to name the same thing, and also to argue in favor of maintaining the possibility of such names. I have done this because logicians working in this field have for the most part been in accord with Quine in adopting the simpler language form. In my view the consequence of adopting such a form is either to exclude natural interpretations by setting an impossibly high standard for vividness, and thus for exportation, or else to make such partial expressions of suspended judgment as (46) inexpressible.

XII

When earlier I argued for Frege's method – seek the intermediate entity – it was on the grounds that a clarified view of the problem was worth at least a momentary ontological risk. But now it appears that to give adequate expression to the epistemological situation requires explicit quantificational certification of the status of such entities. I am undismayed and even would urge that the conservative course so far followed of taking expressions as the intermediate entities is clearly inadequate to

the task. Many of our beliefs have the form: 'The color of her hair is
_____', or 'The song he was singing went _____', where the blanks
are filled with images, sensory impressions, or what have you, but certainly not words. If we cannot even *say* it with words but have to paint it
or sing it, we certainly cannot believe it with words.

My picture theory of meaning played heavily on the analogy between
names and pictures. I believe that the whole theory of sense and denotation
can be extended to apply to pictures as well as words. (How can an
identity "sentence" with the components filled by pictures be both true
and informative?) If we explicitly include such visual images among
names, we gain a new perspective on the claim that we can definitively
settle the question of whether Bernard J. Ortcutt is such that Ralph
believes him to be a spy by confronting Ralph with Ortcutt and asking
'Is *he* a spy?' Ralph's response will depend on recognition, a comparison
of current images with stored ones. And stored images are simply one
more form of description, worth perhaps a thousand words, but thoroughly
comparable to words. Thus Ralph's answer in such a situation is simply
one more piece in the whole jigsaw of his cognitive structure. He might
answer 'yes' for some confrontations (compare – 'yes' for some names),
'no' for others, and withhold judgment for still others.

The suggested extension of the intermediate entities poses an interesting
problem for the ontologist. Must we posit a realm of special mental
entities as values for the variables used in analyzing the relational sense
of belief, or will a variant on the trick of taking sentences as the objects
of belief also account for beliefs involving visual images, odors, sounds,
etc.?[34]

XIII

There are, I believe, two rather different problem areas connected with
the analysis of intermediate contexts. The first problem area, which lies
squarely within what is usually called the philosophy of language, involves
chiefly the more fundamental non-relational interpretation of intermediate contexts. It calls for an explanation of the seemingly logically
deviant behavior of expressions in such contexts and perhaps also for a
more exact statement of just what inferences, if any, are valid for such
contexts. Here I feel that Frege's method outlines a generally acceptable
solution. I especially appreciate the fact that for Frege intermediate

contexts are not seen as exceptions to a powerful and heretofore general logical theory but rather are seen as fully accessible to that theory with the noted anomalies explained as due to a misreading of "initial conditions" leading to an inappropriate application of the laws. This accounting for seemingly aberrant phenomena in terms of the correct application of a familiar theory is explanation at its most satisfying. By contrast, the view I have associated with Quine – that intermediate contexts are referentially inarticulate – contents itself with a huge and unobvious class of "exceptions to the rules". This is shabby explanation, if explanation at all.

The second problem area specifically concerns the relational interpretation of intermediate contexts. Here I have tried to show how Frege's method, though it may provide a basis for unifying the relational and non-relational interpretation of a given intermediate context and though it immediately provides for some form of quantification in, does not by itself necessarily provide the most interesting (and perhaps indispensible) relational interpretation. Further analysis, often specific to the context in question, may be required in order to produce an appropriately discriminating form of Δ which will yield results in conformity with our intuitive demands. Indeed, such an investigation may well lead far beyond the philosophy of language proper into metaphysics and epistemology. I know of no earlier source than 'Quantifiers and Propositional Attitudes' in which relational uses of intermediate contexts are so clearly identified throughout an area of concern more urgent than modal logic. In that article Quine early expressed his remarkable insights into the pervasiveness of the relational forms and the need for a special analysis of their structure. And in fact following Quine's outlook and attempting to refine the conditions for valid applications of exportation, one might well arrive at the same metaphysical and epistemological insights as those obtained in attempting to refine Δ. What is important is that we should achieve some form of analysis of these contexts without recourse to the very idioms we are attempting to analyze.

The problem of interpreting the most interesting form of quantification in, appears in various guises: as the problem of making trans-world identifications, as the problem of finding favored names, and as the problem of distinguishing 'essential' from 'accidental' properties.

The present paper suggests two polar techniques for finding favored names.

237

It is curious and somehow satisfying that they so neatly divide the objects between them, the one applying only to objects capable of being perceived (or at least of initiating causal chains), the other applying only to purely abstract objects. I am well aware of obscurities and difficulties in my formulations of the two central notions – that of a standard name and that of a name being *of* an object for a particular user. Yet both seem to me promising and worthy of further investigation.

Department of Philosophy,
University of California, Los Angeles

BIBLIOGRAPHY

[1] R. B. Angell, *Reasoning and Logic*, New York 1963.
[2] P. Benacerraf, 'What Numbers Could Not Be', *Philosophical Review* **74** (1965) 47–73.
[3] R. Carnap, *Meaning and Necessity*, Chicago 1947, 2nd ed., 1956.
[4] D. Carney and K. Scheer, *Fundamentals of Logic*, New York 1964.
[5] A. Church, 'A Formulation of the Logic of Sense and Denotation', in *Structure, Method, and Meaning* (ed. by P. Henle, M. Kallen, and S. K. Langer), New York 1951.
[6] A. Church, 'On Carnap's Analysis of Statements of Assertion and Belief', *Analysis* **10** (1949–50) 97–99.
[7] A. Church, Review of Quine's 'Notes on Existence and Necessity', *Journal of Symbolic Logic* **8** (1943) 45–47.
[8] G. Frege, 'On Sense and Reference', originally published in *Zeitschrift für Philosophie und philosophische Kritik* **100** (1892) 25–50; translated in *Translations from the Philosophical Writings of Gottlob Frege* (ed. by P. Geach and M. Black), Oxford 1960.
[9] K. J. Hintikka, 'Individuals, Possible Worlds, and Epistemic Logic', *Noûs* **1** (1967) 33–62.
[10] D. Kaplan, *Foundations of Intensional Logic* (Dissertation), University Microfilms, Ann Arbor 1964.
[11] H. S. Leonard, *An Introduction to Principles of Right Reason*, New York 1957.
[12] W. V. Quine, 'Notes on Existence and Necessity', *The Journal of Philosophy* **40** (1943) 113–127.
[13] W. V. Quine, 'Two Dogmas of Empiricism', *Philosophical Review* **60** (1951) 20–43; reprinted in [15].
[14] W. V. Quine, 'Notes on the Theory of Reference', in [15].
[15] W. V. Quine, *From a Logical Point of View*, Cambridge, Mass., 1953, 2nd ed., 1961.
[16] W. V. Quine, 'Three Grades of Modal Involvement', in *Proceedings of the XIth International Congress of Philosophy, Brussels, 1953*, Vol. 14, pp. 65–81, Amsterdam; reprinted in [20].

[17] W. V. Quine, 'Quantifiers and Propositional Attitudes', *The Journal of Philosophy* **53** (1956) 177–187; reprinted (minus 15 lines) in [20].
[18] W. V. Quine, *Word and Object*, New York 1960.
[19] W. V. Quine, 'Reply to Professor Marcus', *Synthese* **13** (1961) 323–330; reprinted in [20].
[20] W. V. Quine, *The Ways of Paradox and Other Essays*, New York 1966.
[21] P. F. Strawson, *Individuals*, London 1959.
[22] A. Tarski, 'The Concept of Truth in Formalized Languages', originally published in Polish in *Prace Towarzystwa Naukowego Warszawskiego, Wydzial* III, no. 34 (1933), pp. vii + 116; translated in A. Tarski, *Logic, Semantics, Metamathematics*, Oxford 1956, pp. 152–278.

REFERENCES

[1] This paper is intended as a commentary on Quine's 'Quantifiers and Propositional Attitudes'. Quine's article was first published in 1956 and I have been thinking about it ever since. Quine has not been idle while I have been thinking, but his subsequent writings do not seem to have repudiated any part of 'Quantifiers and Propositional Attitudes' which remains, to my mind, the best brief introduction to the field. The first half of my reflections was read to the Harvard Philosophy Colloquium in January 1966. Its writing was aided by conversations with Montgomery Furth. The present ending has been influenced by a number of different persons, most significantly by Saul Kripke and Charles Chastain. But they should not be held to blame for it. Furth, who also read the penultimate version, is responsible for any remaining deficiencies aside from Section IX about which he is skeptical. My research has been partially supported by N.S.F. Grant GP-7706.

[2] The quotation is from *Word and Object*, p. 144, wherein the inspiration for 'opaque' is explicitly given. The assimilation of intermediate occurrences to accidental ones might fairly be said to represent a *tendency* on Quine's part. The further evidence of *Word and Object* belies any simplistic characterization of Quine's attitudes toward intermediate occurrences.

[3] In 'Three Grades of Modal Involvement', p. 172 in [20] and other places. An intriguing suggestion for notational efficiency at no loss (or gain) to Quine's theory is to take advantage of the fact that occurrences of variables within opaque contexts which are bindable from without are prohibited, and use the vacated forms as "a way of indicating, selectively and changeably, just what positions in the contained sentence are to shine through as referential on any particular occasion" (*Word and Object*, p. 199). We interpret, 'Hegel believed that x is greater than five' with bindable 'x', as 'x is such that Hegel believed it to be greater than five' which is modeled on (8). Similarly, 'Hegel believed that x is greater than y' is now read as, 'x and y are such that Hegel believed the former to be greater than the latter'. (8) itself could be rendered as, '$\exists x[x = \text{nine}$ & Hegel believed that x is greater than five]', and still not be a logical consequence of (5).

[4] The reader will recognize that I have incorporated, without reference, many themes upon which Quine has harped, and that I have not attempted to make my agreement with him explicit at each point at which it occurs. Suffice it to say that the agreements far outweigh the disagreements, and that in both the areas of agreement and of disagreement I have benefited greatly from his writings.

[5] See especially the end of 'Three Grades of Modal Involvement'. I am informed by

scholarly sources that Aristotelian essentialism has its origin in 'Two Dogmas of Empiricism'. It reappears significantly in 'Reply to Professor Marcus', where essential properties of numbers are discussed, and in *Word and Object*, p. 199, where essential properties of persons are discussed. I will later argue that the two cases are unlike.

[6] In 'A Formulation of the Logic of Sense and Denotation'.

[7] See *Meaning and Necessity*, Section 9, for the discovery of the explicandum, and Section 40 for the discovery of the explicans.

[8] See 'On Sense and Reference' pp. 58, 59 in *Translations from the Philosophical Writings of Gottlob Frege*.

[9] The acute reader will have discerned a certain similarity in function, though not in foundation, between the Frege quotes and another familiar quotation device.

[10] These parallels are exhibited at some length in my dissertation *Foundations of Intensional Logic*.

[11] A drawback to this position is that the resulting *correct* applications of Leibniz' Law are rather unexciting. More interesting intermediate entities can be obtained by taking what Carnap, in *Meaning and Necessity* calls 'intensions'. Two expressions have the same intension, in this sense, if they are logically equivalent. Other interesting senses of 'intension' might be obtained by weakening the notion of logical equivalence to logical equivalence within sentential logic, intuitionistic logic, etc. Church suggests alternatives which might be understood along these lines.

[12] I have approximately followed the notational devices used by Quine in 'Quantifiers and Propositional Attitudes'. Neither of us recommend the notation for practical purposes, even with the theory as is. An alternative notation is suggested in note 3 above.

[13] Also, see *Word and Object*, p. 211, for an implicit use of exportation.

[14] The 'nearly' of 'nearly analytic' is accounted for by a small scruple regarding the logic of singular terms. If a language L containing the name '$\imath y F y$' is extended to a metalanguage L' containing the predicate 'Δ' for denotation-in-L and also containing the logical particles, including quotes, in their usual meaning, then I regard

$$[\exists x \; x = \imath y F y \to \Delta('\imath y F y', \imath y F y)]$$

as fully analytic in L'.

My reasons for thinking so depend, in part, on my treatment of quotation names as standard names, for which see Section VIII below. I am being careful, because Quine suggests disagreement in an impatient footnote to 'Notes on the Theory of Reference' (I am grateful to Furth, who recalled the footnote.) I do not know whether our disagreement, if a fact, is over quotation or elsewhere. The whole question of analyticity is less than crucial to my line of argument.

[15] For a recent expression see *Word and Object*, Section 41.

[16] The same difficulty was noticed, independently, by John Wallace and reported in a private communication.

[17] Quoted from the end of Quine's 'Reply to Professor Marcus'. I fully agree with Quine's characterization of the case, though not with the misinterpretation of Church's review of 'Notes on Existence and Necessity' from which Quine's characterization springs.

[18] See the discussion of what Carnap calls *L-determinate individual expressions* in *Meaning and Necessity*, Section 18, and also Tarski's discussion of what he calls *structural descriptive names* in 'The Concept of Truth in Formalized Languages', Section 1.

[19] The latter wonder is not to be confused with an ontological anxiety concerning the nature of nine, which is more appropriately expressed by dropping the word 'number' in the wonder description.

[20] Benacerraf so concludes in 'What Numbers Could Not Be'.

[21] The present discussion of standard names is based on that in the more technical environment of my dissertation, pp. 55–57.

[22] Given this understanding of **Nec**, it is interesting to note that on certain natural assumptions '$\Delta_n(\alpha, y)$' is itself expressed by '$\mathbf{Nec}(\ulcorner\alpha = \mathbf{x}\urcorner, y)$'.

[23] Note that an attempt to identify the object perceived in terms of resemblance with the perception rather than in terms of the causal chain leading to the perception would seriously distort an account of misperception.

[24] The corresponding principle for determining who it is that a given proper name, as it is used by some speaker, names, was first brought to my attention by Saul Kripke. Kripke's examples incorporated both the indirect path from person named to person naming and also the possible distortions of associated descriptions.

The existence of a relatively large number of persons with the same proper name gives urgency to this problem even in mundane settings. In theoretical discussions it is usually claimed that such difficulties are settled by "context". I have recently found at least vague recognition of the use of genetic factors to account for the connection between name and named in such diverse sources as Henry Leonard: "Probably for most of us there is little more than a vaguely felt willingness to mean ... whatever the first assigners of the name intended by it." (*An Introduction to Principles of Right Reason*, section 30.2), and P. F. Strawson: "[T]he identifying description ... may include a reference to another's reference to that particular ... So one reference may borrow the credentials ... from another; and that from another." (*Individuals*, footnote 1, page 182). Though in neither case are genetic and descriptive features clearly distinguished.

Kripke's insights and those of Charles Chastain, who has especially emphasized the role of *knowledge* in order to establish the desired connection between name and named, are in large part responsible for the heavy emphasis I place on genetic factors.

[25] Although it is useful for scholarly purposes to have a catalogue of such "fallacies" (such as that provided in Carney and Scheer, *Fundamentals of Logic*), the value of such discussions in improving the practical reasoning of rational beings seems to me somewhat dubious. A sensitive discussion of a related form of argument occurs in Angell, *Reasoning and Logic*, especially pp. 422–423.

[26] Such failures may also be due to self-deception, an inaccurate self-concept, but then the purported object does not exist at all.

[27] Insofar as I understand Hintikka's 'Individuals, Possible Worlds, and Epistemic Logic', the domain of values of the bound variables fluctuates with the placement of the bound occurrences of the variables. If, in a quantifier's matrix, the occurrences of the variable bound to the quantifier fall only within uniterated epistemological contexts, then the variables range over possible(?) individuals "represented" by vivid names. If, on the other hand, no occurrences of the variable fall within epistemological (or other opaque) contexts, then the variables range over the usual actual individuals. And if the variable occurs both within and without an epistemological context, then the values of the variables are inner individuals which are also actual. Thus if Ralph believes in Santa Claus, and σ is Ralph's vivid Santa Claus description, Hintikka would treat '$\ulcorner$Ralph believes that $\sigma = $ Santa Claus$\urcorner$' as true and as implying '$\exists x$ Ralph believes that $x = $ Santa Claus', but would treat '$\exists x [x = $ Santa Claus & Ralph believes that $x = $

Santa Claus]' and presumably '$\exists x [\exists y\ y = x$ & Ralph believes that $x =$ Santa Claus]' as false, and not as consequences of '$\ulcorner \sigma =$ Santa Claus & Ralph believes that $\sigma =$ Santa Claus $\urcorner$.

[28] I disregard precognition explained by a reverse causal chain.

[29] We might say in such cases that the name *specifies* its denotation, in the sense in which a set of specifications, though not generated by the object specified, is written with the intention that there is or will be an object so described.

[30] One such weakened notion of representation is that expressed by 'Ralph **Bel** ($\ulcorner \alpha = \mathbf{x} \urcorner$, y)', analyzed as in (44) using our current **R**, which here, in contrast to the situation for $\Delta_{\mathbf{N}}$ (see reference 22 above), is not equivalent to '$\mathbf{R}(\alpha, y$, Ralph)'. Still this new notion of representation, when used in place of our current **R** in an analysis of the form of (44), leads to the same relational sense of belief.

[31] Note especially the "secret identity" genre of children's literature containing Superman, Batman, etc.

[32] At least one author, Hintikka, has seemed unwilling to allow Ralph a belief *about* Ortcutt merely on the basis of Ralph's few glimpses *of* Ortcutt skulking around the missile base. See his 'Individuals, Possible Worlds, and Epistemic Logic', footnote 13.

[33] Another way out is to accept the fact that two names may represent the same person to Ralph though Ralph believes the non-identity, but to put an ad hoc restriction on exportation. For example to analyze (33) as: '$\exists \alpha [\mathbf{R}(\alpha$, Ortcutt, Ralph) & Ralph **B** $\ulcorner \alpha$ is a spy $\urcorner$] & $\sim \exists \alpha [\mathbf{R}(\alpha$, Ortcutt, Ralph) & $\sim$ Ralph **B** $\ulcorner \alpha$ is a spy $\urcorner$]'. This prevents exportation where contradiction threatens. But again much that we would like to say is inexpressible in Quine's nomenclature.

[34] It should be noted that in Church's 'On Carnap's Analysis of Statements of Assertion and Belief' serious objections are raised to even the first step.

GEORGE BERRY

LOGIC WITH PLATONISM

I. LOGICAL ANONTOLOGISM AND ITS MOTIVES

In his 'Logic without Ontology'[1], Professor Ernest Nagel denies that logic attempts to characterize either the way men really think about the world or the real world they think about. In fact, he says, logic is normative only: it seeks to prescribe standards, not to describe the real, and therefor it lacks all ontological implications.

In the present paper I propose to scrutinize this anontological[2] view of logic, to survey several opposing, or ontological, views, and finally to recommend one, which is a form of platonism. Instead of a logic without ontology, I favor a logic with an ontology, specifically a logic with a platonistic one.

Nagel is perfectly aware – and shows it in the cited article, of course – that the term 'logic' is used in at least two senses. Logicians typically deal with certain sentences, for example,

(1) $\quad p \vee \sim p$
(2) $\quad (x)\,(x = x)$
(3) $\quad [(8 = S''7) \,\&\, (7 = S'6)] \supset (8 = S'S'6),$

and so on. These together comprise an object language or languages, and one common usage identifies logic with such an object language or with some group of such. In discussing such sentences, the logician will use others. He may say, for instance,

(4) $\quad$ '$p \vee \sim p$' is a corollary of '$p \supset p$'
(5) $\quad$ '$(x)\,(x = x)$' shows identity reflexive
(6) $\quad$ The consequent of (3) is true.

Sentences like (4), (5), and (6) form a metalanguage or metalanguages, and sometimes it is this or these that, under a second common usage, are called 'logic'. In sense-one, logic is object language; in sense-two, it is metalanguage. Throughout the following I shall use 'logic' in sense-one only; logic in sense-two I shall call 'metalogic'.

Nagel maintains that his anontological thesis holds for both logic and metalogic. When we utter a sentence that is a part of metalogic, he contends, we are talking about idealized discourse. We are saying that in this ideal language something is provable or that one thing validly follows from another. We are not describing the world, or how people do things. Instead, we are laying down norms. The normative character of logic, if less obvious, is – Nagel holds – no less genuine. For instance, if we assert (2) above, we are actually saying something which is, in fact, true only if taken as part of an ideal language. There are plenty of exceptions to (2) once translated into ordinary language. In ordinary English (2) becomes 'Everything is itself'; and frequently we meet exceptions to this: for example, 'The speaker is not himself tonight'. The logician is thus always preoccupied with the ideal, rather than the real, with some never-never language which he holds up as a model of precision and clarity.

This anontologism, or some variant of it flourishes among supporters of empiricism and analytic philosophy generally. Carnap, Ayer, Hempel, Kemeny – these are only some of the names that come to mind.

What are the motives underlying logical anontologism? I think there are two basic ones. The first is the empiricist's and the analytic philosopher's felt need to explain the certainty of logic. Any empirical principle can be wrong, for later observation may disprove it. This uncertainty characterizes all empirical hypotheses. A similar fallibility, in fact, mars every assertion about the world, for the world can always rise up somewhere along the line to veto it. How come, then, that logic *is* certain? The anontologist replies that logic can be certain simply because it is not about the world, so the world can never prove it wrong. The second motive underlying anontologism is a felt need to explain the *a priori* character of logic, its independence, that is, of observation. The pure logician or the pure mathematician works in his study or at his blackboard. He is untroubled by laboratories or experiments, and in his investigations he ignores their deliverances. And well he may, says anontologism, for since his investigations are not about the world at all, no observation of it can guide or correct them.

A third circumstance, though hardly classifiable as a motive underlying logical anontologism, at least renders it more palatable. What

Carnap[3] described as translation of sentences from the material mode into the formal mode of speech, or what Quine[4] calls 'semantic ascent' enables one to convert discussion of objects into a discussion of that discussion of objects. Instead of saying, e.g., '4 is a number', you can say 'The expression "4" is a numeral'. Or, to take the trivial sort of case, instead of asserting sentence A, e.g., '2+2=4', one can always assert the equivalent sentence, 'A is true', e.g., '"2+2=4" is true'. Sentences about numbers thus give way to sentences about numerals or even to sentences about sentences, so that logic itself can be replaced by metalogic. If we can now clear the way by ingesting Nagel's distinction between the real world and language, particularly ideal language, we can swallow the anontologism of metalogic smoothly.

II. APRIORITY AND CERTAINTY IN GRAND LOGICS

We cannot judge this anontological view of logic fairly without first specifying in more detail than Nagel's article does what kind of logic is relevant. Even if the logician should officially confine his assertions *qua* logician to the sentences of metalogic, the character of these will vary with his object language and, indeed – provided only that his metalanguage includes some semantics – with what the object language says of the real world. Accordingly even the replacement of logic by metalogic leaves the pattern, perhaps the very identity, of the logical object language crucial. Surely, it is deductive logic alone which is at issue here, simply because this is the only type of logic which the anontologists have in mind when they maintain that logic has no ontological import. Precision also is required: until he has refined it, the contemporary logician finds imprecise logic pathological and interesting only as a symptom of diseases to be avoided or cured. Precision implies formality – that is, the terms 'sentence', 'postulate' and 'proof' must be so defined for a given language that mechanical, visual inspection of linguistic pattern suffices to decide their application. We have then two requisites, deductiveness and the precision that includes formality. Scope is a third *desideratum*. Logic should be of a maximum utility for science. There are a good many narrow calculi which are well-adapted for special scientific purposes – e.g., the propositional calculus for simplifying circuit design, the calculus of individuals for exploring the limits of nominalism, the first-order functional calculus for axiomatizing the theory of the categorial syllogism or analyzing kinship relations. But for science in general, we need a less specialized calculus. We need something capable of yielding both the common sense principles implicit in all careful reasoning and a goodly segment of classical mathematics, real number theory in particular. From these considerations emerges the conception of what I shall call 'a grand logic'[5] – i.e., a system comparable in strength and at least equal in precision to Whitehead and Russell's *Principia Mathematica*, comprising general calculi governing truth-functionality, quantification, class-membership and class-abstraction or their equivalents.

Let us look again, this time identifying logic with grand logic, at the motives underlying anontologism. The apriority of a grand logic is highly questionable. I shall not argue this in detail, because it has already been done with acuity and penetration by W. V. Quine.[6] He contends that the distinction between the *a priori* (or analytic) and the *a posteriori* (or synthetic) cannot in general be drawn. What has passed for the one differs from what has passed for the other only in being less affected by observation, but this is merely a matter of degree. The logical rule of universal instantiation[7], the Pythagorean theorem and Newton's law of gravitation display in ascending order varying degrees of dependence upon the world of sensory data. Yet these three are similar in that, although none confronts that world directly, each mediates between the so-called observation-sentences that do; witness the fact that each of the three principles may play its role in the single prediction of one observed position from others. Each such principle provides connective tissue invaluable in passing by inference or computation from observation to observation. Each is justified pragmatically for each is tied up with observation by being part of the overarching theory which is science as a whole, itself empirical because at its edges (to use Quine's expression) it *is* immediately responsive to observation. If we adopt Quine's holistic view of science, it seems that we can argue that there is nothing *a priori* about logic and that consequently we do not need to adopt a position which explains its apriority.

What about certainty in grand logics? Certainty in this context is not merely psychological certainty, or cocksureness, or absolute confidence. On the other hand, if such absolute confidence were never even in principle justified, then there would not be any theoretical certainty either. My position[8] is that such confidence in any grand logic is never justified. When people think it is, they give examples like 'If P then P' or the syllogism; and they point out these things as instances of logical certitude. But grand logics include much more questionable items – the Axiom of Choice, for instance, or assumptions guaranteeing the existence of the larger ordinals. When the logician debates, as he frequently does, the truth of such principles, he usually has little faith in his own position and less hope of changing his opponent's; he, at least, knows that he stands on very shaky ground.

While such debatable principles tend to be similarly recondite, they are not always so for the sources of logical uncertainty may emerge in the guise of some famous antinomy at the borders of common sense. As an example, take Russell's Paradox. It can be formulated in the following way. One standard device for constructing class-names is abstraction. This amounts to selecting some necessary and sufficient condition of membership in the class to be named, expressing this condition as a 'condition on' some free variable, and prefixing to the condition the same variable somehow typographically distinguished, say by a circumflex. The resulting expression, called an 'abstract', is then taken as naming the class of all and only those things that satisfy the condition. Thus '$\hat{x}(x > 2)$', and '$\hat{x}(x$ is a horse)' are abstracts which respectively designate the class of numbers greater than two and the class of horses. Now Lassie is a member of this last class precisely if she is a horse, in symbols

$$\text{Lassie } \varepsilon \hat{x}(x \text{ is a horse}) \equiv \text{Lassie is a horse.}$$

Similarly

$$\text{Citation } \varepsilon \hat{x}(x \text{ is a horse}) \equiv \text{Citation is a horse.}$$

More generally

$$(y)(y \varepsilon \hat{x}(x \text{ is a horse}) \equiv y \text{ is a horse}).$$

More generally still

(7) $\qquad (y)(y \varepsilon \hat{x} p \equiv q)$

where 'p' stands in place of any condition on 'x' and 'q' in place of the corresponding condition on 'y'. (7) is sometimes referred to as the Principle of Abstraction. Where 'p' is replaced by '$\sim(x \varepsilon x)$' (7) yields

247

(8) $(y)(y\,\varepsilon\,\hat{x}\sim(x\varepsilon x)\equiv\,\sim(y\varepsilon y))$.

By abbreviating '$\hat{x}\sim(x\varepsilon x)$' as '$R$', we may compress (8) as

(9) $(y)(y\varepsilon R\equiv\,\sim(y\varepsilon y))$.

Invoking universal instantiation, we may take the y of (9) as R itself thereby deriving

(10) $R\varepsilon R\equiv\,\sim(R\varepsilon R)$,

which is contradictory.

Russell's Paradox can be dodged in various ways. One lies in so framing our grand logic's grammar as to leave any expression containing '$x\varepsilon x$' or the like ungrammatical. Lines (8), (9), and (10) are thereby counted-out of the language and the entire argument of the paradox fails by lapsing into nonsense. This in essence is the Theory of Types elaborated in *Principia*[9] and later simplified by Ramsey.[10]

A less sweeping reform consists simply in failing to assume the Principle of Abstraction true for all replacements of 'p'. The requirement, for instance, might be that any such replacement conform to the canons of simplified type-theory. (8) thus remains meaningful but turns false, so that the paradoxical argument fails at that point. This is the line followed by Quine in the system of 'New foundations'.[11]

In *Mathematical Logic*[12], Quine worked out another alternative. Taking the abstraction-prefix '$\hat{x}$' as synonymous not with 'the class of all entities x such that' but rather with 'the class of all *membership-eligible* entities such that', he rewrote the Principle of Abstraction, or line (7), to read

(7′) $(y)(y\varepsilon\hat{x}p\equiv((\exists z)(y\varepsilon z)\,\&\,q))$.

The argument of the paradox now culminates in

(10′) $R\varepsilon R\equiv((\exists z)(R\varepsilon z)\,\&\,\sim(R\varepsilon R))$

which, instead of being contradictory, is simply equivalent to

(11) $\sim(\exists z)(R\varepsilon z)$

or 'Russell's class is a member of nothing'.

Parallel to Quine's distinction between membership-eligible entities and

248

entities in general is the distinction, central to the von Neumann-Bernays system[13], between sets and classes in general. This distinction is there marked by the use of differing variables and the paradox is dodged by in effect rewriting (7) with set-variables. The Principle of Abstraction is thus maintained for sets only, of which Russell's class is not one.

Finally, one might maintain consistency in the face of Russell's Paradox simply by so reconstructing the logic of the truth-functional connectives '$\sim$', '$\equiv$', and so on as to leave some sentences of the form

(12) $A \equiv \sim A$

consistent. But this is difficult. (12) yields '$A \supset \sim A$' and hence

(13) $A \supset (A \mathbin{\&} \sim A)$.

Similarly, (12) yields '$\sim A \supset A$' and hence

(14) $\sim A \supset (A \mathbin{\&} \sim A)$.

Given the Law of Excluded Middle, or

(15) $A \vee \sim A$

a dilemmatic argument yields '$A \mathbin{\&} \sim A$', showing (12) self-contradictory. One might, however, argue that (15) is not self-evident, that 'A' and '$\sim A$' might *both* be false, in which case (12) would be true. Intuitionism, in fact, takes this very course; it holds (15) true only for those cases wherein one of the two disjuncts is provable. Neither '$R\varepsilon R$' nor '$\sim(R\varepsilon R)$', presumably, is such, so that (10) may be defended as a consistent instance of (12).

Here then are five plans for avoiding Russell's Paradox. There are others, equally well-known.[14] In their efforts to preserve consistency they all warp logic away from intuitive obviousness, each drastically and each in its own direction. The result is twofold. First, we are confronted not with a single grand logic appearing in trivially different guises but with five or more fundamentally divergent grand logics. Second, in attempting to choose among them we can scarcely appeal to self-evidence: *that* standard led to the paradox itself. A consistency-proof might end the competition, but none has emerged. Each of the five devices sketched seems to save logic from Russell's Paradox. But this is only to say that each in some way obviates all the familiar versions of the paradox. Perhaps there are other versions capable in some subtle way of slipping into logic past any one of these protective devices. And there are other paradoxes, almost as famous as Russell's.[15] Again, various barriers – the given five for instance – seem to protect logic from them. But the danger, now even greater, of infiltration by unfamiliar versions remains. Indeed, brand new paradoxes different in essence from any antinomy hitherto imagined may even now lie hidden in the labyrinthine implications of every known grand logic like a fatal parasite lodged in the viscera of some majestic animal. Grand logics are no more certain than they are *a priori*.

Unsupported by faith in certainty or the *a priori*, semantic ascent becomes ontologically trivial: *per se* the possibility of it argues nothing. In the first place, it is too general. Surely some sentences imply that extralinguistic objects exist yet even these sentences are replaceable by others that are, on the surface at least, *about* language only: witness the equivalence of any sentence *S* with '*S* is true'. In the second place, semantic ascent is one half of a two way road; the other half is semantic descent. Paralleling the passage from '2 is a number' to '"2" is a numeral' is the passage from '"2" is a numeral' to '2 is a number'. Whatever anontologism gains in the former transition, it loses in the latter.

The anontologist's motives thus appear suspect indeed for he values his view because it explains why logic is certain and *a priori*, when it is in fact neither. It can surely be counted no virtue in a theory that it explains supposed facts which are mere myth. It is as if one were to argue for some *outré* zoological hypothesis on the ground that it accounted for the evolution of the unicorn and the hippogriff.

III. ONTOLOGIZING THE GRAND LOGIC

A grand logic can be given as a purely formal calculus – a set of shapes determined by rules that specify its membership on the basis of pattern alone. Such a purely formal calculus may remain uninterpreted: as long as it does, it has no ontological import since, being meaningless, it lacks import altogether. Clearly the ontology enters the system with interpretation, if at all. There is no mystery in this for it merely amounts to saying that the theorems of the system possess ontological import, because we correctly understand them as asserting that certain things exist. One may even – though doubtless with a shade of artificiality – conceive the endowment of a system with an ontology as a step-by-step process wherein we start with an uninterpreted calculus and proceed by interpreting to ontologize it. To interpret the system, we first separate out from the whole language two groups of expressions, categorematic substantives and (closed) declarative sentences. Then we assign referents or *designata* to all members of the first and truth-conditions to the members of the second. While full interpretation requires both assignments – the first to fix the subject-matter discussed by the system, the second to determine the role of syncategorematic expressions in our discussion of it – the process of ontologizing comprises the first only. We cannot even attempt to assign a given entity as the designatum of a substantive without believing that there *is* such an entity to be designated. Ontologizing is assigning referents to substantives.

In practice, two interpreters can agree in using and even in a large measure in analyzing a language without once agreeing on exactly which entities are designated by its substantives. Consider for instance

(16)   Men are bipeds.

Under one interpretation 'men' and 'bipeds' can be taken as categorematic terms referring to classes and (16) itself as asserting that the first of these classes is a part of the second. So interpreted, (16) thus seems to commit the interpreter to an ontology including classes. Otherwise construed, however, (16) can be taken as short for, say

(17) (x) $(x$ is rational $\supset x$ is two-legged)

where the values of the variable 'x' are limited to animals. Here, it might be held, only the variable is a substantive: the quantifier, the horseshoe, the copula and the two predicates are all syncategorematic particles to be explained in terms of truth-conditions or simply to be taken without explanation as understood. So taken (17), and hence its abbreviation (16), seems to commit the interpreter only to an ontology that includes animals, leaving him free to eschew classes altogether. In translating (16) as (17), the apparently categorematic terms of (16) have dissolved into those, ontologically far lighter, of (17), and (16)'s ostensible reference to certain entities has been explained away as a mere *façon de parler*. Can this always be done? Can *any* expression whatsoever be taken as syncategorematic? Certainly the speaker's metaphysical preferences do not settle the question

– particularly when specific translations, like (17)'s of (16), are lacking. What is wanted here is some standard of ontological commitment, some rule or criterion establishing when a given term may and when it may not be taken as syncategorematic.

Such a criterion has been provided by Quine.[16] Its kernel is that existence or being[17] is the property that we attribute by using the existential or particular quantifier, say '$(\exists x)$', usually translated as 'there is at least one x such that', or 'there exists an x such that', or 'for some x'. Another translation is 'for some value of the variable "x"'. Thus

(18) $(\exists x)\,(x = 2)$

means that for some value of 'x', '$x = 2$' is true. The one who ascribes existence to the number 2 by asserting (18) does so by taking 2 as a value of the bound variable 'x'. More generally, a sentence S imputes existence to those entities that its bound variables must take as values if it is to be true. This principle can stand without further elaboration as the criterion of ontological commitment provided that the language of S contains bindable variables as its sole primitive referential substantives. For simplicity and elegance Quine prefers such languages and confines his attention to them – a limitation legitimate in view of the known procedure for introducing *via* contextual definitions referential substantives other than variables.[18] We may nonetheless, in particular cases, prefer not to define these other substantives; we may prefer to take as primitive not only variables but also, say, abstracts or Russell's definite descriptions or even the '0', '0′', '0″' and so on, used in many versions of Peano's axioms. If so, the ontological criterion must be adumbrated, to wit: a sentence S imputes existence to every entity that some bound variables in S must take as a value or that some other substantive in S must take as a *designatum* if S is to be true. Even in the light of the adumbrated criterion the role of the bound variable remains crucial. For how can we determine whether a non-variable substantive in S *must* take something as a *designatum* for the sake of S's truth? One might, for instance, claim that

(19)   Oddness belongs to 2,

for short,

(20)   *O*2

252

means simply that 2 is odd, where 'odd' is merely an adjective and (hence) syncategorematic. Could we justly make such a claim for '2'? Not if we legitimize the inference from (20) of

(21) $(\exists x)\,(x = 2\ \&\ Ox)$

and thereby successively of

(22) $(\exists x)\,(x = 2)\ \&\ (\exists x)\,Ox$

and

(23) $(\exists x)\,(x = 2)$;

for (23) is the (18) which ascribes existence to 2. Nor can the claim be justly maintained for 'odd' itself, if we permit the parallel inference of

(24) $(\exists \phi)\,(\phi = O)$

from (20). So long, however, as we exclude the inference of (24) from (20), we are free to take 'odd' or 'oddness' or 'O' as syncategorematic and to take (20) as not imputing existence to this property. Alternatively, we might make simple existential generalization our test-inference: treating '2' as categorematic amounts to permitting the inference of '$(\exists x)\,Ox$', for surely if 'there exists an odd thing' follows from '2 is odd', it is because 2 exists.

Ontologizing a formal system, then, is part of interpreting it, specifically that part which consists in assigning referents to its categorematic substantives. Any given theorem of the system commits its asserter to the existence of all such referents required for the theorem's truth. These referents will comprise the values of its bound variables and the *designata* of all of its substantives replaceable by bound variables *via* existential generalization. The grand logic, as I have sketched it earlier, can be so constructed that its sole primitive categorematic substantives, as measured by this criterion, will be bound and bindable variables plus abstracts. It is to the referents of these that we must look for its ontology.

IV. NOMINALISM AND THE SYSTEM G

Let me for convenience here introduce the letter 'G' as the name of some grand logic, as yet unidentified, but having the scope required of any grand logic and restricted in its categorematic substantives as described at the end of Section III above. Incorporating some version of set-theory and hence terms usually translated as 'class', 'relation', 'function' and the like, G will number among its substantives many that ostensibly refer to abstract entities. It accordingly seems natural to scrutinize G's ontology in the light of the major historical alternative viewpoints on the status of the abstract, namely nominalism, conceptualism, and platonism.

Nominalism may be defined as the doctrine that all things are concrete particulars – say, heaps of atoms, or volumes of space-time, or sense-data-complexes, or mental processes. Where within such a mundane world can referents be found able to sustain G's soaring discussion of the abstract? "Nowhere", the conscientious nominalist may reply. Still he will find himself loath to junk G altogether: that considerable segment of it that overlaps classical mathematics seems firmly embedded in modern science as perhaps the most useful of all tools in solving the problems of the concrete. Bur perhaps that is all that classical mathematics and G with it, are; perhaps each is merely a tool, a machine, a giant abacus that in itself says nothing and hence means nothing but nonetheless works.

Although it dodges the difficulties implicit in any interpretation of G, the abacus-theory engenders troubles of its own. The nominalist may refuse to interpret the grand logic, but he can hardly treat his own meta-logical account of it similarly; this metalogic he presumably will insist on interpreting, assigning referents to such key syntactical terms as 'sentence of G', 'expression of G', and the like. Now, for instance, how many expressions are there in G? By the standards of 'classical syntax', as defined by the syntaxical axioms of Tarski's *Wahrheitsbegriff*[19], there are infinitely many, for these axioms guarantee both that the simplest expressions are expressions and that the result of joining any two expressions together is an expression. Confined as he is in his choice of referents to the concrete, the nominalist can maintain his abacus-theory only by either assuming an infinitude of concrete objects or by providing G with a 'non-classical' syntax. He can hardly welcome either alternative. If he accepts the first, he trespasses on ground that, as the most modest of metaphysicians, he would far, far prefer to abandon to the physicist, or astronomer or psychologist. If he accepts the second alternative, he runs the risk of being accused – and with justice – of describing, not G at all, but rather some impoverished imitation thereof.

There are other difficulties, How, for one, can the nominalist explain *why* the meaningless *G* works? Had he accepted it as meaningful, he might have attributed its utility to its truth, but this way is closed to him for truth presupposes meaning.

There is indeed something far-fetched in the claim that *G* is meaningless and hence about nothing. The student of mathematics, even in its most controversial reaches, seems everywhere confronted with a *prima facie* subject-matter. He seems to develop insight into this subject-matter, to acquire knowledge of it, to establish by discovery truth about it. Nor do these achievements appear merely a juggler's dexterity in shifting small senseless objects. If, as when he skirts paradox or confronts the upper infinite, he grows uncertain, it is not because his discourse lacks meaning but because it means so much that, recognizing his inability to fathom all its implications, he waxes sceptical of its truth.

The abacus-theory appears hopeless. But is the nominalist condemned to accepting it or altogether rejecting *G*? Is no nominalistic interpretation of *G* possible? Such would involve taking terms ordinarily dubbed abstract as concrete; abstracts, notably, would perforce be reconstructed as naming non-classes or, alternatively, the classes they name would perforce be reconstructed as non-abstract. Among such will be the numerals designating non-negative integers 0, 1, 2, and so on. Unfortunately classical arithmetic and hence *G*, guarantees an infinite supply of such integers. The nominalist must thus face again the infinity-problem already encountered in the abacus-theory. But now he confronts it in an even more acute form, for he must now choose between hypothesizing infinitely many *concreta* or claiming arithmetic false.

All in all, the nominalist's treatment of *G* seems peculiarly unsatisfactory. Nominalism provides too few objects.

V. CONCEPTUALISTIC INTERPRETATIONS OF *G*

The conceptualist might hope to do better here, for his world is richer. For him reality comes in two *strata*, not one – a bedrock of concrete particulars, like the nominalist's, but supporting a layer of abstract universals. These latter he identifies as concepts, and he asserts that they require the support of particulars, or depend for their existence upon such, by saying that universals exist 'in' particulars only. The universal

255

may inhere in particulars as a property of them, as whiteness in the snow-bank and the seagulls' breast; it may also subsist as a conceived property in the particular mind that thinks it, as in the mind of a Bacon scrutinizing snowbanks or an Audubon painting seagulls. These relations of inherence and subsistence, says the conceptualist, firmly ground the universals in the particular.

There are doubtless many ways that G may be interpreted as referring exclusively to particulars and universals, so depicted. The simplest and most natural suggestion is this: separate G's universe of discourse into classes and individuals[20]; let the latter be particulars and the former universals. A universal can then be defined in G's terms simply as an entity which is either the null-class or has members, and a particular can be defined as a memberless entity other than the null-class. Writing 'Ux' and 'Px' for 'x is a universal' and 'x is a particular' respectively these two definitions become

$$(25) \qquad Ux =_{df} x = \Lambda \vee (\exists y)(y \varepsilon x)$$

and

$$(26) \qquad Px =_{df} x \neq \Lambda \ \& \sim (\exists y)(y \varepsilon x).$$

The universal is thus the class of all the particulars in which it inheres as a property, and the property in question is the very class. Inherence itself is describable within G: under this interpretation

$$(27) \qquad \text{the property inheres in the particular}$$

becomes synonymous with

$$(28) \qquad Px \ \& \ Uy \ \& \ x \varepsilon y.$$

No comparable articulation of subsistence is possible: requisite terms like 'mind' and 'conceives' are wanting. The conceptualist might still take any class he wished as a subsistent class. He might hold some classes only subsistent and essay to formulate within G criteria of subsistence in terms, say, of size or lack of 'impredicative definability'. Or he might hold that every class is conceived by some mind or other – perhaps God's – and so subsists therein. In this event he might, without modifying definition (25), simply translate its *definiens* 'Ux' as 'x is a subsistent universal'. If the first course yields an analysis of subsistence that is strained or partial and the second yields no analysis of subsistence at all, it matters little. *G*'s failure under a given interpretation to analyze or even express this or that conceptualistic notion does not render the interpretation non-conceptualistic; *that* occurs only when *G*, so interpreted, contravenes conceptualism.

The identification of property with class underlying the synonymy of (27) with (28) constitutes a graver discrepancy. Properties, as ordinarily conceived, can differ from each other even when possessed by the same objects. The property of being a legal U.S. silver coin and the property of being a legal U.S. silver coin with milled edges·seem different: an object must have milled edges to possess the second property but not so the first. Yet the class of legal U.S. silver coins is the class of legal U.S. silver coins with milled edges, for a fundamental principle of set-theory asserts that two classes with the same members are the same class.[21] Again, being the first U.S. President and being the second husband of Martha Custis seem two properties, one conferred by the Electoral College and the other by Mrs Custis. Yet the class of first U.S. presidents and the class of Martha Custis' second husbands are the same, for each contains the same solitary member. Can properties be classes when the identity-conditions of the two so differ?

The answer is obvious: no. When in the course of our interpretation we take properties as classes, we are accordingly erasing this difference; by using the old word for the new thing, we substitute the new thing for the old one. The overall justification of this replacement of properties with classes rests on the latter's ability to perform all the needed functions of the former. Is this ability spurious or genuine? Much suggests that it is genuine. Pure mathematics has found itself able to dispense with properties altogether in favor of classes. Perhaps scientific theory as a whole is no more than applied mathematics, therefore susceptible to like economies. Perhaps common sense is only science that is unprecise, uncritical, unsystematic and a century or so behind the times. But these matters call for future investigation. Meanwhile, the 'extensionalized' conceptualism that takes properties as classes differs substantively from traditional conceptualism in so doing.

Despite this streamlining, or perhaps in part because of it, any attempt to interpret *G* conceptualistically uncovers various other stubborn incongruencies. There are two types of conceptualism, or perhaps it would be wiser to call them two strands within conceptualism. Let me call one objective, the other subjective. Objective conceptualism, by far the more common, is ordinarily attributed to Aristotle and Abelard. It holds that the universal first inheres in the concrete particulars that exemplify it as a property, whence the mind abstracts it as a concept. The universal cannot achieve the latter status without having first enjoyed the former, so that there can be no unexemplified universals. If, however, universals are classes and exemplification class-membership, there is one entity which *is* exactly that, namely the null or empty set[22]; for

(29) $(x) \sim (x \varepsilon \Lambda),$

or the equivalent, is a theorem of G. The objective conceptualist, moreover, stipulates that the universal must be exemplified in the concrete particular. Taken extensionally, this requires all members of classes to be individuals. G, on the contrary, provides an endless array of classes-of-non-individuals. A pair is a two-membered class, for instance, so that the class of all pairs – identified by Frege, and following him by the authors of *Principia*, with the cardinal number two – is a class of non-individuals. Analogously for the cardinal number three, and similarly for relations, classes of relations, and so on. Objective conceptualism fits G poorly.

Subjective conceptualism promises better. While cleaving to the core dogma of all conceptualism – that the abstract universal depends for its being upon the concrete particular – subjective conceptualism sees this dependence as the creation of the universal by the particular mind together with its subsequent subsistence therein. The null-class, or any class, thus need not have concrete particular members to exist; the concrete particular mind that by conceiving creates it lends it all the existence it needs. But this variant generates internal difficulties of its own. People do create classifications – acts, that is, of classifying or, perhaps, habits of classifying. But these are concrete, and if conceptualism's universals reduce too such, conceptualism itself lapses into nominalism and falls prey to the same old objections. If on the other hand, the universal is the result or effect of such acts or habits, they will constitute its cause, and it is doubtful that anything so produced can in the end satisfy those explanatory needs that led us to postulate universals in the beginning. Universals, even if produced by minds, are still the properties – recurring throughout space-time and as objective as anything can be – of the concrete entities they characterize. Where two such concrete entities

258

differ it is by virtue of some property possessed by one but lacked by the other. If minds are required in order to produce properties, then no two concrete entities can differ unless the mind creates the difference-property. One galaxy could not be older than another or one atom smaller than another without the efforts of some universal-producing mind. Which mind? It seems the height of vanity and anachronism to lay so heavy a burden upon any human intelligence. The mind of God, then? Perhaps in the beginning and before the advent of man or other intelligent beings, the divine mind created at least some of the properties of things. But such a mentality would require from its beginning certain qualities – say divinity or wisdom – and what (presumably prior) mind created *them*? Theology thus offers the subjective conceptualist a mystery in lieu of an explanation.

The conceptualist might pin his final hopes on some judicious mixture of the subjective and the objective. "The empty class and any class of non-individuals", he might say, "owe their existence to the mind that conceives them; any other class owes its existence to the concrete particulars that are its members". This alternative, it is true, has a certain air of the *ad hoc* about it, but this may be an accident of exposition. The theory itself fails, however, by overlooking the way in which the existence of some classes determines the existence of others. Let me call any class of concrete particulars a first level class; and any class of kth level classes a $k+1$th level class. Now given n concrete particulars, there will be 2^n-1 non-empty first level classes of these; similarly there will be $2^{2^n-1}-1$ non-empty second level classes of these first level classes. Note that it is the number n of the particulars that fixes the number of these second level classes. It is also the identities of the particulars which fixes the identities of the second level classes. The existence of precisely *these* concrete particulars accordingly necessitates the existence of exactly *these* non-empty second level classes. The mind is powerless to affect this relation, yet the eclectic conceptualism in question maintains that the mind causes all such second level classes. How can this be, when the mind cannot influence their identity or number? The mind here is like the spectator who after the finish to a race runs up to the winner and claps him on the back: he is recognizing an achievement that he has not produced.

Further efforts to outfit G with a conceptualist interpretation – whether objective, subjective, or mixed – promise to be no more successful than the foregoing. And why make them? I used to identify constructivism in logic with conceptualism and to include as modern forms of the latter (in order of increasing strength) the intuitionistic systems of Brouwer and Heyting, Language I of Carnap's *Logical Syntax*, and the theory of cumulative types in Quine's 'On Universals'.[23] Such an identification now seems unnecessary. Constructivism can be taken as reflecting a lack of confidence in the mind's ability to fathom the abstract; it need not rest on any real belief that the abstraet must be created by the mind or lodged in the concrete. Taken in this spirit, the constructivist system can be interpreted as a cautious platonism.

VI. PLATONISTIC INTERPRETATIONS OF *G*

In providing *G* with a platonistic interpretation, we may proceed up to a point as under conceptualism, identifying universals with classes, particulars with individuals, and exemplification with class-membership. Because of this similarity, the platonistic will share with the conceptualistic interpretation both an advantage over the nominalistic and a limitation. In recognizing non-particulars, the platonistic interpretation follows the conceptualistic in dodging the nominalist's infinity-troubles as regards both expressions and numbers. Admitting classes of all levels assures a boundless supply of entities. Even so, their variety is limited by reducing properties to classes: no two universals can be exemplified by exactly the same objects, so that our platonism, like our conceptualism, is 'extensionalized'.

The platonist gains power by freeing the universal from its dependence on the particular. For him the universal need not be exemplified in a concrete entity nor indeed in any entity at all. For him the existence of the null set and higher level sets, so troublesome for objective conceptualism, presents no problem. By taking classes as uncaused and eternal, he frees the universal from its genetic dependence on mind and time. It was this dependence that so plagued objective conceptualism, leading universals to revert to the particular or tempting them either to abandon their office as objective characteristics of things or to turn into theological mysteries. Finally, the ills of eclectic conceptualism, which sprang from its charging the mind with the production of upper level classes but not of particulars, vanish once the mind is relieved of all responsibility for creating either. The platonistic interpretation of *G* is immune to all the objections levelled in the foregoing against nominalistic and conceptualistic interpretations.

A platonistic interpretation might, to be sure, encounter difficulties of its own. A likely candidate is the question of how we gain and test our knowledge of universals. The nominalist solves this problem by side-stepping it: no universals, no problem of knowing about universals. Of course, there will be sentences like (16) that may seem to refer to universals; one may ask how we test these sentences. The nominalist can reply that such statements, since like (17) they really deal with concrete particulars only, need embody no extra-empirical beliefs and can therefore be subject to the test of observation. Confronted with the problem of our knowledge of universals, the conceptualist may proceed in like vein. "If the universal is *in rebus*", he might advise, "observe the things; if *in mente*, introspect". The platonist, on the contrary, so sharply separates universal from particular that he may despair of ever learning anything about the first from the second; so, indeed, arose Plato's own doctrine of reminiscence.

How then do we find out about this realm of extra-mental, non-particular, unobservable entities? Our knowledge of them, like our knowledge of the extra-mental, unobservable objects of the physical sciences, is indirect, being tied to perceived things by a fragile web of theory. In both cases – physics and logic – our hypotheses about the unperceived are tested by their success in accounting for the character of the perceived. Misreading this similarity, one might easily conclude that a faculty of non-sensory perception, call it 'intuition', is necessary to play a part in logic parallel to the role of sensation in physics. The conclusion is groundless. Long-run success in dealing with the same old perceptual field of ordinary sensation holistically confirms not only our belief in a force satisfying an inverse-square law but also, if more remotely, our belief in the derivatives used to compute the force. It also confirms our belief in the classes ultimately invoked to so analyze the derivatives as to explain the computations.

G has hitherto been identified with no specific system; it has been described only as some grand logic whose sole categorematic terms are bound variables and the abstracts substitutable for them. Is it possible to pick the best of such logics, thereafter taking that as *G*? Not until after an inquiry many times longer than the present one, and even then not with any reasonable assurance: there are too many logics and too many criteria of selection. A less grandiose project will appear if we limit both. Let us then confine our choice of G to the five logics discussed above, in conjunction with Russell's paradox, and let us make our sole criterion for choosing among them the tenets of platonism. Any G so chosen will not be claimed the best grand logic – only the best of the five from a platonistic viewpoint.

Can we wring from platonism a decision for one of these five logics over the remaining four? The answer is a shaky "yes". Let us criticize each of the five in turn, starting with the intuitionistic.

Intuitionism's rejection of the law of Excluded Middle makes sense under conceptualism. Each of the two disjuncts of '$R\varepsilon R \vee \sim (R\varepsilon R)$', the conceptualist might point out, implies the existence of R. Further, he might hold that R is mind-created and that its very creation is, or at least requires, a direct existence – proof. Lacking such, he is free to regard '$R\varepsilon R \vee \sim (R\varepsilon R)$' as false. Even without accepting the conceptualist's myth of mental creation, one could *doubt* (15) on fallibilistic or generally sceptical grounds. The platonist himself could do as much: his constructivist logic would then appear as one of the 'cautious platonisms' mentioned at the end of Section V above. But minus the myth, the *rejection* of the Law of Excluded Middle is arbitrary to the verge of caprice. Besides, this rejection so cripples proof procedures – especially within real number theory and infinite arithmetic – that the loss in strength of the resulting system almost bars it from the ranks of grand logic altogether. Such weakness bids fair to gall the platonist especially, for it was more than likely the promise of logical power that drew him to platonism in the first place. As a possibility for G, the intuitionist's system strikes the platonist as a bad bet.

For a platonistically interpreted grand logic governed by the Simple Theory of Types, the type of an object might be defined as follows: the type of x is 1 if and only if x is a concrete particular; the type of x is $n+1$ (where $n \geq 1$) if and only if every member of x is of type n. By the canons of the theory, every object must be of some type or other, so that no class can draw its members from more than one type. Sentences asserting the contrary, plus all expressions containing them, are banished from the language of logic by grammatical ukase. This requirement of typical homogeneity embarrasses the platonist on two counts. First it splits the universe into a hierarchy whose lowest rank contains all type-1 objects, whose second rank contains all type-2 objects, whose third rank contains all type-3 objects, and so on: in general, its nth rank is identical with type n. If there are n first-rank objects, there will be exactly 2^n second-rank ones, exactly 2^{2^n} third-rank ones, and so on. The number of objects of lowest rank thus places a ceiling on the number of classes of any given sort, for all classes of any given sort must be alike in rank. This restriction not only strikes the platonist as a repugnant limitation of the universal by the particular; it also leaves standard mathematical items, e.g. that there is no greatest positive integer, un-provable unless infinitely many individuals are assumed. The platonist may be as unwilling to make this assumption as was the nominalist, the more so since he doubtless espoused platonism in the first place with the hope of escaping the nominalist's infinity-troubles.

The requirement of typical homogeneity disturbs the platonist at an even deeper level. In his eyes, the universal confers upon the world whatever unity and order the world possesses. Nor can anything, or any pair of things, exist and escape sharing in this unity and order. To be at all, according to his lights, any two things must be what they are and there-fore have the properties they do. They must share certain qualities the very attribute of being something, for one. Since they are two, not one, some characteristic must distinguish one from the other. And one must be related to the other in some fashion – by blood, or by spatio-temporal position, or by size, or by the fact that one has the other as a member or by the fact that it does not, and so on. Whether called properties, qualities, attributes, characteristics or relations[24], the connecting links here are all universals. Anyone who tells the platonist of two objects which exist without being so connected *via* the universal is going to inspire about as much confidence as the native who told the traveller lost in the New England hinterland that there was no way of getting from there to Boston. Indeed, for the platonist everything, whether concrete or abstract, occupies its own niche in the patterned domain of creation by virtue of the similarities, differences, and other relations that it bears to the rest of reality. Now to say of two entities x and y they that are similar is to say

(30)   there is some universal z exemplified by both x and y.

To say of x and y that they are different is to say

(31)   there is some universal exemplified by x but not by y.

To say that x bears some relation to y is to say[25]

(32)   there is some universal z exemplified by the (ordered) pair of x and y.

When 'ordered pair of x and y' is written '$\{x, y\}$', the three sentences (30), (31), and (32) translate into as respectively

(33) $(\exists z)\,(Uz \ \& \ x\varepsilon z \ \& \ y\varepsilon z)$

(34) $(\exists z)\,(Uz \ \& \ x\varepsilon z \ \& \ \sim (y\varepsilon z))$

(35) $(\exists z)\,(Uz \ \& \ \{x, y\}\varepsilon z)$.

But under type-theory (33), (34), and (35) are all nonsense where x and y are of different types, for in each such case the required universal z would be typically heterogeneous.[26] Yet in all such cases the platonist would want to assert x and y similar, different, or related, invoking the truth of (33), (34), or (35) by way of account. By his standards, type-theory logic thus suffers from a fatal discontinuity and because of this and its infinity-weakness, he will prefer to seek the better G elsewhere. The von Neumann-Bernays system NB admits entities, described as classes that are not sets, which belong to no class whatsoever. The non-elements of Quine's *Mathematical Logic* system ML occupy the same anomalous status: they are incapable of being members of any class. For the platonist who takes universals as classes, such a status is worse than anomalous: it is impossible. For him, things that belong to no class exemplify no universal and have no properties. They cannot be themselves or different from their surroundings. Such things for him, like irrational numbers for the pythagorean, cannot be. He cannot accordingly bring himself to identify either NB or ML with G. This is a pity, for their power and elegance delight his platonic heart.

Of the five logics initially listed only one remains – the system NF of Quine's 'New Foundations'. Surviving unweakened in this system, the law of excluded middle shields it from the ills of intuitionism. Nor is NF subject to type-theory's requirement of typical homogeneity. It thus escapes the latter's infinity-problems and the discontinuities generated by incomparable objects. Within it, entities of diverse levels can be proved similar and different in the sense of (33) and (34). Too, there can be infinitely many classes without there being infinitely many individuals.

Unlike the von Neumann-Bernays system and the system of *Mathematical Logic*, NF acknowledges nothing which is not a member of something. For NF the platonistic nightmare of thing-exemplifying-no-universal remains a morbid dream.

So far, so good. But NF is not without peculiarities of its own. Some are mere eccentricities, hence overlookable. Other must be counted genuine deficiencies. One such is NF's failure to provide a proof of mathematical induction over conditions that contravene type-theory's homogenity requirement.[27] Another is NF's incompatibility with the full-strength axiom of choice.[28] By way of minimizing the first of these two weaknesses, one might claim that mathematical induction is a principle of standard mathematics, that its main importance lies within that area, and that the regions consigned by type-theory to nonsense patently transcend standard mathematics. Pending some definitions of 'standard', this is vague enough. Still, NF is no worse off here than *Principia*: cases of mathematical induction unprovable in the former cannot in the latter even be stated. The gravity of NF's inconsistency with the full axiom of choice is harder to assess. Mathematics hitherto has found some of the consequences of this axiom indispensable, but a weaker form of it compatible with NF might well be found capable of yielding all such required.

Nevertheless, since deductive power is apt to count for so much by his standards, NF's weakness with respect to induction and choice-axioms will very likely weigh heavily against it with the platonist. And doubly so *vis-à-vis* NB and ML, which are surely free of the first of these two deficiencies and presumably free of the second. Only the fatal fault shared by these two systems prevents him from preferring them to NF.

A third deficiency in NF will augment his discomfort. In Section II above, it was pointed out that NF balks Russell's paradox by failing to render provable instances of (7) wherein 'p' infringes type-theory's grammatical fiat. But any instance of (7) can be proved in NF provided it can also be proved that the $\hat{x}p$ of (7) exists. Consistency thus ultimately depends upon the non-existence of Russell's class R. This non-existence weakens the system in ways that compromise manipulative facility. For instance,

(36) $(x)(x = x)$

is provable therein. Hence either universal instantiation or existential generalization must fail; otherwise (36) will yield

(37) $R = R$

which will in turn establish inconsistency *via*

(38) $(\exists x)\,(x = R)$.

Both NB and ML escape the need for any such restriction.

This deficiency in NF can, happily, be removed, but only at the cost of reformulating NF itself. One such revised NF is the following.[29] Its primitive notions are two, abstraction and exclusion. The former, expressed by

$\hat{a}p$

is read

the class of all entities a such that p.

Exclusion, expressed by the Greek[30] letter 'χ', is the relation of one class to another where the two have no members in common. Thus, for instance '$(x\chi y)$' is translatable as 'x excludes y' or more idiomatically 'no x's are y's'.[31] All sentences in the language will be of the form

$(f\chi g)$

where 'f' and 'g' are each replaceable by an abstract or a variable. The principal definitions are these:

(39) $(p/q) =_{\text{df}} (\hat{a}p\,\chi\,\hat{a}q)$

where the instance of 'a' is the alphabetically first[32] variable free neither in the instance of 'p' nor in that of 'q'. Translation of *definiendum*: 'not both p and q'.

The other common sentential connectives '$\sim$', '$\vee$', '$\&$', '$\supset$', and '$\equiv$' are definable in standard fashion in terms of '$/$'

(40) $(a)p =_{\text{df}} (\hat{a}\sim(a\chi a)\,\chi\,\hat{a}(a\chi\hat{a}p))$.

Translation of *definiendum*: 'for all a, p'. The existential quantifier can be defined as usual in terms of the universal one plus negation.

(41) $(f = g) =_{\text{df}} (a)\,(a\chi f \equiv a\chi g)$.

Translation of *definiendum*: '*f* is identical to *g*'.

(42) $[f] =_{df} \hat{a}(a=f)$.

Translation of *definiendum*: 'the class whose sole member is *f* '.

(43) $(f \, \varepsilon g) =_{df} \sim([f]\chi g)$.

Translation of *definiendum*: '*f* is a member of *g*'.

The axioms comprise (47), all instances of (44), plus all specified instances of (45), (46), (48), and (49):

(44) $((p/(q/r))/((t \supset t)/((s/q) \supset (p/s))))$;

(45) $(a) p \supset q$,

where the instance of '*q*' is like the instance of '*p*' except for containing free occurrences of an instance of '*b*' wherever the instance of '*p*' contains free occurrences of the instance of '*a*';

(46) $(a)(p \supset q) \supset (p \supset (a)q)$,

where the instance of '*a*' is not free in the instance of '*p*';

(47) $(x\chi y) \equiv (z)(([z] \chi x) \vee ([z] \chi y))$;

(48) $([b] \chi \, \hat{a}p) \equiv (c)((a)(([a] \chi c) \equiv \sim p) \supset ([b] \chi c))$,

where the instance of '*c*' is neither the instance of '*b*' nor free in the instance of '$\hat{a}p$';

(49) $p \supset (a \varepsilon \hat{a}p)$,

where the instance of '*p*' is stratified. An expression is said to be stratified [33] if it is possible to assign integers to the substantives (the variables and abstracts, that is) of its primitive expansion so that the same substantive is assigned the same integer throughout, any two substantives joined by 'χ' are assigned the same integer, and any abstract is assigned an integer one greater than the integer assigned the circumflexed variable that begins it.

The theorems will be all sentences generated from the axioms *via* these two rules of derivability:

(50)   From corresponding instances of '*p*' and '$(p/(q/r))$' the corresponding instance of '*r*' is derivable.

(51)   From any instance of '*p*' any corresponding instance of '$(a) p$' is derivable.

The axioms (44) combine with the rule (50) to establish all tautologies. Addition of axioms (45), (46), and rule (51) yields all the truths of quantification-theory. Further supplementation by way of (49) produces a version of set-theory.[34]

This revision NNF of NF repairs the original's deficiencies with respect to universal instantiation and existential generalization. Indeed, the first of these is guaranteed immediately, the second almost immediately, by (45). Thus within NNF the existence of Russell's class R is provable. The paradox is nonetheless avoided since within NNF the existence of R does not yield the fatal line (8). More comprehensively, within NNF the general principle of abstraction, which would yield (8) and which may be written

$$(52) \qquad (a)\,(a\,\varepsilon\,\hat{a}p \equiv p)$$

does not follow from the existence of the class designated by '$\hat{a}p$'. Half of what is involved in (50) is, indeed, forthcoming:

$$(53) \qquad (a)\,(a\,\varepsilon\,\hat{a}p \supset p)$$

is demonstrable. The other half, or

$$(54) \qquad (a)\,(p \supset a\,\varepsilon\,\hat{a}p)$$

is apparently not. (49) provides *via* (51) every instance of (54) in which the corresponding instance of 'p' is stratified. But 'R' is not stratified. Accordingly the argument of the paradox falls short of inconsistency and becomes merely a harmless *reductio ad absurdum* proof that (7), and hence (52), fail where the instance of '$\hat{a}p$' is 'R'. Let an instance of '$\hat{a}p$' be called *normal* if the corresponding instance of (52) is true; let it be called *abnormal* if the corresponding instance of

$$(55) \qquad \sim (a)\,(a\,\varepsilon\,\hat{a}p \equiv p)$$

is true. In the terms of this definition, Russell's paradox simply proves 'R' an abnormal abstract. It is easily established that all abnormal abstracts designate the empty class: all instance of

$$(56) \qquad \sim (a)\,(a\,\varepsilon\,\hat{a}p \equiv p) \supset \hat{a}p = \Lambda$$

are theorems of NNF.[35] Russell's class R, non-existent by NF's standards, exists by NNF's but is empty. So for any class condemned within NF by a

268

paradox to non-existence: the same paradox within NNF proves the class null. The presumably many non-existent classes of NF are thus by NNF fused into a single existent one, namely Λ.

Although one of NF's three deficiencies is remedied in NNF, the remaining two survive unmitigated. Still the platonist apparently has no choice but to accept the 'New Foundations' system in its revised version as, by his lights, the best of the five logics considered. Despite misgivings, he will identify NNF with G.

VII. TRADITIONAL PLATONISTIC THESES: THE VIEW FROM G

In the preceding I have attempted to fit, by dint of some tailoring of each, an age-old philosophical doctrine to a modern science. The result is the platonistically interpreted system G. Does this logical platonism or platonistic logic, skeletal and bare as it is, shed any light on traditional platonism? I maintain that it does. I shall attempt to show this by considering in turn various theses that form parts of the platonistic tradition. These are mere examples: my treatment of them is intended only to suggest the direction that a more sustained critical effort might take.

Consider, for instance, the traditional thesis proclaiming that the particular participates in the universal. The sentence

(57)   Particular x participates in universal y

may be translated into G as

(58) Px & Uy & $x\varepsilon y$

– in English 'x is an individual and y a class and x is a member of y'. In the transition from (57) to (58), three vague notions make way for three clear ones. True, set-theory leaves unsettled many questions about individuals, classes and membership, but it settles, insofar as anything can be settled, many others. If we compare this great body of sound theory and intelligible hypothesis with traditional discussions of the universal's exemplification in the particular, it will surely be evident that the replacement of (57) by (58) marks in identifiable ways a clear net gain. For example, it now becomes evident that not only particulars but universals as well participate in universals: classes in general are members of classes. How one universal could exemplify another remained, on the contrary, a mystery as long as exemplification could be misconceived as an act performed, or a process engaged in, by the exemplifying entity. Again, remember the tendency, dominant in Plato himself, to equate exemplification with some sort of approximation so that the particular never possessed properties but only 'imitated' them. This identification, which vitiated the whole platonic epistemology by branding knowledge of the particular impossible, was doubtless encouraged by an unfortunate choice of examples. It may well be that no man is wholly just and no wheel perfectly circular. But 'being partly just' and 'being nearly circular' may also designate properties which particular people and wheels actually have. Plato's error here lay in his failure to recognize that even the most poetic and metaphorical imitation of one quality is the stone-cold, sober possession of another. This far-reaching oversight becomes impossible once (57) is translated as (58). Who could reasonably maintain that particulars, instead of actually being members of classes, only come close to being such?

Consider a second traditional thesis of platonism, that the universal is independent of the particular. Several senses can be attributed to this, and under some of them it is false. It can, for one, be taken to mean that whether universal x is identical with universal y is a question that never turns on what particulars exemplify x and y. So taken, it is false by G, one of whose theorems is

$$(59) \qquad (x)(y)(x = y \equiv (z)(z\varepsilon x \equiv z\varepsilon y)),$$

which is true for *all* x and y, classes of individuals included. Alternatively, the thesis may mean that the identity of universal x with universal y is nowise affected by any relation borne by either to any particular. This also is false according to G, two of whose theorems are

$$(60) \qquad (x)(w)(\exists z)\, z(x, w)$$

and

$$(61) \qquad (x)(y)(w)(z)((z(x, w) \,\&\, \sim z(y, w)) \supset \sim (x = y)).$$

Of these, (60) guarantees that any universal x bears some relation to any particular w, whereas (61) assures us that any universal y will be other than x if y fails to bear that same relation to that same individual. Again, the thesis may amount merely to saying that there are universals unexemplified in particulars. In this sense, G holds it true: Λ, $[\Lambda]$, $[[\Lambda]]$, and so on are all classes without individuals as members, but

(62) $(\exists x)\, x = \Lambda$

(63) $(\exists x)\, x = [\Lambda]$

(64) $(\exists x)\, x = [[\Lambda]]$

and so on are all G-theorems.

A third thesis of traditional platonism proclaims that universals are eternal. Pending some addition of vocabulary, neither this thesis nor any contrary of it can be explicitly articulated in G. But the general analysis of classes embedded in G provides a perspective which displays the thesis as both intelligible and open to reasonable belief. Once universals are taken as classes[36], the thesis merely asserts that classes are eternal. If this is false, it must be because classes have durations. Now the duration of x may be thought of as the set of all instants – call them dates – at which x is: it is the line or line segment that constitutes x's time-span. We date an object when we determine which dates fall within its duration. For concrete particulars, this is the familiar process of discovering when events occur, deciding which periods they occupy and the like. But what is it for something which is *not* particular? How, in general, could one date classes?

For the platonist, the only feasible answer seems to be "By recourse to the classes' members". Where the class has particulars as members, the procedure is obvious: let the dates of x be the dates of those particulars. The rule could even be extended to accommodate a class x which has as its members just non-empty classes of individuals: let the dates of such an x be the dates of the dates of its members. And so on. Where x has members that are particulars, let *the particular corresponding to x* be the smallest single (usually discontinuous) particular whose parts they all are; where x is a set with members that have corresponding particulars; let the particular corresponding to x be the smallest particular whose parts those corresponding particulars all are. Then the general rule for dating a class becomes simply this: let the dates of a class be the dates of the corresponding particular.

271

The rule, of course, fails where there is no corresponding particular: it assigns no date to Λ, or $[\Lambda]$, or $[[\Lambda]]$, or to infinitely many other classes. The lack could be supplied by stipulation: let the dates of a class without corresponding particular be all dates. Or perhaps: let the dates of such a class be all dates after its discovery. But note how arbitrary such stipulations are. It is as if one were to identify the missing burglar's size with the size of his thumb print, or the foundling's birthday with the day of his appearance on the rectory doorstep. Indeed, the arbitrariness is so pronounced that it reveals the motivation underlying the stipulations themselves – the conviction, namely, that everything must, somehow, be dated. How defend this conviction? Perhaps it is an emotive relic of the nominalistic would-be reduction of all things to the particular; perhaps it stems from some buried distrust of the word 'eternal', a discomfort evoked by the term's metaphysical or religious associations. But these are only sentiments and hard to defend. Surely it would be more rational to abandon them and with them the need to date *everything*. The corresponding-particular method, or some variant thereof, of dating classes might still be retained, now unsupplemented by arbitrary stipulations, so that the net effect would be to assign dates to some classes but not others. So viewed, duration appears a property of some classes but not others, hence not essential to a class' being a class. A connection so accidental begs for a second look and upon re-examination the platonist might suddenly find the method of corresponding particulars, which at first seemed so inevitable, now only one more arbitrary stipulation. "Class and corresponding particular", he might point out, "are two quite different things. The correspondence between them no more justifies the assignment of the particular's dates to the class than the quite similar correspondence between parent and eldest child justifies attributing the latter's musical knowledge to the former. Indeed, the seeming inevitability of the method of corresponding particulars rests on *confusing* the set with the corresponding particular. In cold fact, no class has duration." So, at least, the platonist might argue in defending the thesis that all universals are eternal.

As a final instance of *G*'s power in making plausible sense out of something bordering unintelligibility, consider one more traditional thesis, to wit: that being and non-being are both universals and both are. To say of a thing x that it is, amounts to saying that there is something which is it. 'x is' thus translates into G's notation as

(65) $(\exists y)(y = x)$.

Given G's identification of property with class, the property common and peculiar to all things that are, which is the property called 'being', is thus designated by

(66) $\hat{x}(\exists y)(y = x)$.

Now (65) implies

(67) $x = x$

since the only y identical with x will be x itself. Conversely, (65) follows from (67): if x is itself, then some y (namely x) is x. (65) and (67) are thus logically equivalent, and the corresponding abstracts, (66) and

(68) $\hat{x}(x = x)$

are synonymous. But (68) is by definition 'V', the standard name of the universal class. Being, self-identity, and the universal class are for G one and the same. In like vein, to assert of x that it is not, is to deny (63), so that

(69) $\hat{x} \sim (\exists y)(y = x)$

designates non-being. But '$\sim(\exists y)(y=x)$' is equivalent to '$\sim(x=x)$' so that (69) is synonymous with '$\hat{x}\sim(x=x)$' by definition 'Λ', the standard name of the empty set. For G, non-being, self-distinctness and the null-class are one. That being and non-being are universals and that both are, is thus expressible by

(70) $UV \ \& \ U\Lambda \ \& \ (\exists y)(y = V) \ \& \ (\exists y)(y = \Lambda)$,

which is provable within G.

   Examples like the foregoing make it easy to overrate the power of G. The latter is, after all, only a system of logic. Even when supplemented by an appropriately restricted choice-axiom, it will remain, if consistent, mathematically incomplete, embracing a part only of all mathematical truth. Want of vocabulary, if nothing else, insures G's metaphysical incompleteness: whether particulars are sense data or material particles or something else, for instance, is a question whose answer G neither articulates nor directly illuminates. Even more marked is G's poverty with respect to the empirical sciences traditionally labeled such. Yet *G* formulates essential parts of mathematics, philosophy, and science so that it, or some variant thereof, may reasonably be adopted as the framework – strong, definite, examinable and corrigible – of our knowledge as a whole.

Nor is this all. Like the human skeleton, such a framework forms an intimate part of the structure it strengthens. Under any truly rational reconstruction of them, mathematics, philosophy and science will all include some logic or other. If this is to be one single logic shared by all three, it must be a grand logic, for only such can satisfy their diverse needs. So conceived, no one of the three can be true unless the embedded logic is true – and true not because it offers the mind a recognizable self-portrait or because it conforms to some gentlemen's agreement on the rules of the game, but because it describes the world as the world in cold fact is. Each of the grand logics, *G* among them, accordingly emerges as one more of those human efforts, individually uncertain but collectively obligatory, to fathom the nature of things.

Boston University

REFERENCES

[1] Ernest Nagel, 'Logic Without Ontology', in *Naturalism and the Human Spirit* (ed. by Yervant H. Krikorian), New York 1944; reprinted in E. Nagel, *Logic Without Metaphysics*, Glencoe, Ill., 1957.

[2] Compare 'analgesic', 'anastigmatic', 'anesthetic', etc. I owe the neologism to my colleague, Professor Erazim Kohak.

[3] See, for instance, Rudolf Carnap, *Philosophy and Logical Syntax*, London 1935, pp. 58ff.

[4] See W. V. Quine, *Word and Object*, New York and London 1960, pp. 270–276.

[5] I have borrowed the term from Hao Wang. See his 'The Categoricity Question of Certain Grand Logics', *Mathematische Zeitschrift* **59** (1953) 47–56, where he apparently uses the expression in the above sense. Compare 'grand duke', 'grand total' and 'grand larceny'. The latter suggests 'petty logic' as a label for small-bore calculi, but perhaps the suggestion is invidious. Wang's own source may be the title of the unfinished *Grand Logic* of C. S. Peirce. See Peirce's *Collected Papers*, vol. VIII, 278–280.

[6] See W. V. Quine, 'Two Dogmas of Empiricism', in *From a Logical Point of View*, Cambridge, Mass., 1953, pp. 20–46. Also, *Word and Object*, pp. 273–276.

[7] The rule permitting the inference of e.g. '$\alpha = 1$', '$\alpha = 2$', '$\alpha = y$' from '$(x) \alpha \equiv x$'. Its validity stems from the fact that what is true of everything must be true of anything.

[8] For a fuller statement of which see my 'Paradox and Logical Uncertainty', *Philosophical Forum* **15** (1957) 25–40.

[9] See Whitehead and Russell, *Principia Mathematica*, Cambridge, 1st ed., 1910–1913, especially 'Introduction, Ch. II' and the 'Prefatory Statement of Symbolic Conventions' beginning volume II.

[10] See F.P. Ramsey, *The Foundations of Mathematics and Other Logical Essays*, New York and London 1931, pp. 20–29.

[11] W.V. Quine, 'New Foundations for Mathematical Logic', *American Mathematical Monthly* **44** (1937) 70–80.

[12] W.V. Quine, *Mathematical Logic*, revised edition, Cambridge, Mass., 1951.

[13] See Paul Bernays, 'A System of Axiomatic Set-Theory'. This appeared by installments in the *Journal of Symbolic Logic* **2, 6, 7, 8, 13, 19**.

[14] Particularly Zermelo's. See Ernest Zermelo, 'Untersuchungen über die Grundlagen der Mengenlehre I', *Mathematische Annalen* **65** (1908) 261–281.

[15] For an account of the best known ones, see Whitehead and Russell, *op. cit.*, vol. I, pp. 60–65.

[16] See W.V. Quine, 'On What There Is', in *From a Logical Point of View*, pp. 1–19.

[17] In what follows, no distinction has been made between existence and being. Various such distinctions could, of course, be made but none seems relevant to present purposes.

[18] See *Mathematical Logic* §§ 24, 26, 27.

[19] Alfred Tarski, 'Der Wahrheitsbegriff in den formalisierten Sprachen', *Studia Philosophica* **1** (1936) 261–405.

[20] In some systems, in particular the system ML of *Mathematical Logic* and the system NNF introduced in Section VI above, individuals, which would ordinarily be non-classes, turn out to be classes of a certain sort, namely those which are their own sole members. Such odd classes might be termed *improper* classes, all others *proper*. The ordinary distinction of class from individual would then become the distinction of proper class from individual. For simplicity, I have retained the standard terminology; the reader may correct to fit the case. For the systems admitting improper classes, however, definitions (25) and (26) should be replaced as follows:

(25′) $Ux = _{df} \sim (y)\,(y = x \equiv y\,\varepsilon\,x)$

(26′) $Px = _{df} (y)\,(y = x \equiv y\,\varepsilon\,x).$

[21] Sometimes termed 'the principle of extensionality for classes'. In symbols

$$(x)\,(y)\,(x = y \equiv (z)\,(z\,\varepsilon\,x \equiv z\,\varepsilon\,y)).$$

[22] Usually designated by the Greek 'Λ', defined as '$\hat{x} \sim (x = x)$' or the like.

[23] For details and references, see my half of 'The Ontological Significance of the Löwenheim-Skolem Theorem', in *Academic Freedom, Logic and Religion* (ed. by Morton White), Philadelphia 1953, pp. 39–55.

[24] The standard logical analysis of relations ignores the feeling, evidently pretty common, that they are somehow more concrete than properties or classes, and interprets them as classes of sequences. Thus a dyadic relation z is identified with the class of exactly those two-membered sequences or ordered pairs $\{x, y\}$ each of whose first members x bears z to its second member y.

[25] Once the dyadic relation z is taken as a class of ordered pairs, to say "x bears z to y" means that the ordered pair $\{x, y\}$ is a member of z. In symbols, $z(x, y) \equiv \{x, y\}\,\varepsilon\,z$.

[26] It is possible to define relations which are in a sense heterogeneous with respect to type. For example, writing '$[x]$' and '$[x, y]$' for 'the class whose sole member is x' and 'the class whose sole members are x and y' respectively, the Wiener-Kuratowski defi-

275

nition essentially defines '$\{x, y\}$' as '$[[x], [x, y]]$'. See *Mathematical Logic*, § 36 for details. Where x and y are of like type, '$\{x, y\}$' so defined is meaningful under type-theory restrictions: any class of such ordered-pairs $\{x, y\}$ will be a homogeneous relation. Where x is of one type lower than y a new version of ordered pair is wanted: '$\{x, y\}_n{}^{n+1} =_{df} [[[x]], [[x], y]]$' will serve to define it. Any class of such ordered pairs may be taken as a heterogeneous relation joining one object to an object one type higher. The difficulty here is that $\{x, y\}_n{}^{n+1} = \{[x], y\}$, so that the heterogeneous relation of x to y is merely the homogeneous relation of $[x]$ to y, and the system, instead of discussing two different relations, merely contains two different names for the one relation. Similarly with variants and elaborations of such schemes: the net result is to multiply terminology, yet still leave amid the ranks of the missing connections which the platonist would deem present.

[27] See J.B. Rosser, 'Definition by Induction in Quine's "New Foundations for Mathematical Logic"', *Journal of Symbolic Logic* **4** (1939) 80–81.

[28] See E. Specker, 'The Axiom of Choice in Quine's "New Foundations for Mathematical Logic"', *Proceedings of the Academy of Science, U.S.A.* **39** (1953) 972–975.

[29] I have formulated the definitions and axioms to follow in terms of schemata using these schematic letters: 'a', 'b', 'c', 'd', whose instances are variables 'w', 'x', 'y', 'z', 'w''', – etc.; 'f', 'g', 'h', whose instances are variables and abstracts; 'p', 'q', 'r', 's', and 't', whose instances are sentences. ('Variables' here means 'variables to NNF', analogously for 'abstracts' and 'sentences'.) An instance of a schema is any expression formed by uniformly replacing all the schema's schematic letters with instances of them. Two expressions are corresponding instances of two schemata if they are instances formed therefrom by the same replacements.

[30] I have taken the chi, on the suggestion of my colleague, Mr. Walter Emge, from the Greek '$\chi\omega\rho\acute{\iota}\zeta o\mu\alpha\iota$' meaning 'to be separate from'.

[31] Where x or y is an individual, '$(x\chi y)$' is translated as 'x and y are distinct'; the effect in such cases is to make individuals improper classes. See note 20.

[32] Any order will serve as alphabetic; for instance, that in which the variables are listed at the beginning of note 29.

[33] The term was first used in this sense by Quine but the idea goes back to Russell. I have simply adapted Quine's definition to fit NNF's primitives. See *From a Logical Point of View*, p. 90f.

[34] The reduction of NNF's primitives to two was suggested by the similar reduction in Quine's 'Logic Based on Inclusion and Abstraction', *Journal of Symbolic Logic* **2** (1937) 145–152. I have preferred exclusion to inclusion because the former simplifies the structure of alternate denial. Of NNF's axioms and inferential rules, most have appeared in the literature in one status or another. (44) and (50) hark back to Nicod; see his 'A Reduction in the Number of the Primitive Propositions of Logic', *Proceedings of the Cambridge Philosophical Society* **19** (1916) 32–40. (45) and (46) are commonplace theorems of quantification-theory, and (51) is the familiar rule of universal generalization. (49) is simply a weakened form of the Principle of Abstraction. In developing NNF I have been aided considerably by the suggestions of three of my students – Victor Van Neste, Jr., Robert Maydole, and Owen Gallagher. I am also grateful to Prof. Quine for pointing out to me the inadequacy of an earlier set of axioms. The distinction of normal from abnormal abstracts, which dominates NNF's treatment of the logical paradoxes, is implicit in the ancillary system L_2 of Halperin's 'A set of Axioms for logic' [*Journal of Symbolic Logic*, **9** (1944) 1–19], which doubtless suggested it$_n$ to me. Although differing in their axioms, rules of inference, and primitive

notation, NNF and L_2 are equivalent systems in the sense that the primitive expansion of any theorem of either forms the definitional abbreviation of some theorem of the other.
[35] The proof may be sketched as follows. Where the instance of 'c' is as in (48), the latter yields

(A) $\qquad b \varepsilon \hat{a} p \supset (\exists c)(a)(a \varepsilon c \equiv p).$

By substitution

$$(a)(a \varepsilon c \equiv p) \supset \hat{a}(a \varepsilon c) = \hat{a} p,$$

which is to say

$$(a)(a \varepsilon c \equiv p) \supset c = \hat{a} p.$$

This successively implies

$$(a)(a \varepsilon c \equiv p) \supset (c = \hat{a} p \ \& \ (a)(a \varepsilon c \equiv p)),$$

$$(\exists c)(a)(a \varepsilon c \equiv p) \supset (\exists c)(c = \hat{a} p \ \& \ (a)(a \varepsilon c \equiv p)),$$

and

(B) $\qquad (\exists c)(a)(a \varepsilon c \equiv p) \supset (a)(a \varepsilon \hat{a} p \equiv p).$

From (A) and (B) together comes

$$b \varepsilon \hat{a} p \supset (a)(a \varepsilon \hat{a} p \equiv p),$$

thence

$$(\exists b)(b \varepsilon \hat{a} p) \supset (a)(a \varepsilon \hat{a} p \equiv p).$$

From this the desired result follows by transposition since only the empty class has no members.
[36] More accurately, 'proper classes'. See note 20: the distinction made there is crucial here.

277

RONALD BJÖRN JENSEN

ON THE CONSISTENCY OF A SLIGHT (?)
MODIFICATION OF QUINE'S *NEW FOUNDATIONS*

I

Quine's system of set theory, New Foundations (NF), can be conveniently formalized as a first-order theory containing two predicates $\equiv$ (identity) and ε (set membership). One of the most attractive features of NF is its simplicity. Apart from the rules and axioms of first-order identity logic, we need only two specifically set theoretical axiom schemes: the extensionality axiom:

(Ext) $\bigwedge z(z \in x \leftrightarrow z \in y) \rightarrow x \equiv y$,

and the set abstraction schema:

(Abst) $\bigvee y \bigwedge x(x \in y \leftrightarrow \mathfrak{A})$,

where y is not free in $\mathfrak{A}$ and $\mathfrak{A}$ is stratified (as usual, we call a formula *stratified* if indices can be assigned to its variables in such a manner that it becomes a formula of simple type theory).

The adoption of the extensionality axiom (Ext) in NF forces us to identify all objects with sets, leaving no room for non-sets or 'Urelements' which have no members (since any two Urelements would have to be equal by Ext). If we wish to avoid this anomaly we may replace Ext by the slightly weaker version:

(Ext') $\bigvee z(z \in x) \wedge \bigwedge z(z \in x \leftrightarrow z \in y). \rightarrow x \equiv y$.

Let us refer to the so modified system as NFU ('NF with Urelements'). At first sight one might suppose NFU to be but a trivial variant of NF. In fact, Quine himself seems to have held this viewpoint, for he motivates his choice of NF with the following words[1]: "'$(x \in y)$' states that x is a member of y. Prima facie this makes sense only where y is a class. However, we may agree on an arbitrary supplementary meaning for the case where y is an *individual* or non class: we may interpret '$(x \in y)$' in this case as stating that x is the individual y". In a footnote he adds, "This interpretation... results in the fusion of every individual with its unit class;

278

but this is harmless". In this paper we shall prove that NFU is consistent. As a corollary we obtain that NFU is essentially weaker than NF; moreover, NFU remains consistent upon adjoining the axiom of choice (AC), although Specker has shown that AC is refutable in NF. Thus, unexpectedly, the systems NF and NFU prove to be quite different. It is perhaps symptomatic of this state of affairs that we have been unable to extend our consistency result to NF; indeed, we doubt that this can be done with any easy modification of our method.

It is natural to consider the version of NF of NFU which is obtained by adding the following *axiom of infinity*.

(Inf)   There exists a non-empty linear ordering R which has no minimal element.

Inf is easily seen to be stratified. An alternative version of Inf can be given in terms of cardinal arithmetic. Define the *cardinal number* $\bar{x}$ of x as the collection of sets which are in one to one correspondence with x. $\bar{x}$ is a set by the abstraction axioms (Abstr). Call a total ordering R *finite* if R and its converse R^{-1} are both well orderings. Call n a *finite cardinal* if, for some finite R, n is the cardinal of the field of R. Then Inf is equivalent to:

$$\bigvee x(\bar{x} \text{ is not finite}).$$

By Inf it follows in particular that there is no greatest finite cardinal; hence every finite cardinal has an immediate successor. If we define the cardinal operations $+, \cdot$, in the usual manner, it turns out that all theorems of elementary number theory are provable in *NFU* + Inf (hence in NF + Inf) as statements about finite cardinals. On the other hand, $\neg$ Inf implies the existence of a greatest finite cardinal, namely $\bar{\bar{V}}$ (V being the universal set). It follows in particular that V is well orderable, hence $\neg$ Inf implies the *axiom of choice*.

(AC)   Every set of pairwise disjoint non-empty sets has a choice set.

(Note that AC is a stratified statement.) Specker [8] has shown by a highly ingenious proof that AC is refutable in NF. Hence Inf is provable in NF. Specker's proof makes heavy use of the axiom of extensionality and cannot be carried out in NFU. We shall, in fact, show that Inf is not provable in NFU.

We shall reduce the consistency question for NFU to that for the simple theory of finite types (T). T is a many sorted theory containing the two predicates $\equiv$, $\in$, and variables x^i of type i for each non-negative integer i. The primitive formulae of T have the form $x^i \in y^{i+1}$, $x^i \equiv y^i$. As axioms we adopt the extensionality axiom (Ext) and the set abstraction axioms (Abst) (more precisely, we adopt the T-formulae which may be obtained from Ext and Abst by adding indices to the variables). Since Inf and AC are stratified, we may also strengthen T by adopting one or both of these axioms (i.e., by adopting the T-formulae obtainable from them by adding indices to the variables). We shall prove:

THEOREM 1. If $T(T+\text{Inf}, T+\text{Inf}+\text{AC})$ is consistent, then so is NFU (NFU + Inf, NFU + Inf + AC).

Remark. It is known (and can be proven with the help of Gödel's theory of constructible sets) that $T+\text{Inf}+\text{AC}$ is equiconsistent with $T+\text{Inf}$. Hence NFU + Inf + AC is equiconsistent with NFU + Inf.

The proof will be given model theoretically, but could, in principle, be formalized in elementary number theory (Z), since it involves only the construction of specific models, which can be described in Z. If we do not insist on Inf, we can give a model of T consisting of finite sets. This model and its satisfaction relation are (via an appropriate arithmetization) definable in Z.

Following this lead, one can show that the consistency of T is provable in Z. By Theorem 1, then, the consistency of NFU is provable in Z. Gödel's second incompleteness theorem then tells us that Z is not interpretable in NFU; i.e., we cannot in NFU find predicates $N(x)$, $P(y, x, z)$, $M(y, x, z)$ such that all theorems of Z are provable in NFU, interpreting $N(x)$ as 'x is a number', $P(y, x, z)$ as '$y = x + z$' and $M(y, x, z)$ as '$y = x \cdot z$'. Thus, by our previous remark, we conclude that Inf is not provable in NFU.[2]

Specker in [9] has uncovered an interesting connection between NF and certain models of type theory. He considers a language (T^*) which is like T except that its variable types range through all of the integers ($\mathbf{3}$), rather than just the non-negative ones. Hence a model of T^* has the form $\langle U_i, \in_i \rangle_{i \in \mathbf{3}}$, where U_i is non-empty and $\in_i \subset U_i \times U_{i+1}$ for $i \in \mathbf{3}$. Let us call σ a *shifting automorphism* of $N = \langle U_i, \in_i \rangle_{i \in \mathbf{3}}$, if σ is a bijection of $\bigcup_{i \in \mathbf{3}} U_i$ which maps each U_i onto U_{i+1} in such a way that

$$x \in_i y \leftrightarrow \sigma(x) \in_{i+1} \sigma(y) \quad \text{for} \quad x \in U_i, y \in U_{i+1}.$$

We call N a *Specker model* if a shifting automorphism exists. Specker has proved the following theorem (cf. [9]):

LEMMA 1. NF is consistent if there exists a Specker model N in which the axioms Ext and Abst hold.

We obtain Lemma 1 as an almost immediate corollary of:

LEMMA 2. Let $N = \langle U_i, \in_i \rangle_{i \in 3}$ be a Specker model. Let σ be a shifting automorphism of N. Define a model $M = \langle U, \in \rangle$ by:

$$U =_{\mathrm{Df}} U_0 \; ; \; x \in y \leftrightarrow_{\mathrm{Df}} x \in_0 \sigma(y).$$

Then if $\mathfrak{A}$ is a stratified statement and $\mathfrak{A}^*$ is a T^*-statement obtained from $\mathfrak{A}$ by adding indices to the variables, we have

$$\vDash_N \mathfrak{A}^* \leftrightarrow \vDash_M \mathfrak{A}.$$

Proof: We show that if $\mathfrak{A} = \mathfrak{A}(x_1, \ldots, x_n)$ is any stratified formula and if $\mathfrak{A}^* = \mathfrak{A}^*(x_1^{i_1}, \ldots, x_n^{i_n})$ is a T^*-formula obtained from $\mathfrak{A}$ by indexing the variables, then

$$\vDash_N \mathfrak{A}^* [\sigma^{i_1}(u_1), \ldots, \sigma^{i_n}(u_n)] \leftrightarrow \vDash_M \mathfrak{A} [u_1, \ldots, u_n]$$

for all $u_1, \ldots, u_n \in U$. The proof is a straightforward induction on the construction of $\mathfrak{A}$.   Q.E.D.

In particular, if N is a model of Ext and Abst, then these axioms will also hold in M, where M is defined as above; i.e., M is a model of NF. On the other hand, supposing $M = \langle U, \in \rangle$ to be any model of NF, we can define a Specker model

$$N = \langle U_i, \in_i \rangle_{i \in 3}$$

by setting

$$U_i =_{\mathrm{Df}} U, \; \in_i =_{\mathrm{Df}} \in \text{ for } i \in 3.$$

The identity function is then a shifting automorphism of N and, by Lemma 2, N is a model of Ext and Abst. This establishes Lemma 1.

Having resolved to drop NF's extensionality axiom in favor of the weaker axiom Ext', it is natural to consider the system of type theory which results when the same change is made. (This means that each type level admits not only subsets of the previous level, but also new Urelements.) Using Lemma 2 and repeating, essentially, the above proof, we obtain the following analogue of Lemma 1:

LEMMA 3. NFU(NFU+Inf, NFU+Inf+AC) is consistent if there exists a Specker model N for Ext′+Abst (Ext′+Abst+Inf, Ext′+Abst +Inf+AC).

Thus our task reduces to that of constructing appropriate Specker models.

Our starting point for the construction of a Specker model will be a model of a first-order theory S which is equiconsistent with T. S is a weak version of Zermelo set theory. Its predicates are $\in$ and $\equiv$. In the following we use the abbreviations:

$$\bigwedge x{:}\in y\ \mathfrak{A} =_{\mathrm{Df}} \bigwedge x(x\in y \to \mathfrak{A})$$

$$\bigvee x{:}\in y\ \mathfrak{A} =_{\mathrm{Df}} \bigvee x(x\in y \wedge \mathfrak{A}).$$

We speak of such quantification as being *limited*. We call a formula *limited*, if it contains at most limited quantifiers; more precisely, we define the set of limited formulae by the recursion:

   (i) All primitive formulae are limited

   (ii) If $\mathfrak{A}$, $\mathfrak{B}$ are limited, then so is $(\mathfrak{A} \wedge \mathfrak{B})$ (similarly for $\vee$, $\to$, $\leftrightarrow$, $\neg$).

   (iii) If $\mathfrak{A}$ is limited, then so are $\bigwedge x{:}\in y\ \mathfrak{A}$, $\bigvee x{:}\in y\ \mathfrak{A}$.

As set theoretical axioms of S we adopt the axiom of extensionality (Ext) together with the following postulate of set existence:

S2.	$\{x, y\}$ is a set[3]	("pair set axiom")
S3.	$\cup x$ is a set[3]	("sum set axiom")
S4.	$\mathfrak{P}x$ is a set[3]	("power set axiom")
S5.	$\bigvee y \bigwedge z(z\in y \leftrightarrow \cdot z\in x \wedge \mathfrak{A})$,	

where y is not free in $\mathfrak{A}$ and $\mathfrak{A}$ is a limited formula.

We call S5 the *weak Aussonderungsaxiom*. (If we dropped the restriction to limited formulae, we would have the full Aussonderungsaxiom and S would coincide with Zermelo set theory.) We shall show that NFU is consistent relative to S. The consistency relative to T will then result from the following lemma.

LEMMA 4. $T(T+\mathrm{Inf}, T+\mathrm{Inf}+\mathrm{AC})$ is consistent if $S(S+\mathrm{Inf}, S+\mathrm{Inf}+ +\mathrm{AC})$ is consistent.

Lemma 4 is part of the folklore of the subject. For reasons of space (and our own inherent laziness) we shall limit ourselves to giving a sketch of the proof. We first show the consistency of T relative to S. Let

$M = \langle U, \epsilon' \rangle$ be a model of S. Let $u_0 \in U$ be a non-empty set of M (i.e. $\vDash_M u_0 \not\equiv \phi$)[4]. Define $u_i (i = 1, 2, \ldots)$ by:

$$\vDash_M u_{i+1} \equiv \mathfrak{P} u_i.^4$$

Set $U_i =_{Df} \{x \in U \mid \vDash_M x \in u_i\}$ and $\epsilon_i =_{Df} \epsilon' \cap (U_i \times U_{i+1})$. Then $N = \langle U_i, \epsilon_i \rangle_{i < \omega}$ is a model of T, as may easily be verified. Moreover, if AC holds in M, it must also hold in N, since for any $x \in U_{i+1}$, if $\vDash_M$ (y is a choice set for x), then $y \in U_i$ and $\vDash_N$ (y is a choice set for x). If Inf holds in M, we may choose u_0 such that $\vDash_M$ (u_0 is infinite). Inf then holds in N.

We now show that S is consistent relative to T. Let $N = \langle U_i, \epsilon_i \rangle_{i < \omega}$ be a model of T. We define sets $U_i^* \subset U_{i+2}$ and relations $\epsilon_i^* \subset U_i^* \times U_i^*$ as follows:

U_0^* is the set of finite cardinals in U_2[5] (i.e., the equivalence classes of finite $x \in U_1$).

ϵ_0^* is the natural ordering of U_0^*. U_{i+1}^* is the set of $x \in U_{i+3}$ such that $\{y \mid \vDash_N y \epsilon x\} \subset U_i^*$ but $\{y \mid \vDash_N y \epsilon x\} \neq \{y \mid y \epsilon_i^* z\}$ for any $z \in U_i^*$. The hierarchy $\langle U_i^*, \epsilon_i^* \rangle$ ($i < \omega$) is cumulative; in fact we have:

$$U_i^* \subset U_j^* \wedge \epsilon_i^* = \epsilon_j^* \restriction U_i^* \text{ for } i < j.$$

Setting: $\quad U^* =_{Df} \bigcup_i U_i^*; \quad \epsilon^*_{Df} = \bigcup_i \epsilon_i^*,$

it can be verified that $M^* = \langle U^*, \epsilon^* \rangle$ is a model of S. Moreover, if either of the axioms Inf, AC holds in N, then it holds in M^* as well. This completes the proof of Lemma 4.

Let S^* be S extended by the addition of *Skolem functions*; i.e., for each formula $\bigvee y \, \mathfrak{A}(y, x_1, \ldots, x_n)$ we adjoin a new function letter f and appoint the axiom:

(*) $\qquad \bigvee y \, \mathfrak{A}(y, x_1, \ldots, x_n) \leftrightarrow \mathfrak{A}(f(x_1, \ldots, x_n), x_1, \ldots, x_n).$

It is well known that S^* is consistent if S is. Now let us further extend S^* by adjoining new constants c_i ($i \in 3$) and appointing the axioms:

S6. $\qquad c_i \cup \mathfrak{P} c_i \subset c_j \quad (i < j)$

S7. $\qquad \mathfrak{A}(c_{i_1}, \ldots, c_{i_n}) \leftrightarrow \mathfrak{A}(c_{j_1}, \ldots, c_{j_n}),$

where $i_1 < i_2 < \cdots < i_n, j_1 < j_2 < \cdots < j_n$ and $\mathfrak{A} = \mathfrak{A}(x_1, \ldots, x_n)$ is an S^*-formula.

Call the resulting system S_1.

By S_2 we denote the system obtained from S_1 by adding the axioms:

S8. c_i is infinite.

LEMMA 5. If $S(S+\mathrm{Inf}, S+\mathrm{Inf}+\mathrm{AC})$ is consistent, then so is $S_1(S_2, S_2+\mathrm{AC})$.

We prove Lemma 5 with the help of Ramsey's theorem (cf. [7]).[6]

Set: $[A]^n =_{\mathrm{Df}} \{a \subset A | \bar{a} = n\}$ for $n > 0$.

If $B_i \subset [A]^{n_i}$ for $i = 1, ..., m$, we call $X \subset A$ a *collection of indiscernibles* (or an *indiscernible set*) with respect to $B_1, ..., B_m$, when $[X]^{n_i} \subset B_i$ or $[X]^{n_i} \subset [A]^{n_i} \backslash B_i$ for $i = 1, ..., m$. Using this terminology, we can state Ramsey's theorem as follows:

(R_0) If A is infinite and $B_i \subset [A]^{n_i}$ $(i = 1, ..., m)$, then there exists an infinite collection $X \subset A$ of indiscernibles with respect to $B_1, ..., B_m$.[7]

In order to show the consistency of S_1 relative to S^*, it suffices to show that every finite subset of the axioms S6, S7 may be consistently adjoined to S^*.

Let $M = \langle U, \in, \Omega \rangle$ be a model of S (Ω being the interpretation of the Skolem functions). We wish to show that every finite subset of the axioms S6 and S7 is interpretable in M. Choosing an arbitrary $u_0 \in U$, we define a sequence $u_i (i < \omega)$ by:

$$\vDash_M u_{i+1} \equiv u_i \cup \mathfrak{P} u_i.$$

Obviously, we have:

$$\vDash_M u_i \cup \mathfrak{P} u_i \subset u_j \quad \text{for} \quad i < j.$$

Thus, it suffices to show that for any finite sequence

$$\mathfrak{A}_i = \mathfrak{A}_i(x_1, ..., x_{n_i}) \, (i = 1, ..., m)$$

of S^*-formulae, there exists an infinite set $I \subset \omega$ such that:

$$\vDash_M \mathfrak{A}_i [u_{h_1}, ..., u_{h_{n_i}}] \leftrightarrow \vDash_M \mathfrak{A}_i [u_{j_1}, ..., u_{j_{n_i}}],$$

whenever $\langle h_1, ..., h_{n_i} \rangle$, $\langle j_1, ..., j_{n_i} \rangle$ are ascending sequences of elements of I. This follows at once if we take I as being indiscernible with respect to

$$B_i = \{\{j_1, ..., j_{n_i}\} | j_1 < \cdots < j_{n_i} \wedge \vDash_M \mathfrak{A}_i [u_{j_1}, ..., u_{j_{n_i}}]\}$$
$$(i = 1, ..., m).$$

284

Hence S_1 is consistent if S is. If $S+\text{Inf}$ is consistent, we can take M as being a model of Inf and, in the above proof, choose u_0 such that $\vDash_M$ (u_0 is infinite). By the same proof it then follows that each finite subset of S6 to S8 is interpretable in M, hence that S_2 is consistent. Finally, if $S+\text{Inf}+\text{AC}$ is consistent, we can take M as being a model of Inf $+\text{AC}$; hence $S_2+\text{AC}$ is consistent. This completes the proof of Lemma 5.

By a *constant term* of S_1, we mean one of the constants c_i on any term built up from the c_i by the use of Skolem functions. It is apparent that if $S_1(S_2, S_2+\text{AC})$ is consistent, then it has a model

$$M = \langle U, \in, \Omega \rangle$$

in which every $x \in U$ is denoted by a constant term. We may assume without loss of generality that c_i denotes itself ($i \in 3$). By S7 there is an automorphism of $\langle U, \in \rangle$ uniquely defined by: $\sigma(c_i)=c_{i+1}$ ($i \in 3$). Let us set:

$$U_i =_{\text{Df}} \{x \in U | \vDash_M x \in c_i\}$$

and define $\in_i \subset U_i \times U_{i+1}$ by:

$$y \in_i x \leftrightarrow_{\text{Df}} \vDash_M (x \subset c_i \wedge y \in x)$$

(i.e., if $\vDash_M y \not\subset c_i$, then y is to be regarded as an Urelement).

$N = \langle U_i, \in_i \rangle_{i \in 3}$ is then a Specker model, since $\sigma \restriction \bigcup_i U_i$ is a shifting automorphism. In view of Lemma 3 it remains only to prove:

LEMMA 6. If M, N are described as above, M being a model of S_1 (S_2, $S_2+\text{AC}$), then N is a model of $\text{Ext}'+\text{Abst}$ ($\text{Ext}'+\text{Abst}+\text{Inf}$, $\text{Ext}'+\text{Abst}+\text{Inf}+\text{AC}$).

PROOF. Ext' holds in N by the definition of $\in_i$ and the fact that Ext holds in M. In order to show that Abst holds in N, we note that if $\mathfrak{A} = \mathfrak{A}(x_1^{i_1}, ..., x_n^{i_n})$ is any T^*-formula, then there exists a limited S_1-formula $\mathfrak{A}$ such that:

$$\vDash_N \mathfrak{A}[u_1, ..., u_n] \leftrightarrow \vDash_M \overline{\mathfrak{A}}[u_1, ..., u_n]$$

for $u_j \in U_{i_j}$ ($j=1, ..., n$) ($\overline{\mathfrak{A}}$ is obtained by replacing $\wedge x^i (\vee x^i)$ by: $\wedge x{:}\in c_i$ ($\vee x{:}\in c_i$) and replacing $y^i \in x^{i+1}$ by: $x \subset c_i \wedge y \in x$.) Hence, Abst holds in N by the weak Aussonderungsaxiom of M. If M is a model of S_2, then $\vDash_N$ (c_i is infinite) follows by $\vDash_M$ (c_i is infinite). Similarly, if AC holds in M, it must also hold in N.

Q.E.D.

II

A straightforward modification of Hailperin's proof [3] for NF shows that NFU is finitely axiomatizable. By an argument due to Kreisel and Wang[8] [4] we may conclude that the following schema of mathematical induction is not provable in NFU (nor in NFU + Inf or NFU + Inf + AC).

(Ind) $\mathfrak{A}(0) \land \land n{:}{\in}\mathrm{FC}\,(\mathfrak{A}(n) \to \mathfrak{A}(n+1)) \to \land n{:}{\in}\mathrm{FC}\,\mathfrak{A}(n)$

for any NFU-formula $\mathfrak{A}$ (FC is the set of finite cardinals).

Thus the question arises whether NFU remains consistent upon adjoining Ind. The question seems to be open whether, in analogy with the previous results, we can prove the equiconsistency of NFU + Ind with some more traditional type of set theory (e.g. a variant of Zermelo set theory). However, if we enrich our metalanguage by sufficiently strong set theoretical assumptions, we can prove a stronger result: there exists a model of NFU + Inf + AC in which the finite cardinals are standard (i.e. of order type ω). From now on we assume the axioms of Zermelo-Fraenkel set theory[9] (ZF) in our metalanguage. We can then prove:

THEOREM 2. If α is any ordinal, there is a model M of NFU + Inf + AC which contains an ordering of type α.[10]

For $\alpha = \omega$ it follows that the natural ordering of the finite cardinals must be of type ω.

In the following we take α to be a fixed infinite ordinal. Let us extend $S_2 + \mathrm{AC}$ by adjoining new constants $\nu(\nu \leqslant \alpha)$ and by setting up the following axioms:

S9. ν is a (von Neumann) ordinal
       $\nu \in \kappa$ $(\nu < \kappa < \alpha)$

S10. $\nu \in c_i$ $(\nu \leqslant \alpha, i \in \mathcal{3})$.

Call the resulting system S_3. By a *constant term* of S_3 we mean one of the constants c_i, ν or a term built up from these constants by the use of Skolem functions. Given any consistent complete system Q of S_3, we can find a model $M = \langle U, \in, \Omega \rangle$ of Q such that each $x \in U$ is denoted by a constant term. We may assume without loss of generality that each of the constants ν, c_i denotes itself. By S9, S10 there is a term r such that

$$\vDash_M (r \in c_i \land r \equiv \{\langle x, y \rangle \mid x \in y \land y \in \alpha\}).$$

286

If we repeat the above construction of the Specker model $N = \langle U_i, \in_i \rangle_{i \in 3}$, we then obtain:

$$\vDash_N (r \in c_i \wedge r \text{ is a linear ordering})$$
$$\vDash_N \langle v, \kappa \rangle \in r \quad \text{for} \quad v < \kappa < \alpha.$$

Since these statements are satisfied, they also hold in the model of NFU which is derived from N. Thus Theorem 2 will follow if we can ensure that

$$\{ \langle x, y \rangle \mid \vDash_M \langle x, y \rangle \in r \} = \{ \langle v, \kappa \rangle \mid v < \kappa < \alpha \}.$$

Since each element of M is denoted by a constant term of S_3, this is equivalent to a syntactic condition on the complete system Q:

(**) $\qquad Q \vdash \bigvee x : \in \alpha \, \mathfrak{A} \leftrightarrow \bigvee v < \alpha \quad Q \vdash \mathfrak{A}(v)$

for S_3-formula $\mathfrak{A}$. Theorem 2 thus reduces to:

LEMMA 7. There exists a complete consistent system Q of S_3 which satisfies (**).

The proof of Lemma 7 depends on a sharpened form of Ramsey's theorem which applies to uncountable cardinals. Before stating this theorem we extend our earlier terminology. By an *I-partition* of a set A we mean a map $f : A \to I$. If f is an I-partition of $[A]^n$, we call $X \subset A$ *indiscernible* (or a *set of indiscernibles*) with respect to f, if $[X]^n$ lies wholly in one part of the partition (i.e., $\bigvee i : \in I . f[X]^n \subset \{i\}$). We call X indiscernible with respect to a family $\langle f_j \mid j \in J \rangle$ of partitions if X is indiscernible with respect to each f_j. We then have the following counterpart to Ramsey's theorem:

(R_1) Let δ be an uncountable cardinal number[11] such that $2^\beta < \delta$ for $\beta < \delta$. Then for each pair of cardinals $\beta, \lambda < \delta$ and for each $n > 1$ there exists a $\gamma < \delta$ such that any partition $f : [\gamma]^n \to \lambda$ has a set of indiscernibles $X \subset \gamma$ of cardinality β.

(R_1) can be proven with the methods of [2]. For the stake of completeness, however, we provide a sketch of the proof. The proof proceeds by induction on n. Let us call γ *n-adequate* for β, λ if γ satisfies the conclusion of R_1. For $n = 1$ every cardinal $\gamma > \max(\beta, \lambda)$ is adequate. Now suppose the theorem to be proven for n. Suppose that γ is n-adequate for β, λ and that $\lambda^\gamma < \gamma_0 < \delta$. We shall show that γ_0 is $(n+1)$ – adequate for β, λ.

Let $f : [\gamma_0]^{n+1} \to \lambda$. Consider the set G of g such that $g : [H]^n \to \lambda$ for some

$H \subset \gamma_0$; we denote this H by $H(g)$. By $\theta(g)$ we denote the set of $v < \gamma_0$ such that, for every $a \in [H]^n$, $f(\{v\} \cup a) = g(a)$. Let B be the set of $g \in G$ such that for each $v \in H(g)$ holds: $v = \min \theta \, (g \restriction [v \cap H]^n)$. $\langle B, \subset \rangle$ is easily seen to be a *tree*: i.e. for each $g \in B$ the set of $h \in B$ such that $h \subset g$ is well ordered by the inclusion relation $\subset$. In fact, each such h has the form $g \restriction [v \cap H]^n$ for some v. If $g \in B$ and $v = \min \theta(g)$, then the immediate successors of g in $\langle B, \subset \rangle$ are just those $g' \supset g$, such that $g' \in G$ and $H(g') = H(g) \cup \{v\}$. Defining $|g|$ as the order type of $\in \cap H(g)^2$ (i.e. as the order type of the predecessors of g in $\langle B, \subset \rangle$) and setting $B_v =_{Df} \{g \in B \,||g| = v\}$, we obtain by induction on v:

$$\bar{B}_v \leqslant \lambda^{\bar{v}},$$

On the other hand, if $\kappa \not\subset \bigcup_{|g| < v} H(g)$, then there is a $g \in B$ such that $\kappa \in \theta(g)$ (this also follows by induction on v). In particular, since

$$\overline{\bigcup_{|g| < \gamma} H(g)} \leqslant \lambda^\gamma < \gamma_0,$$

there exist a $g \in B_\gamma$. For this we have $g : [H]^n \to \lambda$, whereby $\bar{H} = \gamma$ and

$$(\Diamond) \qquad v = \max(a) \to f(\{v\} \cup a) = g(a)$$

for $a \in [H]^n$, $v \in H$.

By the induction hypothesis, g possesses an indiscernible set $X \subset H$ of cardinality β. By $(\Diamond)$ it then follows that X is indiscernible with respect to f. $\qquad$ Q.E.D.

Consider a family $\langle f_i \mid i \in I \rangle$ of partitions $f_i : [\delta]^{n_i} \to \lambda$. Call a sequence $\langle v_i \in \lambda \mid i \in I \rangle$ *realizable* if for each finite subset $u \subset I$ and each $\beta < \delta$ there is an $X \subset \delta$ of cardinality β such that $f_i[X]^{n_i} = \{v_i\}$ for each $i \in u$. As a corollary to R_1 we obtain the following combinatorial principle:

LEMMA 8. Let δ satisfy the premise of R_1, whereby $cf(\delta) > \lambda$.[12] Let $f_n : [\delta]^n \to \lambda$ for $1 \leqslant n < \omega$. Then the family $\langle f_n | n \geqslant 1 \rangle$ possesses a realizable sequence $\langle v_n | n \geqslant 1 \rangle$.

PROOF. We choose v_n by recursion on n in such a manner that $\langle v_1, \ldots, v_n \rangle$ is realizable for $\langle f_1, \ldots, f_n \rangle$. Suppose v_h to have been chosen for $h < n$. Let U be the set of $X \subset \delta$ such that $f_h[X]^h = \{v_h\}$ for $h < n$. We assume that there are $X \in U$ of arbitrarily high cardinality less than δ. Let U^* be the set of $X \in U$ which are indiscernible with respect to f_n.

288

By R_1, there are $X \in U^*$ of arbitrarily high cardinality less than δ. For $X \in U^*$ let $n(X)$ be that $v < \lambda$ such that $f_n[X] = \{v\}$. Set $n(\beta) =_{\text{Df}} \{n(X) \mid X \in U^* \wedge \overline{X} = \beta\}$. Since $\lambda < cf(\delta)$, there must be a $v < \lambda$ such that $v \in n(\beta)$ for arbitrarily large $\beta < \delta$. Set $v_n =_{\text{Df}} v$. $\qquad$ Q.E.D.

We now turn to the proof of Lemma 7. We may without loss of generality assume the axiom of choice (or, if we wish, even $V = L$) since, if Theorem 2 is provable in $\text{ZF} + V = L$, it is provable in ZF by relativizing the arguments to L. Let S^{**} be S_3 without the constants c_i (i.e. we obtain S^{**} by adding the constants $v(v \leqslant \alpha)$ to $S^* + \text{Inf} + \text{AC}$ and by setting up the axioms S9). Let V_κ denote the collection of sets of rank $< \kappa$.[13] There is then a model M of S^{**} having the form $M = \langle V_\delta; \in, \Omega \rangle$; in this model we take v as denoting v for $v \leqslant \alpha$. The axiom of choice ensures that we can interpret the Skolem functions adequately and that AC holds in M.

Let us consider the set of complete consistent extensions Q of S_3, which contain all true statements of M. We call such an extension Q n-realizable if there exist $X \subset \delta$ of arbitrarily high cardinality less than δ with the following property: If $\mathfrak{A} = \mathfrak{A}(x_1, \ldots, x_m)$ is an S^{**}-formula and $m \leqslant n$, then

$$\vDash_M \mathfrak{A}[V_{\kappa_1}, \ldots, V_{\kappa_m}] \leftrightarrow Q \vdash \mathfrak{A}(c_1, \ldots, c_m)$$

where $\langle \kappa_1, \ldots, \kappa_m \rangle$ is any ascending sequence of elements of X. We call Q realizable if it is n-realizable for every n.

LEMMA 9. There exists a realizable extension Q of S_3.[14]

PROOF. Let A be the set of S_3-statements. We define partitions $f_n : [\delta]^n \to \mathfrak{P}A$ $(n = 1)$ by

$$f_n(\{v_1, \ldots, v_n\}) =_{\text{Df}} \{\mathfrak{A}(c_{i_1}, \ldots, c_{i_m}) \mid i_1 < \cdots < i_n \wedge \vDash_M \mathfrak{A}[V_{v_\lambda}, \ldots, V_{v_n}]\}$$

for $v_1 < \cdots < v_n < \delta$. By Lemma 8 there is a sequence $\langle Q_n \in \mathfrak{P}A \mid n \geqslant 1 \rangle$ which is realizable for $\langle f_n \mid n \geqslant 1 \rangle$. Set $Q =_{\text{Df}} \bigcup_n Q_n$. It is easily checked that Q is a realizable consistent completion of S_3. $\qquad$ Q.E.D.

In view of Lemma 7, all that remains to be proven is:

LEMMA 10. Each realizable extension Q of S_3 satisfies the condition (**).

PROOF. Suppose that

$$Q \vdash \bigvee x\!:\!\in\alpha\, \mathfrak{A}(x, c_{i_1}, ..., c_{i_n})$$

where $i_1 < \cdots < i_n$ and $\mathfrak{A}$ is a S^{**}-formula. By the realizability of Q there exists $v_1 < \cdots < v_n < \delta$ such that

$$\vDash_M \mathfrak{B}\,[V_{v_1}, ..., V_{v_n}] \leftrightarrow Q \vdash \mathfrak{B}(c_{i_1}, ..., c_{i_n})$$

for S^{**}-formula $\mathfrak{B}$. In particular, we have:

$$\vDash_M \bigvee x\!:\!\in\alpha\, \mathfrak{A}(x)\, [V_{v_1}, ..., V_{v_n}],$$

hence:

$$\bigvee \kappa < \alpha \vDash_M \mathfrak{A}(\kappa)\, [V_{v_1}, ..., V_{v_n}]$$

$$\bigvee \kappa < \alpha\, Q \vdash \mathfrak{A}(\kappa, c_{i_1}, ..., c_{i_n}). \hspace{2cm} \text{Q.E.D.}$$

Seminar für Logik und Grundlagenforschung, Bonn

BIBLIOGRAPHY

[1] A. Ehrenfeucht, and A. Mostowski, 'Models of Axiomatic Theories admitting Automorphism', *Fundamenta Mathematica* **43** (1956) 50–68.

[2] P. Erdös, and R. Rado, 'A Partition Calculus in Set Theory', *Bulletin of the American Mathematical Society* **62** (1956) 427–488.

[3] Th. Hailperin, 'A Set of Axioms for Logic', *Journal of Symbolic Logic* **9** (1944) 1–19.

[4] G. Kreisel, and Hao Wang, 'Some Applications of Formalized Consistency Proofs', *Fundamenta Mathematica* **42** (1955) 101–110.

[5] W.V. Quine, 'New Foundations for Mathematical Logic', reprinted in *From a Logical Point of View*, Harvard Univ. Press, Cambridge, Mass., 1953.

[6] F. Ramsey, 'On a Problem of Formal Logic', reprinted in *The Foundations of Mathematics*, Kegan Paul, London 1931.

[7] E. Specker, 'The Axiom of Choice in Quine's "New Foundations for Mathematical Logic"', *Proceedings of the National Academy of Sciences, U.S.A.* **29** (1953) 366–368.

[8] E. Specker, 'Typical Ambiguity in Logic', *Methodology and Philosophy of Science. Proceedings of the 1960 International Congress* (ed. by E. Nagel, P. Suppes and A. Tarski), Stanford University Press, Stanford 1962, pp. 116–123.

REFERENCES

[1] Cf. [6].

[2] The unprovability of Inf can also be demonstrated directly by exhibiting a model, as will be apparent from the proof of Theorem 1.

[3] Written out in full S2–S4 read:

$$\bigvee z \bigwedge u(u \in z \leftrightarrow u = x \vee u = y)$$

$$\bigvee z \bigwedge u(u \in z \leftrightarrow \bigvee y\!:\!\in x \quad u \in y)$$

$$\bigvee z \bigwedge u(u \in z \leftrightarrow u \subset x).$$

[4] We write $\vDash_M \mathfrak{A}[u_1, ..., u_n]$ to mean: $\langle u_1, ..., u_n \rangle$ satisfies $\mathfrak{A}$ in the model M. Frequently we use an even more abbreviated notation; e.g. $\vDash_M u_0 \equiv \phi$ for $\vDash_M (x \equiv \phi)$ $[u_0]$.

[5] i.e. $U_0^* = \{x \in U_2 | \vDash_N (x$ is a finite cardinal$)\}$

[6] Thi.s method of proof appears to have been first used by Ehrenfeucht and Mostowski in [1]

[7] R_0 is provable as a schema in elementary number theory.

[8] If Ind held, we could define the notion $W_n(x)$ of truth for prenex NFU statements with $\leqslant n$ quantifiers. We could also define the notion $P(x)$ of provability in first-order predicate logic. By Herbrand's theorem, if a statement with $\leqslant n$ quantifiers is provable in predicate logic, then there exists a proof in which no formula has more than n quantifiers. Hence, by Ind, we could prove in NFU: $P(\mathfrak{A}) \leftrightarrow W_n(\mathfrak{A})$ for all NFU statements $\mathfrak{A}$ with $\leqslant n$ quantifiers. In particular, taking $\mathfrak{A}$ as an axiomatization of NFU, we have: $W_n(\mathfrak{A})$, therefore: $\neg P(\neg \mathfrak{A})$, which would give us a consistency proof for NFU within NFU itself, thus violating Gödel's second incompleteness theorem.

[9] i.e. Ext, the pair set axiom, the sum set axiom, the replacement axiom, the power set axiom, and the axiom of infinity.

[10] More precisely, there is an r such that, $\vDash_M (r$ is a linear ordering$)$ and

$$\{xy| \quad \vDash_M (\langle x, y \rangle \varepsilon r)\} \text{ is of type } \alpha.$$

[11] We identify cardinals with their corresponding initial ordinals.

[12] $cf(\delta)$ is the smallest ordinal which is cofinal with δ. Thus $cf(\delta) > \lambda$ says that any partition of δ into λ parts must have at least one part of cardinality δ.

[13] i.e. $V_\varkappa = \cup \mathfrak{P} V_\nu$
$$\nu < \varkappa$$

[14] Morley has used similar methods to obtain ω-models with collections of indiscernibles.

REPLIES

TO SMART

In the first half of his paper Smart describes my position clearly, correctly, and approvingly. It is a pleasure to be thus understood and agreed with.

A misunderstanding seems to emerge at the middle of his paper, where he finds me ambivalent on the paradigm-case argument. In fact my attitude toward the paradigm case is univalent but intermediate. What I meant in the misunderstood pages (*WO*, pp. 3f.) was that the paradigm case is not a permanent stopping place, but a point of departure. The expressions 'real', 'exist', 'there is', first come to make sense to us through our observing their commonest uses. So do pronouns, the prototypes of bound variables. The paradigmatic objects of reference of all these devices are, I suggest, visible, tangible bodies. If certain speakers have learned these expressions only from such applications, and then someone proceeds forthwith to deny the reality or existence of bodies, those speakers will find the denial puzzling or absurd. Someone can, on the other hand, intelligibly shift his attributions of existence a little at a time. First he adds some bodies which are invisible and intangible only because absent; then some more which are invisible and intangible only because we are not sensitive enough. At length a systematic usage of the existential idioms thus develops which we find manageable by dint more of system and analogy than of visibility and tangibility. When we have reached that point, we can begin even to understand the denial of existence of visible, tangible things. We understand it as a systematic extrusion of such objects from the range of reference of pronouns, or of values of variables, in some proposed regimentation of scientific theory.

In the beginning we needed the paradigmatic bodies, in order to begin to get the knack of the pronouns themselves and of kindred terms and devices. Paradigm cases confer intelligibility, but continuity of change suffices to preserve intelligibility. Paradigm cases launch our ship, but afterward, in Neurath's figure, we can stay afloat while we rebuild it plank by plank.

292

Apropos of the example 'demonic possession', Smart speaks of "theory-laden" expressions and goes on to suggest that existence in a theory-laden sense could intelligibly be denied of visible, tangible objects. This is very much my view. In a superstitious community one could first learn 'demonic possession' as an observation term, by simple holophrastic conditioning to epileptic fits as paradigm cases. Later, learning an articulate theory about demons and possession, and learning that the theory is false, one could warp the term away from the paradigm cases that originally gave it what meaning it had for him. So it is with 'there is'. Growing up in a community of believers in stones and rabbits, we first learn 'there is' in connection with stony and rabbity sorts of stimulation. Eventually, after mastering the logic of quantifiers and identity or their vernacular equivalents, we invest 'there is' with a theoretical quality and are prepared, in an extremity, to warp it away from its paradigm cases. This is why I have urged the inscrutability of reference[1]; existence in its final estate is theoretical. For convenient communication between persons with unlike ontologies there arises, even, a double usage: the sophisticate who has dismissed rabbits or perhaps numbers as values of variables will still assent to 'There are rabbits' and 'There are large prime numbers' holophrastically, while reserving the right to paraphrase if anyone wants to make ontological capital of the internal constitution of these sentences.[2]

Smart contrasts my "pragmatism and instrumentalism" in *From a Logical Point of View* with the dominant realism of *Word and Object*. Also he senses traces of the earlier attitude lingering in *Word and Object*. Now this appearance of vacillation is a misunderstanding, and one which I was trying to ward off when I wrote this (*WO*, p. 22):

To call a posit a posit is not to patronize it. ... Everything to which we concede existence is a posit from the standpoint of a description of the theory-building process and simultaneously real from the standpoint of the theory that is being built. Nor let us look down on the standpoint of the theory as make-believe, for we can never do better than occupy the standpoint of some theory or other, the best we can muster at the time.

The key consideration is rejection of the ideal of a first philosophy, somehow prior to science. Epistemology, for me, is only science self-applied; Smart describes my view of it very well at the end of his § 2. Science tells us that our data regarding the external world are limited to

293

the irritations of our bodily surfaces, and then science asks how it is that people manage from those data to project their story about the external world – true though the story is. 'Posit' is a term proper to this methodological facet of science. To apply the term to molecules and wombats is not to deny that these are real; but declaring them real is left to other facets of science, namely physics and zoology.

REFERENCES

[1] *WO*, p. 54. See also 'Ontological Relativity', *Journal of Philosophy* **65** (1968) 185–212.
[2] See my 'Existence and Quantification', in *Fact and Existence* (ed. by J. Margolis), Basil Blackwell, Oxford 1969.

TO HARMAN

In 'Two Dogmas of Empiricism' I reflected that interchangeability *salva veritate* is a sufficient condition for synonymy if the language contains, besides standard equipment, a necessity operator that is fulfilled by just the analytic sentences. But I added that a definition of synonymy thus based would offer small comfort, being "not flatly circular, but something like it. It has the form, figuratively speaking, of a closed curve in space".

Kirk recently made an analogous point about translation: there is no indeterminacy if the home language is well equipped for indirect quotation.[1] For my indeterminacy thesis was that two translators could disagree on a translation and still agree in all speech dispositions, in both languages, except translation. Kirk's reflection, to the contrary, is that the conflicting translations would entail conflicting speech dispositions also within the home language, at the level of indirect quotation. This reflection brings as little comfort, regarding determinacy of translation, as my previous reflection brought regarding definability of synonymy. Both situations involve the same quasi-circularity.

I grant Kirk his critical point: the phrase "except translation" in my statement of indeterminacy of translation needs to be elaborated so as to except also indirect quotation and related idioms of propositional attitude. All these devices reflect interlinguistic correlations intralinguistically.

Niceties of formulation aside, however, Kirk's observation can be seen as challenging not the indeterminacy of translation but the determinacy of indirect quotation. Harman makes the point: we can apply indirect quotation and other idioms of propositional attitude to foreign speakers only subject to the same parameter that underlies translation itself, namely, the choice of a scheme of translation.

Harman alluded to this point already earlier.[2] In the present essay he rounds it out into this equation: the doctrine of indeterminacy of translation is equivalent to saying that the so-called propositional attitudes must be seen as not really propositional but sentential attitudes. For, if behind the sentences there were linguistically neutral propositions, translation would of course be determinate. Conversely, if translation were determinate, we could reasonably posit the propositions; we could even define them, somewhat arbitrarily, as the equivalence classes of intertranslatable sentences.

Harman ably defends my indeterminacy thesis. By way of illustrating the point he makes good use of the contrasting explications of number in set theory. The limitation of this illustration is an interesting point too, and a point made by Harman: the sentences about numbers that take on opposite truth values under different explications are sentences that have no clear truth values before explication.

It is a strength of Harman's defense of the indeterminacy thesis that he shows, in the course of it, a tolerant concern for the status of mental entities. His schema for psychology gives beliefs and other mental states the status of hypothetical states of the nervous system. This is just the sort of status I think they should have. To take an easy example, acceptance of a sentence is for me, as Harman remarks, the disposition to assent to it; and for me a disposition, in turn, is a hypothetical state of the internal mechanism.

I am not sure whether my agreement with Harman over mental entities suffices to clear me of the suspicion of philosophical behaviorism, nor whether I want to be cleared. I am not sure what philosophical behaviorism involves, but I do consider myself as behavioristic as anyone in his right mind could be. Writers have sometimes used the word 'behaviorism' pejoratively to denote some doctrine too absurd to admit to; and perhaps the qualifier 'philosophical' serves to identify that usage. But in that sense nobody is a philosophical behaviorist.

Harman quotes from the third paragraph of Chapter II of *Word and Object* with just disapproval. My intuitive idea was that a permutation of the sentence meanings could go forever unreflected in dispositions to use or respond to the sentences. I wanted to say something to that effect without, of course, positing sentence meanings; and I see now that I failed. Harman's suggested remedy is simple and seems adequate: I should appeal at this point not to dispositions to use the sentences in question, but only to dispositions to assent to them or dissent from them.

That passage was lame also in another respect, and of this I was aware at the time: the appeal to "any plausible sense of equivalence however loose". Substantially the same phrase recurs in statements of the indeterminacy of translation where I say that the two translators assign to the jungle sentence English translations that are not equivalent English sentences in any plausible sense of equivalence however loose. I disliked having to appeal thus to equivalence, however apologetically, in the very formulation of a thesis that casts doubt on notions of translation or synonymy or equivalence. But I did better on pages 73f, in a passage that Harman also quotes:

> ... rival systems of analytical hypotheses can conform to all speech dispositions within each of the languages concerned and yet dictate ... translations each of which would be excluded by the other system.

Here there is no appeal to equivalence. As Harman recently put it to me in conversation, it is just that the one translator would reject the other's translation. I have already put this statement of the matter to good use in the second paragraph of the present reply to Harman. As noted in that connection, the formulation does still need hedging against indirect quotation and related idioms. I do not see that it needs also an emendation that Harman suggests, namely, "dispositions to accept sentences" in place of "speech dispositions", though we saw that such an emendation was invaluable elsewhere.

REFERENCES

[1] Robert Kirk, 'Translation and Indeterminacy', *Mind* (forthcoming).
[2] Gilbert Harman, 'Quine on Meaning and Existence', *Review of Metaphysics* 21 (1967) 124–151, 343–367, specifically pp. 142ff.

TO STENIUS

Of his feeling that the things I say are more or less inconsistent with one another, Stenius says that it may be founded on misunderstandings. This proves to be the case. Misunderstanding begins with his reading of the first sentence of *Word and Object*: "This familiar desk manifests its presence by resisting my pressures and by deflecting light to my eyes." "He starts", writes Stenius, "with the familiar Russellian desk and the sense data we get of it."

Having thus willed a sense-datum ontology into my physicalistic opening sentence, Stenius is bound to find things "more or less inconsistent" within my same opening paragraph:

Our common-sense talk of physical things goes forward without benefit of explanations in more intimately sensory terms. Entification begins at arm's length.... The things in sharpest focus are the things that are public enough to be talked of publicly.... It is to these that words apply first and foremost.

The most explicit writing is not proof against stalwart reading; at most it creates a sense of strain, expressed in such comments as "Quine is immediately aware of a difficulty in his outlook" or again "he explains the deviation as the effect of a special 'objective pull'".

Stenius's leading principle, that I posit sense data along with the stimulations, accounts for his notion that I am close epistemologically to Russell. It accounts also for his heading 'In the Beginning was Subjectivity'. The fact is rather that I give linguistic and conceptual primacy to ordinary things, not only on page 1 but steadfastly. The burden that Russell placed on sense data, I place on neural input – adopting thus a black-box model with no awareness presumptions. I am able to take this stance because of my naturalism, my repudiation of any first philosophy logically prior to science. My affinity here is not to Russell but to Neurath. See my adjoining reply to Smart.

Stenius's leading principle aforementioned causes a misunderstanding of what I mean by 'simpler to learn'. The sphere is *simpler* to learn than the objective square, not in being *easier* or less effortful, but as involving less processing of information: all its retinal projections are geometrically similar. What I am comparing in respect of simplicity are unconscious processings of information in the black box which is the human nervous system. And note that 'similar' here is a technical term of geometry.

The gentle but persistent patter of my physicalism does have this much effect: what Stenius had seen as my phenomenal world of sense data, he comes at length to see rather as "a world of surface irritations". "Of course," he concedes, "Quine does not believe that our language really refers to surface stimulations." Of course not; but why the "really"?

I wonder if Stenius was confusing meaning with reference. I use stimulations in meanings – and in meanings primarily of observation sentences. Reference, even on the part of observation terms, is in my view theory-enveloped and thus subject to the indeterminacy of translation. Middle-sized bodies are objects of reference *par excellence*, as urged in the quotation from p. 1. Surface stimulations are seldom referred to except by psychologists, dermatologists, and an occasional philosopher of language.

Misunderstanding comes also of supposing that I intend a one-to-one correspondence between stimulations and meanings. This is behind his objection that "surface irritations are often not internally observable". It was to ward off this misunderstanding that I wrote the paragraph which began:

In taking the visual stimulations as irradiation patterns we invest them with a fineness of detail beyond anything that our linguist can be called upon to check for. But this is all right. He can reasonably conjecture... (*WO*, p. 31).

On the other hand Stenius's accompanying objection that "surface irritations are not socially observable in any relevant sense" is a point on which I disagree, as witness that same page:

We are after his socially inculcated linguistic usage, hence his responses to conditions normally subject to social assessment. Ocular irradiation *is* intersubjectively checked to some degree by society and linguist alike, by making allowances for the speaker's orientation and the relative disposition of objects.

Stenius suggests that the linguist should learn the jungle language from within, and not by translation into English. This suggests to me that he reads Chapter II of *Word and Object* as instructions for field linguists – a sufficiently embarrassing misinterpretation to make me wish I had italicized p. 27, which tells my purpose.

Quoting me thus:

A rabbit scurries by, the native says 'Gavagai' and the linguist notes down the sentence 'Rabbit' as a tentative translation, subject to testing,

Stenius goes on to say that this would be an amazingly good guess. I take issue; it would be an easy guess. It *could* be wrong; hence the further testing. What is worrying Stenius here may be traceable in part to a failure to distinguish between the theoretical or definitional role of stimulus meaning and the linguist's method of discovery. See then my adjoining reply to Hintikka.

In questioning why I call 'Gavagai' a sentence, Stenius overlooks the fact that I speak both of a sentence 'Gavagai' and of a term 'gavagai', and that the latter is enmeshed in the problem of indeterminacy of translation. Evidence for this oversight mounts when, proceeding to the analogical construction of composite sentences, he states some reasonable points which he thinks are at variance with my views. The trouble seems to be that he thinks that I think that 'hurts' and 'my foot' are always sentences and never terms.

Stenius makes a plea for facts, as what make sentences true or false. He seems to agree with me in not wanting to quantify over them, and yet he feels that he is for facts in some sense in which I am against them. "What would be the inconvenience arising from speaking about facts?" If variables are not in point, this issue is not clear.

Of my strictures on intension he writes: "Quine seems to be rather unhesitant about this. To me it seems to be a kind of prejudice." On the contrary, my hesitancy rivaled Hamlet's in its ostentation. I used intensions explicitly in §§ 34, 35, 38, 41, and 42 of *Word and Object*, and introduced special symbols to depict them. When at last I repudiated them in § 43, it was for two strong and explicit reasons unrelated to prejudice. One reason was obscurity of individuation – a point which is bound up with my critique of analyticity and with my doctrine of the indeterminacy of translation. The other reason was referential opacity.

Stenius defends intensions by citing psychological observations on the apprehension of qualities. But such observations have no obvious bearing on the question whether intensional objects, conceived in some sense that would be inimical to extensional substitutivity, should be admitted as values of bound variables. I think it is clear that these, only these, are what I so hesitantly ended up by repudiating in § 43 under the head of intensions.

Of the elimination of names in favor of predicates and bound variables, Stenius writes, "I dispute its claim to be of essential importance for the understanding of how language works." I think I would join him in disputing such a claim, if I were to encounter it. At any rate I see the elimination as independent of one's feeling for English. I make the step for stated reasons and only in the regimentation phase of *Word and Object*, where the identificatory force of singular terms has already lapsed along with the truth-value gaps. See Strawson's paper, adjoining, and the early part of my reply to it. In connection with what Stenius says about singular descriptions in modal contexts see also my reply to Sellars.

TO CHOMSKY

Chomsky's remarks leave me with feelings at once of reassurance and frustration. What I find reassuring is that he nowhere clearly disagrees with my position. What I find frustrating is that he expresses much disagreement with what he thinks to be my position.

1. *Indeterminacy of Translation*

I have stressed, he notes, a contrast between ordinary inductive uncertainty, such as attaches to the identifying of stimulus meanings, and the deeper matter which is indeterminacy of translation. He explains the contrast thus:

Quine has in mind a distinction between "normal induction" ... and "hypothesis formation" or "theory construction" ... What distinguishes the case of physics from the case of language is that we are, for some reason, not permitted to have a "tentative theory" in the case of language (except for the "normal inductive cases" mentioned above).

This misinterpretation of my position was already familiar to me, in the classroom and in discussions with colleagues, before *Word and Object* went to press. Consequently I took special precautions against it, in *Word and Object*. It was in order to obviate this misunderstanding that I wrote the paragraph (pp. 75f.) which began:

May we conclude that translational synonymy at its worst is no worse off than physics? To be thus reassured is to misjudge the parallel.

Yet I cannot charge Chomsky with overlooking this precautionary paragraph of mine. On the contrary, he quoted the rest of it almost in full in the middle of that very paragraph of his own which I dolefully excerpted above. So I must face the fact that the point of my paragraph escaped him, and that it will have escaped others. Let me try again.

In respect of being under-determined by all possible data, translational synonymy and theoretical physics are indeed alike. The totality of possible observations of nature, made and unmade, is compatible with physical theories that are incompatible with one another. Correspondingly the totality of possible observations of verbal behavior, made and unmade, is compatible with systems of analytical hypotheses of translation that are incompatible with one another. Thus far the parallel holds. If you ask a physicist a theoretical question, well out beyond the observation sentences, his answer will be predicated on his theory and not on some unknown and incompatible theory which would have fitted all possible data just as well. Again the parallel holds: if you ask a linguist 'What did the native say?', where the native's remark was far from the category of observation sentences, the linguist's answer will be predicated on his manual of translation and not on some unknown and incompatible manual which would have fitted all possible linguistic behavior just as well. Where then does the parallel fail?

Essentially in this: theory in physics is an ultimate parameter. There is no legitimate first philosophy, higher or firmer than physics, to which to appeal over physicists' heads. Even our appreciation of the partial arbitrariness or under-determination of our overall theory of nature is not a higher-level intuition; it is integral to our under-determined theory of nature itself, and of ourselves as natural objects. So we go on reasoning and affirming as best we can within our ever under-determined and evolving theory of nature, the best one that we can muster at any one time; and it is usually redundant to cite the theory as parameter of our assertions, since no higher standard offers. It ceases to be redundant only when we are contrasting alternative theories at a deep level, e.g. with a view to a change.

Though linguistics is of course a part of the theory of nature, the indeterminacy of translation is not just inherited as a special case of the under-determination of our theory of nature. It is parallel but additional. Thus, adopt for now my fully realistic attitude toward electrons and muons and curved space-time, thus falling in with the current theory of the world despite knowing that it is in principle methodologically under-determined. Consider, from this realistic point of view, the totality of truths of nature, known and unknown, observable and unobservable, past and future. The point about indeterminacy of translation is that it withstands even all this truth, the whole truth about nature. This is what I mean by saying that, where indeterminacy of translation applies, there is no real question of right choice; there is no fact of the matter even to *within* the acknowledged under-determination of a theory of nature.

When someone asks the linguist 'What did the native say?', he thinks the question has a right English answer which is unique up to equivalence transformations of English sentences. He expects this even when the native's remark was far from the category of observation sentences. He expects this insofar as we agree, with him, to neglect the omnipresent under-determination of natural knowledge generally. But in this expectation, even as hedged by this last proviso, he is mistaken.

An unconvincing rebuttal is that everybody who is anybody knows better than to expect even this much factuality of translation. Chomsky hints such a rebuttal in his final sentence: "But why should all of this occasion any surprise or concern?"

Translation is fine and should go on. "All of this" occasions no crisis in linguistics such as the antinomies occasioned in set theory. What "all of this" does occasion, if grasped, is a change in prevalent attitudes toward meaning, idea, proposition. And in the main the sad fact is, conversely, that "all of this" escapes recognition precisely because of the uncritical persistence of old notions of meaning, idea, proposition. A conviction persists, often unacknowledged, that our sentences express ideas, and express these ideas rather than those, even when behavioral criteria can never say which. There is the stubborn notion that we can tell intuitively which idea someone's sentence expresses, our sentence anyway, even when the intuition is irreducible to behavioral criteria. This is why one thinks that one's question 'What did the native say?' has a right answer independent of choices among mutually incompatible manuals of translation. In asking "But why should all of this occasion any surprise or concern?" Chomsky did not dismiss my point. He missed it.

2. *Learning Sentences*

The more absurd the doctrine attributed to someone, *caeteris paribus*, the less the likelihood that we have well construed his words. In *Word and Object* I urged this precept in connection with the notion of a pre-logical people and other examples, and I remarked that it applies not only in radical translation but also at home. I wish Chomsky had considered this precept before attributing to me the absurd belief that the sentences in a man's repertoire are finite in number and generally learned as wholes. For surely it is generally appreciated that generative grammar is what mainly distinguishes language from subhuman communication systems. In a 1951 essay from which Chomsky even quotes, moreover – the one in *From a Logical Point of View* – I had written:

Our grammarian's attempted recursive specification ... will follow the orthodox line, we may suppose, of listing 'morphemes' and describing constructions.

Then I had gone on with further particulars. Also in *Word and Object* there are such passages as "the infinite totality of sentences of any given speaker's language" (p. 27) which might have been expected to preclude Chomsky's strange attribution, though I had not sensed that any such safeguard could be needed. He even notices one such passage (p. 71) himself, but unaccountably refuses to be swerved by it from his systematic misinterpretations.

The nature of his misunderstanding is hinted here:

It ... is clear that when we learn a language we are not "learning sentences".... Rather, we somehow develop certain principles ... that determine the form and meaning of indefinitely many sentences. A description of knowledge of language ... as an associative net constructed by conditioned response is in sharp conflict with whatever evidence we have about these matters.

This sense of conflict is wrong. It comes of taking 'learning sentences' narrowly to mean 'learning sentences outright as unstructured wholes', and taking 'associative net' and 'conditioned response' to refer narrowly to the association of sentences with sentences as unstructured wholes. No wonder he writes "As far as 'learning of sentences' is concerned, the entire notion seems almost unintelligible"; at any rate he has not understood it, or he would have seen in it no conflict with the old familiar doctrine which he sets over against it in the quoted passage. Perhaps my phrases "learning of sentences" and "association of sentences" were obscure, but there were clarificatory passages that should have helped if noted. Thus, in a passage of *Word and Object* (p. 9) which he even cites, I speak of

our learning of sentences ... [in] two modes: (1) learning sentences as wholes by a direct conditioning of them to appropriate non-verbal stimulations, and (2) producing further sentences ... by analogical substitution.

I add that these *two* modes are only a beginning. A page later I write that

mode (2) above is already, in a way, an associating of sentences with sentences; but only in too restrained a way.

Such passages as these cannot be reconciled with the idea that I intended my phrases "learning of sentences" and "association of sentences" to relate to sentences only as unstructured wholes.

3. *Innate Ideas*

Chomsky rightly notes my *penchant* for innate ideas. Rightly, anyway, if we construe 'innate ideas' in terms of innate dispositions to overt behavior. As stressed in *Word and Object*, this *penchant* is one which I share with behaviorists generally. The contrary doctrine in Hobbes, Gassendi, and Locke hinges on the dominance in their day of the idea idea. In an idea-oriented empiricism, the empiricist's premium on external sense would be unfavorable to innate ideas. With Tooke and Bentham, however, there began the serious externalization of empiricism: the shift of focus from ideas, which are subjective, to language, which is an inter-subjective and social institution. Language aptitude is innate; language learning, on the other hand, in which that aptitude is put to work, turns on intersubjectively observable features of human behavior and its environing circumstances, there being no innate language and no telepathy. The linguist has little choice but to be a behaviorist at least *qua* linguist; and, like any behaviorist, he is bound to lay great weight upon innate endowments.

There could be no induction, no habit formation, no conditioning, without prior dispositions on the subject's part to treat one stimulation as more nearly similar to a second than to a third. The subject's 'quality space', in this sense, can even be explored and plotted by behavioral tests in the differential conditioning and extinction of his responses. Also there are experimental ways of separating, to some degree, the innate features of his quality space from the acquired ones. I stressed all this in *Word and Object* (pp. 83f.), and cited old experiments (1923–37) by behavioral psychologists.

Chomsky says I "postulate a pre-linguistic (and presumably innate) 'quality space' with a built-in distance measure". But 'postulate' is an odd word for it, since a quality space is so obviously a prerequisite of learning, and since distances in a quality space can be compared experimentally.

He goes on rather as if my idea were nebulous or obscure.

The handful of examples and references that Quine gives suggests that he has something much narrower in mind, however; perhaps, a restriction to dimensions which have some simple physical correlate such as hue or brightness, with distance defined in terms of these physical correlates.

In fact the denizens of the quality spaces are expressly stimulations

306

(p. 84), any and all, with no prior imposition of dimensions. Any irrelevant features of the stimulations will in principle disappear of themselves in the course of the experimental determination of the quality space. A little advance guessing of relevant dimensions could be handy in practice to economize on experiments, but this need not concern us. In principle the final dimensionality of someone's quality space, if wanted, would be settled only after all the simply ordinal comparisons of distance had been got by the differential conditioning and extinction tests. It would be settled by considerations of neatest accommodation – the sort of thing that Chomsky will have seen in his student days under Goodman. Thus, though Chomsky has a good deal to say about the want of remarks on my part with respect to dimensions of quality spaces, I see no evidence of a problem in this quarter.

In view of the alarming narrowness of the communication margin, I may do well to add here an explicit word of welcome toward any innate mechanisms of language aptitude, however elaborate, that Chomsky can make intelligible and plausible. Innate mechanism, after all, is the heart and sinew of behavior. See Putnam, on the other hand, for remarks on how hypothetical innate mechanism can prove wanting in intelligibility when specified in less scrupulously experimental terms than was the concept of quality space.[1]

4. *Arbitrariness disowned*

Referring to my "definition of 'language' as a 'complex of dispositions to verbal behavior'", Chomsky writes:

Presumably, a complex of dispositions is a structure that can be represented as a set of probabilities for utterances in certain definable "circumstances" or "situations". But it must be recognized that the notion "probability of a sentence" is an entirely useless one .... On empirical grounds, the probability of my producing some given sentence of English ... is indistinguishable from the probability of my producing a given sentence of Japanese.

Later he writes:

Actually, Quine avoids these problems, in his exposition, by shifting his ground from "totality of speech dispositions" to "stimulus meanings", that is, dispositions to "assent or dissent" in a situation determined by one ... arbitrarily selected experiment.

Why does he write "shifting his ground", since "dispositions to 'assent or

307

dissent'" are surely within the "totality of speech dispositions"? I am free to pick, from that totality, whatever dispositions are most favorable to my purpose of distinguishing ostensive meanings. And, this being the case, why does he say "avoids these problems" and not "solves these problems"? The purported equiprobability of his producing a Japanese sentence bears none upon my "arbitrarily selected experiment" in which sentences are queried for native assent and dissent. I venture to suggest that this shows my selection of the experiment to have been less arbitrary than judicious.

Speaking of arbitrariness, I gave also another reason, in *Word and Object* (p. 29), why the linguist must resort thus to query and assent. Passive observation cannot give reasonable evidence even of stimulus meanings of observation sentences, because of an overlap problem.

The main trend of Chomsky's criticism has been to impute to me various hidden, narrow, and arbitrary empirical assumptions. I have tried in foregoing pages to explain how some of these imputations rest on misinterpretation. We find here a further instance of the same:

> It is ... not at all obvious that the potential concepts of ordinary language are characterizable in terms of simple physical dimensions of the kind Quine appears to presuppose. ... It is a question of fact whether the concept "house" is characterized ... as a "region" in a space of physical dimensions, or ... in terms of ... function. ... The same is true of many other concepts ... a knife....

Clearly this criticism is related to the remarks about dimensionality which I answered above at the end of § 3. But one sees also that the generality and studied neutrality of my method of stimulus classes has escaped Chomsky. The method is designed to capture all sensory input and all differences of sensory input, however irrelevant. Whether the stimulus meaning of a given observation sentence has a unifying theme of a spatial sort, or a chromatic sort, or a functional sort, or whatever, is not prejudged; in principle it would be determined afterward, if at all, by sizing up the discovered stimulus meaning. Of course all this is theoretical formulation. In practice we would direct and shortcut our inductions of stimulus meanings by guessing at the unifying theme in advance. And there is no reason not to guess a functional one; there is no bias toward spatial or chromatic traits.

5. *Theories*

So as to close on a more serious theme, I have left the first of Chomsky's criticisms to the end. He remarks my "tendency to use the terms 'language' and 'theory' interchangeably". This tendency is related to my rejection of the traditional distinction between analytic and synthetic statements; or, what comes to the same thing, the distinction between meaning and widely shared collateral information; or, what comes in the end to much the same thing again, the notion that the sentences of a theory have their several and separable empirical contents.

The term 'theory' has a technical sense, as in Tarski, which is not in point here. A set of sentences is a theory, in that sense, if and only if it consists of some subset S of sentences together with all the further sentences that are logically implied by S and do not exceed the vocabulary of S. This concept has its uses when, in proof theory or model theory, we work within a preassigned logical framework – ordinarily the apparatus of quantifiers and truth functions. But it has little evident bearing on general questions of translation and language learning, where we are given no specific logical apparatus nor even any distinction between logical apparatus and other apparatus.

In *Word and Object* and related writings my use of the term 'theory' is not technical. For these purposes a man's theory on a given subject may be conceived, nearly enough, as the class of all those sentences, within some limited vocabulary appropriate to the desired subject matter, that he believes to be true. Next we may picture a theory, more generally, as an imaginary man's theory, even if held by nobody. Theory in this intuitive and somewhat figurative sense is what lies behind Tarski's technical notion; the one goes over into the other when we allow the imaginary man full logical acumen.

One contrast which common sense makes between theory and language is that the same theory can be stated in different languages. I am setting no store by such a translation-invariant notion of theory, because of indeterminacy of translation. Even limiting our consideration to theory within a language, however, we see a contrast of a converse kind: many theories, even conflicting theories, can be couched in one language. Language settles the sentences and what they mean; a theory adds, selectively, the assertive quality or the simulation of selective belief. A language has its grammar and semantics; a theory goes farther and asserts some of the sentences.

But, common sense or anyway traditional philosophy goes on to say, some sentences also are fixed as true already by the semantics of the language, true by virtue purely of meanings, without help of any theory. These, the analytic sentences, could be said to comprise the null theory. Other theories differ from this null one in containing further sentences, and even perhaps in omitting some analytic ones through limitation of vocabulary.

Once I reject the distinction between analytic sentences and other community-wide beliefs, however, my nearest approximation to a null theory is the class of all community-wide beliefs. Still, even from my point of view, theory continues to contrast with language in that many theories are couched in one language. What then of my "tendency to use the terms 'language' and 'theory' interchangeably"? Clearly they are not interchangeable in all contexts, and they are pretty sure to be interchangeable in some. The contexts where Chomsky notices my interchangeable use of these terms are contexts where I speak of language or theory as a fabric or "network of sentences associated to one another and to external stimuli by the mechanism of conditioned response".[2] Such contexts are insensitive to a distinction between language and theory. Such, after all, is the semantic learning of language, once we get beyond observation sentences: we learn truth conditions of some sentences relative to other sentences. We learn thus to use the component words to form new sentences whose relative truth conditions are derivable. Which of these dependencies of truth value are due to meaning, or language, and which belong rather to a substantive theory that is widely shared, is in my view a wholly unclear question. It is no mere vagueness of terminology that makes language and theory indistinguishable in this connection.

Chomsky is right in protesting that I am "surely not proposing that two monolingual speakers cannot disagree on questions of belief". It is only when a belief is shared by the whole linguistic community that a distinction between language and theory runs into trouble.

Even at that point the effect of the distinction is not wholly to be despaired of. The useful effect of a distinction between matters of terminology and matters of fact can still be gained by talking of community-wide acceptance but manipulating the parameter, namely, community width. Thus take the case where, rather than charge someone with an altogether absurd belief, we conclude that his use of a crucial word differs from ours. This is, on the face of it, to conclude that our disagreement with him is verbal rather than factual. Still, our conclusion is no more than a trimming of our speech community to exclude our well-meaning but ill-spoken friend. The negation of the absurd sentence in question is made to count as a community-wide belief, by cutting the community down to size; and our friend's utterance counts then only as a foreign homophone of the absurd sentence. This is all very natural: we demarcate our practical speech community, for particular given purposes, as the community in which all dialogue that is concerned with those purposes runs smoothly and effectively.

One criterion for blaming a disagreement thus on aberrant usage, instead of aberrant belief, is that the tension of disagreement can be relieved by talking in other words. Another basis for imputing aberrant usage instead of aberrant belief is the psychology of learning, intuitively applied: a likelier cause of our friend's seemingly absurd assertion may be found in some phonetic or etymological mechanism of word-switching, say, than in any sufficiently gross misassessment of evidence relating to the subject matter of his sentence.

This same contrast between language and theory, or meaning and belief, dominates radical translation as soon as the linguist's field work reaches the point where he feels he can stop taking every native assertion as true. Instead of further complicating his growing system of analytical hypothesis of translation in order to make a surprising new native assertion come out true, he decides to call the statement false. In so doing he estimates, however undeliberately, which of two psychological processes is likelier to have happened. One is the process whereby this and other natives could have learned a language subject to the new hypothetical kink of syntax or lexicon by which the linguist might hope to accommodate the native's new assertion as true. The other is the process whereby the native might, through faulty observation or false hearsay, have erred about the subject matter of his assertion.

REFERENCES

[1] Hilary Putnam, 'The "Innateness Hypothesis" and Explanatory Models in Linguistics', *Synthese* **17** (1967) 12–22.
[2] When Chomsky finds "this factual assumption far from obvious", he is assuming that the mechanism of conditioned response has to apply simply to each of the innumerable sentences as an unstructured whole. I discussed this misunderstanding in § 2 of the present reply.

TO HINTIKKA

Preparatory to discussing Hintikka's suggestions, let me clarify the intent of those pages of *Word and Object* where I considered the field linguist's initial situation and plausible first moves toward radical translation. I represented him as arriving early, if tentatively, at an identification of the native's ways of expressing assent and dissent. Hintikka suggests at several points that this identification might not be easy, and that we might "find a tribe which did not have any standard expression for assent and dissent". I agree, and can cite three such tribes: the Germans, the French, and the Japanese. 'Yes' goes into 'ja' and 'oui' after affirmative questions but into 'doch' and 'si' after negative questions; 'hai' goes into 'yes' after affirmative questions but into 'no' after negative questions.

There is no reason for the native's sign of assent not to be disjunctive – a 'ja, ja' here, a 'doch, doch' there – and no reason for it not to be elusive. I suggested bases for guessing. "However inconclusive these methods", I continued, "they generate a working hypothesis. If extraordinary difficulties attend all his subsequent steps, the linguist may decide to discard that hypothesis and guess again" (*WO*, p. 30). The linguist's decision as to what to treat as native signs of assent and dissent is on a par with the analytical hypotheses of translation that he adopts at later stages of his enterprise; they differ from those later ones only in coming first, needed as they are in defining stimulus meaning. This initial indeterminacy, then, carries over into the identification of the stimulus meanings. In addition there is in the identification of stimulus meanings the normal uncertainty of induction, though, as stressed in my reply to Chomsky, this is not what the indeterminacy thesis is about. And finally there are the linguist's later adoptions of analytical hypotheses, undetermined still by what he takes to be the native's signs of assent and dissent, and undetermined still by all the stimulus meanings. As Dreben has well remarked, the indeterminacy of translation comes in degrees.

Thus I do not view the recognition of assent and dissent as different in kind from the subsequent higher-level translations, as if the one were firm and good and the other discredited. On the contrary, they are very much of a kind, and anyway I am in favor also of translation, even radical translation. I am concerned only to show what goes into it, and to what degree our behavioral data should be viewed as guides to a creative decision rather than to an awaiting reality. Hintikka seems to have mis-understood me here.

Also he over-estimates the role intended for stimulus meanings. These are quite special bundles of dispositions to verbal behavior, and are meant to reflect ostensive learning. Hintikka is wrong if he supposes that I want to ban behavioral cues that do not figure in stimulus meanings. The expressions of assent, dissent, and greeting are learned, he reminds us, from other behavioral cues. I have been stressing that the expressions of assent and dissent are not fully determined by behavior, and I would say the same of greeting; but still these remain good examples, since behavioral evidence does go into them, and it is not the same behavior that goes into stimulus meaning.

For that matter, even the linguist's evidence regarding a native obser-vation sentence will rest on behavior other than what goes into stimulus meaning. The linguist sees the native looking toward a rabbit and shifting his gaze concomitantly with the rabbit's movement, and he hears him report 'Gavagai'. This behavior is evidence that the stimulus meaning of 'Gavagai' is that of 'Rabbit', but it is very different from the assent-dissent sort of behavior that defines stimulus meaning. Discovering where stimulus synonymy holds is one thing; defining what it is that one thus discovers is another.

My definition of stimulus meaning and stimulus synonymy was meant to individuate what can be learned in ostension. That is, though the ostensive learning of an observation sentence turns upon behavior that is not mentioned in my definition of stimulus meaning, I hold that the particularities of such behavior are indifferent to future usage of the observation sentence thus learned as long as the stimulus meaning stays the same. I was not advising linguists to adhere to assent-dissent tests in learning the jungle observation sentences. Without other behavioral cues they could not even guess what stimulations to test; and they could never test them all.

Various behavioral evidence other than what goes into stimulus meanings will give the linguist clues not only to stimulus meanings, but also to analytical hypotheses. According to my thesis of indeterminacy of translation, many alternative systems of analytical hypotheses will conform equally to all the facts of stimulus meaning and stimulus synonymy; but this does not mean that choice among these alternatives is impossible, nor capricious. Supplementary suggestions, helpful in pointing toward natural choices among alternatives, may well arise from observations of behavior, including perhaps rites and taboos. But I expect that all such further aids, if codified, would still leave a lot of slack, and also that the codification would itself come to look rather arbitrary along the outer edge. Above all, in such a codification of available behavioral aids, every care would need to be taken not to relax behavioristic standards and inadvertently admit any intuitive semantics.

Enough of generalities. I turn now to Hintikka's specific proposal. He proposes a language game as a behavioral criterion for translating quantification. But his game hinges on substitution instances and so is insensitive to the difference between substitutional quantification and objectual quantification.

The difference is that in the substitutional sense an existential quantification is true only if there is a specifiable object fulfilling the given open sentence, whereas in the objectual sense it is true so long as there is any object at all fulfilling the open sentence; and correspondingly for universal quantification. The difference is a real one whenever, as for instance in a theory of real numbers, there are objects in the universe of discourse that are not individually specifiable in the language.

Hintikka wants determinacy of translation for quantification in order to make interlinguistic sense of ontology. But, as I have argued elsewhere, substitutional quantification has no bearing on ontology.[1,2] Anyway, substitutional quantification lends itself to translation by the methods of *Word and Object* quite as determinately as the truth functions do; so it is not clear that his language game adds anything.

Since writing *Word and Object* I have observed[2], by the way, that the determinacy of translation even of the truth functions is less than complete. In the case of conjunction the gap is due to the fact that a speaker may dissent from a conjunction without dissenting from either component. Alternation has a similar gap, dually situated; and substitutional quantification is similarly affected. Still, all these notions enjoy much more determinacy of translation than objectual quantification does.

The gaps in the case of substitutional quantification prove to be gaps for Hintikka's quantification game as well as for my approach. Thus take the case of existential substitutional quantification: a man may be prepared to say that there is a spy on the staff, yet forever unprepared to specify any. A similar remark applies to Hintikka's truth-function game. I grant that it is reasonable and natural to extrapolate across the gap and end up by translating the native idioms into our truth functions and quantification, substitutional or even objectual; but on this score Hintikka's games offer no evident gain over my approach.

My remaining remark aims at clearing up a not unusual misunderstanding of my use of the term 'ontic commitment'. The trouble comes of viewing it as my key ontological term, and therefore identifying the ontology of a theory with the class of all things to which the theory is ontically committed. This is not my intention. The ontology is the range of the variables. Each of various reinterpretations of the range (while keeping the interpretations of predicates fixed) might be compatible with the theory. But the theory is ontically *committed* to an object only if that object is common to all those ranges. And the theory is ontically committed to 'objects of such and such kind', say dogs, just in case each of those ranges contains some dog or other.[2]

REFERENCES

[1] 'Reply to Professor Marcus', in *The Ways of Paradox And Other Essays*, p. 181.
[2] 'Existence and Quantification', in *Fact and Existence* (ed. by J. Margolis), Basil Blackwell, Oxford 1969.

TO STROUD

Stroud's early pages show a gratifyingly sympathetic grasp of thoughts I have tried to convey early and late regarding convention, analyticity, and indeterminacy. Later portions of his paper show a similar appreciation of my case for gradualism and Neurath's plank-by-plank methodology. It is amusing that Neurath, politically so identified with Marxism and Moscow, should emerge as a mainstay of epistemological conservatism. Politics are one thing, epistemology another.

Also there are places where Stroud has missed my intent, and there are points that invite further development also apart from any evident question of right or wrong interpretation. I shall take up these various points indiscriminately, guided only by how they relate to one another.

Between 'Two Dogmas of Empiricism' and *Word and Object* there is in one respect an opposition in emphasis and feeling, though no conflict, I believe, in doctrine. In 'Two Dogmas', concerned to stress general revisibility, I wrote as Stroud quotes me:

Even a statement very close to the periphery can be held true in the face of recalcitrant experience by pleading hallucination.... Conversely, by the same token, no statement is immune to revision.

In *Word and Object*, concerned to stress sensory evidence, I wrote of systems withering when their predictions fail. The sustaining force is observation. The more observational a sentence, the more fully it can be sustained by concurrent observation; the more observational, therefore, the less susceptible to revision. But this does not contradict the 'Two Dogmas' passage, because there is still no claim that the limit, utter insusceptibility to revision, can be reached. On the contrary, the passage from 'Two Dogmas' is even echoed in *Word and Object* (pp. 18f.) thus:

In an extreme case, the theory may consist in such firmly conditioned connections between sentences that it withstands the failure of a prediction or two. We find ourselves excusing the failure of prediction as a mistake in observation or a result of unexplained interference. The tail thus comes, in an extremity, to wag the dog.

The epistemology of *Word and Object* is rather an elaboration than a revision of the view sketched at the end of 'Two Dogmas'. What I alluded to metaphorically as periphery in 'Two Dogmas' reappears as stimulus in

Word and Object, and what were sentences near the periphery reappear as sentences strong in observationality.

Other sentences to think about under the head of immunity to revision are the logically true sentences, or say more specifically the truth-functional tautologies. Stroud connects the question of their immunity interestingly with my rigid semantic criteria for translating truth functions. Now I should say to begin with that the determinacy of translation afforded by those criteria is subject to two limitations, both of which are remarked on in my adjoining reply to Hintikka. One of these limitations, which was noted also in *Word and Object*, is the groping quality of the linguist's early decision as to what to take as the native's signs of assent and dissent. This decision has much the quality of analytical hypothesis, even though it underlies stimulus meaning. The other limitation is a gap in those semantic criteria for translating truth functions; the criteria fail to cover certain cases.

This gap does not need to affect Stroud's problem. He appeals to my semantic translation criteria for truth functions in order to show that I expect translation of truth functions to preserve logical laws. But he could rest assured of that point anyway, quite apart from those semantic criteria and even without confinement to the truth-functional part of logic; for I have insisted unconditionally that translation not conflict with any logical truths (*WO*, pp. 58ff.). Insofar, then, I sustain Stroud's interpretation. And certainly I am prepared to pass over whatever traces of underlying indeterminacy there may be in the signs of assent and dissent themselves.

What is interesting to ponder is the connection between this rigidity of logic in translation and the question of the immunity of logic to revision. For no fixity of dispositions to verbal behavior is assumed; Stroud seems to misunderstand me here. A phoneme sequence which is a logically true English sentence today could sometime cease to be logically true. We would call this change a change not in logic but in English; and what would we mean by so calling it? Simply that in a manual for translating the one phase of English into the other we would provide for translating that logically true string of phonemes into some different string of phonemes, still to be counted logically true. We would do this because of our convention 'Save logical truth'. This convention of translation safeguards logical truth, nominally, against or through all behavioral vicissitudes. In this curious sense logical truth may even be said after all to be true by convention. Yet it is not a sense that gives logic a distinctive epistemological basis.

'Save logical truth' is conventional in character because of the indeterminacy of translation. It is a rule which, compatibly with all stimulus meanings and other verbal dispositions, could be obeyed or flouted. But it is not capricious. The very want of determinacy puts a premium on adhering to this strong and simple rule as a partial determinant.

More generally, we are well advised in translation to choose among our indeterminates in such a way, when we can, that sentences which natives assent to as a matter of course become translated into English sentences that likewise go without saying. This policy is regularly reflected in domestic communication: when our compatriot denies something that would seem to go without saying, we are apt to decide that his idiolect of English deviates on some word. This conclusion in the domestic case contains, as noted in my reply to Chomsky, some amateur psychology. When we carry the same policy over to radical translation, as we would most naturally do anyway, we are in effect assuming general psychological similarities also across the language barrier; and this again is good strategy, where no specific reasons arise to the contrary. Any such happy conformity to native psychological patterns is bound to help us get on more smoothly with the language.

This general policy of translating the obvious (that is, what is assented to as a matter of course) into the obvious is a policy that comes to a head in the logical truths, because of a combination of two circumstances. One circumstance is that the logical truths are all either obvious in the above sense or else potentially obvious, in the sense of being derivable from the obvious by individually obvious steps.[1] The other circumstance is that the translator can deal with them wholesale by abstracting shared skeletal forms. We see, then, how it is that 'Save logical truth' is both a convention and a wise one. And we see also that it gives logical truths no epistemological status distinct from that of any obvious truths of a so-called factual kind.

Proof-theorists and set-theorists, accustomed to contrasting strengths of systems, will point out that a language might turn out to be too poor in logical structure to afford any translations at all of some logical truths. This seems fanciful if we take logic in the strict and narrow sense; less so

318

if we move out to set theory or other mathematics. In linguistics this problem of contrasting strengths of languages tends not to arise, partly because of the margin of vagueness allowable in practical translation and partly because of vagueness as to the boundaries of the languages themselves. Anyway, I may just say for the benefit of those proof-theorists and set-theorists that the convention 'Save logical truth' would have, in the imagined extremity, to be taken in this weak sense: refrain from translating logical truths into falsehoods.

REFERENCE

[1] Cf. 'Carnap and Logical Truth', in *The Ways of Paradox and Other Essays*, pp. 104f.

TO STRAWSON

As Strawson remarks, the schema of predication '*Fx*' and the distinction between general and singular are for me intimately connected. The distinction between general and singular is, at bottom, the distinction between the role of '*F*' and the role of '*x*' in '*Fx*'. This connection of course explains either matter, as Strawson rightly protests, only in terms of the other.

There is also quantification. The crucial thing about the position of '*x*' in '*Fx*' is that it is accessible to variables of quantification. Still we have just this little circle of interrelated devices; and Strawson wants to tie them down. What wish could be more reasonable, considering that by my own account the variable of quantification is ultimately to carry full responsibility for objective reference?

I do tie this little circle of devices down to natural language, ours, after a fashion. Pronominal cross-reference is the prototype of quantification. Occurrence after 'is a' signalizes general terms. "But", Strawson writes, "it is the distinction of role thus signalized, and not the form of signaling, that is important for logical theory."

I am not the one to urge Strawson to settle for ordinary language and to scuttle logical theory. However, I argued in *Word and Object* that objective reference is subject to the indeterminacy of translation. This indeterminacy invests the whole peculiarly referential apparatus of quantification, pronouns, identity, predication, and the distinction between singular and general. This whole apparatus, and with it the ontological question itself, is in this sense parochial: it is identifiable in other languages only relative to analytical hypotheses of translation which could as well have taken other lines.

In a sense, thus, Strawson is right in saying that I explain not the distinction between general and singular, but only the form of signaling it. He would be wrong in supposing that I thought I had or should have done more.

Strawson has an interesting further suggestion of how to recognize a singular term, in its identificatory capacity: use the fact that failure in this capacity engenders a truth-value gap. An attractive thing about this suggestion is that a native's acquiescence in a truth-value gap can be reflected behaviorally in the enterprise of radical translation, by his refusal to assent or dissent. There will of course be the problem of deciding which word of the truth-valueless sentence to blame the truth-value gap on, and there will be other technical problems. If they can be met, we may have here a supplementary behavioral consideration to help govern our choice among analytical hypotheses for translating singular terms.

It could be objected that in radical translation we have no way of knowing whether the jungle words that serve as singular terms in an identificatory way, as checked by appeal somehow to truth-value gaps, are the same words that serve as singular terms in the referential or ontological way that is relevant to quantification. I do not so object, for I consider this question unreal. I hold that in construing terms at all we are working within the indeterminacy of translation. The appeal to truth-value gaps, if it helps us spot singular terms, does so only as a voluntarily added maxim for relieving our indecision among otherwise equally eligible systems of analytical hypotheses.

At any rate, quite apart from any questions of radical translation, the identificatory work of singular terms must be seen as separable from their referential or ontological work. In *Word and Object* a conspicuous effect of regimentation is that a predication of the form '*Fa*', with identificatory singular term in the '*a*' place, goes over into the symmetrical form '$(\exists x)(Fx.\ Ax)$'. A uniqueness clause regarding '*A*' may still be added, but the identificatory work of singular terms has lapsed. A language of this kind can still have indicator words, but they will be general terms: 'here', 'now', 'there', 'then'.

I represented predication, the distinction between general and singular, and even ontology itself, as in a sense parochial. I see the identificatory role of singular terms as parochial too, and independent. Under regimentation according to *Word and Object* it lapses, as do the truth-value gaps.

A notion scarcely separable from the identificatory use of terms is that of aboutness: what thing or things is some sentence about? Under the regimentation this lapses likewise, and good riddance. Sentences quantify over everything, and they fall into one or another special field depending on what general terms occur essentially in them; but the idea of their being about certain things and not others seems dispensable.

I return now, for a further remark, to the distinction between general and singular. These were two of a tight circle of kindred notions which were variously interdefinable, but, as Strawson protested, I showed no

321

way of breaking out of the circle. In this there is something ironically reminiscent of my own old critique of the analytic and synthetic, along with their kinship circle. When Strawson objects that I do not really explain the distinction between general and singular, but tell "only the form of signaling it", he reminds me of my own protest against Carnap: that he did not really explain the distinction between analytic and synthetic, but told only how to spot it in specific languages of his making. What then have I to say for myself?

The distinction between general and singular is clear within our own language, or its regimentations. Equally, Carnap's distinction between analytic and synthetic is clear within some artificial diminutive language L_0 of his own making, for he tells us the analytic sentences of L_0 by an outright recursion. My complaint was that his clearly defined class of sentences called analytic-in-L_0 might as well have just been called K; it threw no light on analyticity as applied to our own language, nor yet to any full-size substitute language adequate to science.[1] On the other hand the distinction between general and singular is expressly tailored to a full-size language adequate to science. What the distinction between general and singular does lack is another quality (lacked also, of course, by the distinction between analytic and synthetic): the quality of applicability to all languages, a quality enjoyed by stimulus synonymy and stimulus analyticity.

A third distinction which in these respects is like the distinction between general and singular is the distinction between logical truth and other truth. Logical truth, it will be recalled, resembles analyticity in holding of 'No man not married is married', but differs from analyticity in not holding of 'No bachelor is married'. Now the notion of logical truth is evidently on a par with that of general *vs.* singular, and superior to the notion of analyticity, in that we can make clear sense of it for a full language adequate to science.[2] For, we can just list an adequate vocabulary of logical particles, and then define a logical truth as a true sentence in which no words other than logical particles occur essentially. At the same time this notion is also like that of general *vs.* singular in its lack of direct applicability to languages generally. The obstacle is that we have no clear notion of logical particle applicable to languages generally.

The word 'evidently', occurring at an inconspicuous point in the above paragraph, is a hedge against an earlier paper of Strawson's to which in conclusion I should like to turn.[3] He there argues that the notion of essential occurrence, which I used just now in defining logical truth, depends in a hidden way on a notion of meaning or synonymy. For, we want to say of some word other than a logical particle that its occurrences in a logical truth are not essential: that they could be supplanted by occurrences of any other one expression without falsifying the whole. The hidden dependence on meaning is this: we have to suppose that the supplanted word, which could be ambiguous, was used in the same sense at all its occurrences in our logical truth, and similarly for the supplanting expression.

Leaning heavily on regimentation, we can assure that all supplanting and supplanted expressions will be general terms. Then we can speak of extensions instead of meanings. We can simply stipulate, it would seem, that the expression to be supplanted in our logical truth have the same extension at all its occurrences therein, and similarly for the supplanting expression. However, Strawson saw this, and more. He saw that to speak of the extension of a term *at* an occurrence is itself not intelligible without appeal to a speaker's changing meaning or intent. To talk of the extension of a term is one thing; the extension of 'table' is simply the class of all tables. But to talk distinctively of the extension of an occurrence of a term is another thing.

Leaning yet more heavily on regimentation, we might content ourselves with the definability of logical truth for language regimentations in which this difficulty does not arise: *univocal* regimentations, in which the extension of a term stays the same from one occurrence to another. But wait: how can I even state this univocality law, without intensionalism? I could say simply and extensionally that '$(x)(Fx \equiv Fx)$' is to hold true for every one-place general term in the 'F' positions, and similarly for many-place general terms; but this is not enough, for it does not preclude shifts of extension in contexts of other forms than '$(x)(Fx \equiv Fx)$'.

There is a long way around. Start out with one of the known complete proof procedures for logic – the logic, specifically, of truth functions, quantification, and identity. It can be fashioned to prove sentences directly – all the sentences that are instances of valid logical schemata – so we may omit any talk of schemata as intermediate devices. By just setting forth this general proof procedure we can define what it is for a sentence to be, as we may say, *logically demonstrable*. Thus far no talk of logical truth, nor

323

validity, nor truth. Indeed some of the sentences that are logically demonstrable in this sense may be false, because (to speak crypto-intensionally) of changes in the extension of a term from one occurrence to another. But now we are in a position to state extensionally an adequate univocality condition: *a regimentation of our language is univocal if all the logically demonstrable sentences are true.* For a regimented language that is in this sense univocal, finally, logical demonstrability is logical truth.

I have not defined 'univocal' in an all-purpose way; a qualification would be prudent, 'weakly univocal'. It seems clearly to serve its specific technical purpose of getting us through to an extensional definition of logical truth. It is remarkable how heavily this definition depends on regimentation, and how heavily also on logical theory, exploiting as it does the completeness theorem itself.

Can the definition be extended afterward to logical truth in some broader sense, or say mathematical truth, so as to cover even a domain that resists a complete proof procedure? I think it can, as follows. Begin tentatively with the old method of definition in terms of essential occurrence; that is, list a mathematical vocabulary, and define a mathematical truth *tentatively* as a true sentence in which no words outside the mathematical vocabulary occur essentially. Then say that, for a weakly univocal language, mathematical truth in this tentative sense is indeed mathematical truth. Weak univocity remains defined as before – hence in terms of a complete proof procedure for mere logic. My conjecture is that this logical modicum of univocity suffices to shield mathematical truth generally from the Strawson effect.

It should be clear that my ventures at defining logical and mathematical truth are and have been epistemologically neutral. I am concerned to demarcate the class of logical or mathematical truths, as I might the class of chemical truths; not to show how or why the evidence for truths in the class differs from the evidence for other truths. Each of my proposed definitions makes use in one way or another of the general notion of truth, and seeks to mark out the appropriate subclass. The general notion of truth thus presupposed is meant in Tarski's way. The question could be raised whether Tarski's truth definition is itself threatened by the Strawson effect; but surely, with our construction limited as it is to a weakly univocal language, we are safe on that score.

There is a final point to notice regarding our dependence upon the completeness theorem. We used it to avoid defining logical truth along the old semantical lines. But the completeness theorem is itself intelligible only as equating demonstrability with logical truth or validity semantically defined. The theorem is deprived of sense, in short, by the very use we make of it. This, however, is a tenable situation. It is a case, in Wittgenstein's figure, of kicking away the ladder by which we have climbed.

REFERENCES

[1] 'Two Dogmas of Empiricism', in *From a Logical Point of View*, p. 33.
[2] I made a point of this superiority in 'Carnap and Logical Truth', in *The Ways of Paradox and Other Essays*, p. 123.
[3] P. F. Strawson, 'Propositions, Concepts, and Logical Truth', *Philosophical Quarterly* 7 (1957) 15–25.

TO GRICE

Grice is interested in a logic of quantification which accommodates primitive names. He prefaces his construction with an interesting list of eight *prima facie desiderata*. I agree with him in finding each of the eight items desirable; though, as he proceeds to point out, some of them are incompatible.

On the heels of showing them incompatible, he proposes "to investigate the possibility of adhering to *all*". How can this be? The answer emerges in distinctions of scope, which suffice to reconcile the incompatibilities.

The system which he then proceeds to develop strikes one as forbiddingly complex. On the whole I am for it, however, and I think its complexity is a surface phenomenon. At bottom the system is closely akin to what I have advocated.

For imagine to begin with that, taking my usual line, we suppress proper names in favor of proper predicates. Instead of a name 'a', thus, naming an object a, we have a predicate 'A' satisfied uniquely by the object a. Imagine next that we restore the names by defining them in terms of the predicates, as abbreviations of singular descriptions; thus $a = (\imath x)\, Ax$. Imagine furthermore that singular descriptions have been contextually defined in Russell's original manner, and accordingly are used both as terms and as prefixes to indicate scope. The proper names, then, being defined as short for descriptions, will likewise figure both as terms and as prefixes to indicate scope.

Finally imagine that, having got up to here, we kick away the ladder of definition and singular description by which we climbed. The resulting theory has the names as primitive, both in their role of terms and in their role of scope prefixes. The laws governing the names are the laws that would have come out of the classical logic of quantification and identity through the medium of the contextual definition of singular description; but they have rather to be codified in express rules of proof now that names are taken as primitive. I think this codification is what Grice is up to. The scope prefixes have given way to a method of numerical subscripts, but this is only a notational departure to facilitate his codification.

Russell dispensed with scope prefixes in practice, on the whole, by stipulating that the scope of a description is to be minimal unless otherwise indicated. For simplicity in my own work I have pressed farther in this same line; I have taken the scope as always minimal, and thus avoided introducing scope prefixes in the first place. If I want to say something that would require a wider scope, I simply dispense with the notation of description and make do with the paraphrase which would be Russell's contextual definition of the wide-scope description. A definitional abbreviation is only a convenience, so, feeling that the convenience is more than offset by the scope apparatus, I have availed myself of the convenience of the notation of description only up to that point.

Grice, however, is directly interested in differences of scope and their bearing on existential import. Given this interest, my line would be the definitional one of three paragraphs back. Despite some polemical literature on the point, I know of no valid objection to my general reduction of names to descriptions. A predicate, after all, can be every bit as "proper", every bit as exclusive and ostensive, as a name. The reduction is primarily a matter of reparsing, as urged in *Word and Object*. Epistemologically it is neutral. But logically it is a boon, certainly, if it enables us, by nothing more than definition, to move from the simple classical logic of quantification and identity to the whole complex theory of scopes of names.

One effect is a consistency proof of the complex theory. To infer the consistency of Grice's system one would have of course to show, which I have not done, that his system agrees with what the definitions would have yielded.

Those who would use prefixes to distinguish scopes of descriptions will be pleased by Richard Sharvy's neat notation: Where Russell would write '$[(\imath x)\,\phi x]\,.\,\psi[(\imath x)\,\phi x]$', Sharvy writes '$(\imath x)\,\phi x\,.\,\psi x$'. The expression '$(\imath x)\,\phi x$' becomes a complex quantifier, 'for the sole object x such that ϕx'.

TO GEACH

Preparatory to taking up the first of two main points of interest in Geach's paper, I want to write a three-page essay on the enterprise of syntax.

Roughly speaking, the task of the syntactician of a given language is to demarcate formally the class of all phoneme sequences belonging to that language. His data, in the observed behavior of his chosen community, are sample members of the class; and what he in the fullness of time produces is a demarcation of the class in formal terms.

The range of the syntactician's data is indeterminate, *prima facie*, in two ways. First, there is the question how wide to take the linguistic community. In practice he will want to include as many people as he can without sacrificing a practical degree of uniformity. In principle, however, he can view his concern as the idiolect of some single native, and regard then his observations of other natives simply as indirect evidence on his paradigmatic individual. Second, there is the question what utterances to disregard as due to inadvertence or playfulness or the effort to communicate with a foreigner. The syntactician may be expected to adjust such decisions in ways conducive to simplicity on the part of his eventual syntax, guarding, however, against procrustean excesses.

By constructing his eventual syntax to fit such samples as he accepts, the syntactician extrapolates to an infinite class of phoneme sequences which he represents as belonging to the language. Simplicity considerations have vast scope here, since an infinite variety of infinite classes all fit the finite samples. There are controls, since the syntactician continues to gather samples and to check his system against them. He produces cases himself, and tries them on natives for bizarreness reactions. But even so he preserves much scope for simplicity considerations, by calling some bizarre cases grammatical, such as Carnap's example "This stone is thinking about Vienna", and others not.

The syntactician's product is, I said, a formal demarcation. By this I mean that it can be couched in a notation consisting only of names of phonemes, a sign of concatenation, and the notations of logic. (Suprasegmental phonemes can be accommodated by an uninteresting adjustment.)

This formal demarcation can be accomplished more particularly, at least in substantial part, by the classical method of substitution classes and constructions. Let us at first ignore the reason for the name 'substitution class', and view these simply as certain classes each of which the syntactician is about to specify recursively. He begins, then, by consigning each single word or morpheme to one or another of these classes. Next he specifies various syntactical constructions, by saying how they are written and what substitution classes they draw their operands from and what substitution classes to consign their products to. Finally he finishes his job of demarcation by saying that the phoneme sequences belonging to the language are simply all the members of substitution classes – or, better perhaps, all segments of such members.

Chomsky holds that the method of substitution classes and constructions is not enough; we need also transformations. Happily this means a departure, not from formality, but merely from the particular mode of formal specification last described. The reason his transformations require no departure from formality is that he does not need to say in general or in principle what it means to be an admissible transformation, any more than we needed to say in principle what it meant to be an admissible construction or a substitution class; it is enough just to specify each specific transformation wanted, if all one wants to do in the end is to demarcate the class of phoneme sequences of the particular chosen language.

If one is interested rather in comparative syntax, then it does become relevant to ask what it means to be an admissible transformation. One may care to rule (unlike Chomsky) that the transformation must leave meanings unchanged; however, I think the only bit of semantics really needed even here is the notion of assent. A transformation is admissible if it always preserves assent; that is, if no sentence commands a speaker's assent but loses it under the transformation. I believe that this condition is adequate because, if a given transformation could ever plausibly be said to 'change a meaning' when applied to some one sentence, I expect that another sentence could be devised which would simply lose assent under that transformation.

Parenthetically it might be remarked that the appeal to meaning in the familiar definition of phoneme can likewise be by-passed in favor of assent, if we can be confident that for every two phonemes there is some sentence that commands a speaker's assent but loses it when the one phoneme is put for the other. But anyway there is another way of getting phonemes without semantics, if with Harris and Wedberg we can believe that for every two phonemes there is some phoneme sequence that belongs to the language and ceases to belong when the one phoneme is put for the other.[1]

An interest in comparative syntax was what gave relevance to the question what it means in general to be an admissible transformation. Equally an interest in comparative syntax gives relevance to the question what it means in general to be a substitution class; a recursive specification of the substitution classes of a specific language ceases to be the whole story. The classical answer to the general question is this: a substitution class is any maximum class of phoneme sequences such that, whenever any member of the class is substituted for another where it occurs as a segment of a phoneme sequence belonging to the language, the result still belongs to the language. In Geach's learned phrase, it is a maximum class whose members are interchangeable *salva congruitate*. Hence the phrase 'substitution class'.

Now the first major point in Geach's paper is that the notion of substitution class, so construed, ill serves syntax. His reason is that terms interchangeable *salva congruitate* can still differ in syntactical role; and his example is the pair 'Copernicus' and 'some astronomer'. How do these differ in syntactical role? In that two constructions can apply indifferently to 'Copernicus' and yet differ from each other in their effects when applied to 'some astronomer'. In Geach's illustration the two constructions give verbally identical sentences, but the sentence is unambiguous in the case of 'Copernicus' and ambiguous in the case of 'some astronomer'. The point I want to make can be expedited by setting ambiguity aside and switching to this example:

(1)   Copernicus was Polish and wrote Latin.
(2)   Copernicus was Polish and Copernicus wrote Latin.

(3)   Some astronomer was Polish and wrote Latin.
(4)   Some astronomer was Polish and some astronomer wrote Latin.

Intuitively the difference in syntactical role between 'Copernicus' and 'some astronomer' is brought out by the equivalence of (1) and (2) as against the inequivalence of (3) and (4). How then ought the concept of

330

substitution class be refined so as to accommodate such differences? With help, I think, of Chomsky's transformation concept. There is an admissible transformation of (1) into (2) but not of (3) into (4). The partitioning of a language into substitution classes could be seen as relative always to some prior listing of transformations; and then a substitution class can be explained as a maximum class whose members are interchangeable *salva congruitate ac transformatione*. Geach's applicational phrases presumably comprise a substitution class in this corrected sense.

Chomsky argued the syntactical inadequacy of the method of construction and substitution class. Geach shows the old notion of substitution class inadequate also in another respect. And now, if my above suggestion is right, Chomsky's transformation device offers a remedy to the second shortcoming as well as to the first.

In passing I would touch on a second and lesser point of Geach's, where he deplores my policy of eliminating singular terms other than descriptions. He is right insofar as one's purpose is analysis of English; the contrast depicted just now in (1)–(4) bears him out. For that matter, insofar as one's purpose is analysis of English, there is something to be said also for truth gaps rather than falsity in the cases where singular terms lack designata. On both points, my deviant course is defensible only insofar as one's objective is a medium having certain advantages over English.

There remains still a second major point in Geach's paper: his well defended analysis of relative clauses. He shows that when a relative clause is appended to a noun, the combination is ordinarily not a coherent whole. He shows that we must not view the relative clause, as I and others have done, as a complex adjective attachable attributively to a noun to form a noun phrase.

Geach's point is of considerable logical interest because relative clauses are what give us abstraction of complex predicates. They are the clauses that so usefully package a complex sentence about x into a single complex adjective attributable to x. This is what they are, that is, as long as we place the cleavages where Geach now shows we must not. He shows that relative clauses are not members of a substitution class; there are greater cleavages within them than at their termini.

What Geach says of relative or 'which' clauses applies equally, as he says, to 'such that' clauses, insofar again as these are in attributive

331

position. But 'such that' clauses, unlike 'which' clauses, can occur also after the copula, in predicative position; and in this position, so Geach has lately written me, a 'such that' clause does cohere as an adjective. This is coolish comfort, since it is rather in attributive position that predicate abstraction is luxurious; 'such that' in predicative position serves no evident purpose beyond the occasional settling of ambiguities of scope.[2]

Geach's analysis leaves predicate abstraction in somewhat the status of Russell's incomplete symbols, or of the differential operators ('d^2/dx^2' and the like) which suggested them to Russell.[3] Knowing that predicate abstraction qualifies as an English construction only by false cleavages, we can continue to prize it for its logical utility. We remain free also of course to develop coherent notations, not English, in which predicate abstractions qualify as coherent wholes.

It remains interesting, precisely because of the logical importance of predicate abstraction, that no such construction is strictly traditional to English. Logic, by trial and error and other expedients, has come a long way. Already within English the 'such that' clause may be seen as a way station; for it is not the most natural English, and moreover it seems to be straining for adjectival status. The 'which' clause, after all, is seen only in attributive position even when wrongly viewed as a coherent adjectival whole. The 'such that' clause, on the other hand, crowds also into predicative position like a full-fledged adjective, and even qualifies, in that position, as truly adjectival.

REFERENCES

[1] See Anders Wedberg, 'On the Principles of Phonemic Analysis', *Ajatus* **26** (1964) 235–253.
[2] See *Word and Object*, pp. 111, 140f.
[3] See *Principia Mathematica*, 2nd ed., I, p. 24.

TO DAVIDSON

What goes by the name of semantics falls into two domains, the theory of reference and the theory of meaning. Truth is on one side of the boundary, meaning on the Other. The two domains are conspicuously distinct, but still there is this fundamental connection between them: you have given all the meanings when you have given the truth conditions of all the sentences. Davidson took the connection to heart and drew this conclusion: the way to develop a systematic account of meanings for a language is to develop Tarski's recursive definition of truth for that language.

To the notoriously flimsy theory of meaning, this idea offers new hope: the discipline of Tarski's theory of truth. Incidentally it clarifies the semantic role of the sentence; we have appreciated since Bentham that sentences were somehow semantically basic, but a truth-directed semantics drives the point home.

What is more impressive, Davidson's idea gives the logical regimentation of language a clear and central role in the theory of meaning. We regimentalists had already been operating under an unswerving conviction that logical regimentation, especially along truth-functional and quantificational lines, was of the essence of the clarification of meaning; but the conviction carried by our excuses (as for instance in a section of *Word and Object* entitled 'Aims and Claims of Regimentation') was, in contrast, swerving at best. In Davidson's picture the urgency of the regimentation becomes clear. The regimentation implements the recursions in a Tarskian truth definition. What we have already been doing becomes imbued with a new sense of purpose and direction.

This effect is striking in connection with extensionalism. The substitutivity of identity, at least as concerns variables, was a clear-cut imperative anyway; to flout it were to play fast and loose with the word and symbol for identity. But extensionalism calls for more: for the substitutivity of coextensiveness. One thing we have long been saying in defense of this demand is that extension is clearer than intension, but this invites retorts about one man's clarity. We said more, too, in defense of extensionalism: the intensional contexts that anybody was wedded to turned out to make trouble even for the substitutivity of identity and to raise problems about quantification. But now from Davidson's idea there issues a powerful further objection against those intensional contexts: they obstruct the recursion of a Tarskian truth definition. If we follow Davidson in equating clarification of meaning with definition of truth, then our old charge that intensions are unclear gains a certain objectivity. So do our scruples against mental entities.

A defense of plain talkers against regimentalists, and so of intensionalists against extensionalists and of mentalists against behaviorists, has been to equate clarity with familiarity and so to declare ordinary language clear *ex officio*. What better can we equate clarity to? A central importance of Davidson's idea is that it offers an answer, thus telling us what is wrong with ordinary language: you cannot launch it into a truth definition.

Does this illumination of the theory of meaning by the theory of truth resolve the indeterminacy of translation? Davidson appreciates that it does not. The reason is that truth itself is immanent to the conceptual scheme: 'Snow is white' is true if and only if snow is white.

What of the well-known dependence of Tarski's truth definition upon a stronger metalanguage? Does this doom the theory of meaning to an infinite regress? No; for the demand for a stronger metalanguage arises, in general, only when we undertake to transform the recursive definition of truth into a direct definition.[1] This we need not insist on doing.

I conclude with a few remarks on Davidson's present special topic, indirect discourse. He agrees with Scheffler[2] that I underestimated the cost of my "final alternative", that of depriving the propositional attitudes of their objects altogether. I also felt that Scheffler made a strong case. Davidson accordingly restores sentences as objects of the propositional attitudes. Choosing indirect discourse as paradigmatic of the idioms of propositional attitude, then, he proceeds to see how far it can be reconciled with definition of truth.

Part of the problem of indirect discourse is the failure of extensionality, but part of it also is the question how far and in what way the content sentence may be allowed to deviate from direct quotation. This is where, as noted in Harman's paper and my reply, the perplexities of translation obtrude on indirect discourse. Davidson does, however, contrive to separate these ills from the other, the failure of extensionality. This is the point of his samesaying relation. It is not supposed to be intelligible, except as indirect discourse in ordinary language is intelligible. It merely packages the problems of indirect discourse that we are not worrying about when we worry about resistance to the truth definition – which is where the failure of extensionality comes in.

Accommodation of indirect discourse to the truth definition is the purpose of Davidson's demonstrative 'that'. This strange device enables him to keep the indirect quoter's quotation in the clear, as the quoter's own pronouncement, however insincere. It can thereupon be construed under the truth definition. And the three-word companion sentence 'Galileo said that' can be construed under the truth definition too, granted that the demonstrative 'that', like 'Galileo', is available in the language in which the truth definition is formulated.

I have thought of the idioms of propositional attitude, like indicator words, as Grade B idiom (*WO*, pp. 218ff.). Now Davidson actually connects them, making indirect discourse accessible to a truth definition precisely by invoking an indicator 'that'.

He does not go into the question of transparent construction in indirect discourse, or the related question of quantifying into indirect discourse. However, my treatment submits directly to his approach. My way of according 'the earth' referential position in the Galileo story would be to say:

Galileo said of the earth that it moves.

This clearly becomes:

Galileo said of the earth that. It moves.

REFERENCES

[1] See 'On an Application of Tarski's Theory of Truth', in my *Selected Logic Papers*, pp. 144f.
[2] *Anatomy of Inquiry*, pp. 108ff.

TO FØLLESDAL

Føllesdal has explained, succinctly but clearly and accurately, my strictures on modalities and how they grew. His account is unusually understanding and sympathetic. And now, turning to set down my comments, I sense an unfortunate disproportion between the satisfaction taken in reading a paper and the length of one's comments upon it. For, whereas disagreements have to be expounded and defended, agreements go almost without saying.

He makes the following point which had not occurred to me before. After showing that extensional transparency implies referential transparency, but not conversely, he points out that it is precisely this failure of the converse that makes quantified modal logic possible at all. He agrees with me that quantified modal logic is possible only at the cost of essentialism, but what he notes further is that it would not be possible even at this price if extensional and referential transparency coincided.

At the end of his paper Føllesdal suggests that the logical modalities are even worse than the propositional attitudes, because of their link to the dubious notion of analyticity. I agree with the somber side of this remark, but am somewhat doubtful about its brighter side: that the propositional attitudes are less obscure. A discouraging vagueness invests all the propositional attitudes, even indirect quotation itself; namely, vagueness as to the manner and degree of variation that is allowable to the subordinate sentence. How far may we go in revising a man's utterance and still be entitled to attribute it to him in indirect quotation? I am not sure that this matter is in better shape than the notion of analyticity on which logical modality depends. What makes me take the propositional attitudes more seriously than logical modality is a different reason: not that they are clearer, but that they are less clearly dispensable. We cannot easily forswear daily reference to belief, pending some substitute idiom as yet unforeseen. We can much more easily do without reference to necessity.

TO SELLARS

Sellars shares my misgivings about quantifying into positions that resist the substitutivity of identity. But he wants still to allow quantification into belief contexts, even of the opaque kind. To this end he adopts Frege's device of reconstruing singular terms as referring, in such contexts, to their senses instead of to their normal designata; hence to individual concepts rather than to individuals. This intensionalizing of objects is meant to restore substitutivity and so to permit the desired quantification.

The move differs from Frege's in applying only to singular terms. But it carries with it a systematic ambiguity of predicates; e.g. 'is wise' ceases to be a predicate of persons and becomes, in belief contexts, a predicate of individual concepts. Sellars shows how his move avoids drawbacks of moves suggested by Hintikka and Chisholm.

Sellars makes this move not only for belief in the opaque sense, but for belief in the transparent sense as well. This is in order to be able to define the transparent sense in terms of the opaque. Here the reader must watch carefully the changing distinctions. There had been the two senses of belief: one was transparent, in the sense of not resisting substitutivity, and the other was opaque, in the sense of resisting it. The point of Sellars's intensionalizing of objects is to render both senses of belief transparent in the sense of not resisting substitutivity; still they continue to be two senses, so he retains the old contrasting terms 'transparent' and 'opaque' to distinguish them; and it is one of the thus adjusted senses of belief, then, that he defines in terms of the other.

His definition of the one in terms of the other has the effect that $^tBf\mathbf{a}$ whenever $\mathbf{a}$ exists and $^oBf\mathbf{a}$. In 1956, I thought the same[1]: that if

(1)   Ralph believes that Ortcutt is a spy

then, assuming that Ortcutt exists,

(2)   Ralph believes of Ortcutt that he is a spy.

Lately, however, Sleigh raised a difficulty that bears on the point.[2] Jones, like all of us, believes there are spies, though, unlike Ralph, he has nobody in particular under suspicion. Also he believes, not unreasonably, that no two births are quite simultaneous. Consequently he believes the youngest spy is a spy. Then, if the inference from (1) to (2) was right, Jones believes of the youngest spy that he is a spy. But then, by existential generalization from this transparent construction, we can infer after all that there is someone whom Jones believes to be a spy. Kripke pointed out to me that this paradox of Sleigh's can be resolved by ceasing to recognize the form of inference that led from (1) to (2).

I have a somewhat similar comment to make on Sellars's stratagem of intensionalizing objects to restore substitutivity. Such a move seemed at one time to solve the substitutivity problem for modal logic, but I more recently offered an argument to show that it does not.[3] The argument applies equally to Sellars's suggestion, as follows. Suppose that $^oBf\mathbf{a}$ but neither fa nor $^oBf\mathbf{b}$. Since $\sim fa$,

$$(3) \qquad \mathbf{a} = (\imath i)(i = \mathbf{a}. \sim fa. \vee .i = \mathbf{b}.fa).$$

However, if Jones has his wits about him,

$$\sim {^oBf}(\imath i)(i = \mathbf{a}. \sim fa. \vee .i = \mathbf{b}.fa).$$

Yet $^oBf\mathbf{a}$; so the substitutivity of the identity (3) has failed.

My objection to quantifying into non-substitutive positions dates from 1942. In response Arthur Smullyan invoked Russell's distinction of scopes of descriptions to show that the failure of substitutivity on the part of descriptions is no valid objection to quantification.[4] He would respond similarly in the present instance. But Sellars would not, for he accepts the substitutivity condition of quantification and has explicitly sought to make his logic of belief safe for substitutivity.

Still, what answer is there to Smullyan? Notice to begin with that if we are to bring out Russell's distinction of scopes we must make two contrasting applications of Russell's contextual definition of description. But, when the description is in a non-substitutive position, one of the two contrasting applications of the contextual definition is going to require quantifying into a non-substitutive position. So the appeal to scopes of descriptions does not justify such quantification, it just begs the question.

Anyway my objection to quantifying into non-substitutive positions can be made without use of descriptions. It can be made using no singular terms except variables. My old example of failure of substitutivity was, nearly enough, this:

> 9 = the number of planets,
> necessarily 9 is odd,
> ~necessarily the number of planets is odd.

Since one and the same object x then evidently fulfills the condition 'necessarily x is odd' or not depending on whether we specify it as 9 or as the number of planets, there is really no sense in the quantification:

(4) $(\exists x)$ necessarily x is odd.

Such was my old argument, using the singular terms '9' and 'the number of planets'. But now let us ban singular terms other than variables. We can still specify things; instead of specifying them by designation we specify them by conditions that uniquely determine them. On this approach we can still challenge the coherence of (4), by asking that such an object x be specified. One answer is that

(5) $(\exists y)(y \neq x = yy = y + y + y)$.

But that same number x is uniquely determined also by this different condition: there are x planets. Yet (5) entails 'x is odd' and thus evidently sustains 'necessarily x is odd', while 'there are x planets' does not.

The point I have just now tried to make is this: (i) *If a position of quantification can be objected to on the score of failures of substitutivity of identity involving descriptions, it remains equally objectionable when no singular terms but variables are available.* My previous point, made in connection with the equation (3), may be put thus: (ii) *Substitutivity of identity for descriptions is not restored by intensionalizing the objects.* I illustrated the one point in terms of necessity and the other in terms of belief, but both apply in both quarters.

What can one do, then, who wants to quantify into contexts of belief or necessity? I say his proper strategy is to reject the hypothesis in (i), and so abandon the objective envisioned in (ii). His proper strategy is to oppose my own stand by condoning quantification into positions that resist substitutivity of identity for descriptions. This does not mean violating substitutivity of identity for variables, which would simply be a wanton misuse of the identity sign; what it does mean is *essentialism*, or the adoption of an asymmetrical attitude toward different ways of specifying the same object. The essentialist's answer to my old objection against (4) would not be Smullyan's appeal to scopes; it would be that '9' designates the number essentially and so is germane to (4) whereas 'the number of planets' designates it accidentally and has no bearing on (4). Or, adapted to my rephrased objection against (4), the essentialist's answer would be that the condition (5) specifies the number essentially and so is germane to (4) whereas the condition 'there are x planets' specifies it accidentally and has no bearing on (4).

What to count as essential specifications would depend on whether one is concerned with necessity or with belief. For belief one requirement would be, vaguely speaking, that the specification hinge on traits by which the object in question is known to Jones. Formally, in systems retaining descriptions, this essentialism would be implemented by not allowing the instantiation of quantifications by terms which designate their objects only accidentally. This restriction is of course needed only for quantifications into opaque contexts. For the logic of belief Føllesdal has worked out this approach in some detail.[5]

My point (ii) does not eliminate all motive for intensionalizing the objects of quantification in modal logic. If a modal logician finds essentialism more congenial in a domain of intensions than elsewhere, then he has reason, when quantifying into modal contexts, to quantify over intensions only. A parallel situation would arise in the logic of belief, if the best version of essentiality for belief purposes turned out to apply rather to individual concepts than to individuals. On the other hand there are strong reasons, connected with doubts about the synonymy relation, for preferring not to admit individual concepts or other intensional objects. Sellars hints a certain sympathy with this attitude himself when he writes, "The mechanics, if not the metaphysics, of the move is comparatively straightforward."

REFERENCES

[1] 'Quantifiers and Propositional Attitudes', in *The Ways of Paradox and Other Essays*, p. 188.
[2] Robert Sleigh, 'On Quantifying into Epistemic Contexts', *Noûs* **1** (1967) 1–31, p. 28. See also Hintikka, *Knowledge and Belief*, pp. 141–144.
[3] *From a Logical Point of View*, 2nd ed., 1961, pp. 152f.
[4] A. F. Smullyan, 'Modality and Description', *Journal of Symbolic Logic* **13** (1948) 31–37.
[5] Dagfinn Føllesdal, 'Knowledge, Identity, and Existence', *Theoria* **33** (1967) 1–27.

TO KAPLAN

This masterly essay is visibly the product of years of ever more subtle thought on referential opacity. It deepens our understanding of these matters in both technical and philosophical ways. It does this, moreover, without enunciating a finished theory; on the contrary, it opens unexpected prospects of future progress. This open-ended character of the work is due to the breadth of Kaplan's philosophical perspective.

I shall begin by remarking on his technical contribution. He analyzes the statement of relative or triadic belief:

(1) z believes 'x is a spy' of y

into terms of absolute or dyadic belief, plus designation, thus:

(2) z believes $\ulcorner \alpha$ is a spy$\urcorner$ for some α which is a standard name of y for z.

Kaplan mischievously leaves it to the reader to recognize, in those "Frege quotes" of his, the "quasi-quotes" or corners that I used in *Mathematical Logic* and earlier writings; the meaning is the same and the shape ends up so. For me the device had been the merest practical convenience; and I am pleased now to see it so neatly assimilated to a Fregean philosophy.

That is by the way. What I want to dwell on is the importance of Kaplan's analysis of (1), here, into (2). One great benefit of this analysis is just that it does reduce triadic belief, or belief-of, to dyadic. But also it throws other light. It opens the distinction between Kaplan's (46) and (47), which my formulations left undistinguished. It accomplishes these things while at the same time meshing nicely with prior theory in other respects. Thus it meshes with Føllesdal's plan of treating some of the names of a thing as standard and others not – the standard ones being admissible as instances of variables in opaque constructions.[1] This plan of Føllesdal's is the formal implementation of the essentialism which, I have held, is the price of quantifying into opaque constructions.

The little matter of exportation which I mentioned with tentative approval in 'Quantifiers and propositional attitudes', but luckily made no use of, has now taken on sizeable dimensions. We now see that such exportation is not generally permissible. In my adjoining reply to Sellars, which went to press before I saw Kaplan's paper, I credited Sleigh and

Kripke with showing this. Now we find Kaplan making the same point independently with help even of substantially the same example. And Furth carries the matter further, by Kaplan's account: he sees names as differing from one another in point of exportability. The exportable ones are precisely the standard names, the names that can instantiate variables within opaque constructions. Clarification and unification are going forward hand in hand.

The question just which of the names of a thing to count as standard, for a believer z, is the open end of Kaplan's theory. He is rightly in no hurry to close it, for it is just here that philosophical significance proceeds to ramify. Already his work on this problem suggests in a sketchy way the foundations of an imposing theory of names, along lines no less relevant to ontology and the philosophy of mind than to logic. A preliminary part of his problem is Neil Wilson's question how wrong a man can be about something and still be said to refer to it.[2] The central part of his problem is, given all the man's names for a thing, to separate the standard ones from the others. I feel that Kaplan's appeal to a "vividness threshold" for this purpose is, for all its vagueness, much the right line, and I find his analogy of names to pictures suggestive.

Toward the end of his reflections on these matters, he argues convincingly that linguistic forms are inadequate as objects of the propositional attitudes and that images or other mental entities must be admitted for the purpose. Since philosophical clarity is so largely a result of avoiding mental entities, we must take care lest this conclusion abet obscurantism. There is some comfort, however, in that images are what are primarily relevant to Kaplan's picture theory of reference, and images are a comparatively innocuous lot as mental entities go.

One place where their comparative innocuousness may be seen is in connection with the problem of meaning. For, recall the rigors of my concept of stimulus meaning, which was my refuge from mental entities. Stimulus meaning gave a satisfying account of meaning over only a limited domain – largely observation sentences. Now an index of the comparative innocuousness of images is that if we were to let them in – if we were to lift the ban on mental entities just that far – we would thereby get no relief from the rigors of stimulus meaning. The terms or sentences for which we can conjure up sensory images are the ones that are already well served by stimulus meaning.

I detect a hint in Kaplan's paper even of how we might hope to legitimize images behaviorally, as dispositions to overt behavior; a man's possession of an image of a thing is his ability to recognize the thing. We may reasonably venture to dabble in mental entities as long as we keep one foot planted on the comparatively firm ground of dispositions to behavior. The way to a full and satisfactory theory of meaning is, I begin to suspect, a phenomenology of act and intension, but one in which all concepts are defined finally in behavioral terms. Such a program, however, is incomparably more visionary than a mere behaviorizing of images. Images promise well as objects of beliefs only of a fairly observational kind, and for these I expect stimulus meanings would serve as well.[3]

Kaplan writes here mainly of belief, but occasionally carries his observations over to the modal logic of necessity. This is where essentialism comes literally into its own; the standard names, for purposes of modal logic, are the names that connote essential peculiarities of the named object. Now I have felt that the unreasonableness of essentialism is most obtrusive when the objects are extensional, and hence that persons bent on quantifying into necessity contexts are apt to be on firmest ground when the values of the variables are intensions.[4] Kaplan expresses a related but somewhat divergent intuition: essentialism is unreasonable for particulars, reasonable for universals. Going intuition one better, he marshals a reason: the universals that enjoy essential traits are universals that admit of standard names of a structural-descriptive kind. This idea of structural-descriptive names as Kaplan sketches it seems to depend on the dubious notion of analyticity; still it is a suggestive idea, and the dependence may prove avoidable.

In any event Kaplan and I see eye to eye, negatively, on essentialism as applied to particulars. The result is that we can make little sense of identification of particulars across possible worlds. And the result of that is that we can make little sense of quantifying into necessity contexts when the values of the variables are particulars. (I keep saying 'little sense' rather than 'no sense' because Kaplan does point to the occasional possibility, in branching worlds, of identifying particulars from branch to branch by continuity of change. But surely this odd case is cold comfort for the quantifying modal logician.)

Kaplan wonders at an asymmetry between my attitude toward belief and my attitude toward modal logic. In my treatment of belief I distinguished between an opaque and a transparent version, but in modal logic I got no further than the opaque. I agree with Kaplan that my treatment was thus asymmetric and that the fact of the matter is symmetric. The distinction between opaque and transparent on the modal side is the distinction between what Chisholm, reviving scholastic terminology, calls *necessitas de dicto* and *necessitas de re*.[5] But I had a reason, as noted in my reply to Føllesdal, for treating belief more fully than necessity. It was that the notion of belief, for all its obscurity, is more useful than the notion of necessity. For this reason my treatment of modal logic was brief and negative; I was content to outline the opacity troubles. Kaplan's charge of "inconsistent skepticism" is off the point; the point is that some obscure notions are, on grounds of utility, more worth trying to salvage than others.

Kaplan suggests twice that I have left what he calls intermediate contexts unanalyzed. I should stress that I have not meant to represent them as without logical or grammatical structure. This would be intolerable, for it would represent us, absurdly, as acquiring an infinite vocabulary. On the contrary, I attributed a logical grammar to the intermediate contexts. I construed 'that' as an operator that attaches to a sentence to produce a name of a proposition.[6] Then, switching to an alternative approach which shunned propositions, I construed 'believes that' rather as an *attitudinative*: a part of speech that applies to a singular term and a sentence to produce a sentence.[7] More complex operators came into play in the analysis of polyadic belief.

In some less obvious sense Kaplan's charge does still seem just, but in what sense? Is it that I do not show how the meanings of intermediate contexts are generated from the meanings of the parts? Or can I protest that I do show just that, by explaining the attitudinatives and other operators? The notion of meaning is so vague that one is at a loss to say what counts here. But I think now that Davidson has hit upon the essential point: we want to be able to carry a Tarskian truth definition recursively through the complex contexts.[8] By this standard Kaplan's treatment of the intermediate contexts could qualify as analysis and mine not.

REFERENCES

[1] Dagfinn Føllesdal, 'Knowledge, Identity, and Existence', *Theoria* **33** (1967) 1–27.

[2] N. L. Wilson, 'Substances without Substrata', *Review of Metaphysics* **12** (1959) 521–539.

[3] In a 1965 lecture 'Propositional Objects', forthcoming in *Critica*, I explored this possibility somewhat.

[4] See the last paragraph of my reply to Sellars.

[5] R. M. Chisholm, 'Identity through Possible Worlds', *Noûs* **1** (1967) 1–8.

[6] *Word and Object*, pp. 164, 168, 192, 194.

[7] *Word and Object*, p. 216. The term 'attitudinative' is a classroom addition.

[8] See my adjoining reply to Davidson, and see his 'Truth and Meaning', *Synthese* **17** (1967) 304–323.

TO BERRY

I agree in general with Berry's admirable survey of the ontological options in set theory. I have nothing useful to add to that aspect of his paper. Instead I shall limit myself to a discussion of the specific system NNF of set theory which he proposes.

Berry partially revives my old pair of primitive ideas, namely inclusion and abstraction, but uses exclusion instead of inclusion. I liked that old starting-point both for the paucity of primitive ideas and for the compactness of my two axiom schemata and three rules of inference; but I had two reasons for turning away from it. One reason was that when I turned from the theory of types to 'New foundations' I ceased to assume a class for every membership condition; and on these terms a primitive notation for class abstraction seemed less suitable than a contextually defined notation for class abstraction. Now Berry meets this objection by letting his class abstracts name the null class when they name nothing else. For that matter, when I got to *Mathematical Logic* I likewise had all class abstracts naming again. But I still had another reason not to revert to my old pair of primitives.

The main advantage of starting rather with membership and a quantifier and a truth function is that the three departments stand separate. You get truth-function theory in all its simplicity and decidability before touching a quantifier; then you get quantification theory in all its classical clarity and completeness without yet having ventured upon the unsettled and forever incompletable domain of set theory. In my system based on inclusion and abstraction, in contrast, the axiom schemata and rules were a tight package of all these things; the three departments had to be disengaged in the course of the deductions.

True, Berry does separate the three departments somewhat in his axioms and rules. This is because, though starting with exclusion and abstraction, he promptly defines membership and quantification and the truth functions and then states his axioms and rules largely in terms of these. His two primitive ideas do not set the tone of his deduction; what they were matters less, therefore, than it otherwise might.

There are strong practical reasons for wanting to maintain, by whatever method, the separation of the three departments. One benefit, of course, is the pedagogical benefit of proceeding by easy stages. Another benefit is simply that of capital, or of machine tools: the machinery of truth functions and quantification can be used in other set theories besides the one at hand, and in other theories besides set theory. And a third benefit is the facility that standardization affords for the comparison of systems, set-theoretic and otherwise.

Thus take, for instance, von Neumann's set theory. Its primitive ideas included functional application and identity. If we want to compare the strength or other virtues of his system with those of another set theory, say Zermelo's, we are well advised first to translate von Neumann's idiosyncratic primitives (as Bernays did) into terms of the epsilon used by Zermelo. Set theory teems with systems that clamor for comparison; and a generally adequate and convenient medium for this purpose is the standard logic of truth functions, one-sorted quantification, and a single two-place predicate, epsilon.

Let us try thus standardizing Berry's NNF. We start, then, with epsilon and quantifiers and a sufficient truth function as primitive notation, and define Berry's 'χ' in the obvious way:

(i) $\qquad (f\chi g) =_{df} (a)\,(a\varepsilon f.\,|\,.a\varepsilon g).$

We have also to define his '$\hat{a}p$', in this sense: $\hat{a}p$ is the x such that $(a)\,(a\varepsilon x.\,\equiv p)$ if such there be, and otherwise Λ. Succinctly, $\hat{a}p$ is the union of all classes x such that $(a)\,(a\varepsilon x.\,\equiv p)$. Thus

(ii) $\qquad \hat{a}p =_{df} (\imath y)\,(z)\,(z\varepsilon y.\,\equiv (\exists x)\,(z\varepsilon x.\,(a)\,(a\varepsilon x.\,\equiv p))).$

Antecedently we may define description contextually as I did in NF (following Russell). Or, as another avenue to the same end, we may bypass description and define abstraction itself contextually. Half of this definition is:

(iii) $\qquad b\varepsilon\hat{a}p.\, =_{df} (\exists c)\,(b\varepsilon c.\,(a)\,(a\varepsilon c.\,\equiv p)),$

which is equivalent to Berry's (48). It remains only to define '$\hat{a}p\varepsilon\zeta$' where 'ζ' stands for a variable or an abstract. A suitable definition can be cribbed from (ii), thus:

(iv) $\qquad \hat{a}p\varepsilon\zeta.\, =_{df} (\exists y)\,(y\varepsilon\zeta.\,(z)\,(z\varepsilon y.\,\equiv (\exists x)\,(z\varepsilon x.\,(a)\,(a\varepsilon x.\,\equiv p)))).$

The existential quantifier and the various truth-function signs in (iii) and (iv) are of course, as in Berry's paper, to be supposed defined in terms

347

of '|' and universal quantification in familiar ways. Berry's definitions (41) and (42) of identity and unit class may likewise be supposed carried over.

To the axiom schemata of NNF, thus standardized, we must reckon not only the primitive expansions of Berry's (44)–(49) according to our adjusted definitions; we must also include, or derive, the biconditionals:

(v) $p|q. \equiv .\hat{a}p\chi\hat{a}q,$ $(p, q$ lacking $a)$

(vi) $(a)p \equiv .\hat{a} \sim (a\chi a) \chi \hat{a}(a\chi\hat{a}p).$

(vii) $f\varepsilon g. \equiv \sim([f]\chi g),$

which correspond to his superseded definitions (39), (40), and (43).

We may now compare the thus standardized NNF with NF. Briefly stated, NF comprises the logic of truth functions and quantification and in addition this axiom and axiom schema:

(viii) $(b)(c)(d)((a)(a\varepsilon b. \equiv .a\varepsilon c).b\varepsilon d. \supset .c\varepsilon d),$

(ix) $(\exists c)(a)(a\varepsilon c. \equiv p)$ $(p$ stratified and lacking $c).$

I think Berry both knows and intends these to be forthcoming in NNF. But what I suspect is that the converse also holds: that NNF as standardized is forthcoming in NF, and therefore differs only in formulation.

I shall leave this as a conjecture, for the proof would be long and laborious. It would require proving (v)–(vii) above and Berry's schemata (47)–(49) all in NF; not under the definitions that were originally in NF, of course, but under the above definitions (i), (iii), and (iv) and Berry's definitions (41)–(42). In addition it would require proving that abstracts, when contextually defined as in (iii)–(iv), can always be substituted for variables; for note that the 'instances' mentioned in connection with Berry's (46) and (51) may use abstracts. The proof of this metatheorem of substitution would be analogous to § 31 of *Mathematical Logic*.

TO JENSEN

NF is, as Jensen says, Ext + Abst. Ext divides in turn into two independent parts. One part is Jensen's Ext', which says that things that have members are identical when their members are identical. The other part says that only one thing lacks members:

C $\qquad (z)(z \notin x . z \notin y) \supset . x = y.$

I am calling this axiom C because it can also be read as saying that everything is a class; that nothing is memberless but the null class. Jensen's NFU, then, is Ext' + Abst, and NF is NFU + C.

Jensen shows that C bears an astonishing burden. He brings out the following contrasts between the strength of NF and that of NFU. The consistency of NF is unknown; the consistency of NFU is provable in elementary number theory. The axiom of choice is incompatible with NF (Specker); it is compatible with NFU. The axiom of infinity follows from NF (Specker); it is independent of NFU.

Early in his paper, Jensen quotes my deviant doctrine of individuals: my trick of taking individuals as their own unit classes, rather than as memberless, and so reconciling C with the existence of individuals. An unwary reader might infer that the perilous excess of strength in NF comes of this. It does not. For, NF does not assume there are any individuals in this sense. Nor, for that matter, does NFU assume there are any individuals in the old sense of multiple memberless objects. NF and NFU differ only in that NF excludes individuals in the latter sense, through C.

Scott showed that NF, if consistent, is independent of there being individuals in my sense; it implies neither that $(\exists x)(x = \{x\})$ nor that $(x)(x \neq \{x\})$.[1] Thus my concept '$x = \{x\}$' of individuals, however bizarre, is harmless; and thus the footnote which Jensen quotes from me is sustained. What is so surprising about Jensen's findings is rather that the great difference in strength between the two systems all comes from humdrum old C, which is simply the extrusion of *Urelemente*, and a commonplace of Zermelo-Fraenkel set theory.

There has indeed already been evidence, in the latter connection, that C is deceptively strong. Fraenkel was able to prove that the Zermelo-Fraenkel system without C is independent of the axiom of choice (if consistent);[2] but his proof used a model containing *Urelemente*, and so

349

could not be extended to include C. It remained to Paul Cohen to prove the more inclusive result, by a very different method. Despite this history, however, one is unprepared for the magnitude of the role of C in NF.

Jensen's brilliant paper contains also other impressive results that I have not mentioned. There are theorems of relative consistency of NFU supplemented by one or more of the axiom of infinity, the axiom of choice, and the schema of mathematical induction. I have not understood all steps. Toward the end of the proof of Lemma 4, for instance, a certain hierarchy is said to be cumulative; yet the inequality stipulated in the immediately preceding sentence seemed designed to obstruct cumulativity. I am doubtless missing something here, as elsewhere. Development of the full details of Jensen's arguments would be a strategic research project for someone, partly because of the remarkable depth and variety of prior theory which his arguments use and relate. Ramsey's theorem, Gödel's constructibility theory, Specker's constructions, Hailperin's finite axiomatization, and the work by Kreisel and Wang on finite axiomatizability, all figure in Jensen's reasoning. I am much gratified to see NF investigated so profoundly.

What of NFU as a working set theory? The assurance of consistency which recommends it also counts against it, since a set theory that can be proved consistent in elementary number theory is too weak to rest with. And indeed Jensen shows that it is too weak for the axiom of infinity, as well as for unstratified cases of mathematical induction. We can of course add these two desiderata; or just induction, since the axiom of infinity then follows.[3] Such an addition is unattractive, however, because of its *ad hoc* character – a character much at odds with the motivation of NF.

NF itself is likewise inadequate to unstratified mathematical induction, even though the axiom of infinity is provable in NF in Specker's diabolically devious way. One may therefore be moved still to supplement even NF with an *ad hoc* axiom schema of mathematical induction. To gain this same effect in a systematic rather than *ad hoc* fashion was a main motive for my supplementing the universe of NF with a domain of ultimate classes in *Mathematical Logic*. This move renders mathematical induction demonstrable independently of stratification. (Incidentally, it undoes the violation by NF of the axiom of choice.[4]) Accordingly the idea suggests itself of a system MLU, related to NFU as ML is related to NF.[5] MLU comes of ML, as did NFU from NF, by dropping C.

Wang proved that ML is consistent if NF is[6]; and his proof seems clearly to carry over, *mutatis mutandis*, to show that MLU is consistent since NFU is. This availability of a consistency proof, this time not just relative to another abstract set theory but outright, is a reason to expect poverty still on the part of MLU, but it is not a reason to expect MLU to be as poor as NFU. The difference is that Wang's proof of the consistency of ML relative to NF used more than elementary number theory; it assumed the consistency of classical analysis. When we carry his argument over to MLU, what we get is a consistency proof of MLU resting on classical analysis; whereas that of NFU needed only elementary number theory.

Both NFU and MLU raise the irksome technical question what to do about the null class. If either system is used where there is occasion to assume individuals, there is no way of saying which of the memberless things is the null class. Zermelo's system and others have faced the same problem, and the usual way of meeting it has been in effect to assume, inelegantly, a primitive name for the null class or a primitive predicate for individuality or for classitude. Fraenkel avoided this inelegance by sacrificing the individuals and imposing axiom C. I did likewise, in NF and ML, but made up the loss by allowing self-unit-classes to serve as individuals when desired. In NFU and MLU, however, C is unavailable. When individuals are wanted in these systems, have we no recourse more elegant than to assume a primitive name 'Λ' and an axiom '$x \notin \Lambda$' to govern it? There is, at least, a sort of way of explaining these additions away contextually. We can explain 'Λ' as an existentially quantified variable whose scope is '$(x)(x \notin \Lambda)$' in conjunction with the totality of our discourse, however extensive. This will be recognized as an application of an idea of Ramsey's. It is unattractive practically in depending upon our setting finite limits to our proposed discourse. But it does enable us to show, at any rate, that 'Λ' and '$x \notin \Lambda$' added no real strength to NFU and MLU.

REFERENCES

[1] Dana Scott, 'Quine's Individuals', in *Logic, Methodology, and Philosophy of Science* (ed. by E. Nagel, P. Suppes, and A. Tarski), Stanford 1962.
[2] A. A. Fraenkel, 'Der Begriff "definit" und die Unabhängigkeit des Auswahlsaxioms', *Sitzungsberichte der Preussischen Akademie der Wissenschaften, phys.-math. Kl.*, 1922, 253–257.

³ See my *Set Theory and Its Logic*, § 41.

⁴ See *op. cit.*, § 42.

⁵ By ML, of course, I mean the system of the revised edition of *Mathematical Logic*, which incorporates Wang's repair of an earlier inconsistency.

⁶ Hao Wang, 'A Formal System of Logic', *Journal of Symbolic Logic* **15** (1950) 25–32. Or see *Set Theory and Its Logic*, § 44.

ACKNOWLEDGMENT

I am grateful to Burton Dreben for reading earlier drafts of these Replies and suggesting improvements.

PUBLICATIONS OF W. V. QUINE

BOOKS

1934: *A System of Logistic*. Cambridge: Harvard, xii + 204 pp.

1940: *Mathematical Logic*. New York: Norton, xii + 344 pp.
  Emended 2d printing: Harvard, 1947.
  Revised edition: 1951.
  Paperback: New York: Harper Torchbook, 1962.
  Translations:
    Spanish by H. Pescador, Madrid: Ocidente, 1972.
    Polish by L. Koj, Warsaw: Panstwowe Wydanictwo, 1974.
  Excerpts reprinted: 1968: pp. 27–33 in Iseminger;[1]
                1971: pp. 23–33 in Manicas;
                1974: same in Zabeeh *et al.*

1941: *Elementary Logic*. Boston: Ginn, vi + 170 pp.
  Revised edition: Harvard, 1966.
  Paperback: Harper Torchbook, 1965.
  Translations:
    Italian by F. Gana, Rome: Ubaldini, 1968.
    French by J. Largeault and B. St.-Sermin, Paris: Colin, 1972.
    Japanese by R. Tsueshita, Tokyo: Taishukan, 1972.

1944: *O Sentido da Nova Lógica*. São Paulo: Martins, xii + 190 pp.
  Translation: Spanish by M. Bunge, Buenos Aires: Nueva Vision, 1958.
  Excerpts translated: 1943: pp. 140–144, 146–158, 179–183 in "Notes on existence and necessity," below.

1950: *Methods of Logic*. New York: Holt, xxii + 272 pp.
  Revised edition: 1959 and London: Routledge, 1962.
  3rd edition, revised and enlarged: Holt, 1972, and Routledge, 1974.
  Paperback: Routledge, 1974.
  Translations:

Italian by M. Pacifico, Milan: Feltrinelli, 1960.
Japanese by S. Nakamura and S. Ohmori, Tokyo: Iwanami, 1962.
Spanish by M. Sacristán, Barcelona: Ariel, 1963.
Hungarian by Urban J., Budapest: Akademiai Kiado, 1968.
German by D. Siefkes, Frankfurt: Suhrkamp, 1969.
French, 3rd ed., by M. Clavelin, Colin, 1973.
Excerpts reprinted: 1971: Introduction in Manicas;
       1973: same in MacKinnon.
1953: *From a Logical Point of View*. Harvard, vii + 184 pp.
Revised edition: 1961.
Paperback: Harper Torchbook, 1963.
Translations:
Spanish by M. Sacristán, Ariel, 1963.
Italian by E. Mistretta, Rome: Astrolabio, 1966.
Polish by B. Stanosz, Państwowe Wydanictwo, 1970.
Japanese by E. Mochimaru and K. Nakayama, Iwanami, 1972.
Excerpts reprinted: 1961: pp. 47–64 in Saporta;
       1964: same in Fodor and Katz;
       1969: same in Olshewski;
       1971: pp. 139–157 in Linsky;
       1974: same in Zabeeh *et al*.
Excerpts translated: 1969: pp. 139–157 in Pasquinelli;
       1973: pp. 47–64 in Eisenberg *et al*.;
       1975: pp. 102–129, 139–159 in Stegmüller.
(For further excerpting see under component articles.)
1960: *Word and Object*. Cambridge: MIT, xvi + 294 pp.
Paperback: 1964.
Translations:
Spanish by M. Sacristán, Barcelona: Labor, 1968.
Italian by F. Mondadori, Milan: Saggiatore, 1970.
French by P. Gochet, Colin, 1974.
Excerpts reprinted: 1960: pp. 5–8 in Sat. Review of Lit., Aug. 6.
       1964: pp. 170–176, 251–257 in Smart;
       1967: pp. 270–276 in Rorty;
       1968: pp. 157–161 in Iseminger;
       1971: pp. 26–79 in Rosenberg and Travis;

1974: pp. 176–186 in Davidson and Harman.

Excerpts translated: 1973: pp. 214–216 in Simpson.

(For further excerpting see under "Meaning and translation.")

1963: *Set Theory and Its Logic.* Harvard, xvi + 359 pp.

Revised edition: 1969 and Taipeh: Mei Ya, 1969.

Paperback: Harvard, 1971.

Translations:

Japanese by A. Ohe and T. Fujimura, Iwanami, 1968.

German by A. Oberschelp, Brunswick: Vieweg, 1973.

1966: *The Ways of Paradox and Other Essays.* New York: Random House, x + 257 pp.

Paperback: 1968.

Translation: Italian by Sant'Ambrogio, Saggiatore, 1974.

1966: *Selected Logic Papers.* Random House, x + 250 pp.

Paperback: 1968.

1969: *Ontological Relativity and Other Essays.* New York: Columbia, x + 165 pp.

Translations:

Spanish by M. Garrido, J. L. Blasco, and M. Bunge, Madrid: Tecnos, 1974.

German, Stuttgart: Reklam, in press.

Portuguese, São Paulo: Abril, in preparation.

1970: *The Web of Belief* (with J. S. Ullian). Random House, v + 95 pp.

1970: *Philosophy of Logic.* Englewood: Prentice Hall, xv + 109 pp.

Paperback: 1970.

Translations:

Portuguese by T. A. Cannabrava, Rio de Janeiro: Zahar, 1972.

Japanese by M. Yamashita, Iwanami, 1972.

Spanish by M. Sacristán, Madrid: Alianza, 1973.

German by H. Vetter, Stuttgart: Kohlhammer, 1973.

Excerpts reprinted: 1972: pp. 35–43, 47–60 in Davidson and Harman (*Logic of Grammar*).

Excerpt translated: 1970: "Sur la tâche de la grammaire," below.

1974: *The Roots of Reference.* La Salle, Ill.: Open Court, xii + 151 pp.

355

Excerpt translated: 1972: "Reflexiones sobre el aprendizaje del lenguaje," below.

ARTICLES

1932: "A note on Nicod's postulate," Mind 41, pp. 345–350.

1933: "The logic of sequences," Summaries of Theses 1932 (Harvard), pp. 335–338.

"A theorem in the calculus of classes," Jour. London Math. Soc. 8, pp. 89–95.

1934: "Ontological remarks on the propositional calculus," Mind 43, pp. 472–476.

Reprinted 1966 in *The Ways of Paradox*.

"A method of generating part of arithmetic without use of intuitive logic," Bull. Amer. Math. Soc. 40, pp. 753–761.

Reprinted 1966 in *Selected Logic Papers*.

1936: "Concepts of negative degree," Proc. Nat. Acad. Sci. 22, pp. 40–45.

"A theory of classes presupposing no canons of type," ibid., pp. 320–326.

"A reinterpretation of Schönfinkel's logical operators," Bull. Amer. Math. Soc. 42, pp. 87–89.

"Definition of substitution," ibid., pp. 561–569.

Reprinted 1966 in *Selected Logic Papers*.

"On the axiom of reducibility," Mind 45, pp. 498–500.

"Toward a calculus of concepts," Journal of Symbolic Logic 1, pp. 2–25.

"Set-theoretic foundations for logic," ibid., pp. 45–57.

Reprinted 1966 in *Selected Logic Papers*.

"Truth by convention," *Philosophical Essays for A. N. Whitehead* (O. H. Lee, ed., New York: Longmans), pp. 90–124.

Reprinted 1949 in Feigl and Sellars; [1]
1964 in Benacerraf and Putnam;
1966 in *The Ways of Paradox*.

Translated 1969 in Cuadernos de Filosofía (Buenos Aires).

1937: "New foundations for mathematical logic," Amer. Math. Monthly 44, pp. 70–80.

Reprinted 1953 with additions in *From a Logical Point of View*.

Translated 1969 in Pasquinelli.

"On derivability," Journal of Symbolic Logic 2, pp. 113–119.

"On Cantor's theorem," ibid., pp. 120–124.

"Logic based on inclusion and abstraction," ibid., pp. 145–152.
Reprinted 1966 in *Selected Logic Papers*.

1938: "Completeness of the propositional calculus," Jour. Symbolic
Logic 3, pp. 37–40.
Reprinted 1966 in *Selected Logic Papers*.

"On the theory of types," Jour. Symbolic Logic 3, pp. 125–139.
Reprinted 1970 in Klemke.

1939: "Designation and existence," Jour. Philosophy 36, pp. 701–709.
Reprinted 1949 in Feigl and Sellars;
1953 partly in *From a Logical Point of View*;
1969 in Olshewsky.
Translated 1972 in Sinnreich.

"Relations and reason," Technology Review 41, pp. 299–301,
324–332.

"A logistical approach to the ontological problem," Jour. Unified
Science 9, pp. 84–89 (preprints only).
Reprinted 1966 in *The Ways of Paradox*.

1940: "Elimination of extra-logical postulates" (with Nelson Goodman),
Jour. Symbolic Logic 5, pp. 104–109.
Reprinted 1972 in Goodman.

1941: "Element and number," Jour. Symbolic Logic 6, pp. 135–149.
Reprinted 1966 in *Selected Logic Papers*.

"Russell's paradox and others," Technology Review 44, pp. 16ff.

"Whitehead and the rise of modern logic," *Philosophy of A. N.
Whitehead* (P. A. Schilpp, ed., LaSalle: Open Court), pp. 125–
163.
Reprinted 1966 in *Selected Logic Papers*.

1942: "Reply to Professor Ushenko," Jour. Philosophy 39, pp. 68–71.

"On existence conditions for elements and classes," Jour. Symbolic Logic 7, pp. 157–159.

1943: "Notes on existence and necessity," Jour. Philosophy 40, pp.
113–127. (Translation of part of *O Sentido da Nova Logica*.)
Reprinted 1952 in Linsky;
1953 partly in *From a Logical Point of View*.

Translated 1972 in Sinnreich;
1973 in Simpson.
1945: "On the logic of quantification," Jour. Symbolic Logic 10, pp.1–12.
Reprinted 1966 in *Selected Logic Papers*.
"On ordered pairs," Jour. Symbolic Logic 10, pp. 95ff.
Reprinted 1966 in *Selected Logic Papers*, combined with next:
1946: "On relations as coextensive with classes," Jour. Symbolic Logic 11, pp. 71f.
"Concatenation as a basis for arithmetic," ibid., pp. 105–114.
Reprinted 1966 in *Selected Logic Papers*.
"Os Estados Unidos e o ressurgimento da lógica," *Vida Intellectual nos Estados Unidos* (R. Amorim, ed., São Paulo: U.C.B.E.U.), pp. 267–286.
1947: "The problem of interpreting modal logic," Jour. Symbolic Logic 12, pp. 43–48.
Reprinted 1953 partly in *From a Logical Point of View*;
1968 in Copi and Gould;
1974 in Zabeeh *et al.*
"On universals," Jour. Symbolic Logic 12, pp. 74–84.
Reprinted 1953 partly in *From a Logical Point of View*.
Translated 1975 in Stegmüller.
"Steps toward a constructive nominalism" (with Nelson Goodman), Jour. Symbolic Logic 12, pp. 97–122.
Reprinted 1969 in Bobbs-Merrill Reprint Series;
1972 in Goodman.
Translated 1967 in Cellucci.
1948: "On what there is," Review of Metaphysics 2, pp. 21–38.
Reprinted 1951 in Aristotelian Soc. Suppl. Vol. 25, appendix;
1952 in Linsky;
1953 in *From a Logical Point of View*;
1964 in Benacerraf and Putnam;
1965 in Nagel and Brandt; partly in Baylis;
1968 in Copi and Gould; in Iseminger; in Margolis;
in Bobbs-Merrill Reprint Series;
1970 in Myers; partly in Loux;
1971 in Manicas;
1972 in Landesman; in Feigl, Sellars, and Lehrer;

1975 partly in Beck.
Translated 1958 in Krzywicki;
 1966 in Krishna (Hindi);
 1971 in Bar-On (Hebrew);
 1972 in Pereira;
 1975 in Stegmüller; as pamphlet (São Paulo: Abril).
1949: "On decidability and completeness," Synthese 7, pp. 441–446.
1950: "On natural deduction," Jour. Symbolic Logic 15, pp. 93–102.
"Identity, ostension, and hypostasis," Jour. Philosophy 47, pp. 621–633.
Reprinted 1953 in *From a Logical Point of View*.
Translated 1975 as pamphlet (Abril).
1951: "Ontology and ideology," Philosophical Studies 2, pp. 11–15.
Reprinted 1953 partly in *From a Logical Point of View*;
 1972 in Feigl, Sellars, and Lehrer.
"On Carnap's views on ontology," Philosophical Studies 2, pp. 65–72.
Reprinted 1966 in *The Ways of Paradox*;
 1972 in Feigl, Sellars, and Lehrer.
"Semantics and abstract objects," Proc. Amer. Acad. Arts and Sci. 80, pp. 90–96.
Reprinted 1953 partly in *From a Logical Point of View*.
Translated 1975 in Stegmüller.
"The ordered pair in number theory," *Structure, Method, and Meaning* (P. Henle *et al.*, eds., New York: Liberal Arts), pp. 84–87.
"[Rejoinder to Mr. Geach] on what there is," Aristotelian Soc. Supp. Vol. 25, pp. 149–160.
"On the consistency of 'New foundations'," Proc. Nat. Acad. Sci. 3, pp. 538–540.
"A simplification of games in extensive form" (with J. J. C. McKinsey and W. D. Krentel), Duke Mathematical Journal 18, pp. 885–900.
"Two dogmas of empiricism," Philosophical Review 60, pp. 20–43.
Reprinted 1951 in small part in "Semantics and abstract objects";
 1953 in *From a Logical Point of View*;

1962 in Aiken and Barrett;
1963 in Lewis;
1964 in Ammerman; in Benacerraf and Putnam;
1965 partly in Nagel and Brandt;
1966 in Rorty;
1968 in Tillman, Berofsky, and O'Connor; in Bobbs-
   Merrill Reprint Series; partly in Margolis;
1969 in Olshewsky;
1970 in Harris and Severens;
1971 in Rosenberg and Travis; partly in Arner;
   partly in Munsat;
1972 in Morick; in Feigl, Sellars, and Lehrer;
1974 in Berlinski; partly in Fodor, Bever, and
   Garrett; in Zabeeh *et al.*;
1975 in Harding.
Translated 1964 in Marc-Wogau;
   1966 in Krishna (Hindi);
   1972 in Sinnreich;
   1974 in Pârvu;
   1975 as pamphlet (Abril).
1952: "On an application of Tarski's theory of truth," Proc. Nat. Acad.
   Sci. 38, pp. 430–433.
   Reprinted 1966 in *Selected Logic Papers*.
   Preface to Joseph Clark, *Conventional Logic and Modern Logic*
   (Woodstock), pp. v–vii.
   Reprinted 1971 in Bynum.
   "The problem of simplifying truth functions," Amer. Math.
   Monthly 59, pp. 521–531.
   Reprinted 1973 in Swartzlander.
   "Some theorems on definability and decidability" (with Alonzo
   Church), Jour. Symbolic Logic 17, pp. 179–187.
   "On reduction to a symmetric relation" (with William Craig),
   ibid., p. 188.
1953: "On ω-inconsistency and a so-called axiom of infinity," ibid. 18,
   pp. 119–124.
   Reprinted 1966 in *Selected Logic Papers*.
   "On a so-called paradox," Mind 62, pp. 65–67.

Reprinted 1966 in *The Ways of Paradox*.

"Mr. Strawson on logical theory," Mind 62, pp. 433–451.

Reprinted 1966 in *The Ways of Paradox*;

1968 in Copi and Gould.

"On mental entities," Proc. Amer. Acad. Arts and Sci. 80, pp. 198–203.

Reprinted 1966 in *The Ways of Paradox*;

1969 in O'Connor.

"Two theorems about truth functions," Boletín Soc. Matemática Mexicana 10, pp. 64–70.

Translated 1953 ibid. ·

Reprinted 1966 in *Selected Logic Papers*.

"Three grades of modal involvement," Proc. XI International Congress of Philosophy 14, pp. 65–81.

Reprinted 1966 in *The Ways of Paradox*.

1954: "Interpretations of sets of conditions," Jour. Symbolic Logic 19, pp. 97–102.

Reprinted 1966 in *Selected Logic Papers*.

"Quantification and the empty domain," Jour. Symbolic Logic 19, pp. 177–179.

Reprinted 1966 in *Selected Logic Papers*.

Translated 1974 in Bencivenga.

"Reduction to a dyadic predicate," Jour. Symbolic Logic 19, pp. 180–182.

Reprinted 1966 in *Selected Logic Papers*.

1955: "A proof procedure for quantification theory," Jour. Symbolic Logic 20, pp. 141–149.

Reprinted 1966 in *Selected Logic Papers*.

"A way to simplify truth functions," Amer. Math. Monthly 62, pp. 627–631.

Reprinted 1973 in Swartzlander.

"On Frege's way out," Mind 64, pp. 145–159.

Reprinted 1966 in *Selected Logic Papers*;

1969 in Klemke.

1956: "On formulas with valid cases," Jour. Symbolic Logic 21, p. 148.

"Unification of universes in set theory," ibid., pp. 267–279.

"Quantifiers and propositional attitudes," Jour. Philosophy 53,

pp. 177–187.
Reprinted 1966 in *The Ways of Paradox*;
　　　　1971 in Linsky;
　　　　1972 in Marras;
　　　　1974 in Davidson and Harman.
Translated 1973 in Simpson
1957: "Logic, symbolic," Encyclopedia Americana.
Reprinted 1966 in *Selected Logic Papers*.
"The scope and language of science," Brit. Jour. Phil. of Sci. 8, pp. 1–17.
Preprinted 1955 in Leary with corruption of text.
Reprinted 1966 in *The Ways of Paradox*.
Translated 1969 in Pasquinelli;
　　　　1973 in Diánoia (Mexico).
1958: "Speaking of objects," Proc. and Addresses Amer. Phil. Assn. 31, pp. 5–22.
Reprinted 1959 in Krikorian and Edel;
　　　　1960 partly in *Word and Object*;
　　　　1964 in Fodor and Katz;
　　　　1966 in Kurtz;
　　　　1969 in *Ontological Relativity and Other Essays*.
Translated 1960 in Bunge;
　　　　1969 in Pasquinelli.
"The philosophical bearing of modern logic," *Philosophy in the Mid-Century* (R. Klibansky, ed.; Florence: Nuova Italia), pp. 3f.
Translated 1969 in Pasquinelli.
1959: "Meaning and translation," *On Translation* (R. A. Brower, ed., Harvard), pp. 148–172.
Reprinted 1960 in large part in *Word and Object*;
　　　　1964 in Fodor and Katz;
　　　　1969 in Olshewsky;
　　　　1971 partly in Rosenberg and Travis;
　　　　1972 in Morick;
　　　　1974 in Berlinski.
Translated 1973 in Bonomi.
"On cores and prime implicants of truth functions," Amer. Math.

362

Monthly 66, pp. 755–760.

Reprinted 1966 in *Selected Logic Papers*.

1960: "Posits and reality," *Basis of the Contemporary Philosophy* 5 (S. Uyeda, ed., Tokyo), pp. 391–400.

Translated 1960 ibid.;

1964 in Rivista di Filosofia.

Reprinted 1966 in *The Ways of Paradox*;

1969 in Landesman;

1973 in Grandy.

"Variables explained away," Proc. Amer. Phil. Soc. 104, pp. 343–347.

Reprinted 1966 in *Selected Logic Papers*.

"Carnap and logical truth," Synthese 12, pp. 350–374.

Preprinted 1956 partly in Hook.

Reprinted 1962 in Kazemier and Vuysje;

1963 in Schilpp;

1966 in *The Ways of Paradox*;

1972 in Feigl, Sellars, and Lehrer.

Translated 1957 in Rivista di Filosofia.

1961: "Reply to Professor Marcus," Synthese 13, pp. 323–330.

Reprinted 1963 in Boston Studies in Philosophy of Science;

1966 in *The Ways of Paradox*;

1968 in Copi and Gould.

"Logic as a source of syntactical insights," Proc. of Symposia in Applied Math. 12, pp. 1–5.

Reprinted 1966 in *The Ways of Paradox*;

1974 in Davidson and Harman.

Translated 1966 in Langages (Paris).

"A basis for number theory in finite classes," Bull. Amer. Math. Soc. 67, pp. 391f.

1962: "Paradox," Scientific American 206, no. 4, pp. 84–95.

Reprinted 1966 in *The Ways of Paradox*;

1968 in Kline.

Translated 1969 in Pasquinelli.

"Le mythe de la signification," *La Philosophie Analytique* (Cahiers de Royaumont IV, Paris: Minuit), pp. 139–169.

1963: "On simple theories of a complex world," Synthese 15, pp. 107–111.

Reprinted 1964 in Gregg and Harris;
1966 in *The Ways of Paradox*; in Foster and Martin.
1964: "On ordinals" (with Hao Wang), Bull. Amer. Math. Soc. 70, pp. 297f.
"Implicit definition sustained," Jour. Philosophy 61, pp. 71–74.
Reprinted 1966 in *The Ways of Paradox*;
1968 in Bobbs-Merrill Reprint Series.
Translated 1964 in Rivista di Filosofia.
"Ontological reduction and the world of numbers," Jour. Philosophy 61, pp. 209–216.
Reprinted 1966 in *The Ways of Paradox*.
"Necessary truth," Voice of America Forum Lectures, Philosophy of Science Series, no. 7; 7 pp.
Reprinted 1966 in *The Ways of Paradox*;
1967 in Morgenbesser.
"The foundations of mathematics," Scientific American 211, no. 3, pp. 113–116, 118, 120, 122, 124, 127.
Reprinted 1966 in *The Ways of Paradox*;
1968 in Kline.
"Henry Maurice Sheffer," Harvard University Gazette 60, no. 14.
Reprinted 1965 in Proc. and Addresses of Amer. Phil. Assn.
"Frontières dans la théorie logique," Etudes Philosophiques, pp. 191–208.
1965: "J. L. Austin, comment," Jour. Philosophy 62, pp. 509f. (A résumé; see 1969.)
Translated 1975 in Muguerza.
1966: "Russell's ontological development," Jour. Philosophy 63, pp. 657, 667.
Reprinted 1967 in Schoenman;
1968 in Klibansky;
1970 in Klemke;
1972 in Pears.
1967: "On a suggestion of Katz," Jour. Philosophy 64, pp. 52–54.
Reprinted 1970 in Woods and Sumner.
"Thoughts on reading Father Owens," Proc. VII Inter-Amer. Congress of Philosophy 1, pp. 60–63.
Introductory notes, *From Frege to Gödel* (J. van Heijenoort, ed.;

Harvard), pp. 150–152, 216f., 355–357.

1968: Comments, *Problems in the Philosophy of Science* (I. Lakatos and A. Musgrave, eds.; Amsterdam: North-Holland), pp. 161–163, 200f., 223.

Replies, Synthese 19, pp. 264–321.

Reprinted 1969 in Davidson and Hintikka.

Translated 1973 partly in Simpson.

"Ontological relativity," Jour. Philosophy 65, pp. 185–212.

Reprinted 1969 in *Ontological Relativity and Other Essays*; 1971 partly in Steinberg and Jakobovits.

"Propositional objects," Critica 2, no. 5, pp. 3–22.

Reprinted 1969 in *Ontological Relativity and Other Essays*.

"Existence and quantification," l'Âge de la Science 1, pp. 151–164.

Reprinted 1969 in Margolis; in *Ontological Relativity and Other Essays*.

1969: "Natural kinds," *Essays in Honor of Carl G. Hempel* (N. Rescher *et al.*, eds.; Dordrecht: Reidel), pp. 5–23.

Reprinted 1969 in *Ontological Relativity and Other Essays*.

"Linguistics and philosophy," *Language and Philosophy* (S. Hook, ed.; N.Y.U. Press), pp. 95–98.

Reprinted 1972 in Morick.

"Existence," *Physics, Logic, and History* (W. Yourgrau, ed.; New York: Plenum), ca. 15 pp.

Foreword to D. K. Lewis, *Convention* (Harvard), pp. ix–x.

"Stimulus and meaning," *Isenberg Memorial Lecture Series 1965–66* (East Lansing: Michigan State), pp. 39–61.

Reprinted 1971 partly in "Epistemology naturalized."

"A symposium on Austin's method," *Symposium on J. L. Austin* (K. T. Fann, ed.; Routledge), pp. 86–90. (For résumé see 1965.)

"The limits of decision," Akten des XIV. Internationalen Kongresse für Philosophie 3, pp. 57–62.

1970: "Philosophical progress in language theory," Metaphilosophy 1, pp. 2–19.

Reprinted 1970 in Kiefer.

"Methodological reflections on current linguistic theory," Synthese 21, pp. 386–398.

Reprinted 1972 in Davidson and Harman (*Semantics of Natural Language*).

1975 partly in Davis.

"Sur la tâche de la grammaire," l'Âge de la Science 3, pp. 3–15, (Author's translation of part of a draft of *Philosophy of Logic*.)

"On the reasons for indeterminacy of translation," Jour. Philosophy 67, pp. 178–183.

"Reply to D. A. Martin," ibid., pp. 247f.

"Grades of theoreticity," *Experience and Theory* (L. Foster and J. W. Swanson, eds.; Amherst: Univ. of Mass.), pp. 1–17.

1971: "Epistemology naturalized," Akten des XIV. Internationalen Kongresses für Philosophie 6, pp. 87–103.

Preprinted 1969 in *Ontological Relativity and Other Essays*.

Reprinted 1972 in Royce and Roozeboom;
1973 in Chisholm and Schwartz.

"Predicate-functor logic," Proc. of II Scandinavian Logic Symposium (North-Holland), pp. 309–315.

"Algebraic logic and predicate functors," pamphlet (Indianapolis: Bobbs-Merrill), 25 pp.

Reprinted 1971 in Rudner and Scheffler.

Homage to Carnap, Boston Studies in Philosophy of Science 8, pp. xxii–xxv.

1972: "Remarks for a memorial symposium," *Bertrand Russell* (D. Pears, ed. New York: Doubleday), pp. 1–5.

"Reflexiones sobre el aprendizaje del lenguaje," Teorema 6, pp. 5–23. (Author's translation of part of a draft of *The Roots of Reference*.)

1973: "Vagaries of definition," Annals N.Y. Acad. of Sci. 211, pp. 247–150.

1974: "On Popper's negative methodology," *The Philosophy of Karl Popper* (P. A. Schilpp, ed.; Open Court), pp. 218–220.

"Paradoxes of plenty," Daedalus 103, no. 4, pp. 38–40.

"Truth and disquotation," Proc. 1971 Tarski Symposium (Providence: Amer. Math. Soc.), pp. 373–384.

"Comment on Donald Davidson," Synthese 27, nos. 3–4, pp. 325–329.

"Comment on Michael Dummett," ibid., p. 399.

In "Mind and verbal dispositions," *Mind and Language: Wolfson*
press: *College Lectures* (Samuel Guttenplan, ed.; Oxford: University
Press).
"The nature of natural knowledge," ibid.
Translated 1974 in Rivista di Filosofia, by author.
"On the individuation of attributes," *The Logical Enterprise* (R.
M. Martin, ed.; New Haven: Yale).
"The variable," Boston Studies in Logic 1.
"Levels of abstraction," Proc. I International Conf. on Unified
Science.
Comments, *Collected Papers of Norbert Wiener* (P. Masani, ed.;
MIT).
Respuestas, *Aspectos de la Filosofía de Quine* (M. Garrido, ed.;
Valencia).
Letter of 1964 to Robert Ostermann, *The Owl of Minerva: Phi-
losophers on Philosophy* (C. J. Bontempo and S. J. Odell, eds.;
New York: McGraw Hill).

ANTHOLOGIES WHERE ARTICLES HAVE REAPPEARED

1949: Feigl and Sellars, *Readings in Philosophical Analysis* (New York:
Appleton).
1952: Linsky, *Semantics and the Philosophy of Language* (Urbana).
1955: Leary, *The Unity of Knowledge* (New York: Doubleday).
1956: Hook, *American Philosophers at Work* (New York: Criterion).
1958: Krzywicki, *Filozofia Amerikańska* (Boston Univ.).
1959: Krikorian and Edel, *Contemporary Philosophic Problems* (New
York: Macmillan).
1960: Bunge, *Antología Semántica* (Buenos Aires).
1961: Saporta, *Psycholinguistics* (New York: Holt).
1962: Aiken and Barrett, *Philosophy in the Twentieth Century* (New
York: Random House).
Kazemier and Vuysje, *Logic and Language* (Dordrecht: Reidel).
1963: Lewis, *Clarity is Not Enough* (London: Allen and Unwin).
Schilpp, *The Philosophy of Rudolf Carnap* (LaSalle: Open Court).
1964: Ammerman, *Classics of American Philosophy* (New York: Mc-
Graw Hill).

Benacerraf and Putnam, *Readings in the Philosophy of Mathematics* (Englewood: Prentice Hall).

Fodor and Katz, *The Structure of Language* (Prentice Hall).

Gregg and Harris, *Form and Strategy in Science* (Reidel).

Marc-Wogau, *Filosofin genom Tiderna, 1900-talet* (Stockholm).

Smart, *Problems of Space and Time* (Macmillan).

1965: Baylis, *Metaphysics* (Macmillan).

Nagel and Brandt, *Meaning and Knowledge* (New York: Harcourt Brace).

1966: Foster and Martin, *Probability, Confirmation, and Simplicity* (New York: Odyssey).

Kurtz, *American Philosophy in the Twentieth Century* (Macmillan).

Rorty, *Pragmatic Philosophy* (Doubleday).

1967: Celucci, *La Filosofia della Matematica* (Bari: Laterza).

Morgenbesser, *Philosophy of Science Today* (New York: Basic Books).

Rorty, *The Linguistic Turn* (Cambridge: MIT).

Schoenman, *Bertrand Russell: Philosopher of the Century* (Allen and Unwin).

1968: Copi and Gould, *Contemporary Readings in Logical Theory* (Macmillan).

Iseminger, *Logic and Philosophy* (Appleton).

Klibansky, *Contemporary Philosophy* (Florence: Nuova Italia).

Kline, *Mathematics in the Modern World* (San Francisco: Freeman).

Margolis, *Introduction to Logical Inquiry* (New York: Knopf).

Tillman, Berofsky, and O'Connor, *Introductory Philosophy* (New York: Harper).

1969: Davidson and Hintikka, *Words and Objections* (Reidel).

Klemke, *Essays on Frege* (Urbana).

Landesman, *Readings in the Foundation of Knowledge* (Prentice Hall).

Margolis, *Fact and Existence* (Oxford: Blackwell).

O'Connor, *Modern Materialism* (Harcourt Brace).

Olshewsky, *Problems in the Philosophy of Language* (Holt).

Pasquinelli, *Neo-Empirismo* (Turin: UTET).

1970: Harris and Severens, *Analyticity* (Chicago: Quadrangle).

Kiefer, *Contemporary Philosophical Thought* (Albany: State Univ.)
Klemke, *Essays on Bertrand Russell* (Urbana).
Loux, *Universals and Particulars* (Doubleday).
Myers, *The Spirit of Analytical Philosophy* (New York: Putnam).
Woods and Sumner, *Necessary Truth* (Random House).
1971: Arner, *Readings in Epistemology* (New York: Scott Foresman).
Bynum, *Frege* (New York: Oxford).
Linsky, *Reference and Modality* (Oxford: Clarendon).
Manicas, *Logic as Philosophy* (Princeton: Van Nostrand).
Munsat, *The Analytic-Synthetic Distinction* (New York: Wadsworth).
Rosenberg and Travis, *Readings in the Philosophy of Language* (Prentice Hall).
Rudner and Scheffler, *Logic and Art* (Indianapolis: Bobbs-Merrill)
Steinberg and Jakobovits, *Semantics* (Cambridge Univ.).
1972: Davidson and Harman, *Semantics of Natural Language* (Reidel).
Feigl, Sellars, and Lehrer, *New Readings in Philosophical Analysis* (Appleton).
Goodman, *Problems and Projects* (Bobbs-Merrill).
Landesman, *The Problem of Universals* (Prentice Hall).
Marras, *Intentionality, Mind, and Language* (Urbana).
Morick, *Challenges to Empiricism* (Wadsworth).
Pears, *Bertrand Russell* (Doubleday).
Pereira, *Significação e Verdade* (São Paulo: Perspectiva).
Royce and Roozeboom, *The Psychology of Knowing* (London: Gordon and Breach).
Sinnreich, *Zur Philosophie der idealen Sprache* (Munich: Deutscher Taschenbuch).
1973: Bleikasten and Birnbaum, *Versions* (Paris: Masson).
Bonomi, *La Struttura Logica del Linguaggio* (Milan: Bompiani).
Chisholm and Schwartz, *Empirical Knowledge* (Prentice Hall).
Eisenberg, Bense, and Haberland, *Linguistische Reihe* (Munich: Hueber).
Grandy, *Theories and Observation in Science* (Prentice Hall).
MacKinnon, *The Problem of Scientific Realism* (Appleton).
Simpson, *Semántica Filosófica* (Buenos Aires: Siglo XXI).
Swartzlander, *Computer Design* (New York: Hayden).

369

1974: Bencivenga, *Logiche Libere* (Turin: Boringhiere).
Berlinski, *The Cutting Edge* (New York: Alfred).
Davidson and Harman, *The Logic of Grammar* (Encino: Dickenson).
Fodor, Bever, and Garrett, *Psychology of Language* (McGraw Hill).
Harman, *On Noam Chomsky: Critical Essays* (Doubleday).
Pârvu, *Epistemologie: Orientari Contemporare* (Bucharest).
Zabeeh, Klemke, and Jacobson, *Readings in Semantics* (Urbana).
1975: Beck, *Perspectives in Philosophy* (Prentice Hall).
Davis, *Philosophy of Language* (Bobbs-Merrill).
Harding, *Can Theories be Refuted? Essays on the Duhem-Quine Thesis* (Reidel).
Muguerza, *Lecturas de Filosofia* (Madrid: Alianza).
Stegmüller, *Das Universalienproblem* (Darmstadt: Wissenschaftliche Buchgesellschaft).

ABSTRACTS

1935: "A unified calculus of propositions, classes, and relations," Bull. Amer. Math. Soc. 41, p. 338.
1937: "Is logic a matter of words?" Journal of Philosophy 34, p. 674.
1940: *Mathematical Logic*, Year Book of Amer. Phil. Soc., pp. 230f.
1947: "On the problem of universals," Journal of Symbolic Logic 12, p. 31.
1950: "Information patterns for games in extensive form" (with W. D. Krentel and J. C. C. McKinsey), Proc. Internat. Cong. of Math. 1.
1951: "Some theorems on definability and decidability" (with Alonzo Church), Journal of Symbolic Logic 16, pp. 239f.
1952: "The problem of simplifying truth functions," ibid. 17, p. 156.
1956: "Unification of universes in set theory," ibid. 21, p. 216.
1959: "Eliminating variables without applying functions to functions," ibid. 24, pp. 324f.
1970: Comments on Belnap, Noûs 4, p. 12.
1971: "Predicate-functor logic," Journal of Symbolic Logic 36, p. 382.

MISCELLANEOUS

1934: Report on Whitehead, "Logical definitions of extension, class, and number," Amer. Math. Monthly 41, pp. 129–131.

1946: Translation (with introduction) of Löwenheim's MS "On making indirect proofs direct," Scripta Mathematica 12, pp. 125–134.

1947: Letter in Carnap, *Meaning and Necessity* (Chicago), pp. 196f.

1951: "It tastes like chicken," Furioso 6, pp. 37–39.

1954: Letter on Griggs, Atlantic Monthly 194, p. 21.

1970: Reply to Mr. Flexner, New York Review of Books 13, no. 12, p. 38.

BOOK REVIEWS

1930: Of Nicod, *Foundations of Geometry and Induction*, Amer. Math. Monthly 37, pp. 305–307.

1933: Of Peirce, *Collected Papers*, vol. 2; Isis 19, pp. 220–229.

1935: Of same, vols. 3–4; Isis 22, pp. 285–297, 551–553.

Of Carnap, *Logische Syntax der Sprache*: Philosophical Review 44, pp. 394–397.

1936: Of García Baca, *Introducción a la Lógica Moderna*; Journal of Symbolic Logic 1, pp. 112f.

1937: Of Weinberg, *Examination of Logical Positivism*; ibid. 2, pp. 89f.

Of Jeffreys, *Scientific Inference*; Science 86, p. 590.

1938: Of Tarski, *Einführung in die mathematische Logik*; Bull. Amer. Math. Soc. 44, pp. 317f.

Of Ushenko, *Theory of Logic*; Philosophical Review 47, p. 94.

Of Hilbert and Ackermann, *Grundzüge der theoretischen Logik*; Journal of Symbolic Logic 3, pp. 83f.

1941: Of Russell, *Inquiry into Meaning and Truth*; ibid. 6, pp. 29f.

Of Serrus, *Essai sur la Signification de la Logique*; ibid., pp. 62f.

Of da Silva, *Elementos de Lógica Matemática*; ibid., pp. 109f.

1946: Of Godinho, *Esboços sobre Alguns Problemas da Lógica*; ibid., 11, p. 126.

1947: Of Toranzos, *Introducción a la Epistemología y la Fundamentación de la Matemática*; ibid. 12, pp. 20f.

1948: Of Reichenbach, *Elements of Symbolic Logic*; Journal of Philosophy 45, pp. 161–166.

1951: Of Goodman, *Structure of Appearance*; ibid. 48, pp. 556–563.

1952: Of Ferrater Mora, *Diccionario de Filosofía*; Journal of Symbolic Logic 17, pp. 129f.

1963: Of *National Geographic Atlas*; New York Review of Books 1, no. 3, p. 8.

1964: Of Mencken, *American Language*; ibid., no. 9, p. 7.
Of *Atlas of Britain*; ibid. 2, no. 2, p. 17.
Of Smart, *Philosophy and Scientific Realism*; ibid., no. 11, p. 3.
Of Geach, *Reference and Generality*; Philosophical Review 73, pp. 100–104.

1965: Of Bagrow, *History of Cartography*; New York Review of Books 5, no. 4, pp. 18f.

1967: Of Russell, *Autobiography*, vol. 1; Boston Globe, April 9, p. B-43.

1968: Of *Times Atlas of the World*; Book World (in Washington Post and Chicago Tribune), May 5, p. 7.

1969: Of *American Heritage Dictionary* and *Random House Dictionary*, College Edition; New York Review of Books 13, no. 10, pp. 3f.; see also no. 12, p. 38, and vol. 14, no. 1–2, p. 54.

1972: Of Munitz (ed.), *Identity and Individuation*; Journal of Philosophy 69, pp. 488–497.

REVIEWS OF ARTICLES

1936: Of Tarski, "Grundzüge des Systemenkalküls"; Journal of Symbolic Logic 1, pp. 71f.
Of Russell, "On order in time"; ibid., pp. 73f.
Short ones (under 400 words): ibid., pp. 43, 68, 113.

1937: Of Saarnio, "Zur heterologischen Paradoxie"; ibid. 2, p. 138.
Of Stone, "Note on formal logic"; ibid., pp. 174f.
Short ones: ibid., pp. 37, 46f., 59, 83f.

1938: Of Chwistek and Hetper, "New foundation of formal metamathematics"; ibid. 3, pp. 120f.
Short ones: ibid., pp. 47–49, 56, 94, 121f.

1939: Of Hermes, "Semiotik"; ibid. 4, pp. 87f.
Short ones: ibid., pp. 102, 125.

1940: Of Bröcker, "Antinomien und Paradoxien"; ibid. 5, p. 79.
Of Leśniewski, "Einleitende Bemerkungen"; ibid., pp. 83f.

Of Church, "Formulation of theory of types"; ibid., pp. 114f.
Short ones: ibid., pp. 30, 71, 84, 157, 168f.

1941: Of Rosser, "Independence of Quine's axioms"; ibid. 6, p. 163.

1942: Short one: ibid. 7, pp. 44f.

1946: Of Barcan, "Functional calculus based on strict implication"; ibid. 11, pp. 96f.

1947: Of Nelson, "Contradiction and existence"; ibid. 12, pp. 52–55.
Of Barcan, "Identity of individuals"; ibid., pp. 95f. [Correction in 23 (1958), p. 342.]
Of Schröter, "Was ist eine mathematische Theorie?"; ibid., pp. 136f.
Short ones: ibid., pp. 55, 95.

1948: Short ones: ibid. 13, pp. 122, 158.

1949: Of Fraenkel, "Relation of equality"; ibid. 14, p. 130.
Of Saarnio, "Der Begriff der Hierarchie"; ibid., p. 131.
Short ones: ibid., pp. 59f., 64, 257.

1950: Of Feys, "Simple notation for relations"; ibid. 15, pp. 71f.
Short ones: ibid., pp. 139, 149f., 215.

1951: Of Myhill, "Complete theory of numbers"; ibid. 16, pp. 65–67.
Of Geach, "Subject and predicate"; ibid., p. 138.
Of Myhill, "Report of investigations"; ibid., pp. 217f.
Short ones: ibid., pp. 138f., 214, 273.

1952: Of Ajdukiewicz, "On the notion of existence"; ibid. 17, pp. 144f.

1958: Short one: ibid. 23, p. 41.

NOTE

[1] See list of anthologies, p. 367ff.